Liberty Power

AMERICAN BEGINNINGS, 1500–1900
A Series Edited by Edward Gray, Stephen Mihm, and Mark Peterson

ALSO IN THE SERIES:

The Making of Tocqueville's America: Law and Association in the Early United States
by Kevin Butterfield

Planters, Merchants, and Slaves: Plantation Societies in British America, 1650–1820
by Trevor Burnard

Riotous Flesh: Women, Physiology, and the Solitary Vice in Nineteenth-Century America
by April R. Haynes

Holy Nation: The Transatlantic Quaker Ministry in an Age of Revolution
by Sarah Crabtree

A Hercules in the Cradle: War, Money, and the American State, 1783–1867
by Max M. Edling

Frontier Seaport: Detroit's Transformation into an Atlantic Entrepôt
by Catherine Cangany

Beyond Redemption: Race, Violence, and the American South after the Civil War
by Carole Emberton

The Republic Afloat: Law, Honor, and Citizenship in Maritime America
by Matthew Taylor Raffety

Conceived in Doubt: Religion and Politics in the New American Nation
by Amanda Porterfield

Liberty Power

ANTISLAVERY THIRD PARTIES
AND THE TRANSFORMATION
OF AMERICAN POLITICS

Corey M. Brooks

The University of Chicago Press   CHICAGO AND LONDON

PUBLICATION OF THIS BOOK HAS BEEN AIDED BY
A GRANT FROM THE BEVINGTON FUND.

The University of Chicago Press, Chicago 60637
The University of Chicago Press, Ltd., London
© 2016 by The University of Chicago.
All rights reserved. No part of this book may be used or reproduced
in any manner whatsoever without written permission, except in the case
of brief quotations in critical articles and reviews. For more information,
contact the University of Chicago Press, 1427 E. 60th St., Chicago, IL 60637.
Published 2016
Paperback edition 2020

29 28 27 26 25 24 23 22 21 20   1 2 3 4 5

ISBN-13: 978-0-226-30728-2 (cloth)
ISBN-13: 978-0-226-71716-6 (paper)
ISBN-13: 978-0-226-30731-2 (e-book)
DOI: https://doi.org/10.7208/chicago/9780226307312.001.0001

Portions of this work, mainly from chapter 2, first appeared in
"Stoking the 'Abolition Fire in the Capitol': Liberty Lobbying and Antislavery
in Congress," *Journal of the Early Republic* 33, no. 3 (Fall 2013): 523–547.

Library of Congress Cataloging-in-Publication Data

Brooks, Corey M., author.
Liberty power : antislavery third parties and the
transformation of American politics / Corey M. Brooks.
pages cm — (American beginnings, 1500–1900)
ISBN 978-0-226-30728-2 (cloth : alk. paper) — ISBN 978-0-226-30731-2 (ebook)
1. Antislavery movements — United States — History — 19th century. 2. Third parties
(United States politics) — History — 19th century. 3. Liberty Party (U.S. : 1840–1848).
4. Free Soil Party (U.S.). 5. Republican Party (U.S. : 1854–). 6. United States — History —
Civil War, 1861–1865 — Causes. 7. United States — Politics and government — 1845–1861.
8. Slavery — Political aspects — United States — History — 19th century.
I. Title. II. Series: American beginnings, 1500–1900.
E449.B766 2016
973.5—dc23
2015018766

FOR LAUREN,
with so much love

Contents

Introduction · 1

CHAPTER ONE · 15
Political Abolition and the Slave Power Argument, 1835–1840

Interlude One · 43
"Bowing Down to the Slave Power":
Northern Whigs, Slavery, and the Speakership, 1839

CHAPTER TWO · 47
Agitating the Congress: Abolitionist Lobbying and
Antislavery Alliances, 1836–1844

Interlude Two · 73
"A Temporary 'Third Party'": Antislavery Whig
Dissidents in the 1841 Speakership Contest

CHAPTER THREE · 77
Building Third-Party Electoral Power, 1841–1846

CHAPTER FOUR · 105
Antislavery Upheaval in the Capitol:
The Wilmot Proviso Debates and the Widening
Sectional Divide, 1846–1848

Interlude Three · 125
"Let the Lines Be Drawn": Conscience Whig Insurgency
and the 1847 Speakership Election

CHAPTER FIVE · 129
Liberty Men and the Creation of an Anti-Slave
Power Coalition, 1846–1849

Interlude Four · 155
"Glorious Confusion in the Ranks":
The Free Soil Balance of Power, 1849

CHAPTER SIX · 161
Free Soil Politics and the Twilight of the
Second Party System, 1849–1853

CHAPTER SEVEN · 187
The Nebraska Outrage and the Advent of
the Republican Party, 1853–1855

Interlude Five · 207
"A New Era in Our History":
The Longest Speakership Contest in American History and
the First Republican National Victory, 1855–1856

CONCLUSION · 213

Acknowledgments · 227
Abbreviations · 231
Notes · 233
Index · 291

Introduction

The feast was sumptuous. Guests fed on nine types of game birds, five different roasted meats, two soups, cold dishes like boned turkey with truffles, and thirteen decadent sides, among them mutton cutlets with Madeira sauce, oyster patties, and calf's head with turtle sauce. Massachusetts Republicans who gathered on February 28, 1856, at the elegant Revere House hotel to hail the election of Nathaniel P. Banks as speaker of the United States House of Representatives had much to celebrate.[1]

Today elections for speaker of the House are quick and uneventful. This was not always the case. In the longest speakership contest in American history, from early December 1855 into February 1856, representatives voted 133 times before a winner emerged. With conflict over slavery destabilizing party loyalties as never before, it was impossible to find a candidate who could unite a House majority, even though congressmen were forced to forgo their pay until the House organized. For two months, the wheels of legislation stood still, as representatives endured roll call after roll call, interrupted only by vitriolic arguments over the root causes of the stalemate or to bandy about increasingly desperate, often absurd, proposals to effect a resolution. One representative even suggested that the entire House resign. Another proposed banning warming fires and all refreshments from the chamber in hopes of making continued gridlock not only politically, but also physically uncomfortable.[2]

Finally on February 2, 1856, Nathaniel Banks of Massachusetts, the moderately antislavery candidate of the fledgling Republican Party, secured the speaker's gavel after a more mundane rule change—one allowing election by plurality. When Joshua Giddings, a militant antislavery House veteran of eighteen years, administered Banks's Oath of Office, thousands cheered from the galleries. Swarms then poured onto the floor to congratulate Giddings, some shedding tears of joy as they clasped the antislavery patriarch's hand. After Giddings returned to his room, the "friends of liberty" besieged him for hours, and once they left around midnight, he passed the remainder of the night writing in bed, recording the triumphant history of this speakership contest for the "coming generations."[3]

For those who had long worked to reverse proslavery control of Congress, Banks's elevation represented a culmination of years of antislavery congressional agitation spearheaded by abolitionist activists. As Ohio Governor Salmon Chase, a longtime political abolitionist leader, congratulated Speaker Banks, Chase paid tribute to the Republican Party's more radical forerunners (presumably including himself): "The friends of Human Liberty will honor as they deserve the faithful men who have so long, so calmly, & so inflexibly maintained the right." Banks's election, to the delight of antislavery men, ensconced the Republicans as the preeminent party in much of the North and ensured the centrality of slavery in future national political debate, a goal towards which abolitionist political activists had been working for decades.[4]

Effective third-party politics have long seemed unfeasible in the American political system. Yet from the mid-1830s through the mid-1850s, a small, radical third-party challenge established the foundation for the most dramatic political upheaval in American history. In the face of the robust Second Party System of Whigs and Democrats, marked by enthusiastic and tenacious partisanship, political abolitionists committed to the goal of ending American slavery worked tirelessly to popularize an antislavery political agenda. Driven by intense moral animus against slavery, political abolitionists, despite their small numbers, skillfully employed third-party activism to reorder a political system designed to muffle any such challenge. In the process, they planted the seeds of Lincoln's Republican Party and ultimately emancipation.[5]

The Northern antislavery consensus embodied in the emergence and then the victory of the Republican Party owed much to those who had been contesting for years against American slaveholders' political power. It was impossible, antislavery activists recognized, to make meaningful inroads against slavery without confronting the political institutions that upheld it. Consistent abolitionist political activism, starting by the mid-1830s, laid the groundwork for the broader antislavery coalitions that became the Free Soil Party and then the Republican Party. Though faced with an entrenched two-party system designed to deter antislavery policymaking, abolitionists shrewdly developed strategies that ensured continued national political attention to slavery.

Among abolitionists' key contributions to the politics of sectional conflict was their effort to elaborate and disseminate the critical rhetorical device of the Slave Power. Within the racist polity of the antebellum North, no other antislavery rhetoric was as persuasive as the claim that slaveholders wielded disproportionate political power and threatened the liberties of white Northern men. Far more so than strict reliance on religious or natural rights arguments for equality, political abolitionists recognized, this capacious political appeal could attract the broad Northern constituency needed to reshape national politics. As the argument's reach expanded, it sometimes assumed new undertones, including gendered, or even racialized, defenses of white male independence. These new valences, though they had the potential to muddle abolitionist demands for racial justice, never overwhelmed the core Slave Power argument that Southern political clout distorted and undermined American democracy.

In the hands of political abolitionists, this argument offered not just alluring political rhetoric, but also a diagnosis of structural flaws in the American political system and an implicit prescription for its repair. Political abolitionists shaped the Slave Power concept into a condemnation of the Second Party System as the crucial political bulwark protecting slavery. Because both the Democratic and Whig Parties relied on cross-sectional support and routinely nominated slaveholders and their apologists for the nation's highest offices, abolitionists castigated even the most ardently antislavery members of those parties as beholden to the Slave Power. This analysis became the justification and then the most compelling argument for the abolitionist Liberty Party, founded in 1840. Abolitionist political activism successfully thrust this Slave Power idea into the Northern mainstream in hopes of promoting a national political reorganization that would array the friends of freedom against the Slave Power and accelerate the demise of American slavery.

Scholarly narratives of antebellum politics have routinely treated political abolitionists as minor players in national political crises over slavery, perhaps in part because even historians of abolitionism have downplayed their contributions. Scholarship emphasizing William Lloyd Garrison and his vocal inner circle has long diverted attention from the influence and accomplishments of the much larger group of political abolitionists.[6] More recent abolitionist scholarship has focused heavily on uncovering the important abolitionist contributions of women and radical black reformers.[7] As a by-product of both this overdue attention to groups marginalized by nineteenth-century politics and the older focus on Garrisonians, who opposed partisan political action, we have lost sight of many vital dimensions of political abolitionism that have only recently begun to come back into focus. Consequently, as James Stewart notes, the fields of abolitionist studies and national political history remain so disconnected that "to read in them simultaneously is to slip back and forth between alternate universes." Recent scholarship is beginning to answer Stewart's call, but political abolitionism still has not been fully reintegrated into the mainsprings of antebellum political history. This book aims to meet that challenge.[8]

Perhaps in part because generations of scholars of abolitionism have understated the significance of antislavery third-party politics, many political historians have also found it easy to downplay abolitionists' role in the wrangling that ultimately precipitated the Civil War. After all, as late as 1860, few Americans considered themselves abolitionists, many Northern voters detested abolitionists as self-righteous fanatics, and even many Republicans seemed interested only in limiting the expansion of slavery into federal territories. As histories of the most progressive and militant abolitionists established the ideological gulf separating them from the Northern mainstream, political historians studying sectional conflict and the rise of the Republicans sought explanations beyond antislavery. In the process, they have illuminated important facets of the sectional conflict, but have in most cases marginalized political abolitionism. Instead, the rise of the Republican Party has been portrayed as best attributable to a number of causes only loosely related to abolitionist political agitation: the popularization of a free labor ideology that rejected competition with slave labor in western territories; an antimonopolistic libertarian ideology that "grew straight from the roots of the Democracy's long-standing commitment to egalitarianism"; or the breakdown of the Second Party System because of "ethnocultural" divisions and fears of antirepublican conspiracies unrelated to slavery.[9]

It might seem surprising that so many modern historians, including those who sincerely admire abolitionist radicalism, have given political abolitionists such short shrift. But we can perhaps better understand this scholarly blind spot as a legacy of older, deeply-flawed interpretive traditions that had taken abolitionist political influence more seriously.[10] First among these were histories of the sectional conflict penned by politicians who had participated in it, such as longtime Ohio antislavery congressman Joshua Giddings and Henry Wilson, an early Republican senator and later vice president. These histories written by the victors uncritically celebrated Civil War–era politics as a crusade against slavery, eliding the prevalence and intensity of racism and anti-abolitionism in the antebellum North.[11] Decades later, "revisionist" Civil War histories of the 1930s and 1940s unflatteringly returned abolitionism to the center of the sectional crisis. Irresponsible, shortsighted politicians, revisionists argued, appealed to sectional passions and unwittingly plunged the nation into an otherwise "repressible" conflict. Reserving especial vehemence for abolitionists, revisionists charged them with recklessly infusing antebellum politics with the high-stakes emotional rhetoric that made further compromise intolerable. One prominent revisionist even likened antislavery activists to Nazi and Stalinist propagandists.[12]

Histories penned in the wake of the mid-twentieth-century black freedom struggle thankfully dispensed with this denigration of abolitionism, instead depicting abolitionists as heroic forerunners of modern civil rights activists. Among the revisionist school's more enduring influences, however, was the extended scholarly debate it spawned over abolitionists' underlying motivations. Much of that abolitionist scholarship, both favorable and unfavorable, focused more on *who* the abolitionists were and what they *thought* than on what they *did* and the effectiveness of their tactics.[13]

Modern historians have rightly shunned the self-righteous triumphalism of slavery-centered histories penned by antislavery politicians like Wilson and Giddings and the racist hyper-conservatism of most Civil War revisionists. Both of these outdated schools, with all their many flaws, were perceptive, however, in calling attention to the powerful influence of political abolitionists. Understanding how maintaining a political system half-slave and half-free became increasingly untenable over the antebellum period demands a careful reconsideration of influential political abolitionist agitation.

American abolitionism developed as a modern mass movement in the early 1830s. Spearheaded especially by Boston newspaperman William Lloyd Garrison, this newly radicalized "immediatist" antislavery movement called for immediate action to abolish American slavery. Spurred not only by moral revulsion at slavery's violence and dehumanization, antebellum abolitionists were also responding to profound changes in Northern society and in the broader Atlantic world, including the evangelical revivalism of the Second Great Awakening, the example of Parliament's 1833 legislation to emancipate British colonial slaves, and an accelerating "market revolution" that led many to reevaluate American labor relations. Most importantly, early white immediatists drew inspiration from a longstanding black protest tradition. In prior decades, white abolitionists working for black freedom and moral uplift had often emphasized deferential appeals to political elites who might have recoiled at more combative tactics. At the same time, however, urban free black activists increasingly boldly urged the complete eradication of American bondage and racism. In the

1820s, this free black activism coalesced in opposition to the American Colonization Society and its disingenuous "antislavery" project of encouraging Southerners to free their slaves and deport them to West Africa. Ultimately, black political mobilization against colonization helped persuade many white abolitionists, including Garrison, of the need for a more radical, organized, and uncompromising abolitionist movement.[14]

To directly challenge slavery as undemocratic, sinful, and anti-American, though, was to call into question one of the nation's most central institutions. Through the antebellum period, enslaved African Americans made up between an eighth and a sixth of the nation's population and an even larger share of the country's wealth. Abolitionists thus often faced popular derision, social ostracism, and in some cases physical violence, all of which underscored the overwhelming obstacles confronting their quest to convert Southerners or even large numbers of Northerners to their antislavery doctrines. Along with the massive economic investment in slave labor, pervasive racism, indifferent or diffident national church organizations, and the support slaveholders derived from the national political system all combined to further safeguard slavery.[15]

Since the inception of the American republic, slavery had represented a source of social and political discord. Given slavery's seeming incompatibility with the egalitarian ideals announced in the Declaration of Independence, the post-Revolutionary decades saw every Northern state abolish the institution or establish a plan to gradually wind it down. So even as slavery lingered in the Middle Atlantic region, it was possible by the 1789 convening of the First Congress for many Northerners to conceive of their "free states" as fundamentally unlike the slave societies further south. Consequently, the Early National North harbored respectable antislavery reformers who argued for federal policies to curtail slavery's growth in hopes of the eventual emancipation of all American slaves. A swift and angry reaction against antislavery petitions to the First Congress made clear, though, that Southern politicians considered their autonomous control of slavery the critical condition for union.[16]

This 1793 Fugitive Slave Act affirmed the federal commitment to sectional harmony, but also faced ongoing challenges in Northern communities bordering the slave South. In response to the problem of antislavery Pennsylvanians, white and black, aiding and encouraging slave runaways, Congress, during its decade stint in Philadelphia, had passed this 1793 law to spell out requirements for how Northern state governments should execute the constitutional obligation to "deliver up" slaves escaping across state lines. Though governed by federal law, these conflicts generally played out, occasionally violently, among the individuals and states that were forced to navigate conflicting legal and moral terrains along the Mason-Dixon Line and on opposite sides of the Ohio River. As enslaved people fled to post-emancipation Pennsylvania, or into the Old Northwest, they found numerous allies, white and black, in their self-liberation efforts. Thus the related issues of fugitive slave rendition and free black abduction repeatedly forced Northern individuals, and occasionally state governments, to confront the demands and power of Southern slaveholders.[17]

These conflicts, along with others over the ongoing implementation of gradual emancipation, continued to generate controversy at the state level, but in *national* politics, slavery usually remained a secondary issue under the First Party System of Federalists and Jeffersonian Republicans. At several junctures, Northern politicians did complain of disproportionate Southern political power resultant from the Constitution's three-fifths clause, which allocated congressional representatives and Electoral College votes based on total free population plus three-fifths of slaves. But such controversies were typically episodic and transitory. As the early nineteenth-century Federalist Party became an overwhelmingly Northern organization, its members leveled charges of slaveholder dominance at Jefferson's coalition. The Jeffersonians themselves later experienced intraparty rancor over slavery in the Orleans Territory (present-day Louisiana) and over enforcement provisions for the 1808 international slave trade ban, but the War of 1812 muffled hyperpatriotic Northern Jeffersonians' attacks on their party's Virginian leaders. By 1819, however, the challenge of slavery's westward expansion incited a new, more pitched sectional controversy. In the crisis over slaveholding Missouri's application for statehood and the fallout thereafter, Northern sectionalist arguments proliferated and threatened to unravel the now-dominant Jeffersonian Democratic-Republican Party.[18]

It was this "fire-bell in the night," as Jefferson himself famously termed it, that inspired New York wirepuller Martin Van Buren to seek a new mechanism for organizing national politics. Hoping to avert future sectional crises, Van Buren envisioned a revived Democratic coalition uniting "planters of the South and plain Republicans of the North" and suppressing "prejudices between free and slaveholding states." When slave-owning war hero Andrew Jackson emerged in the mid-1820s as a champion of the common man, Van Buren hitched his wagon to the Tennessee general and began the process of building a new Democratic Party, and ultimately a second American party system. Within a few years, the Whig Party had established itself as a formidable challenger focused on demanding activist federal economic policies that Jackson and Van Buren rejected. While Whigs incorporated a wide range of evangelical reformers and veterans of the anti-Masonic movement, with their well-known fears of concentrated power, the new opposition party, on the whole, relied, like the Jacksonians, on maintaining cross-sectional accord and avoiding national disputes over slavery.[19]

As leaders of the budding antebellum abolitionist movement surveyed the society around them, many quickly recognized that the political arena, now structured by this Second Party System of Whigs and Democrats, represented a key venue for antislavery activism. Though most abolitionists conceded that Northerners had no constitutional authority over slavery in Southern states, it seemed equally clear that the federal government could combat slavery elsewhere, including most obviously in the District of Columbia, where the Constitution gave Congress the power to "exercise exclusive Legislation in all Cases whatsoever." Political abolitionists thus came to articulate the objective of divorcing the federal government from slavery, a policy vision grounded in legal interpretations that freedom was national while slavery should be confined only to states that had expressly legalized the institution. If they could achieve this denationalization of slavery, many abolitionists hopefully anticipated that the immoral, allegedly unproductive institution would soon wither away. As James Oakes has shown, political abolitionists, antislavery moderates, *and* slaveholding adversaries all came to be convinced that if the federal government ceased to treat slaves as property, the institution would become so enfeebled as to ultimately induce voluntary state abolition.[20]

As abolitionists worked to shift the federal government's orientation toward slavery, many concentrated especially on Congress. Congress possessed the jurisdiction to promote key components of the antislavery movement's national political agenda, among them immediate emancipation in the District of Columbia, rejecting the admission of new slave states, barring slavery from U.S. territories and federal property such as forts and custom houses, repealing federal fugitive slave legislation, and, most controversially, ending the interstate slave trade. At least as importantly, though, political abolitionists could capitalize on the wide reach of congressional debates to transmit their arguments to a broad Northern audience. Even if congressmen didn't always give their undivided attention to colleagues' floor speeches (as Rachel Shelden shows), constituents, abolitionists appreciated, often did. Additionally, the quirky calendar for antebellum congressional elections—spanning many months and with some states choosing congressmen over a year before the first session of their term—meant that national political circumstances sometimes evolved dramatically between members' elections and swearing in, and that a substantial portion of House business was conducted by lame ducks; antislavery activists were often closely attuned to these anomalies of the nineteenth-century Congress. To reach congressional policymakers, abolitionists initially employed a tool that was presumably open to all American men, women, and children—the congressional petition. By sending thousands of petitions requesting immediate emancipation in the District of Columbia to the U.S. House in the mid-1830s, abolitionists forced politicians from all parts of the nation to address the slavery question.[21]

Beginning in 1836, the House of Representatives adopted the infamous gag rule to rebuke antislavery petitioners by automatically and indefinitely laying their requests on the proverbial table. Undaunted, political abolitionists linked their movement with a defense of Northern civil liberties and thereby mobilized the stunning new restriction to recruit droves of converts. Many abolitionists soon concentrated especially on claims that slaveholders' disproportionate political influence perverted national policymaking and the democratic process.

As abolitionists sharpened this argument, they declaimed against a sinister "slaveholding power" comprising slave master politicians and their Northern allies. This rhetoric soon evolved into a systematic argument that the Southern "Slave Power" dominated the national government through its control of the Second Party System, with disastrous results for not only enslaved African-Americans, but also free white Northerners. Because the Democrats and Whigs were cross-sectional parties that were competitive in both sections, nearly every state, and most congressional districts, both relied on cooperation between slave state and free state politicians. Consequently, meaningful antislavery policy could never be expected from either party. Both Whigs and Democrats, abolitionists contended by the late 1830s, were complicit in the Slave Power. Even ostensibly antislavery politicians from those parties would consistently prioritize partisan obligations over antislavery convictions, as was born out repeatedly in national elections for president and speaker of the House (the two contests with a national electorate).

This Slave Power argument thus spurred many abolitionists to insist that they could achieve their ultimate goal of destroying American slavery only by first upending the proslavery party system. Initially, political abolitionists sought to identify and endorse acceptable antislavery candidates. But as political abolitionists faced repeated disappointment, and their Slave Power argument evolved into an increasingly thorough denunciation of the Second Party System, many edged toward independent abolitionist politics. By the end of the 1830s, a small but swelling chorus among the abolitionist leadership called boldly for an abolitionist third party to confront the powerful Whig and Democratic organizations.

After establishing the Liberty Party, political abolitionists skillfully identified and capitalized on institutional openings for third-party influence created by the contours of the Second Party System. Liberty leaders particularly recognized the value of Congress as a public forum and worked to coax congressional politicians to take more advanced antislavery stands. As abolitionists lobbied and sometimes collaborated with (primarily Whig) antislavery congressmen, they provoked aggressive proslavery responses. Then, political abolitionists celebrated the ensuing fireworks that dramatized Slave Power control of the federal government.

In electoral politics, meanwhile, Liberty partisans worked to generate voter pressure that would expose the major parties' commitments to the Slave Power and compel Northern politicians to assume increasingly antislavery positions. Through their congressional and electoral tactics, political abolitionists nudged slavery and the Slave Power ever closer to the center of national political debate. By the mid-1840s, Congress could no longer hope to avoid antislavery polemics. In the face of the Mexican-American War, Northerners from across the political spectrum delivered anti–Slave Power diatribes, and divisive disputes over the prospect of slavery's westward expansion came to dominate congressional debate. As the circle of anti–Slave Power politicians widened, some new proponents, especially former Democrats, focused on the defense of free white manhood. Though such rhetoric may have discomfited political abolitionists, most accepted that any revolt against Southern political power boded well for their goal of redeeming the federal government. Indeed, political abolitionists had already demonstrated their awareness that the reach of anti–Slave Power politics could be broadened through appeals to white manhood, though preferably not through the sorts of openly racist formulations later espoused by Democratic congressmen.

After helping create the growing anti–Slave Power tide, political abolitionists strove to channel it into ever broader antislavery political action in hopes of toppling the proslavery Second Party System. In the process, political abolitionists became vital, if sometimes ambivalent, architects of the Free Soil Party and then the Republican Party. Political abolitionists had long argued that only by tearing down the Second Party System and organizing national political debate around issues of slavery and freedom could they rescue the federal government from the Slave Power. Despite the relative moderation of the Free Soil and Republican Parties, both offered the chance to elect increasing numbers of anti–Slave Power officeholders who would not be constrained by party affiliation with slaveholders. When the bulk of the nation's electorate divided between the proslavery Democratic Party and the antislavery, however cautiously, Republican Party, political abolitionists saw success near at hand. As the Republican ascendancy led down the ominous road to civil war, most veterans of the Liberty and Free Soil Parties confidently embraced the opportunity to overthrow the Slave Power, end slavery, and, some hoped, transform American society and promote racial equality.

Across this decades-long political conflict, abolitionist strategy developed in conjunction with slaveholding politicians' rising apprehensions about their institution's security. As the abolitionist movement grew, its initiatives seemed to elicit excessive Southern wrath. Counterproductive Southern efforts to suppress antislavery speech and political action won abolitionists new sympathizers (which in turn lent further credibility to proslavery extremists' forebodings of an abolitionist conspiracy that might one day sweep the North). Learning quickly, abolitionists soon began working to consciously incite Southern overreactions, especially in Congress. To a degree, extreme proslavery politics and political abolitionism relied on each other. Increasingly common confrontations between proslavery and antislavery radicals made it harder and harder for mainstream politicians to ignore the slavery issue. Proslavery zealots, in their efforts to repel all antislavery incursions against a political system that was, on the whole, fairly friendly to slaveholders' interests, provided political abolitionists with valuable opportunities to further destabilize that system. Despite the best efforts of sectional moderates to paper over deepening discord, anti-abolitionist and anti–Slave Power politics together fed a cyclical dynamic that continually escalated the political conflict over slavery.[22]

This book explores political abolitionists' indispensable influence on the dramatic rise of antislavery politics and employs a roughly, but not entirely, sequential organization, with some significant chronological overlap across chapters. The first chapter demonstrates how abolitionist arguments about overbearing Southerners' disproportionate political power developed into a sophisticated analysis condemning both the Democratic and Whig Parties. The chapter then shows how the Slave Power argument shaped political abolitionists' move toward third-party politics.

The second chapter illuminates political abolitionists' strategies for building collaborative relationships with prominent antislavery politicians, especially the handful of potential Whig allies in the U.S. House of Representatives. Antislavery representatives served as conduits through which abolitionists might broadcast portions of their message to a national audience. As political abolitionists lobbied and cooperated with antislavery congressmen, together they helped spread an anti–Slave Power message to an ever more receptive Northern public.

Chapter 3 explains how Liberty partisans also used electoral politics to draw attention to the Slave Power's influence over both major parties. Capitalizing on intense competition between Whigs and Democrats in many Northern constituencies, abolitionists marshaled balances of power to impede major-party attempts to evade the slavery question. These efforts were especially productive in New England's majority-rule elections, where Liberty men forced repeated runoffs as a way to further expose Democrats' and Whigs' responsibility for upholding the Slave Power.

The next two chapters demonstrate how the Mexican-American War provoked an explosion of anti–Slave Power sentiment across the North, and how political abolitionists exploited this popular upsurge. Heated congressional debates over slavery's westward extension powerfully exhibited the growing appeal of antislavery arguments developed by political abolitionists. Coalition-minded Liberty men then seized on this widespread anti-extension feeling to make the case for a new, broader anti–Slave Power party. While antislavery Whigs and Democrats still clung to faint hopes that their parties might nominate anti-extensionist presidential tickets, Liberty coalitionists laid the groundwork for the Free Soil Party. With its expanded ranks, third-party antislavery emerged more powerful than ever in Congress.

The final chapters illustrate how Free Soil congressmen deftly used the toolkit developed by political abolitionists in the 1830s and early 1840s to further combat the Slave Power in the first half of the 1850s. Chapter 6 focuses on Free Soil opposition to the so-called Compromise of 1850 and demonstrates how political abolitionists strove, through state-level coalition politics and congressional agitation, to sustain anti–Slave Power opposition to the newest efforts to silence debate over slavery. Thus, as chapter 7 explicates, when the 1854 Kansas-Nebraska Act triggered a new crisis, Free Soil leaders in and out of Congress stood ready to organize and promote the anti-Nebraska coalition that quickly evolved into the Republican Party and became a powerful anti–Slave Power force in congressional and electoral politics.

Vignettes describing five elections for speaker of the House punctuate this story at key moments and highlight political abolitionists' efforts to reshape congressional politics. As a crucial component of their assault on the Slave Power's national ascendancy, political abolitionists emphasized Southern domination of the House speakership. Abolitionists aptly perceived the formidable policymaking role of antebellum speakers of the House, who determined all committee assignments without resort to the sorts of formalistic seniority rules that have shaped later congressional committee appointments. A closer look at a series of antebellum speakership contests provides another window into how antislavery politicians first imagined they could, and then eventually did, control the organization of the House of Representatives—often *the* pivotal battleground for the future of slavery in the American polity.

The book's conclusion explores the persistent role of political abolitionists' antislavery policy agenda and anti–Slave Power rhetoric in the politics of the late 1850s and early 1860s, as the national government lurched towards disunion, Civil War, and finally, emancipation.

The story that follows then is among the more impressive examples in American history of a social movement that found itself shut out from national policymaking and thus moved into political activism to bring its issues before the nation. Political abolitionists' strategic decisions led to perhaps the most successful and important third-party political mobilization in American history. To better examine this remarkable development, this book will shine a light on numerous arcane legislative and electoral rules, obscure convention maneuvering, internal dissent among political abolitionists, and many disappointing or unexpected political reverses. This was the complicated and occasionally unseemly labyrinth political abolitionists were compelled to navigate. The degree to which many of them came to resemble conventional politicians, with somewhat loftier aspirations, underscores their pragmatism and evolving tactical sophistication. Liberty and Free Soil leaders appreciated that transforming national politics first required an understanding of how to operate effectively within that institutional milieu.

Political abolitionists incubated an anti–Slave Power politics that perceptively assessed the roots of slavery's power in American politics and simultaneously offered greater promise for capturing the imagination of Northern voters than any other antislavery appeal offered by white or black abolitionists, whether Garrisonians, Liberty men, Whigs, or Democrats. Political abolitionists rightly saw the rise of the Republican Party as a vindication of their years of contesting the Slave Power's control of national politics, even if the party fell short of their most ambitious aims. Political abolitionists had worked for decades to make slavery and the Slave Power the central issues in national political debate, and by the mid-1850s, they seemed to have succeeded. By concentrating on political abolitionists' adroit tactics and use of the Slave Power argument to challenge the two-party system of Whigs and Democrats, we can better understand how they conceived of national political reorganization and then strove, with significant success, to make their vision a reality.

* CHAPTER ONE *

Political Abolition and the Slave Power Argument, 1835–1840

Abolitionists comprised a tiny fraction of the Northern populace in the 1830s. Widely reviled, disparaged, and sometimes physically threatened, abolitionists nevertheless quickly devised ways to recruit new adherents to the small but burgeoning movement. Among their most important and effective strategies, abolitionists crafted a persuasive analysis identifying a Southern "Slave Power" that controlled national politics and corrupted American democracy. To understand and ultimately overcome the Slave Power's stranglehold on federal policymaking, abolitionists argued, one first had to recognize its domination of both the Whig and Democratic Parties. Historians have long appreciated the importance of this anti–Slave Power rhetoric in the rise of moderate, popular antislavery politics in the second half of the 1850s. In seeking this argument's roots, however, we have often missed the degree to which abolitionist activists developed and shaped this concept as both a rational analysis of American party politics and an *abolitionist* partisan political argument.

Too often the abolitionists' Slave Power argument is characterized as rooted primarily in either an irrational paranoid anticonspiratorial style in American politics,[1] or in the populist impulses of Jacksonian antimonopolism.[2] A more general tendency to see the Slave Power concept as an appeal to amoral anti-Southernism has further combined to dissociate the argument from its abolitionist pedigree.[3] These prevailing perspectives have shrouded abolitionists' roles in pioneering this argument. Abolitionists recognized that opposition to the Slave Power could encompass a broad spectrum of Northern political opinion. Abolitionists gradually accepted the potential alliances this elasticity promoted because they increasingly believed that Slave Power control over the government constituted the primary obstacle to emancipation. If they could wrest the support of the federal government from slavery, they argued, the institution would soon crumble. In campaigning against the Slave Power, political abolitionists incorporated a sometimes underappreciated policy program based on a constitutional interpretation formulated especially (but not exclusively) by Ohio Liberty Party leader Salmon Chase. Holding that the U.S. Constitution did not sanction *federal* action to establish or protect slavery, Liberty men charged that the Slave Power had diverted the federal government from its constitutional responsibility to promote freedom everywhere within its jurisdiction.[4]

The crucial *political* innovation within abolitionists' Slave Power argument, though, was their analysis of the cross-sectional Whig and Democratic parties as structured to advance the proslavery agenda of Southern political elites. By the late 1830s, political abolitionists characterized these parties as the central mechanisms through which the Slave Power maintained political dominance. With even avowed antislavery Whigs and Democrats routinely privileging partisan obligations and supporting slaveholders and their sympathizers for the nation's highest offices, abolitionists perceptively identified the party system's fundamental role in sustaining the Slave Power's supremacy.

Motivated by a profound commitment to weakening and eventually eradicating American slavery, antebellum political abolitionists' Slave Power argument was both a strategic rhetorical device and a central component of their policy agenda. This Slave Power argument informed nearly all of their tactical decisions and convinced many of the need for an independent abolitionist party. As they demanded a thorough restructuring of national political debate around the issues of slavery and freedom, political abolitionists ultimately concluded that to combat the Slave Power they would have to extricate themselves from the two parties it controlled. By the time the phrase "Slave Power" was popularized in 1839, abolitionists were already well on their way to making this argument the basis of a platform for the embryonic political grouping that became the Liberty Party.

Antebellum abolitionists' comprehensive and sustained institutional analysis differentiated their Slave Power argument from the earlier anti-Southern political rhetoric on which it seems to have drawn. During the mid-1830s, abolitionists updated old arguments to emphasize new aggressions: especially the House gag rule against antislavery petitions, postal censorship of abolitionist mailings, and proslavery expansionists' designs on Texas. While Early Republic forerunners had reacted bitterly to specific affronts like the 1793 Fugitive Slave Act or Missouri's admission as a slave state, antebellum abolitionists, by contrast, mobilized each new offense to build an enduring antislavery politics aimed not merely at stopping the next incursion, but at destabilizing the national political system as a vital step towards vanquishing Southern slavery.[5]

Confronting the Slaveholding Power in the mid-1830s: Postal Censorship, the Gag Rule, and Texas

Through energetic postal and petition campaigns, abolitionists challenged Southern slaveholders and their Northern accomplices, who responded with antidemocratic efforts to smother abolitionism. As antislavery activists confronted a proslavery federal government, they embroiled themselves ever more deeply in the political process. Both the inaugural issue of William Lloyd Garrison's Boston-published *Liberator* in 1831 and the Declaration of Sentiments issued at the American Anti-Slavery Society's founding meeting in 1833 had urged constitutional federal restrictions on slavery, underscoring abolitionists' early commitment to political action. In the second half of the 1830s, slaveholders' efforts to censor abolitionist mailings and gag antislavery petitions, as well as to augment their political power by annexing Texas, led abolitionists to foreground claims about the political dangers slavery posed to free white Northerners.[6]

Even their ostensibly apolitical "moral suasion" brought abolitionists into the maelstrom of national politics. Most famously associated with Garrison and the *Liberator*, moral suasion initially presupposed that abolitionists must convince liberal Southerners of the immorality of slavery and convert them to the antislavery cause. This model of inducing conversions evoked the preachers of the Second Great Awakening, who converted thousands to a new, more proactive evangelical Protestantism. By 1835, the American-Anti Slavery Society's moral suasion campaign had churned out reams of pamphlets, tracts, and newspapers and sent lecturing agents traveling across the North to spread their antislavery gospel.[7]

That year, the American Anti-Slavery Society embarked on its most impressive expansion of the moral suasion campaign. Capitalizing on the sophisticated national postal system and discounted mailing rates for newspapers, the society's New York office circulated mounds of antislavery literature to potential Southern converts. This postal onslaught mailed at least 175,000 separate items into the slave states in the summer of 1835 alone. Outraged Southerners alleged that abolitionists sought to incite slave insurrection, and the conflict came to a head when South Carolina vigilantes broke into the Charleston post office to seize and publicly burn a sack of mail their postmaster had detained.[8]

Keenly aware that postal censorship discomfited many who had previously spurned antislavery agitation, abolitionists railed against federal complicity as President Andrew Jackson's slave-owning postmaster general, Amos Kendall, deliberately looked the other way while subordinates ignored federal law. New York City's Democratic postmaster, Samuel Gouverneur, deferred to his slaveholding bosses and asked the American Anti-Slavery Society to put their campaign on hiatus pending formal instructions from Kendall. When the society refused, Gouverneur took it upon himself to withhold their mailings. Soon after, President Jackson sought congressional legislation barring "incendiary" materials from the mails. Although Congress rejected the president's proposal, the request itself corroborated abolitionist arguments that proslavery politicians had "*determined to annihilate American liberty altogether!*"[9]

South Carolina governor George McDuffie's response to the postal campaign especially substantiated abolitionist charges about slavery's antagonism to open political discussion. McDuffie's November 1835 address to the state legislature eulogized "domestic slavery" as the "CORNERSTONE OF OUR REPUBLICAN EDIFICE" and pronounced that abolitionists deserved to be punished "BY DEATH WITHOUT BENEFIT OF CLERGY." McDuffie even went so far as to demand Northern penal laws to squelch antislavery activism. Four other Southern legislatures endorsed similar resolutions, and several Northern politicians, including New York governor William Marcy (a Democrat), expressed sympathy—though no Northern states actually criminalized abolitionism. Noting Northern revulsion at such outrageous Southern ultimatums, abolitionist James Birney, a reformed ex-slaveholder himself, commented, "McDuffie's Message is doing a great deal for the salvation of the Country." Abolitionists learned quickly that they could advance their own movement by deliberately provoking Southern overreactions.[10]

The petition controversy that gripped the House of Representatives from 1835 through 1844 even more dramatically influenced the growth and politicization of abolitionism. This petition controversy grew directly out of the main political strategy advocated by abolitionists in the early 1830s: targeting congressional abolition of slavery in the District of Columbia as an *initial* policy goal, one they hoped would be the first in a long line of federal legislative inroads against American slavery. Other policy changes that abolitionists assumed would follow included abolition in federal territories, a ban on new slave states, prohibition of slavery at federal forts and on the high seas, and most potentially revolutionary, prohibition of the extensive interstate slave trade—"the great door to the slave Bastile, left in the side of the constitutional temple," as Utica abolitionist lawyer Alvan Stewart described it. This prospect of domestic slave trade interdiction, with its radical challenge to property rights and questionable constitutionality, lurked in the background of federal conflicts over slavery, but abolitionists more often emphasized first abolishing slavery where clearly under federal authority, most conspicuously in the District of Columbia. Treating such proposals with deadly seriousness, slaveholding congressmen went to great lengths to avert any such entering wedge for the abolitionist legislative program.[11]

No Southern offense did as much to inspire the Slave Power argument as the infamous gag rule. Even more egregious than efforts to censor abolitionist mailings, in the spring of 1836, proslavery House majorities inaugurated a policy of systematically silencing antislavery petitioners. The political storm that erupted over abolitionist petitioning would dominate debate over slavery and the Slave Power for the next nine years. Imperious Southern tactics to suppress antislavery petitions became abolitionists' clearest evidence of the troubling political power of slavery. Through this experience, abolitionists further apprehended the allure of a Slave Power argument.[12]

This "Pearl Harbor of the slavery controversy," as historian William Freehling aptly described it, came on unexpectedly, during a routine round of petition presentation in December 1835. Abolitionists had been submitting petitions since the very first Congress, but after a pitched initial debate in 1790, most subsequent Congresses had managed to ignore these pleas. Beginning in 1834 though, the newly founded American Anti-Slavery Society spearheaded an expanded, organized drive that gathered at least 34,000 signatures on antislavery petitions, most of which called for a House bill to end slavery in the District of Columbia. In the early days of the 1835–36 session, South Carolina freshman James Henry Hammond impetuously demanded that Congress refuse to even *receive* such petitions.[13] For almost two months, the House debated the merits of receiving petitions for abolition in the District, with a small group of Northern Whigs, led by ex-president John Quincy Adams (who had returned to Congress as a representative from Massachusetts in 1831) and Vermont representative William Slade, defending abolitionist petitioners against both proslavery extremists like Hammond and Democratic allies of Vice President, and presidential hopeful, Martin Van Buren (of New York). Finally, Charleston's Henry Laurens Pinckney, trying to "arrest discussion of the question of slavery," "harmonize the Union," and "put down fanaticism," proposed that Congress refer antislavery petitions to a select committee chaired by himself. This committee returned with a report declaring abolition of slavery in the capital inexpedient but constitutional, and recommending the first gag rule, which stipulated that all petitions or resolutions "relating in any way, or to any extent whatsoever, to the subject of slavery or the abolition of slavery" were to be automatically and indefinitely "laid on the table." Cries of "Order!" silenced Adams's lone protest, and the Democratic leadership rammed through Pinckney's resolution, soon to be known as the gag rule, or just the gag, by a 117–68 vote.[14]

As abolitionists followed the debate over petitioners' rights, they quickly discerned its potential to bolster their arguments about the incompatibility of slavery and freedom. While the Senate managed to quietly bypass antislavery petitions through an esoteric procedural mechanism, abolitionists fulminated against the more barefaced House restriction, warning that "the oppression that has so long robbed the slave of his rights and liberties, is now grasping at the rights and liberties of all." Henceforth abolitionists would cast their movement as "the conflict of liberty with slavery—the issue of which is to be universal freedom or universal bondage." "Let no one think for a moment," the American Anti-Slavery Society admonished, "that because he is not an abolitionist, his liberties are not and will not be invaded." In their calls for antislavery political mobilization, abolitionists questioned the honor, independence, and (implicitly) manhood of the Slave Power's "servile" Northern abettors, whom abolitionists besmirched with the derisive epithet "doughface" (which eccentric Virginia congressman John Randolph of Roanoke had famously, cryptically coined during the 1820 debates over Missouri's admission as a slave state).[15]

The House gag on antislavery petitions, along with Southern contempt for sanctity of the mails, led abolitionists to increasingly emphasize the coherence and power of the slaveholding interest in the federal government. Anticipating language abolitionists would soon deploy about a voracious Slave Power, the American Anti-Slavery Society lamented in 1836 that "the broadest and highest bulwark of our liberties already lies prostrate to make room for the grasping monster." Alvan Stewart, in a letter to the founding meeting of the Pennsylvania Anti-Slavery Society, similarly anticipated future personifications of the Slave Power by describing slavery as "a dreadful monster" preying on slaves' labor and Northerners' freedoms.[16]

The great strength of these arguments was their ability to both target a wider audience and remain persuasive to immediatist abolitionists. Addressing a convention of committed activists, the eloquent antislavery lecturing agent Henry B. Stanton stressed his paramount concern for "the rights of free citizens," cautioning that the apparent "spirit of slavery at the North would not only prevent freeing the slaves of the South, but would make us slaves." In raising the specter of slavery's threat to white freedom, Stanton's remarks underscore many abolitionists' understanding of, and immersion in, a political culture in which white male independence was so jealously guarded. Stanton, however, also exhorted antislavery activists to capitalize on the Northern outrage at Southern encroachments as a tactic for inducing new conversions to abolitionism.[17]

Antislavery activists keenly noted that proslavery efforts to curtail Northern civil liberties paralleled the mid-1830s wave of anti-abolitionist rioting in the North. Easily connecting this mob violence to their political argument, abolitionists perceived and publicized the fact that local political elites often encouraged, and sometimes outright led, the hostile crowds. Among the foremost advocates of antislavery politics, Birney faced threats of personal violence and riotous mobs as he published an abolitionist newspaper in free Ohio. When an 1836 riot destroyed Birney's press, Cincinnati lawyer Salmon Chase offered his first public defense of the antislavery movement. Chase exemplified how threats to free discussion drew thousands into antislavery activism: "Much as I have deprecated the course of the abolitionists, I regard all the consequences of their publications, as evils comparatively light when contrasted with the evils produced by the prevalence of the mob spirit." Chase soon became one of the most effective champions of an abolitionist legal argument and political strategy designed to unite opponents of the Slave Power.[18]

As anti-abolitionist mob violence convinced growing numbers that slavery threatened republican freedom, the martyrdom of Reverend Elijah P. Lovejoy in late 1837 further galvanized the abolitionist movement. Lovejoy's religious newspapers spoke out against slavery first in St. Louis (where the institution was legal) and then in Alton, Illinois (where it was not). Anti-abolitionist crowds destroyed three of his printing presses, so when the fourth arrived in Alton, Lovejoy insisted on defending it and was shot to death by an angry mob. Abolitionists decried this lawlessness as "pregnant with destruction to our free institutions." However, they also recognized that "this event has opened eyes and ears heretofore closed" and could be used to "rouse up, and unite the freemen of the non-slaveholding states . . . whatever may be their sentiments respecting southern slavery and its immediate abolition."[19]

By the time of Lovejoy's murder, these were familiar arguments that fit neatly into the narrative abolitionists were crafting about how proslavery interests endangered freedom of discussion. Over the 1830s, abolitionists elaborated a response to Southern political power that formed the foundation of the Slave Power argument. As early as 1837, abolitionists denounced slaveholding congressmen and their congressional doughface allies as a nefarious "slaveholding power in the national councils." Indiana abolitionists seeking to create a statewide antislavery society warned, "The slaveholding power is *aiming to extend* itself into all the states; and . . . it will never rest satisfied with a less sacrifice than the dearest rights of free men." Facing this "slaveholding power," abolitionists enjoined an organized political response from the "friends of freedom."[20]

Abolitionists pursued their strategy of highlighting slaveholders' tyrannical assaults on Northern liberties through a vigorous effort to ensure that the gag rule remained in the national political spotlight. Antislavery societies across the North continued to inundate the House, and especially Adams, with petitions against slavery in the District of Columbia, and Congress repeatedly passed new rules to stifle them. In the spring of 1837, the American Anti-Slavery Society implemented an ambitious new petitioning campaign designed to further accelerate the congressional controversy, appreciating that the more names they amassed for the House to silence, the more they would dramatize the antislavery cause. Convening at the New York office to oversee the centralized operation, celebrated Quaker poet John Greenleaf Whittier and Henry Stanton, two of the most highly politicized abolitionist spokesmen, joined the indefatigable Theodore Dwight Weld, who had been the most prolific and moving antislavery lecturing agent before his voice gave out in 1836. Together, this committee disseminated instructions to every county society, requesting the names of abolitionists who could be entrusted to circulate petitions in each town in their county. Trumpeting the importance of congressional agitation, the committee reminded local organizers:

> The success which has attended the exercise of the right of petition thus far, in producing discussion in legislative bodies, in arousing the people... has shown, that it is one of the most efficient instrumentalities which the friends of the slave can employ. The voice of the people, thus expressed, can arouse the nation.

At the same time, the Anti-Slavery Convention of American Women ran a similarly extensive women's petition campaign with central boards in Boston, New York, and Philadelphia.[21]

Striking grassroots mobilization combined with the administrative feats of petition drive coordinators like Stanton, Weld, Whittier, and South Carolina–born abolitionist sisters Sarah and Angelina Grimké to swell the antislavery petition tide to unprecedented levels — 415,000 signatures on petitions to Congress in the centralized campaign's first year by the Anti-Slavery Society's accounting. This impressive output ensured the continued salience of congressional debates over antislavery petitions. From 1836 through 1844, the gag rule provided the most consistent and compelling evidence for arguments about the potent and sinister influence of slavery in Congress, and in American politics generally.[22]

Abolitionists also inserted the politics of the gag into the state legislative arena by petitioning state legislatures to send antislavery resolutions to congressmen who might find it more difficult to ignore the voices of "sovereign states." The Massachusetts House of Representatives responded to such state-level petitions by inviting Stanton in 1837 to address a committee considering resolutions opposing the gag and advocating abolition in the District of Columbia. Over two days, Stanton ranged across topics as varied as the constitutionality of abolition in the District, the immorality of property in man, federal jurisdiction over the domestic slave trade, and the diplomatic embarrassment caused by slavery at the capital. Returning frequently to proslavery control of Congress, Stanton charged, "In our National Legislature, freedom of speech is struck dumb, by the omnipotence of slavery," and the assemblymen responded with resolutions assailing the gag rule and affirming congressional power over slavery in the District.[23]

Abolitionists speaking to state legislative committees soon became commonplace. In 1837 Birney addressed the Vermont legislature and found a receptive audience containing many "abolitionists ... of the most thorough stamp." The following year, Birney and, more remarkably, Angelina Grimké were called before the Massachusetts legislature to expound on slavery in the District of Columbia. A year after that, New York abolitionists Alvan Stewart and William Chaplin spent two nights addressing the Judiciary Committee of the New York Assembly on the same topic.[24]

State legislative hearings provided an additional stage from which abolitionists could broadcast their goals. Abolitionists also pressured state legislatures for African American civil and political rights, but the discussions that called prominent abolitionists before state legislatures in the 1830s mostly pertained to congressional proceedings on the gag rule and slavery in the District of Columbia, the "foul cancer on the breast of the body politic." Consequently, abolitionist political organizers often viewed state legislatures as another route into national political debate, believing that "the action of Congress will be but the echo of the action of the State Legislatures."[25]

Abolitionists' antipathy to the slaveholding interest in Congress also heightened their attention to proslavery designs on the newly independent republic of Texas. Abolitionists viewed the recent Texan war of independence from Mexico as part of a proslavery conspiracy and claimed that Southern politicians advocated annexation primarily for the purpose of increasing slaveholders' congressional representation. The expansive Texan territorial claims made abolitionist anxieties about increased Southern representation particularly acute. Indeed, they feared Texas could be carved into as many as six to eight new slave states.[26]

From early on, the writings of Benjamin Lundy alerted fellow abolitionists to the machinations of slaveholders working in concert as a pro-annexation "party." Lundy's detailed knowledge of Texas (acquired while scouting the region for sites for potential freedmen colonies) shaped abolitionists' perceptions of the Lone Star republic, and his widely disseminated pamphlets argued that Texans revolted to protect slavery. Asserting that the "influence of the SLAVE HOLDING PARTY in the United States is now so completely in the ascendant, and so thoroughly sways the deliberations and proceedings of our Federal Government," Lundy cautioned that admitting Texas would imperil the American union.[27]

Reiterating arguments about Southern demands to control the national government, abolitionists warned that slaveholders' efforts to safeguard slavery against dissent extended even beyond suppressing Northerners' civil liberties. Southerners now demanded a bellicose and dangerous foreign policy designed to guarantee their national supremacy in the face of rapid Northern population growth. If successful, the annexation project could give "the slaveholding power" a "permanent ascendancy" over national policymaking.[28]

Proslavery responses confirmed abolitionists' apprehensions. Unabashedly promoting annexation to shore up slaveholders' political power, Mississippi's state legislature, for example, openly advocated the measure as a means to maintain the South's "equipoise of influence" in Congress. The Cincinnati abolitionist newspaper the *Philanthropist* angrily retorted: "Are the people of the free States prepared to see al[l] their political power and influence unjustly wrested from them? . . . Are they ready to be thrown into the balance as a mere make-weight, an 'equipoise,' to the rogues and renegades of Texas?" If the United States annexed Texas, the *Philanthropist* admonished, the South would soon "have concentrated the *whole political power* of the Union in its own hands." Abolitionists quickly followed these forebodings to their logical conclusion that the additional Southern representation gained from Texas would enable slaveholders to further stifle Northern liberty. "What will hinder them," American Anti-Slavery Society corresponding secretary Elizur Wright, Jr., queried, "when by the annexation of Texas they have secured a Southern majority in the federal legislature . . . from crushing the very life of liberty throughout the entire republic?"[29]

To the abolitionists' delight, Northern sentiment responded to their alarm. By 1838, the Rhode Island, Vermont, Ohio, and Massachusetts legislatures along with the lower houses in New York and Maine had passed resolutions opposing annexation and demanding that their congressmen vote against it. In the report accompanying the Massachusetts resolutions, state senator James Alvord characterized the annexation proposal as a "flagrant wrong" designed to extend slavery and "increase the relative power and weight of the Southern States." This outpouring of Northern opposition helped stanch (at least temporarily) Southern ambitions for an annexation treaty. Abolitionists' arguments against the aggrandizing slaveholding power seemed to have worked. The North writ large had rejected annexation. The Massachusetts Anti-Slavery Society rejoiced, "Thanks to the abolitionists, the free states have been roused to the disgrace and ruin of becoming a partner in the crimes of that bloody and slave-trading republic." While thrilled with their success, abolitionists remained vigilant, aware that Southern politicians would likely seize "the first favourable opportunity of making war on Mexico" to secure Texas.[30]

The Anti–Slave Power Basis for Abolitionist Political Action

Over the course of the late 1830s, political abolitionists arraigned the major parties' dependence on the Slave Power increasingly frequently and forcefully. Consequently, as political abolitionists further elaborated and disseminated their analyses of proslavery control of American politics, they also began to explore new tactics, including, ultimately, abolitionist electoral strategies.

In 1839, abolitionist judge William Jay's *View of the Action of the Federal Government in Behalf of Slavery* provided the most comprehensive analysis yet of the structural underpinnings of slaveholders' political dominance. The second son of John Jay, the Revolutionary-era diplomat, New York governor, and first Chief Justice of the U.S. Supreme Court, William inherited his father's Federalist social conservatism, but also deep religious devotion and moral antipathy to slavery. A West Chester County judge for over two decades before being ousted in 1843 on account of his abolitionism, Jay laid out an especially systematic exposition of slavery's impact on federal policy. Dedicating particular attention to the "slave power in Congress," Jay's 1839 treatise demonstrated how Southerners controlled national politics through their disproportionate congressional numbers (supplied by the three-fifths rule), united "anxiety to protect and perpetuate slavery," and abilities to intimidate with threats of disunion or to co-opt Northern politicians "acting from party views" or "their love of southern trade."[31]

That same year, Ohio Democratic senator Thomas Morris helped broadcast these ideas to a national audience by encapsulating the detailed analyses of abolitionists like Jay in the epithet "slave power." Reaching a broad Northern readership, Morris's valedictory firmly ensconced the phrase in national political discourse. Morris boldly declared, "The slave interest has at this moment the whole power of the country in its hands." Although at times conflating the "the slave power of the South, and banking power of the North," Morris saw no reason for hope in the alleged democratic principles of his old party (nor in the Whig Party): "Both political parties . . . courted them [abolitionists] in private and denounced them in public, and both have equally deceived them." Echoing abolitionist arguments, Morris implored Northerners to join him in contesting "the insatiable grasp of the slaveholding power as being used and felt in the free states."[32]

Notwithstanding the clarity with which Morris dissociated his anti–Slave Power stance from the proslavery major parties, some modern historians have viewed his Senate activism as indicative of the Democratic origins of the Slave Power idea. Linking the concept to Jacksonian opposition to the Second Bank of the United States and its affiliated "Money Power," as Morris sometimes did, Jonathan Earle, for example, contends that Morris himself "formulated and popularized the concept of a Slave Power." Closer scrutiny of abolitionists' political arguments in the late 1830s, however, reveals that rather than being a direct outgrowth of Democratic populism, the Ohio senator's anti–Slave Power sentiments likely drew at least as much on the political thought of southern Ohio abolitionists, many of whom did not share Morris's economic views (much less his partisan affiliation). Not long after Morris's first antislavery Senate oration, in which he had worried publicly over Southern attempts "to overwhelm us with the power of this Government," Morris joined leading Ohio abolitionists James Birney and John Rankin at the November 1836 founding of the Clermont County Anti-Slavery Society, whose members resolved "[T]hat the recent encroachments by the South on the Indisputable rights of the North . . . are fearful omens of the utter prostration of our liberties, if slavery be long continued." Moreover, from the vantage point of Morris's southern Ohio, the threat slavery posed to Northern rights had been made all too real in the repeated incursions of Kentucky kidnappers seeking to seize black Ohioans as fugitive slaves. It seems probable that Morris learned far more of his anti–Slave Power political argument from moralistic associates like Birney than from fellow Democrats who repeatedly sought to stifle his antislavery outbursts and jettisoned him for antislavery heterodoxy even before his 1839 speech—which he delivered as a lame duck.[33]

By the summer of 1839, assaults on the Slave Power saturated abolitionist publications. After Morris helped publicize the phrase, abolitionists widely adopted "Slave Power" as the most prevalent, pithy name for the critique of Southern political clout that had been elaborated in Jay's *View of the Action of the Federal Government* and propagated in abolitionist writings and speeches for years prior. Many now championed termination of Slave Power control over the federal government as the first, fundamental step towards eradicating American slavery. This argument thus became the basis of political abolitionists' case for deeper involvement in electoral politics.

Abolitionists across the North emphasized Congress as the linchpin in their anti–Slave Power program. Abolitionists had long recognized Congress as a locus of slaveholders' national power, because of the extra representation Southern states received for three-fifths of slaves. This added influence afforded to "the slave power in Congress" assured the protection of slavery over "all *the other* interests of the country." Enough free state representatives invariably acquiesced to this dominating Slave Power's demands and compromised away "the liberties as well as the interests of northern freemen."[34]

In the second half of the 1830s, some abolitionist leaders thus began to insist that abolitionists could conscientiously vote only for candidates who could be trusted to resist this Slave Power in Congress. These abolitionists framed right political action as both moral duty and a practical strategic departure. As early as the summer of 1836, the American Anti-Slavery Society had responded to the gag by recommending that abolitionists "give your suffrages hereafter only to such men as you have reason to believe will not sacrifice your rights." By late 1838, wealthy abolitionist philanthropist Gerrit Smith advocated that abolition societies require members to withhold votes from candidates who did not support immediate abolition and rebuked "sham abolitionists" who cast ballots for proslavery candidates.[35]

As the battle over the gag rule involved abolitionist leaders ever more deeply in political action, many became convinced that the national two-party system represented the most important source of slavery's political power. Abolitionists began to publicly renounce earlier political affiliations and independently evaluate each individual candidate. For example, Whittier, a one-time local Whig operative, increasingly perceived that, on the national level, Northern Whigs were, like their Democratic counterparts, beholden to slaveholding co-partisans. Already by 1836, Whittier envisioned, however overoptimistically, the abolitionists as a powerful independent bloc: "No party in the country is now so thoroughly organized, and so united as the abolitionists. . . . They move in a mass . . . So long as they remain thus, they are invincible." But the next few years would demonstrate all too clearly the naiveté of expecting abolitionists to "move in a mass" without any institutionalized political organization.[36]

Putting antislavery above partisanship became a tactical necessity once abolitionists came to view the two-party system as integral to slaveholders' control of the national government. Initially abolitionists across the North advocated interrogation of candidates for state and national offices. Embracing a strategy previously employed by British abolitionists, American antislavery organizers developed policy questionnaires and then publicized which, if any, candidates furnished acceptably antislavery answers. In contests where no candidate offered satisfactory responses, abolitionists advocated "scattering" their votes to write-in candidates: "Let every friend of the slave nominate his own candidate in all those places where the political parties refuse to put up worthy men." In the many New England elections that required a majority, "scattering" abolitionists could demonstrate their influence by preventing an election anywhere they could marshal even the narrowest balance of power.[37]

The questionnaire strategy transformed the relationship of abolitionists to the party system. By publicly proclaiming which candidates were worthy of abolitionist support, antislavery societies demanded that abolitionists abandon, or at least loosen, former party ties. They could no longer act as Whigs or Democrats; they would now vote their antislavery convictions first. If abolitionists could make it widely "understood that whatever may be their individual political sentiments, they will not vote for any candidate of any party who is ready to sell their rights to the Slaveholders," then many abolitionists believed the parties would soon select antislavery candidates. Too often though, candidates failed to respond, gave noncommittal answers, or reneged on their promises once in office.[38]

Whittier and the abolitionists of Essex County, Massachusetts, attempted the questionnaire strategy as early as 1834, with Whittier pushing his old Whig ally Representative Caleb Cushing to pledge support for abolition in the District of Columbia. In 1838, Cushing's ambiguous responses to the county antislavery society convinced the group that abolitionists should vote against him. Cushing observed these proceedings silently and undetected in the back of the society's meeting. When Whittier arrived the next morning to implore him to take a bolder stance, Cushing, still in his nightclothes, hurriedly drafted a letter in support of abolition in the District. He was then safely reelected with abolitionist backing.[39]

Identifying Congress as one of the most important bastions of Slave Power influence, abolitionists especially targeted elections for the House of Representatives. Antislavery publications disseminated model interrogatories to be posed to congressional candidates across the North. Although the 1838 annual meeting of the American Anti-Slavery Society declaimed against forming an abolitionist political party as "suicidal," the society urged abolitionists "to vote, irrespective of party, for those only who will advocate the principles of universal liberty." The society particularly directed abolitionists to interrogate congressional candidates and publish the answers across their districts. Through vigorous, organized interrogations, abolitionists hoped to "send many able advocates of our cause to Congress, where above all places they are now most needed." If abolitionists could influence the Northern parties to nominate antislavery candidates, the next Congress might well "agitate slavery to its foundation." An *Emancipator* correspondent averred, "Congress is but a weathercock. It veers with the wind . . . let it blow strongly towards abolition."[40]

By 1838, abolitionists in Massachusetts's Fourth Congressional District (Middlesex County) had constructed the nation's best-organized vote scattering campaign. Neither the incumbent Democrat nor his Whig challenger adequately answered the interrogatories posed by local abolitionists. Consequently, they withheld support from both. This scattering strategy could be highly effective in close races where victory required an absolute majority—as in Massachusetts congressional contests (and most other antebellum New England elections). The American Anti-Slavery Society sent Stanton to canvass the district to thwart the election of either candidate. Over five months and three ballots, abolitionists prevented an election. Whittier congratulated Stanton, predicting that this obstruction would "establish conclusively the fact, that there is power in our principles to break down the despotism of party." Abolitionists elsewhere attentively followed the contest as "one of surpassing interest, not to the electors of Middlesex merely, but to the free states at large." Unfortunately, at the fourth election, Democrats mustered an increased turnout and narrowly reelected their candidate, with many who had previously scattered votes to abolitionists returning to old loyalties. Still, abolitionists had demonstrated that they could be politically formidable and that officeholders risked defeat if they disregarded antislavery constituent pressure. As Bruce Laurie has argued, this impressive scattering campaign convinced many Massachusetts abolitionists that direct political action would be essential to the future of abolitionist tactics.[41]

Abolitionists in the West similarly recognized the importance of direct political action, even though they could not exploit the sort of majoritarian electoral rules that had made vote scattering so attractive in Massachusetts. Gamaliel Bailey, Birney's successor as editor of the Cincinnati *Philanthropist*, urged Ohio abolitionists to use their votes to reward friends and punish enemies, recognizing that such pressure might force politicians to adopt stronger antislavery positions. Bailey interrogated local candidates, believing that "politicians in this community *are* greatly concerned as to how we vote"; in 1838, Cincinnati Whigs even admitted to Bailey that abolitionists' votes might well "control the fate of the elections."[42]

In the run-up to Ohio's 1838 contest, candidates from both parties ignored abolitionist questionnaires, but with Senator Morris's term expiring, Bailey recommended that abolitionists vote for Democratic state legislators to promote the antislavery spokesman's reelection. After Bailey highlighted Whig governor Joseph Vance's extradition of an abolitionist indicted in Kentucky for abetting a slave escape, even more Ohio abolitionists abandoned the Whigs. The Ohio Democracy swept into office with this newfound, short-lived abolitionist backing. Ohio abolitionists had shown they "know how to *vote*" and "preached a sermon to the politicians that will not soon be forgotten." Although Ohio abolitionists had clearly manifested their electoral will, the Democratic legislators they had helped elect disregarded their contribution and dumped Morris. These Democrats also bolstered the state's discriminatory Black Laws, ignored abolitionist petitions, and voted against Whig state senator Benjamin Wade's resolution supporting Congress's right to end slavery in the District of Columbia. This betrayal at Columbus pointedly illustrated both the anti-abolitionist leanings of most Northern Democrats and the manifest shortcomings of nonpartisan electoral strategies.[43]

The 1838 New York gubernatorial contest elicited the most widely publicized, controversial, and ultimately disappointing abolitionist use of the questionnaire system. In 1838, New York State Anti-Slavery Society leaders William Jay and Gerrit Smith interrogated Democratic incumbents governor William Marcy and lieutenant governor John Tracy and their Whig challengers William Seward (for governor) and Luther Bradish (for lieutenant). Focusing on issues directly under the purview of the state government, abolitionists asked the candidates whether they would support a state law guaranteeing jury trials for alleged fugitive slaves, repeal of the law allowing Southern masters to keep their slaves in New York for up to nine months, and elimination of the property qualification restricting black male suffrage. While the Democratic candidates answered all three queries unfavorably, Seward and Bradish had to juggle the support of both antislavery and anti-abolitionist Whig constituents.[44]

Facing continued abolitionist pressure, Bradish finally answered Jay and Smith less than a month before the election. Seward's request that Bradish visit his home to confer came two days too late. Bradish answered all three queries so favorably that abolitionists claimed the letter would "diffuse joy through all the anti-slavery associations in the land."[45] Once Bradish answered, Seward felt compelled to respond, but Seward did not join in Bradish's support for equal suffrage. New York Whig leaders despaired over Bradish's more radical letter, as Jay and Smith advised abolitionists to vote only for Bradish and cast no gubernatorial vote. Smith implored abolitionists to "convince these [political] parties . . . that you are not hypocrites" by rejecting candidates who "like Governor Marcy and Mr. Seward, speak out for slavery." Seward's advisor Thurlow Weed feared abolitionism's electoral "influence may be *pervading*, and if so, must prove disastrous." Weed, like many Whigs, presumed political abolitionists sought to destroy the Whig Party and "build an Abolition party" on its "ruins."[46]

Both Seward and Bradish won with a victory margin just shy of 3 percent, and, to abolitionists' dismay, Seward narrowly outpolled Bradish. To many abolitionists, this election proved "the impossibility of wrenching off the adherents of party on the *scattering system*." This "terrible Election" convinced Alvan Stewart and his closest allies that abolitionists could promote antislavery policies only "by forming a 3d party & breaking down one of the great parties."[47]

By early 1839, a small cadre of upstate New York abolitionists, led by Stewart and former Erie Canal commissioner Myron Holley, demanded a new political strategy. These two were soon joined by New York State Anti-Slavery Society president Gerrit Smith, who marveled at the "monstrous . . . inconsistency of talking & writing & praying *against* slavery, at the same time, that we are voting *for* it!" While few abolitionists agreed as yet with Stewart and Holley's third-party project, most shared their interest in combating the Slave Power through politics.[48]

At a well-attended national gathering in Albany, New York, in July 1839, abolitionists resolved to focus on political action and withhold their votes from anti-abolitionist candidates. William Goodell's keynote address fulminated against the "encroachments of the Slaveholding Power," including the gag rule, mails controversy, and efforts to annex Texas. "The events of last five or six years," Goodell asserted, "leave no room for doubt that the SLAVE POWER is now waging a deliberate and determined war against the liberties of the free States." Goodell importuned abolitionists to vote only for avowed opponents of slavery, and the convention, after some controversy, advocated nominating "distinct anti-slavery candidates in case no tried and true friends of emancipation are offered by either of the political parties," but stopped short of supporting a national abolitionist party.[49]

This Albany meeting clearly reflected the increasing politicization among the abolitionist leadership, but Stewart had thus far failed to persuade many colleagues of the need for an independent party. As late as September 1839, Stewart worried about the lack of support from even Joshua Leavitt and Goodell, editors respectively of the American Anti-Slavery Society's *Emancipator* and New York Anti-Slavery Society's *Friend of Man* (and soon to be two of the most dedicated third-party proponents). Applying the Slave Power argument to all Democratic and Whig politicians,

Stewart predicted that any "milk and water abolitionist" nominated by the major parties would "surrender his abolition as a debt of gratitude to the party for his election." By the next month, Stewart and Holley had enlisted Leavitt, whose *Emancipator* became the most important mouthpiece for abolitionist third-party politics. Goodell soon followed. Earlier in 1839, Elizur Wright and Reverend Charles Torrey had split Massachusetts abolitionism over the question of antislavery political action. Before the year's end, Wright was convinced Holley was "above half right" and touted the need for a "HUMAN RIGHTS PARTY" unless the Whigs nominated a decidedly antislavery presidential ticket in 1840.[50]

Making the Case for an Abolitionist Third Party

The approach of the 1840 presidential election powerfully accelerated simmering divisions in the abolitionist movement. The famous and complicated rift between William Lloyd Garrison and political abolitionists deepened in 1839 and 1840, and a pitched debate over the prospect of an abolitionist third party erupted among those who supported political action. With both parties nominating proslavery presidential tickets, a small but committed group of activists worked vigorously to erect an independent abolitionist political party in the crucible of the 1840 campaign.

Conflicts had emerged within the abolitionist movement as early as 1837 over constitutional interpretation and antislavery political activism. At one extreme, Alvan Stewart argued that the Constitution sanctioned federal emancipation in the Southern states, and at the other, Garrison declared the Constitution irredeemably proslavery and rejected voting altogether. Confronting these two politically untenable approaches, national organization leaders like Stanton and Wright fretted about potentially divisive controversies over political tactics. Compounding these tensions were accelerating disputes over the role of women as antislavery lecturers and society officers. For many of the most politically inclined leaders, this "woman question," over which Garrisonians and a number of evangelical abolitionists seemed all too eager to do combat, was beside the point—a distraction that could prejudice Northern public opinion against the more important cause of eradicating slavery. "You never can prevail on the American people to be abolitionists," Gamaliel Bailey worried, "if they become impressed with the notion that in so doing, they must break down a clergy, make women *men*, abolish the Sabbath, and set aside all family and civil government." Elizur Wright, a multitalented former math professor and tireless if sometimes irascible organizer, likewise found controversy over women's activism dangerous and distracting. While believing that "the tom turkeys ought to do the gobbling," Wright expressed disgust at the idea that the national antislavery society should refuse "to employ well qualified agents to address all who will hear, *because they are women*." But "that this question should be brought up by some of our friends as though it were a twin sister of anti-slavery" struck Wright as "mortifying in the extreme." Stanton, while somewhat sympathetic to the women's cause that his new bride Elizabeth Cady Stanton was just beginning to embrace, shared Wright's view that the woman question presented a potentially dangerous diversion from the antislavery crusade.[51]

Garrison, along with his strident anticlericalism and controversial support for women's rights, also championed increasingly radical views about political participation. Garrison's opposition to organized political action has been well-chronicled in both sympathetic and unsympathetic accounts. By the decade's end, he espoused a nonresistant philosophy that condemned all human government as rooted in the implicit threat of violence. Garrison and his acolytes thus refused to implicate themselves in the sin of coercive government.[52]

Tensions escalated as many Massachusetts abolitionists, led by Stanton, Torrey, Wright, and Amos A. Phelps, demanded concrete political action and condemned Garrison's efforts to foment dissension over the "woman question." In the face of this mounting discord, Wright and Stanton made an abortive attempt in 1839 to commit the Massachusetts Anti-Slavery Society to political action. After they failed, they established the Massachusetts Abolition Society, which published the *Massachusetts Abolitionist*. Paralleling the rift among male counterparts, Bay State women abolitionists also divided, with those who rejected Garrison's apparent impiety and expanding reform agenda founding a new Massachusetts Female Emancipation Society, a valuable ally for the Massachusetts Abolition Society and later the Liberty and Free Soil Parties. By late 1839, as controversy reheated, many political abolitionists strove to disassociate the widening conflict over political tactics from earlier friction over women's activism. And indeed some who sympathized with Garrison on women's rights prioritized "the *duty* of political action" and supported the new, political Massachusetts society.[53]

Massachusetts abolitionists exported their divisions to the national society at the 1839 anniversary meeting, which adopted a controversial resolution casting antislavery political action as moral duty. The following year the American Anti-Slavery Society split, this time ostensibly over women's appointment as officers after Garrisonians assembled a larger delegation than their opponents and forced that issue. Still, the schism can be understood only with similar attention to politics. The Massachusetts rift that presaged the national rupture revolved around quarrels over political strategy. When the "woman question" ultimately rent the national society, the debate over political tactics represented an equally crucial fault line, as evidenced by the presence of several women's rights advocates in the American and Foreign Anti-Slavery Society. Almost all leaders of this new organization, founded mainly by evangelicals who had bolted the old society, either supported, or at least accepted, organized abolitionist political action.

For many, though, political action still meant using questionnaires to identify acceptable candidates, but by 1839 the general failure of the interrogatory system contributed to rising interest in independent nominations, and ultimately an abolitionist political party. But that new strategy stemmed as much from abolitionists' evolving analysis of the Slave Power as from specific disappointments with interrogation. By the eve of the 1840 presidential election, the most compelling antislavery political appeal was the Slave Power argument. Political abolitionists argued increasingly vocally that both the Whig and Democratic Parties, as cross-sectional alliances, incentivized Northern politicians to compromise with slaveholders to secure national power. Antislavery Whigs as well as well as doughface Democrats perpetuated a system in which those controlling national policy were invariably slaveholders or their most pliant apologists. To effectively combat the Slave Power, abolitionists would have to construct their own organization. The interrogatory tactic had become necessary when abolitionists insisted on voting for antislavery candidates; a third party became necessary when abolitionists concluded that even committed antislavery politicians would inevitably be beholden to the Slave Power as long as they remained Whigs or Democrats.

Abolitionists, as well as many Northern Whigs, had long criticized Democrats', and especially the Van Buren administration's, friendliness to Southern interests. President Van Buren's opposition to abolition in the District of Columbia, pro-Southern distribution of patronage, and vigorous prosecution of the costly Second Seminole War in Florida (in which U.S. troops were fighting, in part, to recover fugitive slaves under Seminole protection) all attested to the doughfaced character of the Northern Democracy. Van Buren's handling of the *Amistad* case especially infuriated abolitionists. When illegally enslaved Africans aboard the Spanish ship *Amistad* rebelled against their Cuban captors and arrived in the Long Island Sound, the Van Buren administration initially sought to remand the Africans to Spanish authorities. When the case instead went to federal court, abolitionists aided and defended the accused Africans while the Van Buren administration worked to return them to Cuban slavery. Assuming the captives would lose in court, President Van Buren covertly deployed the *U.S.S. Grampus* to Connecticut to spirit the Africans away before their abolitionist allies could appeal, a fact that came to light after the judge surprisingly ruled in the captives' favor.[54]

With Van Buren and the Democrats so obviously pursuing proslavery policies, third-party proponents strove to disabuse "Whig Abolitionists" of the "utter delusion" that "the Whig party are almost an abolition party." As Leavitt explained, "So long as the men in office are 'nominated and elected' members on the ground of adhesion to one party or the other, they will deem their honor virtually pledged to regard the success of their party," and not abolitionism, "as the first object." Alvan Stewart characterized both the Whigs and Democrats as "pro-Slavery parties who hate us more than they do each other," but predicted hopefully that "this nation will, in a short time, be divided into two great parties which will swallow all others up, to wit: an anti-slavery one on one side, and a pro-slavery one on the other."[55]

Political abolitionists even attacked the smattering of abolitionist Whig officeholders, men like Slade and Congressman Seth Gates, a former secretary of the Genesee County (New York) Anti-Slavery Society, for their willingness to support their party's proslavery leadership. By 1840, leading abolitionists dismissed Whigs' claims "to be the friends of the freedom of discussion, the right of petition, [and] the cause of universal liberty," given their continual prioritization of party obligations over antislavery principles. And indeed Whig managers in antislavery Vermont privately admitted to fearing "political abolitionism" as "the darkest cloud in our political horizon."[56]

Henry Clay especially symbolized Whigs' unreliability. Into 1839, Senator Clay was the frontrunner for the Whig presidential nomination. Like Van Buren, Clay had been a key architect of the Second Party System and stood as his party's preeminent national leader, a man who could appeal to both Northern and Southern voters. In his younger days, Clay had developed a modest antislavery reputation, advocating gradual emancipation for Kentucky in 1799, and espousing in the Senate, as late as 1832, a vague hope for slavery's eventual termination. As he prepared for a possible presidential run in 1840, Clay, notwithstanding his ownership of dozens of slaves, felt pressured to convince fellow slaveholders of his sectional loyalty. To allay Southern doubts, Clay's lengthy February 7, 1839, Senate oration recorded his opposition to abolition in the District of Columbia, vilified "ultra abolitionists," and proudly attested that neither of "the two great parties in this country has any designs or aims at abolition." Abolitionists quickly condemned Clay's "abject prostration before the slaveholding power" as confirmation "that both parties are at this time making it the leading object of their movements to identify themselves with slavery." Clay's speech, the *Emancipator* averred, had "opened the eyes of thousands of [Whig] abolitionists" and, abolitionists hoped, "thus weaned them from their long cherished man-worship" of the famous Kentuckian. Indeed, many antislavery Whigs did spurn Clay after his offensive oration, and Whig officeholders representing antislavery districts, like Slade and Gates, worried that a Clay nomination would cause third-party abolitionism to spread "like wild fire."[57]

The abolitionist movement's increasing politicization and attention to the Slave Power's corruption of the Second Party System, however, gave third-party advocates reason for optimism. Myron Holley was even elected to chair a well-attended American Anti-Slavery Society convention in Cleveland in October 1839—a clear vote of confidence for abolitionist politics. Holley helped push attendees to support resolutions committing abolitionists to political action, but failed to pass a resolution advocating nomination of a presidential ticket. Still, Stanton reported that most convention goers appeared to support an abolitionist "nomination at some future time." Ever-persistent, Holley the next month spearheaded an enthusiastic Warsaw, New York, convention, which tendered a nomination to James Birney. Still ambivalent about the viability of a third party, Birney chose ultimately to neither formally accept nor reject the premature nomination.[58]

Not long after the Warsaw meeting, the Whig Party met and selected General William Henry Harrison of Ohio as its presidential candidate. Delighted to see Clay "laid upon the shelf," the *Emancipator* attributed his defeat to "the Anti-Slavery feeling of the North," which Clay's "ostentatious and infamous pro-slavery demonstration in Congress" had so inflamed. Most antislavery men, however, recognized that Harrison, a Virginia-born anti-abolitionist, promised little more than Clay. The "unanimity of the Convention" in giving the vice presidential nod to Virginia planter John Tyler, "a more bigoted devotee of . . . slavery than even Henry [Clay]," offered further confirmation that the Whig Party remained "anxious as ever to testify its unshaken allegiance to the SLAVE POWER." As vice president, Tyler's tie-breaking vote would ensure slaveholding control of the Senate. Even if Northern Whig attempts to cast Harrison as the less proslavery presidential option contained a kernel of truth, third-party advocates could never support Tyler, who, they maintained, could only "be elected by the votes of the abolitionists."[59]

Soon after the nominations of Harrison and Tyler, slaveholding congressional Whigs further antagonized abolitionists with a new permanent gag rule. To defend his party's commitment to slavery, Maryland Whig

William Cost Johnson proposed the most stringent gag to date: a standing rule rejecting petitions outright, instead of the session rules automatically tabling them in past Congresses. After securing the floor, Johnson also took the opportunity to endorse William Henry Harrison and to contemptuously advise that Northern co-partisans "tell their women petitioners to attend to knitting their own hose and darning their stockings, rather than come there and unsex themselves, be laid on the table, and sent to a committee to be reported on." Notwithstanding, or perhaps aided by, his condescending remarks, Johnson's more egregious gag passed the House, though with only a six-vote majority. While Johnson attempted to (salaciously) challenge the gender norms of Northern Whigs who permitted their wives and daughters to enter the political fray, abolitionist responses proposed different criteria for masculine honor in the antebellum North. Emblematizing abolitionist rhetoric that extolled politicians who resisted Southern bullies and questioned the manhood and independence (and perhaps the racial identity) of doughfaces who did not, the *Pennsylvania Freeman* derided as "*white slaves*" the dozen Northerners whose "aye" votes passed the Johnson Gag.[60]

To abolitionists' further chagrin, antislavery Whigs who vehemently opposed the gag still joined Johnson in lauding Harrison's presidential candidacy on the House floor. Even militantly antislavery William Slade capped an unprecedented two-day, five-and-a-half-hour speech demanding immediate abolition of slavery in the District of Columbia with an exhortation that Whig abolitionists cast presidential ballots for a Southern sympathizer. Abolitionism, Slade contended, was not yet ready "to be rocked in the whirlwind of a presidential election."[61]

The prospect of having to choose between two clearly proslavery political parties provided the primary motivation for increasing numbers of abolitionists' interest in establishing their own national party. By late 1839, political abolitionists assailed both parties' shared "determination ... never to resist the shameful encroachments of the slave power." Abolitionists, they argued, must "range ourselves in a separate organization, based on a sacred regard for the inalienable rights of man." As the presidential election approached, political abolitionists stridently insisted that "the slave power controls the national government," and the fact that both parties consistently nominated slaveholders and their sympathizers for the nation's highest offices confirmed that neither would ever advance antislavery policy. Accurately assessing the rising importance of presidential ambitions in American politics, political abolitionists grasped that "the President is the very incarnation of the party that supports him" and his "politics are, for the time being, the politics of the nation" and "control, to a great extent, the politics of the states, the counties, the cities, and the towns, insomuch that the State and local elections are made to turn chiefly on the presidential question." Since "the SLAVE POWER . . . controls . . . the presidency," it "controls likewise THE NATION."⁶²

Finally on April 1, 1840, an Albany abolitionist convention formally nominated a national abolitionist presidential ticket. But even then, the weak support this decision received cast doubt on the legitimacy of the meeting, which opponents derided as the "April Fool convention." Only 121 men participated, over 100 of them New Yorkers, and many abstained on the vote that authorized independent nominations by a 44 to 33 tally. Still, third-party advocates celebrated as the convention tapped James Birney for president and Philadelphia's Thomas Earle for vice president with what an observer described as "great unanimity." Scattered meetings across the North, but especially in upstate New York, emphatically approved the new ticket. This time Birney proudly accepted in hopes "of concentrating the votes of abolitionists" to commence "the rescue of the country from the domination of the slave power."⁶³

To meet objections to the New York–centric Albany Convention making national nominations, the convention appointed a Central Corresponding Committee, which called a ratification meeting in New York City in May while many abolitionists were already in Manhattan for the aforementioned divisive anniversary meeting of the American Anti-Slavery Society. Attended by delegates from ten of the thirteen free states, the New York City gathering blessed the Birney-Earle ticket and initiated the process of consolidating the inchoate political abolitionist forces. Third-party abolitionists arranged conventions to nominate state and local tickets and established newspapers to promote their candidates. That summer, Massachusetts, Vermont, Illinois, Michigan, New York, New Jersey, and Ohio abolitionists chose presidential electors, and other states followed shortly before the election. Still, abolitionists faced an uphill battle in the 1840 contest, in which partisan tempers ran so famously high.⁶⁴

Through 1840, many voting abolitionists clung to interrogation as their preferred way to avoid moral responsibility for supporting proslavery candidates. Lewis Tappan, the deeply pious, morally rigid Yankee businessman who was perhaps the antislavery movement's most assiduous organizer, fretted that if abolitionists formed their own party they would sacrifice their moral stature, their influence with members of the major parties, and their emphasis on bringing slaveholders to repent. Also, they risked broadcasting their numerical weakness, a criticism Tappan shared with nonvoting Garrisonians. While Tappan sympathized far more with political abolitionists than with Garrison's anti-government heresies, Tappan still hoped in 1840 to avoid a third party, vainly advocating continued use of questionnaires. Though he voted for Birney, Tappan refused to publicly support the Liberty Party until 1843.[65]

Still others who accepted the wisdom of independent political action initially questioned the timing of launching a new party in the heat of the 1840 campaign. John Greenleaf Whittier penned a letter for the April 1840 Albany Convention, declaring it inexpedient to nominate. Nervous that the political disaster of the 1838 New York gubernatorial election would be replicated across the free states, Whittier had hoped the Albany Convention would instead "settle" the legitimacy of independent political action and advise abolitionists to oppose Harrison and Van Buren, while waiting for a future contest to field a formal abolitionist ticket. Henry Stanton shared Whittier's apprehensions, convinced that "at least 19/20ths of the Abolitionists" in Massachusetts "are decidedly hostile to an independent national nomination this year."[66]

Elsewhere, several leading political abolitionists continued voting Whig, or simply abstained. William Jay was not alone in supporting a policy of choosing the lesser of evils. Vermont's secretary of state and leading abolitionist newspaper editor Chauncey Knapp, who had long hoped to abolitionize the Whig Party and enjoyed some success in his home state, refused to campaign for either Harrison or Birney. Knapp instead preferred to sit the presidential election out, an example many seemingly followed, as Vermonters cast over five thousand more votes for governor than for president (a difference of almost 10 percent). In Ohio too, leading political abolitionists, including Birney's former partner Gamaliel Bailey, at first opposed independent nominations. Finally endorsing Birney in the summer of 1840, Bailey barely persuaded a convention of southern Ohio abolitionists to do the same in September. Several of Bailey's Ohio allies though, including Salmon Chase, Samuel Lewis, and Edward Wade, all of whom would soon become key third-party leaders, adhered to the Harrison ticket. Chase, already during the summer of the campaign felt disgusted with both parties, despite his election to Cincinnati's city council "last spring as a Harrison man." Chase further foreshadowed his future involvement when he privately admitted his sympathy for the third party, even though he considered its founding "premature."[67]

The small but growing group of third-party advocates meanwhile dismissed this circumspection as tactically imprudent, and once the Albany Convention nominated its ticket, even Stanton and Whittier avidly supported it. Much in the way that feelings of shared responsibility for slavery spurred their original commitment to immediatist abolitionism, many abolitionists came to consider antislavery voting a binding moral duty. To bear honest testimony against slavery meant voting for abolitionist candidates untainted by association with the Slave Power. Alvan Stewart chided, "To vote for either of the pro-slavery candidates, is to take the deep guilt of slavery on your souls." Charles B. Ray, editor of the leading black abolitionist newspaper, thus justified "political action" as "a necessary fruit of our abolition principles . . . and an *independent political abolition party*" as "a necessary fruit of political action."[68]

Scholars often stress the moral and religious impetuses for the formation of an abolitionist third party, but a false dichotomy between moral purity and pragmatic politics has obscured the strategic vision of the third-party movement. Third-party advocates construed their political program as both a moral protest *and* a practical tactical move. "The question of Independent Anti-Slavery Nominations" was as much "a mere question of expediency" as one of moral responsibility. The third party aimed "to dethrone the inexorable SLAVE POWER from its present political ascendancy . . . a very strong, if not the strongest citadel of slavery in this land"—a goal that could be achieved only through "a direct, and determined" effort to make "the question of slavery the grand question of *national* politics—which of course, requires a corresponding national nomination." Political abolitionists thus valued third-party politics as both a means to maintain their moral probity by providing nominees for whom abolitionists could conscionably vote *and* as a strategy for toppling the Slave Power.[69]

These political upstarts understood that their party would begin weak, unable to even unite voting abolitionists (not to mention the obvious opposition it faced from Garrisonians). Not "disheartened by the smallness of the beginning," they believed that antislavery Whigs and Democrats could gradually be "disabused of party ties." In the meantime, the abolitionist party might act "as a STIMULUS to one or both of the other parties to be as favorable as they possibly can . . . to the cause of freedom, in order to catch the votes of half-way abolitionists."[70]

Even many who did not fully support the move into third-party politics agreed that Harrison and Van Buren were "equally obnoxious" to "consistent abolitionists." As the campaign heated up, Birney supporters dredged up old votes and anti-abolitionist speeches to prove that Van Buren and Harrison were incurably proslavery. Abolitionist newspapers particularly strove to debunk "wide-spread delusions" about Harrison's pretended antislavery sympathies, printing his aspersions against "the schemes of abolitionists" as "fraught with horrors upon which an incarnate devil only could look with approbation."[71]

In addition to combating Whig arguments that ousting Van Buren should be antislavery voters' highest priority, abolitionists also had to dissuade antislavery Whigs who acknowledged Harrison's proslavery sympathies but supported him anyway to promote Whig economic policy. Third-party proponents insisted that slavery must trump all other issues, and some also retorted with an economic argument that blamed the nation's economic crisis on "mal-administration of the National Government . . . by the Slave Power." Criticizing slaveholders for promoting an unstable economic policy, the New York State Anti-Slavery Society decried the Slave Power's "fluctuating, changeful, and deranging measures of political economy" as designed to "disturb and cripple the free States." Recognizing the challenge of confronting voters' varied economic policy preferences, third-party abolitionists argued that the only way to reverse the "ascendancy in the national councils" of the "SLAVOCRACY" would be through insistence that "the ONE IDEA of abolishing slavery" control abolitionist voting. Until abolitionists put antislavery above other political concerns, "*the people* of the North" would continue "to be dictated to by the Slave Power, and to be humbugged" into concentrating on "mere questions of money getting."[72]

Many Whig abolitionists, in addition to voting their economic interests, were swept up in the "perfect mania" of the Harrison campaign and seemed willing, third-party men grumbled, to "wade to their armpits in molten lava to drive Van Buren from power." These forebodings proved correct as Harrison won in a landslide, running especially well in antislavery districts. In several Northern states, the third party, lacking sufficient time to coordinate, could not even organize to field state tickets. Nationwide, the Birney ticket mustered barely seven thousand votes, a mere 0.3 percent of the total popular vote.[73]

As the new third party came out of this electoral disaster, its leaders reaffirmed their commitment to abolitionist politics. Despite the meager vote total, third-party men insisted they had exerted more influence than they could have by scattering. During the campaign many had also conceded that "when the Presidential election shall have been settled . . . abolitionists will be truer," at which point "the liberty party will have numerous advocates." The Committee of Correspondence for the Birney presidential ticket, effectively the national campaign committee, celebrated the new strategy: "The power which will overthrow slavery has been discovered; it is the terse literature of the northern ballot box." The committee urged continued organizing and called on abolitionists to nominate third-party candidates for local office and to elect delegates to attend an 1841 national convention to tap presidential and vice presidential nominees for 1844. Many leaders believed that fielding a ticket (which most expected would again be headed by Birney) early would help generate interest in the new party. While the party had not been formally named, its adherents increasingly adopted Gerrit Smith's preferred moniker, Liberty Party, which soon became official.⁷⁴

Liberty men now sought to erect a party at the grassroots. At the same time, political abolitionists focused ever more closely on Congress. "The greatest good can be done to the cause of Liberty and the slave," Joshua Leavitt argued, "by placing *one man* in Congress, who owes no allegiance or obligation to either of the great proslavery parties, and who can be relied on as true to principle under all contingencies." As they attempted to build their party, abolitionist leaders, especially Leavitt, strove to further infiltrate congressional debate to promote the antislavery cause. While they hoped to elect Liberty men to Congress, abolitionists' careful lobbying efforts nurtured important collaborative, if often tense, relationships with antislavery congressmen (mostly Whigs). This, along with the continued growth of the Liberty Party organization, would ensure that conflicts over the reach of the Slave Power edged ever closer to the center of national political debate.⁷⁵

* Interlude One *

"Bowing Down to the Slave Power": Northern Whigs, Slavery, and the Speakership, 1839

The 26th Congress opened in December 1839 with especially acrimonious partisan jockeying. In the first House scheduled to select a speaker by voice vote (instead of secret ballot), tensions ran high, especially as it became clear that five disputed seats from New Jersey could swing control of the closely divided House. It took nearly two weeks of bitter, mostly unproductive debate, before a narrow majority of the members resigned themselves to excluding both sets of claimants and letting the House organize first.[1]

Meanwhile, both parties prepared for the dispute's eventual resolution by caucusing to select speaker nominees well before the House was ready to open the voting for its chief office. Whig partisans easily settled on former speaker (1834–35) John Bell of Tennessee. The Democratic caucus proved less harmonious. Displaying dissension mirroring the wrangling occupying the full House, Democratic members descended into disruptive personal squabbles and heated arguments over which slaveholding speakership candidate could best satisfy the party's extreme proslavery States' Rights faction. Virginia's John Jones ultimately emerged with the support of a bare majority of his fractious caucus.[2]

Finally on December 14, the long-postponed speakership battle commenced. Among the many intently awaiting the results were political abolitionists who were now beginning to mobilize against both major parties. In the months leading up to the congressional session, Joshua Leavitt's *Emancipator* had called readers' attention to the fact that "the two parties, who will be very evenly balanced, are looking forward with much anxiety to the choice of speaker." Stressing the agenda-setting power of antebellum speakers, with their authority over all committee appointments, Leavitt forewarned that "of course neither party will dare to run any other than a slaveholder." Leavitt continued sarcastically, "It would be contrary to all rule and comity, *and would greatly endanger our happy union, were a freeman and the representative of freemen to be elected to preside over the most august republican assembly in the world."*[3]

As the House began balloting, an intractable, proslavery States' Rights minority confirmed Leavitt's forebodings. Rejecting both Bell and Jones, eighteen Southerners, Whigs and Democrats, scattered their votes to candidates deemed more acceptably proslavery than either slave-owning caucus nominee. After five more fruitless roll calls, each lasting about an hour, the House seemed no closer to an organization, and members finally ventured into the rainy Washington streets at nine o'clock that Saturday night. What had become clear in the evening votes, however, was that when members returned from their Sunday respite, Robert M. T. Hunter would stand, surprisingly, as a serious Whig contender. Hunter, a young States' Rights Virginian with ambiguous partisan loyalties, had begun to gather support on the fourth ballot, including from a number of Northern Whigs, antislavery Ohioan Joshua Giddings among them. Hunter's vote totals had mounted on subsequent ballots, though at the adjournment he remained far short of a majority.[4]

As voting resumed Monday, the confusion multiplied, with leading Whigs retrying and then re-abandoning Bell. Even the penultimate tenth ballot was so chaotic that members divided their votes among sixteen candidates, six (five of them Southerners) receiving over ten votes. However, once enough of the States' Rights men united with the mass of the Whig Party to bring Hunter within striking distance of a majority, Adams and every other antislavery Whig duly fell in line and helped Hunter reach a three-vote majority on the eleventh roll call. Even former Genesee County (New York) Anti-Slavery Society secretary Seth Gates, who had resolutely voted for Northern candidates (usually Adams) on the third through tenth ballots, switched his vote to Hunter.[5]

This disturbing denouement seemed to substantiate abolitionists' charges that participation in the Second Party System necessarily entailed subservience to the Slave Power. It was a "great pity," the *Massachusetts Abolitionist* lamented, that "whig abolitionists in Congress" had proven so unreliable. Attacking sixteen putatively antislavery Whigs who supported Hunter, Leavitt similarly bemoaned "that the elevation of a slaveholder to the Chair of the House of Representatives, was the act of the abolitionists." "Had they been only as much opposed to slavery," Leavitt continued, "as they are true to their party, they might with ease have secured the election of a man unstained at least with the open crime of slaveholding." The fact that, unlike Bell, Hunter was not even a dependable Whig made this treachery all the worse. After the Whig Party had "called on the [many] abolitionists" who opposed Van Buren's financial policy to put aside their abolitionism to promote Whig political economy "or the country would be ruined," Whigs elected by abolitionists' votes proceeded to vote for a speaker "diametrically opposed to all their doctrines."[6]

As political abolitionists made their case for a third party, they emphasized antislavery Whigs' speakership votes as particularly damning evidence of the Slave Power's dominance of both major parties. The votes "to place a slaveholding Speaker in the chair" by Whig congressmen who had been elected "on the ground of their anti-slavery professions" provided irrefutable testimony that genuine antislavery victories could never be achieved within the major parties. The New York State Anti-Slavery Society especially chastised abolitionist representatives Gates and William Slade for "bowing down to the slave power" at the Whig Party's "bidding."[7]

Further confirmation for abolitionist charges that antislavery Whigs' speakership votes buttressed the Slave Power can be found in proslavery champions' jubilance at Hunter's election. George Fitzhugh, who later achieved notoriety as slavery's preeminent social theorist, was "elated and delighted." South Carolina States' Rights Democrat John Calhoun likewise gloated over the power of States' Rights men to dictate the choice of speaker. "The only reason" Calhoun could ascertain "why they [Whigs] should prefer" Hunter to a States' Rights Democrat was his refusal to pledge support for President Van Buren's impending reelection bid. "On this slender ground the whigs claimed him," but Calhoun, like the abolitionists, recognized that "in every other respect," Hunter's politics were "identical with . . . other State rights men."[8]

Despite the disappointing result, the stalemate that preceded Hunter's triumph helped abolitionists discern institutional dynamics favorable to third-party action. Because of the competitiveness of the two parties, the requirement of a majority for election, and the importance the parties placed on controlling the organization of the House, a determined minority in Congress could hold the parties hostage by denying both the majority necessary to elect a presiding officer and begin legislating. The fact that a small States' Rights bloc had essentially handpicked the speaker suggested that antislavery representatives might one day do the same. This further supported the case for an abolitionist political organization. Leavitt saw the power exerted by proslavery extremists, and thought, why not us?

> There are in the House as many abolitionists as State Rights men, who, if they had been equally united, and equally firm, and equally ready to sacrifice their party predilections to their higher principles, could have gained their end . . . and thus have broken up, probably forever, one of the prerogatives of the Slave Power—that of appointing all the presiding officers of our national legislature.[9]

Even abolitionists who initially opposed a third-party strategy recognized the force of these arguments. Lewis Tappan desperately hoped to avoid third-party politics but privately chastised Gates, Giddings, and "the abolitionists in the H. of R." for failing to unite on an antislavery candidate. Of course, Tappan was already acknowledging the institutional logic that would encourage a third-party strategy when he insisted that antislavery politicians disregard party dictates while organizing Congress—one of the most pivotal partisan contests. Yet Joshua Giddings had a point when he cautioned that abolitionists should be careful not to repel their few potential congressional allies. These developments thus also made clear just how important it would be for abolitionists to cultivate working relationships with antislavery Whig congressmen, even as political abolitionists erected the Liberty Party and challenged them in the electoral arena.[10]

* CHAPTER TWO *

Agitating the Congress: Abolitionist Lobbying and Antislavery Alliances, 1836–1844

The Liberty Party's poor showing in the 1840 election suggested to critics its futility, but abolitionists continued to develop political strategies that allowed them to exert political influence far out of proportion to the vote totals they polled (which did increase continually after 1840). Liberty men coupled their third-party electoral strategy with concerted efforts to build partnerships with congressmen who could help thrust slavery and the Slave Power argument into national political debate.

Beginning in the mid-1830s, political abolitionists skillfully exploited Congress as a forum through which they could publicize their cause. They worked energetically on the ground in Washington, and through copious correspondence, to cultivate allies among a small cadre of mostly Whig antislavery congressmen, headlined by ex-president John Quincy Adams. Abolitionists lobbied, and sometimes directly cooperated with, these men, to provoke proslavery belligerence that dramatized the Slave Power's sway over national politics.

After creating an independent party, however, political abolitionists had to further renegotiate their alliances with men who were ostensibly partisan opponents but at the same time represented the most promising and visible antislavery collaborators. Political abolitionists, even as they publicly denounced all Whigs as accessories to the Slave Power, capitalized on the predicament of officeholders who strained to reconcile sincere antipathy to slavery with the countervailing pressures of membership in the bisectional Whig Party. For their part, this coterie of vocally antislavery congressmen relished opportunities to incite controversy over slavery, often appreciating, and sometimes relying on, abolitionist support. Abolitionists could be counted on to publicize any antislavery activity in Congress, especially when Washington papers like the *National Intelligencer* (the capital's Whig paper of record) would not.

The abolitionist approach to lobbying potential congressional partners represented a unique strategy in antebellum politics. Contemporary lobbying was typically non-ideological and focused on private bills, also known as special legislation. Since private bills represented an overwhelming proportion of the legislative output at the state level, antebellum lobbyists predominantly worked in state capitals to secure government contracts, patronage appointments, and corporate charters. Political abolitionists, by contrast, concentrated on Congress for both jurisdictional and strategic reasons. Unlike professional lobbyists paid to advance specific special interests, political abolitionists engaged in broad issue-oriented lobbying on an unprecedented scale. Quaker abolitionists in the 1790s had anticipated these practices, but their antebellum counterparts far exceeded the organization and sophistication of those earlier efforts. Many proponents of abolitionist lobbying (especially Lewis Tappan and Joshua Leavitt) had also gained experience integrating lobbying with mass petitioning in the Sabbatarian campaign against Sunday mail service (1828–1831). These antecedents notwithstanding, antebellum abolitionists developed an innovative form of congressional advocacy that helped instigate new floor controversies over slavery despite both major parties' desires to avoid them.[1]

Political abolitionists' lobbying often aimed simply at generating antislavery debate in Congress, and, to a lesser extent, Northern legislatures, for consumption by a national audience. Although antebellum abolitionists experienced few substantive policy victories at the federal level, lobbying provided a key tactic through which they could amplify their opposition to the Slave Power and induce new conversions. Members of Congress have often powerfully influenced national political history by "taking stands" intended more for swaying public opinion than for affecting the disposition of particular legislation. Political abolitionists perceived this fact and strove to exploit congressional debate to magnify and disseminate their arguments about slavery's disproportionate influence in the federal government, especially since newspaper coverage of Congress was so extensive in this era.[2]

These sorts of extra-electoral practices have often been associated with those excluded from conventional political participation (such as reform-minded women). Liberty strategy, however, incorporated *both* formal partisan politics—operating a political party and voting against the Slave Power—and extra-electoral strategies. While Liberty men possessed, and employed, the franchise, they never elected enough of their own partisans to shape national politics without resorting to other tactics too. In lobbying quasi-abolitionist Whig congressmen, political abolitionists identified a bloc of representatives sympathetic to their aims but constricted by partisan obligations and then learned to deftly manage these complicated, precarious relationships.³

Cultivating Congressional Partnerships and Courting Controversy

As abolitionists increasingly turned towards political action in the second half of the 1830s, they began to seek out congressional partners, well before the formation of the Liberty Party. Controversy over the gag rule especially offered abolitionists new promise for cultivating alliances with frustrated Northern congressmen. When Congress restricted antislavery petitions, abolitionists saw more than just an opportunity to bolster their arguments about the threatening power of slaveholders. By working with antislavery congressmen and encouraging them to circumvent the rule, abolitionists could ensure continued public scrutiny of this most blatant manifestation of the Slave Power. The gag rule fight provided a shared project in which immediatist abolitionists and antislavery congressmen relied on each other for effective resistance. Congressional debates, now replete with contentious showdowns featuring eloquent, combative antislavery representatives, popularized the abolitionists' political message to a much broader audience than had joined the movement. Realizing this, many political abolitionists concentrated closely on Congress and the few allies they found there.

John Quincy Adams's well-chronicled battle against the gag made him the prized target of political abolitionist lobbying. As abolitionists presented Adams with mounds of petitions, they also lobbied him, in person and through the mail, to precipitate new controversies. Antislavery societies formally eulogized Adams's "upright and manly course," and their accolades strengthened his resolve. Though he eschewed direct involvement in the abolitionist movement, Adams embraced the role of anti–Slave Power agitator and came to be praised across the North as "Old Man Eloquent" and by some abolitionists as an "inflexible opponent of the baneful system of slavery." Reflecting widespread abolitionist sentiment, Sarah Grimké "cordially" thanked Adams for his efforts against the gag, but criticized his opposition to immediate abolition in the District of Columbia as "a surrender of moral principle." Abolitionists importuned Adams to avow support for emancipation in the District, which many viewed as an antislavery "test question," but he consistently disappointed them.⁴

Though he expressed "regret to lose their good will," Adams complained that "the abolitionists generally are constantly urging me to indiscreet movements." Initially ambivalent about his antislavery congressional stands, Adams confided to his diary in 1837, "The exposure through which I passed at the late session of Congress was greater than I could have imagined possible; and, having escaped from that fiery furnace, it behooves me well to consider my ways before I put myself in the way of being cast into it again." But pressed by abolitionists and their numerous petitions, Adams, despite his misgivings, continually plunged back into that fiery furnace. Adams routinely attempted to present armloads of prohibited petitions. Moreover, his efforts to ridicule the gag rule and its proponents precipitated congressional strife that made him the epicenter of sectional political conflict in the late 1830s and early 1840s.[5]

Adams honed a gift for humiliating his proslavery adversaries, such as in early 1837 when he told the chair he had a petition purportedly sent by slaves and asked if it would fall under the ambit of the gag. Adams remained coy about the possibly forged petition's contents as irate Southerners demanded to burn the paper on the House floor and suggested the ex-president be indicted for fomenting slave insurrection. Once Adams revealed that the petition did not, as all had assumed, advocate abolition, Southerners attempted to censure him for committing "a flagrant contempt on the dignity" of the House. The ensuing debates lasted nearly a week as Adams mocked Southerners' suggestions that he be indicted, attacked the institution of slavery and immorality of slave owners, and defended the right of slaves to petition. By the time his remarks concluded, the censure motion was hopeless. Adams's dramatic rebuke to the slaveholding interest on the House floor cemented his role as the leading antislavery sympathizer in Washington and further dramatized Southern repressiveness.[6]

Abolitionists applauded Adams for his "faithful and fearless resistance to the usurpations of the Slaveholding power" and urged him to continue to provoke this sort of commotion. William Jay explained to Adams that his congressional stands "sowed much precious seed" from which abolitionists expected to reap a "glorious harvest." Abolitionists, not the Massachusetts Whig Party, consequently cooperated with Adams to further publicize the slave petition feat. Boston abolitionist Isaac Knapp (printer of William Lloyd Garrison's *Liberator*) published a pamphlet edition of Adams's epic House speech on the slave petition, along with his related letters to his constituents (first printed in the *Quincy Patriot*). John Greenleaf Whittier added an introduction extolling Adams's "graphic delineation of the slavery spirit in Congress." The next summer, as new petition drives got underway, the *Emancipator* republished Adams's letters and urged that they be read publicly to inspire antislavery activists.[7]

Abolitionists reveled in the congressional attention generated by debates over their petitions, appreciating that these disputes broadcast abolitionists' arguments far more effectively than they could on their own. Lewis Tappan underscored this benefit of the House debates when he explained to Adams that abolitionist petitioners did "not expect so much to convert members of Congress as their constituents." As Theodore Dwight Weld recognized, antislavery congressmen were "in a position to do for the A. S. cause by a single speech more than our best lecturers can do in a year." The Massachusetts Anti-Slavery Society similarly emphasized this benefit of infiltrating congressional debate: "Never is agitation so thorough and effectual, as when it begins in the halls of legislation." "The country," the society continued, "has learned more of the dangerous tendencies of slavery" from "discussions in Congress, than we could have instilled directly for years."[8]

The slave petition ruse especially highlighted the value of cooperating with sympathetic congressmen to goad Southern congressmen into embarrassing overreactions. An *Emancipator* correspondent mocked the Southern response to antislavery petitions: "The effect is electrical. The House is in commotion at once. If a nest of rattlesnakes were suddenly let loose among them, the members could manifest but little more 'agitation.'" This congressional chaos, as William Jay later wrote a Georgia congressman, "so augmented the strength of the Abolitionists, that they themselves have found it good policy to keep up the irritation." The *Emancipator* concurred: "A hundred thousand undisturbed lecturers on abolition, at all events, could not have done half so much to spread their doctrines, as has been effected by the violence of those who sought to suppress them." Abolitionists thus continued furnishing petitions and lobbying Adams for further attacks likely to elicit additional Southern hysterics.[9]

As Adams's tirades against the gag rule endeared him to many abolitionists, they identified him as a potential ally on a number of other antislavery political issues. Proslavery designs on Texas in the mid-1830s sparked one of the earliest and most fruitful collaborations between abolitionists and Representative Adams. In the midst of the tumultuous session that eventuated in the first gag, Quaker abolitionist editor and Texas expert Benjamin Lundy sought out Adams's aid in publicizing the proslavery aims of the Texan Revolution. As Adams requested information on Texan slavery, Lundy delightedly obliged, furnishing pamphlets, maps, a history of Texas, and translations of Mexican abolition laws. Adams marshaled this evidence to charge the Jackson administration and its supporters with pushing the country toward an acquisitive, proslavery war with Mexico.[10]

Lundy quickly realized the efficacy of Adams's congressional stands and urged him on: "No man, occupying the station in [the] community which has fallen to thy lot, ever had a better opportunity to establish an imperishable fame." Adams for his part made sure that "a huge pile" of diplomatic documents about Texas was placed on every congressman's desk in late 1837. These, an abolitionist observer remarked, would "speedily open the great subject now agitating the country." Adams corresponded regularly with Lundy, who continued to prevail on him to serve as a congressional watchdog against renewed efforts to annex Texas. Together Adams and Lundy, and the abolitionist movement more broadly, helped generate the pervasive Northern anti-annexation sentiment that shelved the Texas issue until the Tyler administration revived it in the early 1840s.[11]

To further promote their policy aims and, as importantly, antislavery controversy in Congress, abolitionists repeatedly attempted to establish a lobbying presence at the capital. Even amidst the financial panic of 1837, the American Anti-Slavery Society pledged sparse resources for a congressional lobby. The society requested that Weld "repair to the City of Washington, when the discussions on Slavery shall come up," but he declined, and the society never appointed a substitute. In the winter of 1838 Henry B. Stanton attended Congress as an abolitionist lobbyist to confer with Adams and "look after the imperiled right of petition," and in 1840 Whittier visited Washington to discuss the slavery issue with congressmen from both sections. As Lewis Tappan explained, "Our great object now should be to get anti Slavery before the intelligent mind of the community." For this purpose, Tappan visited Washington multiple times and tried to establish an antislavery book depository there.[12]

Seeking to attract new allies, or at least generate publicity, Tappan also hoped the *Emancipator* could reach the desk of every congressman, a goal editor Joshua Leavitt strove to meet. In 1837, the American Anti-Slavery Society's executive committee adopted an official plan "to send a copy of the Emancipator, weekly, to each Senator and Representative in Congress," and also offered to provide "any gentleman in Congress" copies of "any books, pamphlets, or papers" in the society's collection. Long continuing to value this tactic, Leavitt put a donation from his mother toward the same purpose in 1841. The Cincinnati *Philanthropist* likewise sporadically sent papers to members of Congress, and Vermont Whig William Slade advised Amos A. Phelps of ninety-two representatives and six senators who would be likely to at least peruse free copies of Phelps's *Massachusetts Abolitionist*. In 1840, the national society also developed a plan to distribute William Jay's *View of the Action of the Federal Government* to at least fifty congressmen, with the aid of Representative Seth Gates.[13]

In 1840, ex-senator Thomas Morris suggested, more ambitiously, that abolitionists in every Northern state select a delegate to "form an organized body" that would conduct "daily sessions" in Washington concurrently with Congress. Morris hoped such a group could "collect all possible information on the subject of American Slavery" and provide accurate reports on congressional debates and national political news. While the abolitionist movement never established a Washington organization as systematic as Morris envisioned, abolitionist newspaper editors and correspondents, most importantly Joshua Leavitt, soon served a similar function, providing an influential abolitionist lobbying presence in Washington.[14]

As political abolitionists moved in and out of the capital city, they also shaped national debate through their interactions with the District's sizable black population. Abolitionist visitors, along with several antislavery congressmen, worked with local African Americans to create what Stanley Harrold has described as a biracial subversive community. A small group of radical political abolitionists in Washington, sometimes supported by Gerrit Smith and his upstate New York associates, promoted aggressive antislavery activity in this rare Southern locale that abolitionists could safely frequent. These efforts, many of them spearheaded by radical political abolitionist newspaperman Charles Torrey (of the Albany *Tocsin of Liberty* and then the *Albany Patriot*), further polarized the Washington community. Torrey collaborated with black Washingtonians to organize extensive Underground Railroad operations. When he died in 1846 while serving time in a Maryland penitentiary for abetting slave escapes, Torrey became a martyr for abolitionists of all political persuasions. This combative brand of often illegal antislavery subversion at times influenced congressional debate by raising the stakes of the abolitionist threat for slave-owning officeholders. Leavitt and a few antislavery congressmen were sometimes aware of these activities and on occasion exploited them to emphasize the horrors of slavery and the slave trade in the capital city, but Leavitt and the congressmen focused on congressional debate as their main venue for confronting the Slave Power.[15]

While Adams remained the most visible antislavery collaborator in Congress, political abolitionists also worked intently to build partnerships with the handful of younger congressmen who openly identified as abolitionists. A small group of antislavery Whig representatives led by Seth Gates of Le Roy, New York, Joshua Giddings of Jefferson, Ohio, and William Slade of Middlebury, Vermont, thus became central to political abolitionist strategy. Many of these men represented strong Whig districts, some from the highly evangelized areas of the "Burned-over District" in western New York and the northern Midwest and several from the uniquely antislavery state of Vermont. A smaller number, like textile manufacturer Nathaniel Borden, hailed from industrializing regions, where skilled workers and small proprietors made up much of the "antislavery rank and file." This collection of antislavery congressmen worked closely with abolitionists, as well as with Adams, to pinpoint openings in House rules that allowed for disruptive dilatory tactics. They especially capitalized on "the wide range of debate" in the Committee of the Whole, a parliamentary device constituting the entire house as a committee on the state of the Union. In the whole House a simple majority could cut off debate and immediately bring a measure up for a vote, but the Committee of the Whole provided antislavery representatives far more latitude.[16]

Slade, initially the House's most militant antislavery voice, especially earned the admiration of political abolitionists. From early on, they lavished Slade with praise and pressed him to challenge the Slave Power at every opportunity. Although Slade lacked Adams's proclivity for extemporaneous invective (in part because Adams's greater prestige and parliamentary expertise made it harder for the House to silence him), Slade prepared at least one blistering antislavery diatribe for each congressional session. Lamenting his choice of a life in politics instead of the ministry, Slade felt morally impelled to use his office to help reform "this degraded guilty, suffering world." Though a loyal Whig until 1848, Slade proudly avowed his abolitionism, boldly advocated racial equality, and fought unflinchingly for emancipation in the District of Columbia.[17]

Like the abolitionists, Slade relished the fact that his antislavery speeches "produced no small excitement in the House" and "disturbed the nerves of the slaveholders." The opposition he faced from "foolish hot heads of the South," Slade recognized, would cause his oratory "to be read by thousands, who, but for that would have felt little or no interest to see it." Slade praised the abolitionist movement as a "noble cause" and hoped to have "the pleasure of aiding its advancement." Slade was so devoted to his antislavery calling that he refused to abandon his congressional post even to return to his sick and grieving wife after the death of their daughter (Lewis Tappan, but not Slade himself, attended the funeral). Slade, like Adams, faced occasional death threats, but dismissed them as mere "growling" with no "bite." Never able to achieve Adams's political independence, Slade worried intensely about juggling the support of his abolitionist Whig constituents and those loyal to the party's Southern leadership. When political abolitionists began condemning all Whig politicians as the Slave Power's accessories, Slade, to his deep dismay, absorbed some of the sharpest criticism, especially from the *Emancipator*, of which Slade was a "constant reader."[18]

Giddings even more skillfully emulated Adams's penchant for inciting Southern hysteria, and in time would assume his mantle as the House's leading antislavery gadfly. When the physically imposing forty-three-year-old first arrived in Washington in 1838, abolitionists in his Western Reserve district warily pinned their hopes on the staunch Whig. It did not take long before Giddings revolted at the "self important airs" and "overbearing manners" of the "southern bullies." Far more appalling still was the "drove of human male & female" Giddings witnessed "driven past the Capitol."[19]

Disgusted by his firsthand encounters with slavery in the District and coaxed on by abolitionist correspondents at home, Giddings became determined to take a stand in the winter of 1839. He consulted Gamaliel Bailey, the leading abolitionist editor in the West, to cultivate abolitionist support for his first antislavery congressional incursion. Bailey's encouragement reassured Giddings as he prepped his antislavery speech. Having secured Bailey's support, Giddings proceeded by attacking a bill seemingly unconnected to slavery—a tactic for obtaining the floor that would become a staple of antislavery congressional agitation. Opposing an appropriation to build a new bridge over the Potomac, Giddings repudiated any expenditure for the District not absolutely necessary for the functioning of the federal government. No Northerner, he claimed, could "consent to continue the seat of Government in the midst of a magnificent slave-market." Congressmen, Giddings asserted, should move the capital to a locale where they could look out the window without seeing innocent "men, women, and children, indiscriminately chained by the neck." Outraged members from both sections clamored for the floor and "the greatest confusion prevailed" before a majority ruled Giddings out of order.[20]

Along with producing controversies that highlighted slaveholders' congressional influence, antislavery congressmen could also use their political access and national platform to raise alarms about the Slave Power's newest aggressions. Abolitionists highly appreciated their congressional allies' ability to serve as antislavery watchdogs. For example, in the face of the seven-year-long Second Seminole War, abolitionists and antislavery congressmen worked together to expose the "ulterior object" of this "Florida war with its enormous expenditure of property and human life"—all aimed apparently at eliminating the fugitive slave haven that Seminole territory had become. Giddings expounded for three hours "with the most perfect calmness" on the proslavery aims of the costly guerilla war, "although the House was nearly all the time agitated like the waves of the sea." Seeking to enlighten and rouse the Northern public, Giddings cast the war as a grand slave-hunting expedition that transformed American soldiers into "slave-catchers." Edward Wade, Giddings's frequent Liberty challenger on the Western Reserve, praised the polemic as "the most important" speech "ever delivered in congress on the subject of Slavery." Abolitionists widely lauded the oration and gladly purchased the pamphlet version as the best available source of information on the Florida war.[21]

Adams similarly worked with abolitionists to transform the House into a platform from which to apprise the nation of the federal government's proslavery machinations. After conferring in the spring of 1840 with Lewis Tappan and Roger Baldwin, the *Amistad* Africans' lead counsel, Adams vocally demanded an inquiry into executive documents that included a "scandalous mistranslation" seemingly designed to prejudice the case against the accused Africans. (Later, however, the proofreader claimed the mistake resulted from sloppy handwriting.) To Adams and the abolitionists, the error seemed indicative of the administration's calculated attempt to evade the question of whether the captives had been taken illegally from Africa.[22]

As a public champion of the abolitionists' case on behalf of the illegally enslaved Africans, Adams spotlighted the Van Buren administration's flagrant attempts to manipulate the judicial process to predetermine a proslavery outcome. When the case reached the Supreme Court, Tappan enlisted Adams as cocounsel to generate added publicity. Although Tappan admitted that Adams, who had spent little time in court, was "not probably a very good lawyer," abolitionists and antislavery Whigs both recognized that he could use his Supreme Court appearance "to make a speech for the country." Adams did not disappoint. "He showed," Congressman Seth Gates reported, "how all the National sympathies were in favor of slavery" with "biting, burning, blistering sarcasm." When the Supreme Court freed the Africans, Adams assured Leavitt it was "one of the happiest events of my life."[23]

Along with exploiting the occasional high-profile Supreme Court case on slavery, political abolitionists' activism at the state level could also complement their congressional lobbying and capitalize on the visibility of sympathetic state officeholders. Many political abolitionist leaders thus lobbied close to home too, especially when they had personal relationships with local elites. From early on, John Greenleaf Whittier perceived that local politicians might be able to "take hold of the cause without essentially endangering their popularity." Whittier knew he had "some influence with this class," since his earlier work as a National Republican journalist had "gained me a large number of political friends" through whom "the higher classes of our statesmen, etc. may be reached." By 1837, Whittier lobbied not only Whig friends, but also prominent Massachusetts Democratic state representative Robert Rantoul. Whittier assured Rantoul even at that early date that abolitionists would put antislavery before party. Increasingly distrustful of Whig partisanship, Whittier exhorted Rantoul to sponsor antislavery resolutions in the legislature, so that the Whigs could not, as a party, receive credit.[24]

On rare occasions abolitionist state legislators could generate the kind of attention that made political abolitionists all over the North take notice. Antislavery newspapers lauded Massachusetts state senator James Alvord's 1838 "sterling" legislative reports, the first against annexing Texas and the second in support of almost the entire political abolitionist program, even prohibition of the domestic slave trade. Both of Alvord's reports passed with overwhelming support. Abolitionists forcefully advocated Alvord's nomination to Congress and rejoiced when he was nominated and then elected with broad antislavery support. To their great sorrow, Alvord died before his term commenced.[25]

Perhaps the most provocative abolitionist state legislator was Thaddeus Stevens, a Pennsylvania Anti-Mason who eventually made peace with, and joined, the Whig Party. In Stevens, abolitionists found an ally who enjoyed goading anti-abolitionists in Harrisburg as much as Slade and Adams did slaveholding congressmen in Washington. Like Adams and his abolitionist admirers, Stevens had a flair for the dramatic. In 1837, Stevens got himself elected a delegate to a Harrisburg Convention of "Friends of the Integrity of the Union"—intended as a euphemism for anti-abolitionists. At the convention, though, Stevens argued that slavery, not abolitionism, endangered the "Integrity of the Union." "The house, thus made up of materials as repellent and incongruous as the north poles of magnets," abolitionist Jonathan Blanchard jeered, "was constantly fluctuating between roars of laughter and almost out-breaking rage." When Stevens offered resolutions declaring all men created equal and that Congress had the right to abolish the interstate slave trade and slavery in the District of Columbia, the convention adjourned rather than be forced to record a vote. Abolitionists delighted in this spectacle, and soon after praised Stevens for his (unsuccessful) efforts to prevent the 1838 Pennsylvania Constitutional Convention from excluding black men from the franchise. Stevens actively participated in abolitionist meetings and expressed regret at being unable to attend the 1839 national antislavery convention at Albany.[26]

Promoting state-level agitation and political partnerships became a particularly high priority for black abolitionists, both Garrisonians and Liberty men. This was especially true in Pennsylvania, where black suffrage was eliminated in 1838, and New York, where black men who owned less than $250 worth of property had been disfranchised in 1821. In Pennsylvania black abolitionists convened from across the state multiple times to protest their 1838 disfranchisement. In Michigan, which barred black suffrage in its initial 1835 constitution, Henry Bibb, an escaped slave turned Liberty Party activist, played a leading role in organizing black abolitionists to demand equal suffrage. There and across the Midwest, black and white Liberty men and women fought discriminatory Black Laws that included restrictions not only on suffrage, but also on testifying in court, serving on juries, and attending public schools, and in the most egregious cases, rules excluding or discouraging African American settlement by requiring that black immigrants post costly bonds against their becoming a public burden.[27]

Among the diverse African American efforts to contest codified Northern racism, the sophisticated suffrage campaign of New York's black abolitionists especially resembled the national abolitionist movement's strategy for influencing Congress. Black abolitionists' New York Association for the Political Elevation and Improvement of the People of Color strove to flood the New York Assembly with petitions for equal suffrage, beginning in 1838. The New York *Colored American* urged not only extensive petitioning, but also the appointment of an "agent in Albany" to oversee the petitions. Black Liberty Party activist Henry Highland Garnet executed this plan in 1841. After spearheading a new petition drive, Garnet spent the winter at Albany lobbying the legislature for equal suffrage. Garnet even spoke before the Judiciary Committee, but the suffrage restrictions survived.[28]

Already possessing the vote in Massachusetts (as in most New England states), black Liberty men worked with white co-partisans to contest other forms of discrimination there. The Massachusetts Liberty Party pushed for repeal of the legislative ban on intermarriage and for legislation banning segregation on railroads and mandating public school integration. However, in Massachusetts, unlike New York, most African Americans initially remained loyal to Garrison. Nonetheless, black Liberty partisans and black Garrisonians worked together to fight railroad and school segregation. In those efforts both groups collaborated with antislavery Whig legislators, including John Quincy Adams's son Charles Francis Adams.[29]

In the exceptionally antislavery state of Vermont (where African Americans were few), politicians like Slade especially felt justified in their insistence that Whig partisanship need not contradict their abolitionism. Both parties in Slade's home state claimed a strong abolitionist membership. Whig and Democratic officeholders worked alongside each other in the Vermont Anti-Slavery Society, which counted among its active members Whig lieutenant governor David Camp, Whig secretary of state Chauncey L. Knapp, and three-time Democratic lieutenant gubernatorial candidate Edward D. Barber. Whig and Democratic leaders alike condemned proslavery national chieftains and supported both political and social equality for the state's small free black population—a suicidal position for party politicians in nearly every other state. Vermont abolitionists from both parties celebrated that "a large majority" of Vermonters shared their aspirations of repealing the gag rule and abolishing slavery in the District of Columbia. The bipartisan Vermont Anti-Slavery Society also advocated that abolitionists vote only for antislavery candidates, paying lip service at least to the goal of avoiding any "alliance with either of the political parties of the day." In 1840, though, political abolitionists still denigrated Vermont politicians, notwithstanding the presence of "many of the most prominent abolitionists in the state" on both parties' tickets. Holding fast to the Liberty position that the major parties were the mainstays of the Slave Power, the *Emancipator* griped that "Slade, Camp, Barber, & c, will, of course, uphold pro-slavery men in the General Government." While third-party proponents routinely assailed the partisanship of major-party abolitionists, they understood that in antislavery bastions like Vermont, Whigs and Democrats could both aid the abolitionist cause immensely by sending antislavery legislative resolutions and, more importantly, earnest antislavery representatives like Slade to Congress.[30]

Joshua Leavitt and the Washington Liberty Lobby

After embracing third-party politics in the early 1840s, leading political abolitionists deepened their commitment to a concerted lobbying strategy. Even while disparaging antislavery Whigs as submissive to the Slave Power, Liberty men simultaneously worked to convert them. At a minimum, third-party abolitionists had to be careful not to completely repel their most important political allies. To nurture Liberty-Whig congressional alliances, Joshua Leavitt established an influential abolitionist lobbying presence in Washington. The son of a local notable who had represented his western Massachusetts community in the state legislature, Leavitt trained as both a minister and lawyer but became a career activist. With fervent evangelical passion, rigorous work habits, and an incisive, if sometimes dogmatic, analytical mind, Leavitt had served diligently in New York's benevolent reform network for nearly a decade before he was called to the *Emancipator*'s editorial chair in 1837. An experienced editor in his early forties, Leavitt provided the *Emancipator* a professional though polemical editorial voice. With the founding of the Liberty Party, Leavitt's *Emancipator* soon became the de facto party organ and perhaps *the* venue in which the Slave Power's control of the major parties was most consistently and thoroughly assailed. Leavitt's abolitionist journal, like major-party papers of the time, was highly attuned to congressional politics, and Leavitt clearly appreciated the value of reporting in person on heightening congressional wrangling over slavery. During his repeated Washington sojourns in the early 1840s, Leavitt cooperated with antislavery congressmen to instigate controversies that forced Congress to grapple over slavery and drew further attention to the overweening Slave Power.[31]

The collaboration of Liberty leaders, particularly Leavitt and Gerrit

Smith, with two-term New York congressman Seth Gates especially demonstrates the advantages of, and obstacles to, Liberty attempts to build congressional alliances. Gates's immediatist background and his break from the Whig Party in 1843 differentiate his political evolution from most other prominent antislavery Whigs. A former secretary of the Genesee County Anti-Slavery Society, Gates had a longstanding relationship with Smith, and the two corresponded frequently to compare tactics. Also a prominent local Whig, Gates accepted the editorship of his town's Whig paper, the *Le Roy Gazette*, in 1838. In that capacity, Gates applauded the election of Southern Whigs, even some of Adams's rabid congressional adversaries, and uniformly sided with his party in its clashes with abolitionists during the 1838 gubernatorial campaign. After this faithful editorial service, the Whig Party nominated Gates for Congress. Abolitionists hailed his election in 1838, before the Liberty Party's founding, as an abolitionist triumph.[32]

By the fall of 1839, however, as Gates prepared to depart for Congress, many upstate abolitionists insisted stridently on complete independence from the major political parties, even as abolitionists continued privately courting Whig officeholders. Gates's future law partner F. C. D. McKay admonished, "Even our friend Gates must be either *abolition, or Whig*. To be both is impossible." To Gerrit Smith, although surely not to fellow Whigs, Gates portrayed his partisanship as instrumental, swearing that once he could "see that duty or expediency required it" he "would swing clear of party." Gates worried independent action would "unite both parties against us," but already, Gates insinuated he might eventually abandon his party if convinced of Liberty assertions it bolstered the Slave Power.[33]

As he wavered, Liberty partisans pursued Gates ever more vigorously. Before departing for Washington, Gates beat back an effort to pledge a Genesee County antislavery convention to abolitionist voting. Gerrit Smith responded by publicly deprecating his friend as exerting a "most disastrous" influence on the antislavery cause. To Gates's great personal offense, the Liberty Party quickly circulated Smith's denunciatory letter in 1,500 handbills, many in Gates's district. Gates, even while working loyally for the Whig Party, viewed himself as a dedicated abolitionist. Having twice braved anti-abolitionist mobs alongside abolitionist lecturing agent Amos Phelps, Gates deeply resented Smith's public condemnation. Gates's lengthy published retort dismissed the abolitionists' third-party strategy as "*utterly impracticable.*" Smith realized he had offended a powerful friend and softened, but did not rescind, his criticism. Smith assured Gates, "My own judgment of you is that you are a genuine abolitionist—a sincere friend of the slave—but that being blinded and misled by political party feelings, you have, on one point, gone widely astray from the requirements of our holy cause." Representative Gates's experiences exemplify the fraught relationships that would develop between Liberty partisans and antislavery congressmen.[34]

The 1840 presidential campaign powerfully exacerbated tensions between third-party abolitionists and Whig fellow travelers. In addition to witnessing the founding of the abolitionist Liberty Party, the approaching election raised the stakes of the petition question, led to Maryland Whig William Cost Johnson's permanent gag rule, and generated conflict that Leavitt celebrated as "abolition fire in the Capitol." Slaveholding Democrats attacked the Whig Party by grousing, as abolitionists well understood, that antislavery Whigs were "drumming up recruits" for the abolitionist movement. To defend his party's commitment to slavery, Johnson proposed his new standing gag rule. Abolitionists condemned the House majority for passing Johnson's gag but welcomed the heated debates that preceded its enactment: "This body professes not to discuss the subject of slavery. . . . Yet, it nevertheless happens for the last fortnight the House of Representatives has been entirely engrossed with this prohibited subject." John Greenleaf Whittier assured Adams that the more audacious Johnson Gag would kindle Northern antislavery sentiment to an even greater degree than had previous gag rules.[35]

Though abolitionists valued the intense debate over petitioners' rights, they castigated antislavery Whigs who prioritized Harrison's election over the assault on the Slave Power. While Slade exulted "What hath God wrought!" at being permitted to deliver a two-day argument for abolition in the District of Columbia in the "very den of slave holders and slave traders," political abolitionists assailed the speech's gratuitous presidential endorsement. "Mr. Slade . . . attacked the Monster Slavery like a man . . . showed the system to be hellish & monstrous, and that its influence in our country was all powerful," but then "bowed down and licked the boot of oppression," despite being "fully aware of" Harrison's "determined deadly hostility to the principles of Liberty."[36]

As political abolitionists embarked on their maiden third-party campaign, they aimed to undermine abolitionist support for Harrison by denigrating his leading antislavery Whig adherents. "The slaveholders will listen patiently to Mr. Slade, and let his speech circulate all over the South," Leavitt chided, "if he will wind up by giving his vote for Speaker and for President as slavery dictates," even though Leavitt recognized the slaveholders' alarm at Slade's speeches and their usefulness for the antislavery cause. Leavitt did not spare even the venerable ex-president: "Of what avail are the whinings of John Quincy Adams . . . about the encroachments of slavery" when he tacitly supported Harrison? At times Leavitt berated abolitionist Whigs so relentlessly that Giddings suggested he needed a "straight jacket." By directing such venom at even obviously antislavery officeholders, third-party abolitionists affirmed their commitment to mobilizing a political force uncontaminated by major-party influences. Since abolitionists' anti–Slave Power invective threatened to seriously strain their relationships with potential congressional mouthpieces, personal lobbying became all the more crucial.[37]

At the same time that political abolitionists publicly chastised antislavery Whig congressmen, they privately worked to exploit these representatives' ability to generate congressional controversy. The two groups came to respect each other, if at times grudgingly, and both benefited from their collaboration. Abolitionist petitions provided the basis for many of the stands taken by antislavery Whigs, and Liberty partisans' private support encouraged them to voice their antislavery convictions and sometimes achieve celebrity (and notoriety) in the process.

Despite their weak showing in the 1840 election, Liberty men remained confident of future success if they could continue to precipitate antislavery congressional disruptions. With this goal in mind, Leavitt established himself as a lobbyist on the ground in Washington. Leavitt quickly became a Washington fixture, the leading abolitionist in the capital. Even as he flayed antislavery Whigs in his party press, Leavitt personally encouraged and aided their efforts in Congress. Leavitt arrived in the winter of 1841 to report on the Supreme Court trial of the *Amistad* Africans and assist Adams in preparing for oral arguments. Leavitt also spent as much time as possible observing congressional debate and buttonholing antislavery representatives. Leavitt frequently alleged his desire to avoid returning to the "hotbed of politics and sin," but for four years, the *Emancipator* repeatedly beseeched contributions to support him in Washington, for the good of the antislavery cause. His presence on the floor, and unsolicited distribution of his paper to all members, even became a subject of House debate, exposing Leavitt to a threat of censure and expulsion. Leavitt claimed that many congressmen enjoyed reading the *Emancipator*, though it certainly irritated some Southerners. Earlier, when John Calhoun had received a copy in his Senate mail, he "deliberately held it out at arms length—tore it in pieces & threw it on the floor."[38]

Many abolitionists who remained staunch Whigs valued Leavitt's presence at Washington, since the reports he disseminated provided an important abolitionist perspective on congressional debate and Supreme Court proceedings. The Whig abolitionist editor of the Xenia, *Ohio Free Press* praised Leavitt as "one of the most vigilant and indefatigable politicians in all our acquaintances," notwithstanding his *"third partyism."* Antislavery

Whig congressmen too appreciated Leavitt's work, despite his frequent attacks on their partisanship. Slade, though he publicly complained about the *Emancipator*'s "bitter censure" of Whig abolitionists, praised Leavitt's "talent and industry" and privately defended his impatience. Gates assured his friend Gerrit Smith that Leavitt was "doing good of course." Conceding the validity of some Liberty Party criticisms, Gates confidentially wrote Smith "as though . . . not a political opponent!" and admitted that President Harrison would likely "be pro slavery enough" given that he was so "very proud of his Virginia birth, whereas," Gates continued acerbically, "if I had a dog born in that state, it would afford a strong inducement to shoot it, rather than be proud of it."[39]

Abolitionist lobbyists and antislavery congressional coadjutors thus found much common ground and developed close relationships, even as the two butted heads over electoral tactics. Leavitt sometimes requested advice from Giddings about when he should return to Washington and relied on Giddings and Gates to receive his mail through their franking privilege and also to reserve a room for him. As these antislavery Whigs staked out increasingly aggressive stances, Liberty partisans grew hopeful of converting them. Ohio Liberty manager Salmon Chase attempted to cajole Giddings into acting with Ohio Liberty men in support of ex-Whig judge and state senator Leicester King for governor in 1842, in part by pretending that Chase had supported the independent nomination only because he expected Giddings would approve. Chase urged that if Giddings would "give us the weight of your name & influence," the Liberty Party's "triumph will be sure & soon." To Chase's chagrin, though, most prominent antislavery Whigs, including Giddings, persisted in supporting their party's state and national nominees. The fact that the Whigs finally controlled Congress in the early 1840s only increased the cross-pressures on antislavery Whig congressmen.[40]

Even at the special session President Harrison had called to address the persistent economic depression, the Whig Party could not avoid the issue of antislavery petitions. Leavitt did his best to make sure of that. Before this session commenced, Harrison had died, making Virginia proslavery extremist John Tyler the new president—the "melancholy issue," Leavitt lamented, of strenuous Whig efforts to persuade abolitionists to vote for Harrison. The *Emancipator* urged increased petitioning to force abolitionism into the special session and to sustain Adams, who had already "thrown himself once more into the breach, for the rescue of the Right of Petition." By contrast, stauncher Whigs like Slade, eager to confront the national financial crisis and implement the Whig economic agenda after years in the minority, advocated that abolitionists reserve their petitions for the regular session. The *Emancipator*, however, predicted that Southerners would attempt to reenact the previous Congress's rules, including the Johnson Gag, at the special session. Leavitt thus implored abolitionists to use their petitions to overturn the gag or at least to provoke a new controversy before the House adopted rules. Leavitt appreciated that antislavery Whigs imagined they could best aid the cause by aiming "first at the specific points of policy" they considered "beneficial to free labor," such as a protective tariff and national bank, but Leavitt rejected any deferral of direct political action against slavery and the Slave Power. Leavitt ultimately proved correct in his belief that no meaningful challenge to proslavery policymaking could succeed under the Second Party System, but antislavery Whigs had a point too. The Republican Party would later win national power by effectively conjoining antislavery ideals with economic policies appealing to Northern farmers, workers, and industrialists—an achievement, however, that became possible only with a party divorced from slaveholder control, as Liberty men had long prophesied.[41]

By the time Leavitt scraped together funds to return to Washington, antislavery Whigs had again disappointed Liberty partisans. Adams seemingly expunged the gag, but the House reconsidered and ultimately passed special session rules that tabled *any* petitions not pertaining to the specific policies the session had been called to enact. Antislavery Whigs (excepting Adams) defended this compromise as discontinuing extraordinary treatment for antislavery petitions. But even temporarily silencing antislavery petitions out of benign motives, abolitionists lamented, diverted political debate away from slavery. Furthermore, abolitionists contended, "this special rule" had been "adopted at the instance of slaveholders" and "modelled according to their views" so as to proscribe debate over "whether Congress is constitutionally bound to receive abolition petitions." Still, because of Adams's initial struggle for repeal, abolitionists could view the proceedings "with the liveliest satisfaction."[42]

Despite Adams's narrow defeat during the special session, Liberty partisans urged added pressure on Congress and continued to count on support from antislavery congressmen. In preparation for the regular session, the American and Foreign Anti-Slavery Society (a politically independent organization led primarily by northeastern Liberty men) disseminated a comprehensive plan calling for increased petitions and for abolitionists to personally engage their representatives "openly, face to face." The society instructed petitioners to also address a separate letter to Gates, inventorying the request, location, and signers of petitions to aid political abolitionists' efforts to tabulate them. "The discussions in Congress," the society asserted, "greatly promoted our righteous cause, and prove that legislative bodies are not immoveable." As desired, the abolitionists' efforts once again incited shrill House debate. Virginia proslavery extremist Henry Wise, one of Adams's more adroit combatants in the gag rule debates, even responded with a speech denouncing the "carefully and skillfully laid" plan coordinated with "Seth M. Gates, the agent of the abolitionists on the floor of Congress."[43]

Wise's forebodings at the burgeoning collaboration between the Liberty Party and antislavery Whigs reflected a keen awareness that third-party leaders were increasingly channeling grassroots abolitionist activism into national politics. To further facilitate congressional assaults on the Slave Power, Leavitt intensified his lobbying efforts by moving into Ann Sprigg's boarding house with Giddings, Slade, Gates, and several other antislavery Whig congressmen. Over the next few years, lodging and dining together, this group, which Giddings styled an antislavery "select committee," strategized to circumvent the gag. Leavitt planned tactics with these representatives and pressed them to challenge slavery on the House floor and privilege antislavery convictions over party obligations. While Leavitt believed Whigs like Gates and Giddings to be misguided, he understood that they considered themselves "sincerely opposed to the slave power" and hoped that on practical tactics they could be "of one mind."[44] Leavitt urged other political abolitionists to "visit Washington for the purpose of sustaining . . . those of our representatives who are disposed to do right." Leavitt especially hoped for assistance during the session's opening month, which he correctly anticipated would be dominated by debates over antislavery petitions.[45]

In response to Leavitt's entreaties and Giddings's request for help compiling evidence for antislavery floor speeches, famed semi-retired abolitionist lecturer Theodore Dwight Weld joined Leavitt and the congressmen at Sprigg's for parts of two sessions. This "abolition house" eventually became so crowded that Weld had to share Leavitt's bed. Weld also shared Leavitt's commitment to mobilizing congressional testimony against proslavery influences in American politics, even though they disagreed about third-party tactics. While Weld avoided embroilment in electoral politics, he wholeheartedly supported antislavery lobbying, in large part because antislavery congressional speeches would be published in newspapers "scattered all over the south as well as the North." Outspoken abolitionists Angelina Grimké Weld and Sarah Grimké (now Weld's wife and live-in sister-in-law, respectively) similarly reminded him that, beyond just "collecting facts," the real importance of his presence at the capital was "the influence" he could exert through "counsel & conversation" with antislavery politicians.[46]

Upon Weld's arrival at Sprigg's, he and Leavitt immediately began preparing ways for their messmates to elude the gag. Before these designs came to fruition, though, Adams precipitated a new scuffle that required Leavitt's and Weld's full-time involvement as political advisers. Following Adams's attempt to present an abolitionist petition for dissolution of the Union, enraged slaveholders called for censure (and, as in the proceedings five years earlier, one advocated burning the petition on the House floor).[47]

This new controversy gave Leavitt and Weld an even stronger voice in House debate. Gates, Giddings, Slade, and six other antislavery Whigs conferred with their abolitionist housemates and deputed the two of them to assist Adams in what became a dramatic two-week arraignment of slavery's role in national politics. Through the ordeal, Weld served as Adams's research assistant. Giddings secured him an alcove in the Library of Congress, and Weld spent countless hours assembling materials Adams could use in his defense. At night, Weld, Leavitt, and Adams met to plan arguments he would air to the nation the next day. Adams's tirades sounded strikingly similar to Liberty rhetoric as he denounced the "conspiracy . . . against himself, and, through him, against the right of petition, and all the rights and liberties of the free people of this union." Gates gleefully reported to abolitionist friends that the House was "in the midst of abolition excitement." After occupying the House for a full six days (spread over two weeks) and using his personal defense to deliver a withering excoriation of slavery's power in national politics, Adams offered to forgo the remainder of his intended remarks if the House would table the censure motions. If not, though, "he had a great deal of time yet to require." A House majority thus decided it would be prudent to "lay the whole subject on the table" — a defeat that left many Southern congressmen, Leavitt recounted, "dreadfully mortified."[48]

After throwing out the censure motions, the House returned to its outstanding business of petition presentation, and the floor reverted to Adams. He promptly offered almost 200 more antislavery petitions. Giddings marveled at "the power of his eloquence" and reported to Ohio Liberty manager Salmon Chase that "I have with my own eyes seen the Southern Slaveholders literally shake and tremble through every nerve and joint, while he arrayed before them their political and moral sins." "The last two weeks," Giddings continued, "have done more in congress on this subject than the last ten years previous." Giddings proudly averred "that the charm of the Slave power *is now broken*," and confidently predicted that "a moral revolution in this nation will take its date from this session of Congress." And yet, the Washington Whig newspaper, the *National Intelligencer*, refused to print Adams's speeches. Instead, Leavitt took copious notes, despite objections to his presence on the House floor, and then sent them off to not only his *Emancipator* publisher, but also his antislavery Whig competitor, the more widely circulated *Boston Courier*.⁴⁹

Liberty partisans eulogized the antislavery representatives' efforts and encouraged them to go further. William Jay congratulated Adams on his "glorious triumph" over censure and observed that "multitudes have sided" with Adams, many of whom "till now have held little sympathy with the abolitionists." Edward Wade assured Giddings that the congressional strife was "opening the eyes of the people to the fact that there is something more radically rotten in the administration of public affairs than our political doctors have been willing to admit." By Wade's appraisal, "The Whigs are up full river above canoe navigation" and could be saved only in the unlikely event that the party welcomed abolitionists and cast slaveholders "overboard to be swallowed by sharks or whales or any thing else that won't vomit them up again." The *Emancipator* similarly joked that "some of our northern members [of Congress] are in *great danger* of becoming LIBERTY MEN!"⁵⁰

Seeking to widen the congressional rift over slavery, Leavitt, Weld, and their fellow boarders at Sprigg's followed up on Adams's triumph by proceeding with their original plan to focus congressional debate on slavery: a set of resolutions drafted by Weld for Giddings to present in support of the slaves who had overtaken the crew of the coasting ship *Creole* and sailed to the Bahamas, where British authorities affirmed the mutineers' freedom. Giddings attempted to assert Weld's "municipal theory of slavery," contending "that slavery being an abridgement of natural law" was only legal in the jurisdiction of the states that had explicitly enacted laws protecting it. Consequently the *Creole* slave rebels "violated no law" and were, Giddings told Congress, "justly liable to no penalty" for "resuming their natural rights" through violent uprising. Proslavery representatives angrily censured Giddings without allowing him to defend himself, after which Giddings promptly resigned and returned home to campaign for reelection and prove that he had faithfully represented his antislavery constituency.⁵¹

Leavitt and Gates sent Giddings regular updates from Washington warning him not to expect support from fellow Ohio Whigs: "The Lord send you deliverance, for your Whig colleagues won[']t. I hope I can scare you pretty well, so you will never trust much to slaveocrats again." The Ohio delegation scuttled Gates's efforts to organize a meeting of Northern Whigs in support of Giddings, since many Ohio Whigs were wary of being too closely connected to abolitionism. As Ohio Whigs deserted Giddings, Gates feared they might even pressure Ohio's Whig governor to delay the special election. In contrast, "Leavitt & all the third party folks" were, Gates reported, "deeply anxious for" Giddings's return to Washington—a telling indication of the common ground that antislavery radicals like Giddings and Gates shared with Liberty men but not with Whig co-partisans.[52]

Abolitionists found the censure of Giddings "producing a happy effect," persuading antislavery voters to abandon their old political parties. Despite the timidity of his Ohio colleagues, support for Giddings mounted across the North. William Slade remarked in response to a fervent pro-Giddings meeting in Philadelphia:

> This outrage will it is evident, wake up a spirit in the country, such as has not been waked up before. It will be worth one hundred thousand,—yea, a million abolition lectures. The slaveholders are taking the business of abolition out of our hands. We have nothing to do but to stand still, and see the salvation.[53]

Liberty partisans, of course, had no intention of standing still. While the Whig Party disdained Giddings's abolitionism, Liberty men embraced him more than ever before. Even without support from the Whig machinery, Giddings won reelection resoundingly. With the special election a referendum on Giddings's congressional opposition to slavery, the Ohio Liberty Party provided its full support, this once, and Liberty gubernatorial candidate Leicester King stumped across the district for Giddings. Salmon Chase celebrated Giddings's resolutions as almost identical to the Ohio Liberty Party's position that "slavery cannot be extended one inch beyond state limits." Giddings's triumph indicated to Liberty partisans that "we have now reached a point at which the slave question in its thousand & one relations *must & will be met.*" Finally "the *North*" was ready to "make a stand against the domineering *encroachments* of slavery." One sign of the improving prospects of antislavery politics was the difficulty Southerners had defeating Adams's attempts to repeal the gag in late 1842 and 1843 (the gaggers clung to majorities of five votes or fewer both years). Giddings claimed (reflecting years later) that the odious rule had "morally ceased to operate" once he overcame his party's hostility and won reelection in the spring of 1842.[54]

Neither Liberty men nor Whig congressmen had time to rest on their laurels, though. As the Tyler administration plotted a renewed push for Texas annexation, abolitionists again worked with their congressional watchdogs to warn the Northern public. In 1842, Adams attempted to alert the North to plans for "the dismemberment of Mexico, and the annexation of an immense portion of its territory to the slave representation of this Union." Lewis Tappan likewise feared a new Southern congressional attempt "to smuggle Texas in" and urged the importance of abolitionist lobbyist Joshua Leavitt's presence at Washington in late 1843: "Do not . . . sleep upon your post. You are now *the watchman* at head-quarters."[55]

Working with Leavitt, Seth Gates kept abolitionists informed of Tyler's covert maneuvering. Gates consulted Gerrit Smith on anti-annexation strategy, and encouraged abolitionists to lobby their state and national representatives, especially Democrats Gates could not reach. In Washington, Gates joined Leavitt and Weld in drafting an anti-Texas speech for another New York Whig to deliver. Then Gates rallied antislavery voters with his 1843 "Address to the People of the Free States," signed ultimately by twenty-one Northern Whigs. This address, printed in antislavery-leaning newspapers across the North, aimed to alert the nation to the Tyler administration's designs on Texas. Gates drew heavily on abolitionist rhetoric as he warned that annexation would ensure "*the undue ascendancy of the slaveholding power in the Government.*" Leavitt's *Emancipator* praised this "admirable exposition of the danger of this infamous conspiracy," but also questioned Northern Whigs' attempts to claim the anti-annexation mantle for their party, when only twenty-one had signed the address, eight of them belatedly. As Gates continued to feed political abolitionists crucial information about the annexation scheme, he veered gradually toward Liberty partisanship.[56]

Congressman Gates's disgust at his party's course through Giddings's censure and reelection campaign especially suggested the potential efficacy of Liberty efforts to coax antislavery representatives to abandon their party. Working closely with Leavitt and Weld, Gates soon believed, "We must inevitably come to a northern party ere long," but in 1842, Gates still wistfully hoped Northern Whigs might yet "stand up vigorously for the rights of the North & the slave." By late 1843, Gates had given up on his party, and Liberty men proudly touted his defection. Gates's decision conveniently coincided with his withdrawal from political office (he returned home to tend to his health), but his rupture with the Whigs is best explained by his disgust at the party's apparent devotion to slaveholding anti-abolitionist and presidential heir apparent Henry Clay, whom Gates deemed "rotten as a stagnant fish pond on the subject of slavery." Once absent from the "sinful metropolis" of Washington, Gates missed his daily scheming with messmate Leavitt, "with his iron pen, invincible zeal & indomitable courage, unretiring faith & indefatigable labors," and praised him as "the safest & strongest Liberty party man in America." With support for Clay's presumptive 1844 presidential candidacy the new test of Whig loyalty, Gates conceded that abolitionists could no longer operate within the party. His health excused him from accepting Smith's suggestion that he run for lieutenant governor, but Gates did attend the 1843 national Liberty Party convention.[57]

While Liberty men beset partisan antislavery Whigs, Adams received more lenient treatment. By 1843 abolitionists who had worked with Adams came to tolerate, if not condone, his refusal to support immediate abolition in the District of Columbia. Increasingly distant from national party contests, Adams's political renown made him an important symbol of antislavery politics. His leadership in the gag battle, along with his role in the *Amistad* trial, earned him many political abolitionists' "warmest gratitude." Leavitt praised "Mr. Adams' sincerity and deep devotion to the cause of Liberty," proclaiming him "one of the greatest of living men" and "one of the truest patriots that ever lived" and asserting "that he is as fully bent on doing whatever he thinks best calculated to hasten the overthrow of slavery as any abolitionist in the land." Adams reciprocated this respect and told political abolitionists that his "sentiments, I believe very nearly accord" with members of "Abolition societies, Anti-slavery societies, or the Liberty Party."[58]

With this mutual understanding, Liberty men worked ever more closely with the ex-president to facilitate his provocative theatrics. In one of the most impressive of these collaborations, Adams and a Boston abolitionist committee together brought national attention to antislavery arguments against the 1793 Fugitive Slave Act. The stakes of the fugitive issue, always a source of simmering sectional tension, had risen considerably in light of the Supreme Court's 1842 *Prigg* v. *Pennsylvania* decision, which established the supremacy of federal fugitive slave legislation over any state laws that might interfere. However, by declaring fugitive slave recaption exclusively under federal jurisdiction, the Court opened the door for new varieties of personal liberty laws aimed at disentangling state authorities from the rendition process. For Liberty men, the decision also made clear that the fugitive slave issue could, and should, be contested at the federal level.[59]

Not long after *Prigg*, the seizure of Virginia fugitive George Latimer in Boston precipitated an antislavery groundswell across Massachusetts as abolitionists formed a statewide "Latimer Committee" to prevent his rendition. This committee helped purchase Latimer's freedom, published a short-lived antislavery newspaper, and led a massive petitioning campaign across the state. Drawing from a cross-section of antislavery Bay Staters, the 1843 petition drive garnered almost 52,000 signatures (the first of which was Latimer's) on a congressional petition requesting that the state "be freed from its connexion with slavery." A similarly impressive state petition demanded a new personal liberty law, which Massachusetts legislators passed later that year, prohibiting state officials and state jails from being utilized by Southerners seeking to recover fugitive slaves. As for the federal petition, organizers William F. Channing (son of famous Unitarian minister William Ellery Channing) and Liberty Party activist Henry I. Bowditch contacted Adams to coordinate the logistics of transporting the massive document into the House. Once the House gagged it, Adams displayed the enormous petition—three feet in diameter spooled around a wooden wheel and nearly a half-mile long if unrolled—on his desk. The giant petition, indeed, was so large that Adams had to vacate his ordinary seat to be seen over the roll. Latimer Committee organizers observed with satisfaction that "it attracted great attention from all who entered the Representative hall, and from attention arose discussion of the whole system of slavery and anti-slavery, which, of course, is all that is wanted." Giddings gloated at embittered Southern representatives' "cold sweat" at viewing the monumental petition, and a Whig Party press that clearly grasped the abolitionists' strategy complained of the "good deal of ostentation in thus parading a memorial before the House" simply for the purpose of trying "to agitate—agitate—agitate the country."[60]

By the mid-1840s Lewis Tappan could rejoice that "everybody is talking about the movements in Congress." And when, as the winter of 1844 wore on, neither Leavitt nor Weld could be present in Washington, Giddings genuinely lamented their absence. Tappan meanwhile became fixated on revitalizing their lobbying strategy. Leavitt returned in December 1844 for one final session at the capital, where he was able to witness the rescinding of the gag rule, though his relationship with Giddings had somewhat chilled in the wake of the recent presidential contest. That same winter, the New York State Anti-Slavery Society dispatched William Chaplin to succeed Charles Torrey as "a watch-dog" there "to *see* what may pass before my eyes, and make a true report to the good Liberty public" (and Chaplin, like Torrey, became involved in organizing slave escapes). Tappan, however, hoped to fund a more permanent political abolitionist presence in Washington.[61]

In 1844, to the Liberty Party's consternation, many of the most progressive antislavery Whigs, including Giddings, had campaigned vigorously for slaveholding presidential candidate Henry Clay. After that divisive 1844 election, Lewis Tappan pushed for a national Liberty Party convention at Washington while Congress was in session, but the plan was postponed because it did not leave enough time for winter travel to Washington. Abolitionists celebrated the long-awaited repeal of the gag rule (by a vote of 108–80) in December 1844 but fretted over the imminent annexation of Texas and the possibility of war with Mexico. Those developments, though, would ultimately make the Slave Power argument all the more convincing and provide the impetus for Tappan to establish the Washington *National Era* in 1846. The *Era* would not only provide the Liberty Party with a newspaper at the capital, but also would enable editor Gamaliel Bailey to create a permanent abolitionist congressional lobby. Bailey's continued pursuit of the lobbying strategies pioneered earlier in the decade would play a crucial role in strengthening abolitionist alliances with antislavery congressmen in the late 1840s.[62]

Since 1839, political abolitionists had rejected any party connection with slaveholders or their advocates. They combined electoral opposition to antislavery Whig congressmen like Adams, Gates, Giddings, and Slade with lobbying efforts designed to precipitate congressional debate that drew national attention to slavery and the Slave Power. Liberty leaders benefited immensely from the assistance of Whig allies who could win national office and ensure a broad audience for antislavery. In rare cases, Liberty leaders convinced prominent politicians like Gates to repudiate their old party connections and espouse political abolitionism. Most of Gates's antislavery Whig colleagues, however, clung to their party until the 1848 presidential election again forced them to choose between supporting a slaveholder and deserting their party. Despite their refusal to join in Gates's break with the Whig Party, political abolitionists and antislavery congressmen would continue to cooperate to incite controversies that could further illustrate the reach of the Slave Power.

Challenging the Slave Power together, political abolitionists and antislavery Whig congressmen collaborated to repeatedly inject slavery into congressional debate, even as both dismissed each other's electoral strategies. It was for this express purpose of building such congressional alliances that abolitionists had established a presence in Washington, and their efforts helped make slavery an ever more central question in national political debate. The increasing attention to proslavery influence in Congress aptly complemented Liberty electoral strategies that similarly sought to expose the Slave Power's control of national politics.

* Interlude Two *

"A Temporary 'Third Party'": Antislavery Whig Dissidents in the 1841 Speakership Contest

In 1841, Congress convened early, under the weight of the Washington heat and an economic crisis that had been festering for nearly four years. In the face of an unsustainable federal deficit, General William Henry Harrison's first (and only) substantial presidential action had been to call a special session to right the nation's finances. Before the congressmen arrived, Harrison had contracted pneumonia and died.

Though they doubtless mourned the deceased president and pondered the direction Vice President John Tyler's administration might take, Whig representatives elected on Harrison's coattails could look forward nonetheless to a hefty forty-vote majority. This time, there would be no need for the party to accept an unreliable speaker like Robert Hunter. Northern Whigs, the sectional majority within the preponderant party, now eagerly awaited their chance to finally select a speaker from the free states after slaveholders had presided over the seven previous houses. Abolitionists thus had been "well assured" that many Northern Whigs intended only to "vote for a free Speaker." As the Washington correspondent for Congressman Seth Gates's hometown Whig paper the Le Roy Gazette (of which Gates was former editor) noted, "the Slave States have given us the Speaker for 27 out of the last 30 years," so "there was every where an expectation and desire in the free States that a northern Speaker should be selected." Touting Buffalo's Millard Fillmore, who had developed a modest antislavery reputation (which he would eventually negate entirely), the Le Roy Gazette urged that New York, by far the largest state, with representatives comprising about a sixth of the House, deserved her turn in the speaker's chair.[1]

Both "out of doors" preceding the Whig caucus and then within it, antislavery Whigs Gates, Giddings, and Slade strove to promote a Northern candidate "on the ground that the speakership was due to the free states." To their *frustration, Kentucky slaveholder John White, a Henry Clay lieutenant, beat out the Northern candidates in caucus. As a response, the antislavery dissidents resolved to "make a demonstration that there were men who would no longer vote for a slaveholder when we had good candidates of our own," but the three insurrectionists persuaded only Adams and John Mattocks of Vermont to join them, and Nathaniel Borden of Massachusetts followed their example in casting his own Northern protest vote. Whig leaders, not needing those six votes to elect White, grudgingly tolerated the defection.²

Leavitt, not yet in Washington, erupted when he learned that House Whigs had selected another slaveholding speaker. Uninformed of the six protest votes, Leavitt savaged "Slade, Giddings, Gates, and numerous other members who at home appear to have a deep abhorrence of slavery, and a fixed determination to resist the further encroachments of the slave power," but once in Washington "quietly succumbed"—or so Leavitt assumed. These antislavery Whigs angrily complained of the "great injustice" done by Leavitt's precipitate, unfounded criticism. After learning the truth, Leavitt apologized and commended the small band who had determined that Southern "overseers had ruled the House long enough."³

Leavitt's initial accusation, though, evinced political abolitionists' continued suspicion of antislavery Whigs, which would persist as long as the Whig Party did. Northern Whigs had previously insisted it was their section's turn to choose the speaker, but once the caucus selected White, all except six dutifully voted for a slaveholding disciple of Henry Clay. Liberty men bemoaned that the "Slave Power has again triumphed." The six antislavery dissidents' act of independence further highlighted the perfidy of the many other Northern Whigs who had yet again "yielded to party dictation." Unlike with Hunter's election, another few antislavery defections would not have defeated White, but free state Whigs collectively controlled more than enough votes to have demanded a Northern speaker. Liberty men chastised known abolitionists who helped elevate White, especially those who had directly rebuffed private entreaties from Gates, Giddings, and Slade to join in their protest.⁴

The votes repudiating White, however, suggested that political abolitionists might further loosen antislavery Whigs' partisan fetters. A Brooklyn Liberty meeting chaired by Arthur Tappan, for example, hailed "the vote of the six members of Congress" who would not support "a slaveholder for Speaker" as "the beginning of a continued and united effort in Congress against the further encroachments of the slave power." Liberty men applauded these congressmen's flouting of party discipline and anticipated that abolitionists might soon sever antislavery Whigs from their proslavery party. Leavitt maintained "great respect . . . for those who formed a temporary 'third party' in the election of Speaker, in despite of all the solicitations of party interest," but warned* that political abolitionists would neither "countenance what they do against" liberty, nor excuse them for "things left undone."[5]

The 1841 election for speaker of the House was emblematic of the shifting politics of the antislavery congressional vanguard, demonstrating how heavily Southern power wore on some Northern Whigs. The obvious anxieties of antislavery congressmen struggling to reconcile their partisanship with moral disgust for slavery offered Liberty men a promising indication that they might soon detach these politicians from the Whig Party. Striving to convince receptive Whigs that the Slave Power controlled their party as much as it did the Democrats, Liberty men urged desertion as the only course consistent with their 1841 speakership votes. This goal undergirded the vigorous lobbying discussed in the last chapter and further induced Liberty managers to structure third-party electoral campaigns around exposing the impossibility of meaningful antislavery progress within the major parties, as discussed in the next chapter. With Gates at least, the Liberty men succeeded. Those who remained active office seekers proved more reluctant. Liberty partisans thus strove to also use electoral politics to highlight the major parties' subservience to the Slave Power. By generating antislavery constituent pressure at the same time that abolitionist leaders were refining their lobbying strategy, Liberty partisans hoped to further sway antislavery politicians to abandon their proslavery parties.

* CHAPTER THREE *

Building Third-Party Electoral Power, 1841–1846

As they worked to accelerate debate over slavery in Congress, Liberty Party leaders simultaneously strove to create a formidable electoral force. Careful examination of Liberty electoral strategy makes clear that third-party leaders did not view their organization as a mere protest party, nor was political abolitionism simply moral suasion by other means. Liberty men knew it would be difficult to build a viable party that might win electoral victories, but they believed it was possible. Because antebellum parties printed and distributed their own electoral "tickets," Liberty men did not face the substantial impediment that formal state-sanctioned ballots today present for third-party organizing. Liberty men also knew that the competitiveness of the Second Party System created valuable opportunities for third-party influence. Liberty men skillfully used electoral politics to pressure the major parties *and* to attract new third-party converts by dramatizing Northern Whig and Democratic complicity with the Slave Power. Observing a slaveholding minority manipulating the political system to create a daunting Slave Power, abolitionists reasoned they could rouse latent antislavery sentiment in the North to produce a similarly potent "Liberty Power."[1]

The Aims and Arguments of the Liberty Organization

Historians have labeled the final two-thirds of the nineteenth century the "party period," pointing to the rise of mass political parties as the main institutions organizing American political behavior. Third parties during this period have often been glossed over or marginalized as antiparty protests. Most Liberty activists, however, were not fundamentally antiparty. Liberty leaders built party structures and participated in partisan politics. (Indeed, more than a few abandoned promising careers as major-party operatives when they joined the Liberty Party.) The goal of most Liberty action was not necessarily to offer an alternative to Jacksonian-era hyperpartisanship, but rather to provide a rival organization that could direct popular political fervor into antislavery channels. Notwithstanding the intense party loyalty of many Northern Whigs and Jacksonians, Liberty men believed they could function effectively as a third party by emphasizing their Slave Power argument and seizing opportunities to control balances of power between the two parties.[2]

Both potential strategic goals of Liberty Party activism—achieving national political victory or pressuring one or both of the major parties to adopt an unequivocally antislavery platform—required construction of an organized party. Still, most scholarship on American abolitionism, as well as much of nineteenth-century political history, portrays the Liberty Party as thoroughly unlike the party organizations against which it competed. Historians who extol Garrisonian radicalism have unsurprisingly scoffed at meager Liberty vote totals as evidence that third-party political action was not only morally debasing but also strategically ineffectual.[3] For many years, though, historians sympathetic to the more "conservative" evangelical wing of the movement shared this low estimate of Liberty politics.[4]

Competing at all levels within the American political system, and focusing especially on congressional races, Liberty men quickly sought to develop organizations mimicking the major parties by establishing party committees at the county and congressional-district level and later at the town level. Within a year and a half of the party's founding, some political abolitionists even envisioned an institutionalized party reaching down to individual school districts. The pro-Liberty New York State Anti-Slavery Society, for example, hoped to implement quarterly planning meetings in every county in the state, and Liberty men elsewhere professed similar organizational aspirations.[5]

The many abolitionist women who embraced the Liberty Party strategy also contributed to the party's efforts to nurture local organizational structures. Though they appeared in leadership roles far less than Garrisonian counterparts, Liberty women circulated petitions, attended meetings, distributed literature, raised much-needed funds, and endorsed candidates, and a handful, among them Peoria's Mary Davis and Pittsburgh's Jane Grey Swisshelm, lent important journalistic services to the third party. Women's antislavery society meetings across the lower Midwest were often scheduled to coincide with Liberty Party conventions, and attendants intermingled extensively, even if women did not speak at party conclaves or sit on platform committees. While circumscribed by traditional norms of domesticity, third-party women nonetheless mobilized their moral commitments against slavery to justify intensive involvement in grassroots political organizing aimed at swaying men to cast their votes against the Slave Power.⁶

The ambivalence about the morality of abolitionist party politics that some Liberty men (and women) expressed only underscores the degree to which party managers were building a party to operate within the partisan order rather than merely register protest against it. Often Liberty leaders even suggested that, upon gaining control of the national government, they would promote abolition by deploying federal patronage to empower antislavery voices in the South, much in the way Democrats and Whigs used patronage to stanch Northern antislavery. Abolitionists shunned neither patronage nor partisanship in and of themselves; the abolitionist critique instead centered on the ability of slaveholders to control both parties and thereby barter patronage for acquiescence in proslavery policies.⁷

By refocusing the nation's attention on slavery and institutionalized racial discrimination *as political problems*, Liberty men aimed ultimately to construct a party large enough to counterbalance the Slave Power. In the meantime, Liberty voters could pressure major-party politicians in those constituencies where elected representatives could ill afford to be seen as toadying to overbearing slave masters. Political abolitionists hoped to compel antislavery Whigs and Democrats to join their ranks, but more immediately, Liberty electoral challenges could force Northern officeholders to aver antislavery stances that would help foreground the slavery issue in national debate. Third-party leaders declared that they would happily unite in any organization fully committed against the Slave Power, but that the Liberty Party as yet remained the only such vehicle. Joshua Leavitt explained in 1843:

> Whether the Liberty party is destined to come into the possession of political power, or whether it is to serve only as a means of driving up the other parties to their duty, we have never undertaken to prophecy, nor are we very anxious to be able to foresee. We have always told the politicians that it was in their power at any time to annihilate the Liberty party. Let them do their duty, and the Liberty party dies . . . Such an issue we contemplate with perfect complacency. At the same time, we have not the remotest expectation of such a result.⁸

Many political abolitionists also fantasized about enlisting antislavery Southerners. The Liberty creed insisted that the third party was a national, not a sectional, party, and a select group took bold initiatives in the Border

South to combat slavery on its own ground. Still, even many who hoped the Liberty Party could one day develop a cross-sectional following understood the need initially for a nearly exclusively Northern political party. While inclined to spurn "geographical political parties," Gerrit Smith wrote in 1842 of his "growing conviction that a northern political party will be found indispensable for the overthrow of American slavery," and that "the nucleus of that party is the little 'Liberty party.'" Ohioans Salmon Chase and Gamaliel Bailey were among the most vigorous advocates of an antislavery vision that would incorporate nonslaveholding Southerners. But by demanding a new political party freed from all connection with the Slave Power, they effectively demanded a movement, at least temporarily, disconnected from most of the South. Chase imagined that "there are many, very many slaveholders who believe slavery to be a curse" and "look to the Liberty Party with great interest," hoping its success might enable them to promote emancipation "without the fear of being crushed by the weight of the local slavery party." Chase firmly believed that if Northerners "would act as Liberty Men against National Slavery consistently, unitedly and efficiently, they would find themselves soon reinforced by the friends of Liberty in slave states." Thus, even the vision of a truly national Liberty Party first required political change in the North.[9]

As an electoral force, the Liberty Party indeed started small, but the mere seven thousand Liberty votes polled in the 1840 presidential election did not discourage party leaders. The decision to move into partisan politics had been a momentous one, subjecting political abolitionists to bitter condemnation from foe and friend. The intensity of their commitment to third-party action had been quite deep for them to brave such overwhelming opposition; so their anticipation of eventual triumph should come as no surprise. Genuinely believing that slaveholders drew moral authority and political strength from their control of national policymaking, political abolitionists charged that the Second Party System enabled the Slave Power to protect slavery by co-opting Northern leaders through patronage and by directing national attention to economic issues that seemed trivial compared to the sinful enormity of slavery. If Liberty men could effectively pitch this message, they anticipated that Northern voters would feel compelled to abandon old party connections. Liberty Party men may have been overly sanguine, but few were naïve or impractical. They studied the machinations of national, state, and local political systems, and quickly learned how to exploit rare openings for third-party influence.

In doing so, most Liberty leaders espoused the "one-idea" principle, arguing that the only condition for partisan allegiance should be opposition to slavery and the Slave Power—the one idea that united them. At times some Liberty men advocated broadening the party program to incorporate other reforms, but most adhered to the one-idea strategy as best enabling them to recruit from *both* major parties. As Pennsylvania political abolitionists asserted, the one idea was sufficient to "cover the entire ground of national policy, that the country now needs." Moreover, since abolitionists viewed slavery as an all-encompassing total institution that impinged on every facet of the nation's political, economic, and social life, concentrating on this one idea seemed the best strategy for promoting liberty and prosperity more generally.[10]

The main corollary to the "one-idea" principle was a demand for civil and political equality for black Northerners. Many prominent black abolitionists consequently championed Liberty partisanship, although historians still debate the extent of African American representation among the rank and file. Among the small subset of free black men permitted to vote, some remained allied to Garrison or preferred to support the Whigs, with their more credible promise of controlling state legislation to repeal discriminatory statutes. Still, several leading black activists, including Henry Highland Garnet, Henry Bibb, Martin Delany, James W. C. Pennington, Charles B. Ray, Samuel R. Ward, and Theodore S. Wright, played important roles in third-party politics and gradually directed much of free black male abolitionism towards an increasingly close affinity with the Liberty Party by the mid-1840s. This was especially true in locales where black spokesmen figured prominently in the third-party leadership, as in Bibb's Michigan, Delany's Pittsburgh, Pennington's Connecticut, and especially in upstate New York, where Liberty activists Garnet, Ward, and Jermain Loguen all preached at points during the 1840s. Among white political abolitionists, the Slave Power idea did tend to overshadow black civil and political rights as time passed, but the two lines of argument remained compatible, and the Liberty Party continued to fight institutionalized racism and attract black votes, even as its campaign rhetoric often prioritized more popular attacks on slaveholders' political power.[11]

Focusing on combating "the pestiferous rule of the Slave Power," the Liberty Party enjoyed substantial growth. Liberty vote totals increased steadily from 1840 to 1843 in every free state. In Maine, for example, where only 195 men cast Birney votes in 1840, the Liberty Party polled 1,662 votes in 1841, 4,080 in 1842, and 6,746 in 1843. New York abolitionists exulted at holding the balance of power in four counties in 1841 and believed that they might soon mobilize this "balance power" to secure "Liberty representation on the floor of the [state] capitol." Though that success did not materialize, Liberty partisans controlled 4.5 percent of the Empire State's electorate by 1843. In Vermont, the growth was especially dramatic, with the 1843

Liberty gubernatorial candidate capturing 7.5 percent of votes cast. Even in New Hampshire, where the doughfaced Democratic machine reigned unrivalled, Liberty men polled about 3,000 votes and elected four state representatives in 1842; the following year Liberty partisans sent ten legislators to Concord. While major-party votes still dwarfed Liberty totals, the increase was dramatic.[12]

The Liberty Party's primary appeal relied on continued reiteration of the Slave Power's control over both political parties, and through them, national policymaking. Both were "pledged to the Slave Power" and "arrayed against the friends of Liberty." No mere segment of the Liberty program, this analysis was *the* justification for abolitionist political organization. The 1842 Massachusetts Liberty Party Convention thus asserted "that under all political changes of parties and administrations, the slave power still maintains its ascendency, in controlling the legislation, patronage and diplomacy of the government." At that convention, Garnet chastised the hypocritical antislavery professions of those still "clinging to the old proslavery parties" and predicted that, as abolitionists further exposed the "Slave Power," the Liberty Party would soon become the "most powerful party in our country." Identifying the major parties with the Slave Power not only served as an effective campaign tactic; political abolitionists genuinely believed that "the prospect of overthrowing American slavery will be *precisely* in proportion to the inroads, which, under the Divine blessing, we shall make upon our proslavery parties." Each Whig and Democratic electoral victory, Liberty leaders argued, reinforced a party system used by slaveholders to secure sway over Congress and the White House. Furthermore, the "servile lickspittle [partisan] press" continuously deceived Northern voters into supporting the Slave Power-dominated parties.[13]

This Slave Power argument also incorporated an economic analysis of how slaveholders had destroyed the national finances at great cost to free labor. In Liberty hands, this line of attack aimed to further strengthen the case for a single-minded, one-idea focus on slavery and the Slave Power. Liberty men insisted that slavery must preempt other issues, not only because it was of greater moral and political import, but also because it would be futile to address other economic concerns before the slavocracy had been checked. Joshua Leavitt's speech on the "Financial Power of Slavery" during the 1840 presidential campaign articulated these arguments most comprehensively, and many subsequent Liberty discussions followed his lead. "Slavery is the chief cause of our present commercial embarrassments," he argued, since fickle, indebted slaveholders promoted a "fluctuating policy," particularly on banking, that inhibited the nation's financial stability and drained Northern capital. And while such abolitionist arguments consistently overstated the economic inefficiency of the South's slave labor system, it was true, as Edward Baptist has shown, that many overleveraged cotton planters relied on Northern and foreign credit markets to underwrite their high-risk ventures in expanding southwestern slavery. Liberty leaders suggested that by 1844 Southern debts to the North exceeded $300 million. During the 1844 campaign, the New York State Anti-Slavery Society urged laboring Northerners to defend their own economic interests by casting third-party ballots, since "both of the [major] political parties, in submitting to the dictation of the *Slave Power*, are doing all they can to enable the slaveholder to live through our commercial, social, and political relations, upon the results of Northern industry." In these polemics, Liberty men cast free labor as virtuous and efficient and slave labor as demoralizing and wasteful. Such analyses, as Eric Foner has explained best, would become crucial to the broadening of antislavery politics in the 1850s.[14]

Notwithstanding the Liberty Party's attention to Northern economic interests, the Slave Power concept remained first and foremost an argument about slaveholders' disproportionate political power, wielded through the Whig and Democratic organizations. As Liberty partisans made "Slave Power" a household phrase, they observed that if slaveholders could control the nation, a similar power on behalf of liberty might one day challenge the Slave Power for national primacy. Seeing "the slave power, in the persons of the 250,000 slaveholders of this country" (a standard Liberty estimate), exert such overweening influence, Liberty leaders envisioned themselves similarly manipulating the nation's political institutions. Cincinnati *Philanthropist* editor Gamaliel Bailey predicted: "Their power will augment from year to year, till the politicians of the country will be compelled to pay the same respect to its will, that they now do to the commands of the Slave-Power." This was of course the goal of antislavery politics—transforming a political system in which Northern acquiescence to slaveholder demands was a prerequisite for advancement into one in which it would guarantee defeat. Liberty men increasingly characterized national political action as a contest between "two Antagonist Forces . . . the Slave Power and the Liberty-Power," or more commonly, the Slave Power and the Liberty Party. Liberty publications predicted dramatic growth, frequently extrapolating from the proportional increases of the Liberty Party's first few years that the party could control a presidential election by 1848, although leaders often privately acknowledged such forecasts to be overly optimistic.[15]

Ohio (and particularly southern Ohio) Liberty leaders like Bailey became especially known for their emphasis on "deliverance of the government from the control of the slave power." Among the foremost political abolitionist journalists, Bailey, though deeply religious, tended to more strictly demarcate religion and politics than other Liberty journalists. After a peripatetic youth that included a medical degree from Philadelphia's Jefferson Medical College and a Pacific sea voyage, Bailey found his calling with Birney's Cincinnati *Philanthropist*. By the end of 1836, Bailey was basically running the paper, which soon became the preeminent antislavery journal west of the Appalachians. Living on the murky borders of slavery and freedom, Bailey sometimes employed comparatively measured abolitionist rhetoric, perhaps in hopes of appealing to potentially antislavery Southerners and staving off the sort of mob violence that nearly killed the *Philanthropist* in 1841. Bailey's brand of practical antislavery politics balanced moral abolitionism, deep commitment to individual rights, and tactical emphases on the Slave Power and on targeting slavery where it was most vulnerable to federal intervention. In this approach, Bailey accorded closely with the legal analyses of his Cincinnati lawyer friend Salmon Chase, who blended abolitionist religious convictions with unremitting ambition.[16]

Chase had commenced his antislavery political crusade in the courtroom. Working with his client Birney, the towering young attorney helped refine constitutional arguments for slavery's illegality outside Southern state limits as he defended fugitive slaves and white Northerners who had harbored them, including Birney. Enforcement of the 1793 Fugitive Slave Act was unconstitutional in Ohio, Chase argued (though unsuccessfully) in the 1837 *Matilda* case (and in the related case against Birney), as that law presumed a right of property in persons that could not exist in free Ohio. In subsequent years, as one of the West's most active Liberty partisans, Chase continued to litigate against federal involvement in fugitive slave recaption, to the point that critics dubbed him the "Attorney General for Runaway Negroes," an insult he rather relished. Chase's reasoning in these fugitive cases helped solidify the legal groundwork behind Liberty demands for divorcing the federal government from slavery.[17]

With political abolitionist calls for denationalizing slavery so closely entwined with resistance to federal fugitive slave legislation, it is perhaps unsurprising that many Liberty partisans directly abetted slave escapes. Though this illegal activity was never officially part of the Liberty program, many black and white Liberty leaders worked consistently, if surreptitiously, to aid runaway slaves. Those who risked the most by venturing South to organize mass escapes, like Charles Torrey, drew the greatest attention, but a far larger number of Liberty men played vital roles in Underground Railroad efforts in the North, including by offering their homes as "depots." Well-known black Liberty partisans like Loguen, Ray, Delany, and

Pennington, along with white political abolitionists like Smith, Lewis Tappan, perennial Connecticut gubernatorial nominee Francis Gillette, Pennsylvania's Francis LeMoyne, Michigan *Signal of Liberty* editors Theodore Foster and Guy Beckley, and brazen northern Illinois radical Owen Lovejoy (brother of the martyred abolitionist editor Elijah Lovejoy) represent just a fraction of the prominent Liberty men who repeatedly aided slaves running for freedom.[18]

Given the manifest radicalism of many Liberty operatives, some found it troubling when Chase suggested that any "man who adopts & acts upon" the goal of wresting control of the government from the Slave Power "and severs himself from the slavery parties is a Good Liberty man," even if "adverse" to the name "abolitionist." This was the sort of crass political calculation that Garrisonians (and their modern enthusiasts), along with several eastern Liberty men, deprecated as illustrating the corrupting influence of partisan politics. Still, Ohio Liberty leaders made clear to eastern colleagues their "hope that if success shall crown our efforts to divorce the government from slavery, that State after State will speedily and voluntarily emancipate." The December 1841 Ohio Liberty Convention's address, penned by Chase and adopted unanimously by two hundred delegates, forcefully advocated the "ABSOLUTE AND UNQUALIFIED DIVORCE OF THE FEDERAL GOVERNMENT FROM SLAVERY."[19] A shared commitment to overcoming the Slave Power by defeating the major parties united Liberty men with varying degrees of abolitionist radicalism. Joshua Leavitt understood that the Ohio men's goal of overturning Slave Power control over the government was effectively the same program as more radical easterners' calls for "'employing all honorable and constitutional means to hasten the removal of slavery.'" Even so dogmatic a moralist as Lewis Tappan could accept the program of "aiming only to divorce the general Govt from all participation in Slavery & the Slave Trade," and praise the "truly National" principles of the Ohio Liberty leaders.[20]

Chase's trenchant appraisal of the Slave Power argument's political allure, at least in Ohio, is borne out in the writing of embattled antislavery Whigs there. Albert G. Riddle, a key Western Reserve ally of Joshua Giddings, agreed "that the time is not far distant when the issue must be made directly between the North & South." While Riddle feared that the "Self Styled Liberty Party" was "making great effect" in efforts aimed at "destruction of the Whig Party," he also "wish[ed] most sincerely that we *were* all with them." Though Riddle and his supporters "heartily ... dislike[d] the name of abolitionist," he understood that "their eyes" would "flash" and "their faces burn" as soon as one spoke to them of Southern control over national politics. Riddle thus celebrated, despite his Whig affiliation, that it "would require but little to annihilate party distinctions" and unite opponents of the Slave Power.[21]

The Liberty Attack on Whig Partisanship: The Specter of President Henry Clay

Incessant Liberty attacks on both major parties especially targeted, and angered, antislavery Whigs. Since their party nominated more antislavery candidates and attracted more antislavery voters than the Democrats (who often openly campaigned on white supremacy), Northern Whigs responded angrily to Liberty attempts to smear them as proslavery. Whig politicians across the North portrayed their party as the party of moral reform, and many ran as antislavery candidates, or even characterized the Whigs as "the true 'liberty party.'" Thus Liberty men faced the dual challenge of disabusing voters of these Whig professions and reassuring them that the Liberty Party would not weaken the antislavery cause by aiding proslavery Democrats. Abolitionists worried far less about persuading antislavery voters to oppose Democratic politicians, since so few flaunted antislavery credentials (at least before 1846).[22]

Continually having to defend themselves against Whig aspersions that Liberty men were covertly serving the Democrats, many Liberty leaders came to prefer "the open, above-board baseness of the Democracy on the subject of abolition, to the hypocrisy and treachery of the Whigs." Because both parties supported slavery at the national level and placed slaveholders and doughfaces in positions of national power, neither could be trusted, regardless of which harbored more antislavery voices. Abolitionist publications described the Democrats as "mortgaged soul and body to slavery," but more frequently assailed "*Janus-faced*" Whig attempts to present their party as "*anti* slavery in (some portions of) the North and slaveocratic in the South."[23]

While political abolitionists deplored the continued alliance of antislavery Whigs with proslavery national leaders, Liberty papers pointed to the increasing prominence of abolitionist Whig officeholders as evidence of Liberty influence. Self-described abolitionist John Mattocks had been elected governor of Vermont in 1843. Roger Baldwin, the abolitionist lawyer who had represented the *Amistad* Africans, ran as the Connecticut Whig gubernatorial candidate unsuccessfully in 1843 and victoriously in 1844 and 1845. While Liberty men preferred to see their own ranks swelling, they took solace in the degree to which they had pushed segments of the major parties toward antislavery stances. Even Giddings's renomination in 1843 came to be seen as evidence of Liberty Party power on the Western Reserve. After reapportionment, Giddings's district had been stripped of many antislavery Whig voters, encouraging some party leaders to consider dumping Giddings, but the Liberty challenge made such a move impossible. While it "was very humiliating" for leading Cleveland Whigs "to come down on their knees and nominate Giddings for their representative," a refusal might have pushed the district's many abolitionist Whigs into the Liberty ranks.[24]

The best example of Liberty influence coercing antislavery nominations from the Whig Party came when Vermont Whigs gave their 1844 gubernatorial nomination to William Slade, the most "thorough abolitionist" that ever "spoke in Congress" (by the *Philanthropist*'s estimate). Political abolitionists reproached Whig leaders' apparent designs to mobilize Slade's antislavery influence to help the proslavery national party secure the presidency in 1844. Nonetheless, abolitionists exulted that "the nomination of William Slade by the Whigs, *was forced upon them by the existence of the Liberty party*." Slade himself privately conceded that many Vermont Whigs had only "been willing to *use me* to keep down the third party."[25]

Liberty leaders boasted that their political pressure had made support for abolitionism "the sure way to promotion" for Whig politicians who once would have viewed it as "political suicide." Such developments demonstrated "that politicians have already discerned that there is a Liberty Power at the North, as well as a Slave Power at the South." But Liberty men also bemoaned the fact that "all these [Whig] Abolitionists are supporters of a pro-Slavery national party, and use all their influence to promote the election of a Slaveholder [for president]." As the Liberty Party forced increasingly antislavery nominations on Northern Whig organizations, Liberty men had to work ever more strenuously to persuade antislavery Whig voters to forsake their party.[26]

The Liberty Party's best evidence of the Whig Party's commitment to proslavery policymaking was its clear intention to run Henry Clay for president in 1844. In addition to his substantial investment in slave property, Clay was anathema to Liberty men for his prominent anti-abolitionist Senate speeches, which Liberty men interpreted as barefaced attempts to curry Southern favor for his presidential candidacy. Clay was particularly dangerous, Utica Liberty editor William Goodell insisted, precisely because his "cunning, calculating, and apparently compromising" action "excites little opposition." Liberty men campaigned by implicitly challenging the manhood of opponents who took direction from leaders like Clay and "yielded submissively to the Slave Power." Liberty candidates, in contrast, could not "be bullied, bought nor flattered, nor yet overseerized." Harsher Liberty rhetoric characterized Northern Whigs as "white Charlies," kowtowing to Henry Clay no less meekly than his enslaved personal servant Charles—an insult that likely resonated especially for antebellum voters who so prized their identities as independent white men.[27]

Throughout the early 1840s, Liberty leaders deployed the specter of Henry Clay and predicted (correctly, as it turned out) that Whig officeholders would be called upon to campaign for the Kentucky planter in 1844. The widespread acceptance of Clay's claim to the presidential nomination came to exemplify the Slave Power's control over the seemingly Northern-dominated Whig Party. As early as January 1841, even before President Harrison's inauguration, Liberty men had begun preparing for the next presidential contest, assuming that "Clay, Van Buren and Birney will stand before the people until 1844." Since both Clay and Van Buren had "linked themselves irrevocably with slavery," there could be no hope for effective antislavery policymaking from either Whigs or Democrats. Clay's anticipated candidacy became a powerful symbol of the hypocrisy of Whig antislavery professions and provided tangible support for abolitionist contentions that Whigs, like Democrats, were institutionally beholden to the Slave Power.[28]

Leavitt's *Emancipator* did not spare any antislavery Whigs from these attacks. Almost remarkably, Leavitt managed to connect nearly every antislavery Whig action back to Clay and the Slave Power. Leavitt portrayed even the gubernatorial nomination of Roger Baldwin as a way to dupe Connecticut abolitionists into supporting Clay. By passing a resolution praising the Kentuckian, the 1843 Connecticut Whig nominating convention illustrated "that Mr. Baldwin's known opposition to slavery, his spotless morals, and his faithful professional services in the Amistad case, are held up by the Whig party" solely for the object of "drawing in a certain class of voters to the support of the party, who could [otherwise] not now be induced to vote for" Clay. Liberty journalists cast Democrats as similarly beholden to proslavery national leaders but more frequently emphasized that "the present leading object of the managers of the Whig party is to destroy the Liberty political movement," so as to ensure antislavery support for "Henry Clay, the chief of slaveholders."[29]

Vermont, where antislavery sentiment was most pervasive, provided Liberty partisans with especially conspicuous examples of the Whig tactic of nominating abolitionist candidates "in order to wheedle the friends of impartial liberty into the support of Henry Clay for the Presidency." The 1843 Vermont Whig convention that nominated abolitionist John Mattocks for governor also selected two pro-Clay delegates to represent the state at the next national nominating convention. Liberty assessments of the Whigs' strategy of using antislavery men like Mattocks or Slade to mobilize antislavery votes for Clay are borne out in the correspondence of Whig managers. As early as 1840, Vermont Whig strategists touted the political value of nominating Slade for governor because he was "an Abolitionist, tho not so much so as to sink his character as a sound Whig." By late 1843, Vermont Whig leaders worried that the Liberty Party constituted the key threat to Whig dominance there. Testifying to the organizational sophistication of the state's political abolitionists, Erastus Fairbanks (a future governor) warned of Liberty plans for "ingratiating themselves with the people" during the winter "*interregnum* of political action." Fairbanks, having identified a political imperative that Whigs demonstrate their commitment to "the principles of Abolition and the rights of the free states," advocated a counteroffensive Whig abolitionist lecture series, to be led by William Slade, "so well known as a good Whig & yet a thorough abolitionist." Fairbanks similarly urged that Whig newspapers represent "their own cause" as "the Anti Slavery cause" in an effort to "destroy the 3rd party influence." Fairbanks's assessment of the Liberty threat clearly proved compelling, as Slade finally received the gubernatorial nomination in 1844 and 1845 and won both times.[30]

By repeatedly emphasizing the partisan connections between state and national politics, Liberty politicians shrewdly worked to direct political attention to the Slave Power's national supremacy. Ohio Liberty men exemplified this tack in framing Whig Thomas Corwin's 1842 gubernatorial campaign as a direct referendum on Clay's impending presidential bid. The *Philanthropist* wrote that "the fates of Henry Clay and Thomas Corwin are indissolubly linked in this State." If Corwin was defeated, the *Philanthropist* contended (wrongly it turned out), the Whigs would "hardly dare try" Clay. Thus, "Every vote given then for Corwin is a vote that Henry Clay shall be President." And when 5,500 Liberty votes contributed to Corwin's 3,000-vote defeat, political abolitionists proudly took credit, and boasted that the result might well have killed Clay's chances for the 1844 nomination. Even Giddings, notwithstanding his and Leavitt's fruitful collaborations at the capital, could not escape the *Emancipator*'s censure that he was "nominated, plainly for no other object but to secure his influence and the votes of those who respect him, in favor of the election of Henry Clay, in 1844." Private correspondence of a Cleveland Whig manager corroborates that Ohio Whigs appreciated that Giddings would win "the abolition vote ... and exert a good influence [for the Whigs] throughout the state by outmaneuvering" the growing Liberty movement in northeastern Ohio.[31]

This emphasis on the major parties' proslavery presidential aspirants became the leitmotif of Liberty campaign discourse and the crucial evidence of the parties' ineluctable corruption by slavery. Moreover, the political threat that this Liberty refrain posed in the strongest antislavery constituencies had clearly induced the nomination of increasingly radical Whigs, including the sorts of congressional candidates likely to provoke floor controversies that abolitionists knew so valuably dramatized the Slave Power.

Majority Rule and Minority Power in New England

Liberty partisans also appreciated that by marshaling balances of power in local, state, and congressional elections, they could transform losing campaigns into vital opportunities to expose the Slave Power's sway over both major parties. Regardless of the election outcomes, the opportunity to publicly challenge major-party Northerners' antislavery professions was a crucial benefit Liberty men gained from contesting so many races they had no chance of winning. Liberty balance-of-power tactics were particularly fruitful in the five New England states (Rhode Island being the regional exception) where election to any state office or to the U.S. House of Representatives required an absolute majority (as opposed to a plurality) of votes cast. On occasion, political abolitionists might be able to effectively bargain for concessions, but more often, Liberty partisans maintained an unwavering commitment to their own candidates. In doing so, the Liberty Party forced uncomfortable standstills that could only be concluded with significant abstentions from one of the major parties, often at the expense of their professed principles. Even though the major parties usually resolved these deadlocks and eventually elected one or the other of the primary candidates, the process was time-consuming, painstaking, embarrassing, and most importantly, newsworthy.[32]

New England Liberty men enthusiastically practiced dilatory electoral tactics. Liberty Party efforts to forestall electoral choices, potentially indefinitely in some cases, served two functions: preventing effective governing by a plurality antithetical to Liberty interests and offering time for Liberty men to further articulate their message in hopes of attracting new adherents. The Liberty Party's aggressive efforts to produce extended delay in these electoral contests thus served many of the same functions as dilatory parliamentary tactics do for legislative minorities. Liberty partisans often saw value in delay simply for the sake of delay. By creating additional elections in which Liberty votes could play a decisive role, they generated added opportunities to voice arguments about the Slave Power's corruption of both major parties. And all of these strategic benefits were augmented by the annual occurrence of statewide elections. At times it must have felt to New England politicians like one Liberty-induced stalemate had barely been resolved before yet another beckoned.[33]

Even for the many majority-rule elections that were settled by state legislators when no candidate won a popular majority, as with gubernatorial contests in all five majority-rule New England states, the devolution of the choice on a state legislature sometimes offered similar advantages for political abolitionists. At a minimum, Liberty men could further demonstrate Whigs' and Democrats' complicity with the Slave Power as they worked to resolve the impasses. In rarer situations, Liberty men could elect enough legislators to wield a balance of power either for bargaining or dilatory purposes within a state legislature, usually in the lower house. Liberty men understood that with majority requirements and the parties often so evenly matched, a tiny fraction of the electorate could erect formidable roadblocks for the major parties.

From the outset, the third-party strategy seemed promising. Liberty vote totals mounted each election cycle, and third-party leaders saw Northern Democrats and Whigs tacking toward Liberty positions in hopes of stemming the flight from their parties. Outright Liberty victories remained few, but there was no denying the party's growing influence, especially in comparison to its inauspicious beginnings in the 1840 presidential campaign. For example, in five of the seven Vermont gubernatorial elections featuring Liberty candidates, the third party forced the legislature to choose the governor.[34]

Massachusetts Liberty men were especially well organized to exploit these rules. Already by 1841, they had trebled their 1840 vote total, and party leaders looked forward to recruiting the state's many committed abolitionists who yet remained tethered to the major parties. Massachusetts Liberty activists vigorously strove, with occasional successes, to promote civil rights, personal liberty, and prolabor laws, as Bruce Laurie has described well. Equally importantly, third-party leaders aimed to use local and state elections to unmask proslavery interests in both major parties and establish a beachhead for political abolitionist efforts to infiltrate national politics.[35]

When the struggling finances of the *Emancipator* (during a deep economic depression) forced editor Joshua Leavitt to move his paper from New York to Boston and absorb the Boston *Free American*, it trained the attention of one of the abolitionists' most incisive strategists on the opportunities Massachusetts afforded for balance-of-power politics. Leavitt immediately recognized the value of publishing in a location where he could highlight majority-rule elections' openness to third-party manipulation: "Every one can see that the rule of voting in Massachusetts, and the decided strength and union of abolition voters, . . . point to this glorious old Commonwealth as the State that is most likely to be first in taking its position, as a State in favor of universal and impartial liberty." Leavitt appreciated the value of this majority-rule electoral system for third-party action at all levels of New England government. Because state senate and state executive races in which no candidate received a majority were decided by the legislature, it proved especially important that Liberty men exert their electoral power even in town elections for state legislators. If Liberty men could control a balance of power in the lower house of the legislature, they could hope to control state politics. Furthermore, legislators selected United States senators, and Liberty men desperately hoped to place an antislavery voice in the Senate.[36]

With the Liberty Party's continued focus on wresting control of the federal government from the Slave Power, Massachusetts Liberty campaigners cast state elections as proxy battles over slavery's role in national politics. Even though Whig and Democratic gubernatorial candidates John Davis and Marcus Morton may "have professed Anti-Slavery principles," both, the *Emancipator* asserted, had "shown themselves, on every occasion, ready to sacrifice their Anti-Slavery for the good of their party." Although the Liberty Party failed to control a balance of power statewide in 1841, Davis achieved his majority by less than one percent of the vote, and the Liberty Party wreaked havoc in political contests across the state. Already enough Liberty voters rejected the major-party candidates to deny initial elections of state representatives in over eighty Massachusetts towns. In some, the parties were so closely matched that a prominent abolitionist who could poll even a smattering of votes, such as John Greenleaf Whittier's thirty-four in Amesbury, could repeatedly deny a majority choice. Unable to cajole the Whittier bloc after three elections, exasperated town leaders decided not to send an assemblyman to Boston that year. The town of Holliston similarly chose to forgo representation "because [according to the *Emancipator*] a little band of 17 true hearts, after several trials, could neither be bought nor intimidated." Leavitt gloated that even New Bedford (perhaps not incidentally a major destination of fugitive slaves), with a population of 13,000, held four unsuccessful elections before deciding to go "unrepresented in the legislature this year, because . . . a chosen few loved liberty more than party."[37]

Having won over 3 percent of the vote in 1841, barely a year after the party's inception, Massachusetts Liberty men looked forward to the next year's contest, which would include congressional races. In 1842, Liberty men increased their popular vote to over 5.4 percent and sent six representatives to Boston, enabling them, as hoped, to briefly control a balance of power in the state house. After a series of complicated political maneuverings with ambiguous results for Liberty men, the legislature organized with a narrow Whig plurality and an avowedly antislavery Whig speaker in the lower house and a Democratic majority in the senate.[38] The split legislature, however, meant that gubernatorial balloting would offer Liberty men a showdown that could either elect a Liberty governor or at least clearly demonstrate both parties' deference to the Slave Power. Under Massachusetts law, since no one won a popular majority, the state house of representatives would choose two candidates, one of whom the state senate would select for governor. The house would determine the senate's two options by first balloting until one candidate received a majority and then again until a second received a majority. Given the Democratic senate and closely divided house, any Whig votes for Morton in the lower house would guarantee his election and belie Whig professions that other partisan issues trumped (anti-)abolitionism. In this scenario, many Liberty men hoped that division between the major parties would force the election of their candidate Samuel Sewall, who himself placed a surprisingly high estimate on his chances for victory. Ultimately, two Whigs voted to send Morton's name to the senate, virtually assuring his election as governor. Those votes, Leavitt argued, exemplified Whig desires to appease Southern co-partisans by avoiding support for Liberty men at all costs. On the (meaningless) ballot for the candidate to face Morton, Davis received 271 of 292 votes cast. Nearly every Democrat had selected the Whig candidate rather than give credence to the Liberty Party. The *Emancipator* proclaimed these results as "proof" of the shared "HOSTILITY TO LIBERTY" of both "GREAT PARTIES WHICH HAVE SO LONG CURSED THE COUNTRY."[39]

Congressional races in majority-rule states provided especially telling opportunities for Liberty men to highlight the Slave Power's influence over both major parties, not least because state legislatures could not resolve undecided contests. Unlike with state executive officer elections, most New England congressional seats remained unfilled until voters elected a representative. And unlike for assembly seats, no one could simply call off an election and leave the seat vacant. Congressional electorates had to ballot continually until someone achieved a majority, sometimes leaving numerous seats empty when Congress opened. Liberty men understood that these bizarre rules created valuable openings for a third party that knew how to take advantage of them. By disrupting congressional races in the majority-rule states and extending the election season, Liberty men could continue to publicize their arguments about major-party submissiveness to the Slave Power.

In elections beginning in 1842 for the Congress opening in December 1843, Liberty men delayed choices in eleven New England districts (four in Maine, six in Massachusetts, and one in Vermont), up significantly from three that had required runoffs for the previous Congress. Furthermore, the number of runoffs, or "trials" as contemporaries called them, reached dramatic new levels. One Massachusetts district required seven trials before a Whig won with just over 51 percent of votes cast. Liberty men forced six separate elections in two other Massachusetts races and one Maine race, and four trials in another district in each of those states. Three Massachusetts representatives were not seated until after the Congress was well underway, and a Maine Democrat missed the entire first (longer) session of his term.[40]

The protracted campaigns for the unresolved Massachusetts races particularly illustrate how Liberty men exploited electoral gridlock to expose the "two desperate parties" as "pledged to the Slave Power" and "arrayed against the friends of Liberty." After the third round of voting, the strong Liberty showing had left half of the ten Massachusetts congressional seats still unfilled. As Liberty vote totals mounted and major-party support often dwindled, Leavitt projected that "none but Liberty men can represent those five districts in the next Congress," unless one party abandoned the contests. Liberty men increased their percentage of the vote from the previous trial in sixteen of the twenty-one runoffs held across Massachusetts congressional districts that election cycle. In each district, though, ultimately enough major-party voters abstained to enable either Whigs or Democrats to elect their candidate. But this result simply vindicated Liberty contentions that Whig and Democratic politicians were more concerned with suppressing political abolitionism than with the supposedly paramount issues dividing the major parties. This was dilatory electoral politics at its finest. For months the state had been unable to fill half of its congressional seats—one election had been delayed for nearly a year and a half—all because of the little Liberty Party. This Liberty obstructionism became so irritating to major-party leaders in Massachusetts that some attempted, unsuccessfully however, to abolish the majoritarian electoral rules in 1843. In light of Liberty partisans' effective exploitation of majority-rule voting systems, their confidence approaching the 1844 presidential election seems understandable if a bit too optimistic.[41]

The Election of 1844 and the Texas Issue

By early 1844, the Whig and Democratic national conventions had validated Liberty forebodings that both would nominate proslavery presidential tickets. Clay, as long expected, received the Whig nomination. To abolitionists' dismay, New Jersey's Theodore Frelinghuysen was added to Clay's ticket as Southern Whigs' preferred choice for a Northern vice presidential candidate. William Jay chastised Frelinghuysen, known as the "Christian Statesman" for his opposition to Indian removal and support for temperance and other reform causes: "You have lent the influence of your name, associated as it is with the religious zeal and benevolence of the nation, to the cause of slavery." The Democratic nomination proved more contentious. Southern demands for Texas annexation disrupted party unity and scuttled the expected nomination of Martin Van Buren, who had publicly opposed a potential war to secure Texas. Instead the party chose "dark horse" candidate James K. Polk, an expansionist Tennessee planter and former speaker of the House.[42]

Leading up to the election, some Liberty men also began to rethink their presidential nominee, hoping to find a candidate with broader appeal. Birney had been renominated by a national Liberty convention in May 1841, over three years prior to the election. Since then the party had won massive new accessions in each intervening canvass. Through the early 1840s, several Liberty leaders privately conspired to replace Birney with a more renowned candidate. Leading this effort to find a new nominee were Cincinnati Liberty managers Chase and Bailey. Thinking practically about how to broaden the Liberty Party, they, like mainstream politicians, considered electability an important criterion for their national standard-bearer. First they put out feelers to Birney to see if he would permit a new nominating convention to replace him. Fearing it would be "difficult to persuade any considerable body of the people to unite in the support of one so little known as Mr Birney," Chase instead suggested prominent antislavery Whig politicians like John Quincy Adams or William Seward. Some local organizations agreed, such as an August 1842 Miami County (Ohio) Liberty Convention that similarly proposed nominating Adams. Birney, however, sharply rebuked Chase: "It seems strange to me that any abolitionist conversant with our cause could have thought . . . of going *out* of our ranks for candidates for any office." Birney also cautioned Chase against pushing the Ohio Liberty Party towards overemphasizing "opposition to Slavery" on economic and political grounds rather than "as a matter of religious duty." Several eastern party leaders, including Leavitt and New York's Alvan Stewart, backed up Birney, and Chase's efforts seemed to have been quieted.[43]

In 1843, Chase and Bailey, attuned to many rank-and-file Liberty men's desire to balance political pragmatism and moral idealism, again urged Birney to consider whether he was "the most eligible candidate," suggesting that Jay might garner more votes without morally compromising the party. Sharing Chase's assessment of Birney's inadequacy as a national candidate, Lewis Tappan and numerous other eastern abolitionists joined in pushing

Jay as a more appealing choice who (unlike Adams) *was* a member of the abolitionist ranks. Jay, however, quickly threw water on the idea. Moreover, many leading political abolitionists feared that abandoning Birney could seem too great a concession to expediency. Even among Liberty men who preferred Jay, there were few who would support the change unless Birney stepped aside willingly. Eventually, Birney privately suggested he would acquiesce, but given his and Leavitt's reluctance, Birney remained the 1844 nominee. A more "eligible" candidate would have to wait for the next election cycle.[44]

As the 1844 election approached, President Tyler's efforts to annex slaveholding Texas became the preeminent national issue. In response, Henry Clay initially presented himself as anti-annexation, but later partially backtracked, while Polk consistently called for immediate, unconditional annexation of the slaveholding Texan republic. Clay's April 1844 "Raleigh letter," penned when Van Buren remained his presumptive opponent, articulated a cautious position, opposing annexation unless concluded with Mexico's approval *and* widespread consensus across the United States—nearly impossible preconditions. A few months later though, Clay issued his "Alabama letters," hedging against the Raleigh letter by suggesting support for annexation at some future time. Clay's equivocation further impaired Northern Whig efforts to persuade abolitionists to support him as an anti-annexation candidate. Liberty men reminded antislavery voters that preventing Texas annexation was only one of many important ways to check the Slave Power, and that Liberty men would be most "disheartened to see abolitionists striking hands with their proslavery opponents, and voting for their slaveholding candidates, in the vain hope of [Texas's] exclusion." Scoffing that electing Clay to protect against annexation was "like setting the wolf to guard the sheep," Liberty men contended that Birney represented "the only anti-annexation candidate." A strong Liberty vote, moreover, could "speak in thunder-tones in the ears of Northern Congressmen," "keep Texas out of the union," and help reclaim the national government "from the grasp of the Slave Power." But antislavery Whigs like William Slade, who "concur[red] . . . with the ultimate aim of my friends of the 'Liberty Party,'" made a plausible case that electing the Whig ticket remained "the only effectual barrier against the speedy consummation of the dangerous and suicidal scheme of Annexation for the purpose of perpetuating Slavery."[45]

While Liberty men hoped that a sufficient third-party turnout would send Northern politicians a compelling antislavery message, some presciently predicted that even if Polk won and proceeded to annex Texas, that result might stir complacent Northern voters. Though they opposed annexation, Liberty men were "not blind to the possibility that this same iniquitous scheme" might well facilitate "the more speedy downfall of slavery, by arousing the North." As the election approached, Lewis Tappan predicted privately to his senator brother Benjamin (an Ohio Democrat) that "the cause of emancipation will prosper more under President Polk's administration than under President Clay's," since, "if Polk is elected all the Whigs of the North will be opposed of course to the extension of slavery & many of the democrats. Whereas if Clay is elected he will carry nearly all the North with him & all the South." Tappan, at least, "prefer[red] an out & out fiend & advocate of slavery" like Polk, "to an intriguer" like Clay.[46]

Riding a wave of expansionist fervor among Democrats in both sections, Polk won the Electoral College vote 170 to 105 but won only a plurality in the popular vote. The Liberty Party polled about 62,000 votes, just over 2 percent of the national total and far below expectations of many Liberty leaders who had hoped for large increases over 1843 state elections. Still, the party multiplied its 1840 total almost tenfold. More dramatically, continued Liberty control of the balance of power in New York famously denied Clay the state's thirty-six electoral votes, which would have won him the White House. While Liberty men quickly shifted toward new efforts to pressure Northern Democrats to oppose annexation, Northern Whigs widely assailed New York Liberty voters for defeating Clay. In one of its many fits of bitter postelection invective, the North's leading Whig organ, the *New-York Tribune*, complained, "It is this Liberty party which has willfully, wickedly given a new life-lease to Slavery in our country." Lame-duck president Tyler meanwhile claimed Polk's narrow victory as an annexation mandate. And since a Texan-American treaty had failed to receive the sanction of two-thirds of senators, congressional Democrats conspired with the outgoing president to pass a constitutionally questionable joint resolution for annexation. Whig leaders held Liberty partisans responsible and vocally reprised the campaign strategy Whigs had employed in the "Garland forgery," a fraudulent letter depicting Birney as working for the Democrats. Though Liberty managers had predicted just this sort of "monstrous" campaign trick and felt confident the letter was a fake (so confident in fact that cash-strapped Liberty leader Elizur Wright bet Whig stalwart Daniel Webster $200 when they met on a Massachusetts train car), it had appeared too late in the campaign to be properly discredited and likely dissuaded some Whiggish abolitionists from casting Liberty ballots.[47]

In the face of the incessant Whig attempts to blame Liberty men for annexation, political abolitionists retorted that Whigs should have instead nominated an antislavery candidate. Perhaps, Liberty men suggested, Whigs might have then swept the free states. Liberty men "organized to elect *anti-slavery men* to office, not to choose the least guilty of two hoary slaveholders." Gerrit Smith explained in a public letter to ex-governor William Seward that the fact "that Mr. Clay is a slaveholder, is reason sufficient why the Liberty party could not vote for him." Slaveholders in both national parties, Smith added, still insisted on "making slavery" the parties' "paramount interest," and that "of itself" provided "abundant and conclusive evidence that the Whig party is proslavery." Moreover, Liberty men viewed the continued Whig harassment as "a concession to our power" that would only "make us more confident" in attacking the Slave Power "until pro-slavery parties are broken down."[48]

Outside of New York, Clay won several of the more highly abolitionized states, including, to Leavitt's dismay, Massachusetts with a clear majority. Even with Clay's majority there, Liberty men still defeated an election in four of the state's ten congressional districts. Birney's vote showed a gain of over two thousand from Sewall's the previous year, and Birney ran ahead of Sewall, showing that many Whigs and Democrats at least rejected their party's proslavery presidential nominees if not the entire parties. In one of the unfilled Massachusetts districts it took nine trials to elect a representative well after the opening of Congress, and even in the conclusive election, the Liberty candidate polled a higher total than any Liberty candidate (the party had switched its candidate multiple times during the year of balloting) in the previous eight votes. Three Maine seats, one in Vermont, and one in New Hampshire (of which more below) also required runoffs.[49]

Northern reactions to the Texas annexation campaign, both before and after the election, evinced evidence of welling disaffection among antislavery Democrats too. Theodore Sedgwick III's scathing New York *Evening Post* series denounced the proslavery annexation project. Lewis Tappan then coordinated printing and distribution of thousands of copies of an 1844 pamphlet version of Sedgwick's polemic against expanding and perpetuating "slavery and the slave-holding power." Most Northern Democrats, though, accepted Polk's expansionist candidacy. A great many endeavored to portray Texas as a strictly partisan, and not a sectional, issue, including through suggestions that Texas might ultimately be divided between free and slave states, or that annexation would speed the gradual end of slavery and racially purify the nation by "diffusing" America's black population southward and westward. After the 1844 election, though, a number of Democrats who had run ahead of Polk became convinced that the incoming president's Southern expansionism represented an electoral millstone in antislavery constituencies. About a third of Northern Democratic representatives voted against the joint resolution for annexation, with a particularly pronounced revolt among the New Yorkers. Highlighting both the virulence of Northern Democratic racism *and* the growing political cost of association with the Slave Power, New York congressman Lemuel Stetson forewarned: "Before one year is over, democracy will have so strong a smell of niggers that ¼ of our friends will be drawn to the abolition ranks." Notwithstanding the admonitions of men like Stetson and the joint resolution's passage, most New York Democrats remained reluctantly loyal to the incoming president, even as misgivings continued to percolate among them.[50]

But in New Hampshire, known as "the South Carolina of the North" for its dominant pro-Southern Democratic machine, the uncompromising anti-annexation stance of Congressman John P. Hale opened the first enduring rift over slavery among Northern Democrats. The ensuing months of high political drama provided a tantalizing model of how Liberty partisans might further their anti–Slave Power agenda by combining with dissidents from the major parties. By the time New Hampshire held its congressional elections, months after the presidential contest, Congressman Hale had already spoken and voted against annexation in the House of Representatives. To explain this dissent, Hale issued a public letter "To the Democratic Republican Electors of New Hampshire" in January 1845. Attacking Texas annexation as a barefaced plot to expand slavery and advance the interests of Deep South slaveholders who feared the prospect of an emancipated Texas, Hale inserted the Texas issue into the center of his reelection campaign. State Democratic chair (and future U.S. president) Franklin Pierce, once a college chum of the rebellious congressman, threw the party's full weight against Hale. Party operatives fell into line, and a special nominating convention jettisoned Hale for party loyalist John Woodbury.[51]

Abolitionists, by contrast, cheered Hale's letter as "one of the boldest and noblest words ever spoken for Liberty" and assured Hale that he would receive many Liberty votes, even though the third party could not yet openly endorse him. Hale's schismatic Democratic allies similarly anticipated him winning nearly "all the abolition votes," and predicted that "this question of slavery" would soon "be the dividing point between the parties," much as Liberty men had long hoped. Amos Tuck, a key lieutenant, envisioned a long political future for Hale as an antislavery champion, urging, "Let your abhorrence of [slavery] be as notorious of that of J. Q. Adams." In private correspondence, Liberty men and antislavery Democrats from outside New Hampshire alike expressed their shared admiration for Hale's "bold and manly" stand, offering decidedly martial words of encouragement: "The hand which has so bravely dashed its gauntlet at the feet of Slavery must now do manly and vigorous battle." Even Garrisonians sent prominent lecturers, including Frederick Douglass, to New Hampshire to advocate Hale's reelection. Already at that point, some Hale supporters began to imagine that if they could not return him to the House they might instead force his selection for the state's U.S. Senate seat that would open in 1847.[52]

Three of the four congressional nominees on the Democratic ticket (this was the final election in which New Hampshire elected congressmen on a statewide ticket) won reelection easily, but support for Hale ensured that Woodbury failed to receive the necessary majority. Hale supporters, who adopted the moniker "Independent Democrats," now gained the spring and summer to organize. After the first election, Hale's allies assured him that he could expect support from the "*Leaders* of the *Abolition party*" going forward, and in subsequent runoffs the Liberty Party declined to field its own challenger. Many anti-annexation Whigs now also seemed to back Hale. Fighting for his political life, Hale traversed the state speaking against the proslavery implications of annexation, and his lieutenants established a newspaper, the *Independent Democrat*, to publicize his efforts. Again in September and again in November Woodbury failed to achieve a majority, as Hale's combined support from Liberty men, Whigs, and anti-annexation Democrats continued to mount.[53]

With the next trial scheduled to coincide with the March 1846 state general election, Independent Democrats, Liberty men, and Whigs now found added incentive to work together, not only to support Hale, but also to deny the Democratic Party control of the state government for the first time in years. With the anti-Democratic forces more or less openly cooperating in many locales, the combined totals of the Whig gubernatorial nominee and the joint Liberty and Independent Democratic candidate threw the election into the state legislature. From Congress, Joshua Giddings wrote Hale of the "woe-begone countenances" of "the slaveholders and servile doughfaces" at the news of regular Democrats' defeat in their former stronghold. United in opposition to slavery expansion, Whig, Liberty, and Independent Democratic legislators cooperated to divvy up available offices, including sending Hale back to Washington, now for a six-year term in the U.S. Senate. Hale's refusal to "bow down to the 'dark spirit of slavery'" promised Liberty men a congressional sympathizer entirely independent of major-party leaders for the very first time. As Hale built his reputation as a potent antislavery firebrand in the national legislature, some Liberty leaders would soon begin to imagine emulating the successful anti–Slave Power coalition strategies that had elected him.[54]

While Hale's triumph seemed an auspicious sign that a significant number of Northern Democrats might soon refuse further complicity in proslavery expansionism, the fact of Texas annexation revealed an emboldened

Slave Power. In response to proslavery politicians' increasingly aggressive program, Liberty leaders undertook ever more vigorous efforts to broaden their party. The ensuing war with Mexico (1846–48) soon heightened national attention to the power of slavery in the national government and created further opportunities for anti–Slave Power political action.

In an effort to reenergize the Liberty Party and recruit new supporters of a broad anti–Slave Power agenda, Salmon Chase organized the June 1845 Southern and Western Liberty Convention in Cincinnati. This time the Liberty Party would not make the same mistake of nominating a presidential candidate years before the next election, but without a national convention, this Cincinnati gathering could serve an important organizing function by bringing together Liberty men from across the West, along with some from the East and a handful from Kentucky and western Virginia. Thousands of enthusiastic abolitionists descended on a Cincinnati tabernacle, overflowing the hall and crowding at the windows in a meeting one New Yorker characterized succinctly as "a *rouser!*" Though the convention ecumenically invited all who sought to deliver the country from the Slave Power, and, as its name implied, aimed to attract Upper South sympathizers, convention speakers by and large championed the Liberty Party as the only true means of opposing the Slave Power. The convention called Birney to the chair, but Chase oversaw the all-important resolutions and address committee. Chase's wide-ranging address drew on religious, economic, and constitutional arguments against slavery. As usual though, Chase especially emphasized the Liberty Party's Slave Power argument, beseeching all antislavery men to "renounce at once all proslavery alliances" and "vote for no man, [and] act with no party politically connected with the supporters of slavery."[55]

Impressed by the Southern and Western Liberty Convention, New England Liberty men organized a Boston "Convention of the Friends of Freedom in the Eastern and Middle States" that similarly attracted thousands to protest new Slave Power depredations. In comparison to the Cincinnati meeting, speakers at Boston drew more directly on antislavery religious fervor, and the eastern convention also generated an inconclusive debate on federal constitutional authority over slavery in the states—a new fault line within the Liberty movement. Despite the airing of differences over antislavery constitutionalism and the relatively greater emphasis at Boston on the third party's religious mission, similarities between the two conventions highlight the continued commitment among all wings of the third party to a concerted political assault on the Whig and Democratic organizations. In their first formal resolution, convention goers asserted "that slavery is the greatest political evil which afflicts the nation . . . and that the Liberty party is nothing more or less than a united political effort to throw it off." Perennial Massachusetts Liberty gubernatorial candidate Samuel Sewall drafted a call for fierce opposition to any legislation consummating the admission of Texas, and the convention created a series of committees aimed at igniting a cross-party anti-Texas movement. The convention address, penned by Gerrit Smith (who subscribed personally to the more radically antislavery interpretations of the U.S. Constitution), concluded that the major parties, "made up of slave-owners as well as non-slave owners," had in effect transformed the North into "the servant of the South." Consequently, Smith declared, "Slavery is a monster to be overcome only in direct encounter and deadly grapple."[56]

The next summer, Illinois political abolitionists called a similar regional North-Western Liberty Convention. A crowd of thousands gathered under a tent in downtown Chicago to cheer Liberty leaders' perorations on the immorality of slavery. Among the most celebrated speakers was African American Michigan Liberty leader Henry Bibb. In forceful resolutions, the convention reprobated the "heinous sin" of slavery" and reiterated the longstanding Liberty mantra on overthrowing Slave Power control of the federal government:

> That as a national party, our purpose and determination is to divorce the Federal Government from Slavery, to prohibit slaveholding in all places of exclusive national jurisdiction, to abolish the domestic slave trade, to restore the balances of the federal Government—in a word, to step to "the verge of our constitutional powers" for the destruction of Slavery itself.

The Chicago proceedings also featured spirited debate over introducing other liberal reform planks to the third-party program, but a clear majority rejected any departure from the one-idea strategy, agreeing in principle with Chase's plea (in a letter to the convention) that there be "no party test except the abolition of slavery." Other parts of Chase's letter foreshadowed new sources of internal controversy, as the Ohioan suggested support for some sort of "antislavery League irrespective of party." At this point, early in the summer of 1846, the North-Western Liberty Convention's resolutions made clear that most attendees considered "inflexible adherence to the great practical principles of Christianity by the Anti-Slavery party . . . their only hope of healthful success," and communicated their anxiety that recruiting "Liberty voters" who were "not thoroughly indoctrinated into" the party's "pure principles, will assuredly induce corruption, destroy its vitality, and end in its destruction."[57]

Despite the latent fissures glimpsed in these regional conventions, many

Liberty leaders during this period were growing hopeful for the imminent collapse of the proslavery Second Party System, as they observed slaveholders' increasing audacity and further articulated anti–Slave Power arguments to ever broader audiences. By 1844 the Liberty Party had developed a well-established and growing influence across the North, as Whittier affirmed:

> The Liberty Party is no longer an experiment. It is a vigorous reality, exerting already a powerful influence upon the policies of the country. It has had no hot-bed growth, but has risen up slowly and steadily under adverse circumstances, and against the contempt, *prejudice* and desperate opposition of both old parties.

Even in the heat of the 1844 presidential campaign, some Liberty men imagined that the days of proslavery party unity were numbered. By late 1845, many Liberty men were convinced that "the old parties have had their day" and that there would soon "be a new combination of the political elements for other and higher objects." Thus, "a full and increased Liberty vote" would "have an incalculable power in spreading the cause of freedom" and in expediting "the crisis when there" would "be but two parties in the country—one an anti-slavery party and the other a pro-slavery party."[58]

Liberty men hoped eagerly for sectional cleavages in the major parties and saw reason for optimism in the continued rumblings of dissatisfaction over Texas annexation and in Hale's elevation to the Senate. Exploiting their balance of power between two closely matched parties in many locales and trumpeting their arguments about the major parties' corruption by the Slave Power, Liberty men strategized to bring together an ever larger political constituency dedicated to destroying the Slave Power. The aggressive Southern expansionism that became a guiding policy of the Polk administration made this sort of broad antislavery political mobilization seem increasingly possible, and eventually, almost certain.

* CHAPTER FOUR *

Antislavery Upheaval in the Capitol: The Wilmot Proviso Debates and the Widening Sectional Divide, 1846–1848

The Mexican-American War dramatically raised the stakes of the slavery debate and gave further credence to Liberty charges that the Slave Power controlled national politics. As Congress prepared to adjourn in August 1846, the likelihood of American conquest of Mexican territory intensified fears of slavery's continued westward extension. Earlier that year, President Polk had provoked a war that critics denounced as a proslavery land grab. Unwilling to compromise on Texas's dubious claims to the sparsely populated territory between the Rio Grande and her traditional southern boundary at the Nueces River, the president deployed American troops to the disputed territory and hostilities ensued. The U.S. Army's speedy occupation of Mexican Alta California and New Mexico quickly introduced into national political debate the question of slavery's future in conquered territories. This issue was further complicated by the fact that in California and New Mexico, unlike in Texas, the 1829 Mexican emancipation edict had largely succeeded in extinguishing chattel slavery. The prospect that the United States might reestablish slavery where it had been previously prohibited horrified Northerners across the political spectrum.

These fears became crystallized in the Wilmot Proviso, an 1846 legislative amendment authored by Representative David Wilmot, a hitherto little-known and fiercely partisan Democrat from remote northeastern Pennsylvania. On August 8, 1846, the sweltering second-to-last day of the congressional session, President Polk sent the House of Representatives an appropriation bill seeking $2 million to be used in peacemaking. This unexpected requisition confirmed widespread Northern suspicions that Polk intended to negotiate for territory beyond the disputed Texas boundary region. Taken aback by the eleventh-hour request, the House postponed the vote until after a dinner recess, during which several Northern Democrats prepared an amendment that slavery should be forever banned in any territory captured or purchased from Mexico. When debates resumed, several Whigs condemned Polk's apparent plans to augment the nation's slaveholding territory, and one called upon Northern Democrats to offer precisely the sort of amendment that Wilmot, an "ultra-democrat, who had heretofore voted with slave-holders" (John Greenleaf Whittier's characterization), had sitting on his desk. Wilmot easily secured the floor, perhaps because of his pro-administration record, and moved to amend Polk's "Two Million Bill" by adding the proviso that became his namesake, stipulating that slavery should be forever prohibited in any territory the United States was to acquire in the peace process.[1]

As Congress hurried to finish its business, the amendment occasioned only brief debate. The Proviso and then the amended appropriation bill both passed the House on almost purely sectional votes. Though the appropriation was designed to fund expansion, Northern Whigs who had opposed territorial acquisitions almost unanimously supported the amended bill, while nearly every Southern expansionist voted against it because of the antislavery rider. Ultimately, though, the appropriation, and with it the Proviso, died in the Senate.[2]

The Proviso's language drew explicitly on the slavery ban of the 1787 Northwest Ordinance, passed under the Articles of Confederation and later upheld by Congress. Equating the new proviso with the slavery prohibition in the Northwest Territory helped legitimize the non-extensionist demand, not least because the 1787 ordinance had been penned by Democratic luminary and Virginia slaveholder Thomas Jefferson. Liberty partisans, especially Salmon Chase, had previously referenced the Northwest Ordinance as the "most significant and decisive" evidence that the founders intended that "slavery would be excluded from all places of national jurisdiction" before the Slave Power had perverted this design. Liberty men, Whigs, and Democrats alike cast the Proviso as the sequel to the 1787 non-extension ordinance and therefore "an essential indispensable principle in the administration of the general Government."[3]

Wilmot's proviso soon came to encapsulate the festering division over slavery's extension and seemed to portend the sort of sectional organization of national politics that the Second Party System had been designed to avert. The revolt of anti-extension Northern Democrats reflected the simmering sectional tensions that political abolitionists had worked so hard to exacerbate. The congressional arguments that this legislative amendment then ignited plainly demonstrated how fully anti–Slave Power rhetoric had infiltrated national political discourse. Generating sectional friction within both major parties, the Proviso debates marked a transformative moment in antebellum politics. A potential touchstone for reorganizing national political conflict into a division between the Slave Power and a new Liberty Power, the Wilmot Proviso offered political abolitionists their best opportunity yet to further unravel the Second Party System.

Interpreting the Proviso

Most interpretations of Wilmot's apparently unforeseen amendment focus on divining the motives of the rotund Pennsylvania backbencher and the small band of Northern Democrats with whom he conspired. Several accounts (notably Chaplain Morrison's) view intraparty conflicts and personal vendettas as best explaining the Proviso's introduction and persistence. In contrast, Eric Foner persuasively describes the Proviso as arising from its authors' compulsion to inoculate themselves against charges of support for a proslavery war. While disagreeing about the causes of the Proviso's introduction, Foner and Morrison both concentrate on discerning its authors' rationale, and subsequent scholarship has often shared this preoccupation with the measure's surprising origins.[4]

Because of the tendency to focus on the Proviso's authors, leading histories of the antebellum Democracy treat the Proviso as a distinctly Democratic measure, subsuming its appeal under some core Jacksonian ideology that can explain the newly vocalized antislavery convictions of numerous Northern Democrats. Historians who focus on the party's antimarket economic radicalism emphasize contemporary arguments that the Proviso would secure western land for free labor.[5] Those who view white supremacy as binding Democrats together concentrate on the racism of some, including Wilmot, who hoped to reserve any territorial conquest exclusively for whites. Both sides of this debate about the ideological content of Jacksonian Democracy make room for the Wilmot Proviso, and in doing so exaggerate its specifically Democratic character.[6]

Historians' close attention to the Proviso's *introduction* has tended to obfuscate the most intriguing features of the protracted *debates* it engendered. Those debates illustrate the growing antislavery commitment among Northern politicians and register the anti–Slave Power constituent pressure they faced. By threatening the sectional harmony that was the hallmark of the Second Party System, the Proviso constituted an acute threat to both Democratic and Whig unity. More so than even their votes against slavery, Northern congressmen's oratory belied claims that they prized sectional accord. The increased use of antislavery and anti–Slave Power rhetoric by mainstream politicians marked a breaking point for many Jacksonian Democrats. Their party had long prided itself on evading slavery when possible and protecting it when necessary. While Whig leaders tolerated greater heterodoxy on slavery (perhaps in part because they so rarely controlled the national government), they too recognized that the intensity of Northern Proviso support undermined party unity. Even though the Proviso appeared to be an abstract issue and not a pressing governmental measure, members of both houses, of both parties, and from both sides of the Mason-Dixon Line went to great lengths to divert discussion to this suddenly paramount question, long before the United States actually acquired any of the territory under consideration. As abolitionists had long warned, neither major party could ever brook any genuine threat to focus national politics on slavery. When the Wilmot Proviso did just that, political abolitionists saw both a culmination of their efforts to put slavery at the center of national political debate and an unprecedented opportunity to better organize the anti–Slave Power ranks.

Liberty partisans celebrated the free states' standing "shoulder to shoulder for the limitation of slavery" as a portent of "Liberty's coming triumph." Encouraged Liberty newspapers predicted that, even if the Proviso did little more than attract "general and earnest attention to the great questions involved, this of itself" would hasten the "contest between the slave power and the friends of liberty." The expected resumption of debate over the Proviso would, Liberty men asserted, "be of incalculable value to the cause of human freedom, and render us, the abolitionists, an immeasurable service." Gamaliel Bailey's *Philanthropist* thus predicted that antislavery sentiment "out of doors" would "penetrate Congress" and ensure that "the great struggle between Liberty and Slavery, between the Propagandists of Eternal Slavery, and its Antagonists, will inevitably take place in the next session of Congress."[7]

Though Giddings and other insurgent antislavery Whigs still hoped to convert their party to antislavery, he nonetheless relished the chance to be "in the midst of a revolution" in which "we shall find all party calculations deranged, and all political expectations uncertain." Apparently welcoming the prospect of a sectional reorientation of national politics (though vainly hoping it could be overseen by Northern Whigs), Giddings and his local organ the *Ashtabula Sentinel* extolled the Proviso and declared "the subject of *Northern Rights* . . . paramount to all others." The antislavery *Boston Daily Whig* (edited by John Quincy Adams's son Charles Francis) joined Giddings and the Liberty men in foreseeing the Proviso's significance: "As if by magic, it brought to a head the great question which is about to divide the American people." To the dismay of antislavery radicals, the Proviso seemed to have little effect on the fall 1846 elections, but the next congressional session soon validated their optimism that the Proviso would transform national debate.[8]

The Uncompromising Rhetoric of Congressional Anti-extension

When Congress reconvened, antislavery New York Democrat Preston King reintroduced the Two Million Bill on his own authority as a way to renew the Proviso agitation, even though Wilmot himself had promised Polk not to broach the issue. King's move precipitated acrimonious debate and ensured that the Proviso would remain at the center of national politics. A month later, Polk requested a new appropriation (now $3 million) for making peace. At this point King, Wilmot, and most free-state congressmen vehemently insisted on prohibition of slavery in any territory ever acquired by the United States. Northerners repeatedly lined up in favor of the Proviso, so frequently indeed that Abraham Lincoln later claimed (perhaps with some exaggeration) to have voted for it forty-two times during his single congressional term. The House again attached the Wilmot Proviso to Polk's requested appropriation and again passed the amended appropriation—both on sectional votes. The Senate, however, excised the Proviso and returned the original bill to the House. At that point, President Polk began "moving heaven and earth to prevent the Wilmot amendment from being adopted." With this presidential arm-twisting and, by Liberty and Whig accounts, liberal distribution of executive patronage, the Proviso-less Senate bill narrowly passed the House.[9]

Notwithstanding this defeat for the Proviso's many advocates, the question of slavery's extension dominated ongoing debates over the Mexican War, territorial expansion, and organization of the Oregon territory. The vast majority of Northern congressmen refused to countenance any increase in the nation's slaveholding territory, and Congress became consumed with sectional strife. The fact that a fundamental threat to partisan unity had been touched off by an obscure representative's failed appropriations amendment reveals just how entrenched Northern antipathy to Slave Power expansion had become. Wilmot's legislative rider had turned Congress into an arena of intense moral and political debates about the legitimacy of American slavery. In doing so, the Proviso profoundly disturbed the cross-sectional comity that was a hallmark of the Second Party System and, abolitionists argued, the mainstay of the Slave Power.[10]

For this reason, Liberty partisans, long accustomed to temporary legislative defeats, emphasized the Proviso as a positive sign of rising antislavery sentiment, rather than dwelling on the narrow failure of its adherents to engraft it as a condition on further military appropriations. The *Emancipator* thus concluded that "the cause of freedom has lost nothing in this struggle. It has not gained as much as we desired, yet it has gathered strength, which will yet increase until slavery shall not only be checked in its march, but entirely overthrown." The *Annual Report of the American and Foreign Anti-Slavery Society* similarly noted: "In no year since the commencement of the anti-slavery effort in this country has there been so much discussion on the subject of slavery as during the past year. In the halls of the National and State Legislatures, in newspapers, in ecclesiastical assemblies, and among the people, the question of slavery has occupied unusual attention." The *Emancipator* further exulted that "the anti-slavery excitement which has been rocking the nation . . . these ten years past, has wrought a mighty change" so that "public sentiment in the north, demands the limitation of slave territory." Wisconsin's leading Liberty paper boasted too that the Proviso, while unanticipated, reflected "the silently pervading influence of right principles" disseminated by the political influence of "Liberty men . . . ringing the truth for years." "Up to the time the proviso was introduced into Congress," the paper continued, "none but antislavery men had advocated such a measure."[11]

Even if these Liberty outlets likely exaggerated their influence on mainstream Democratic politicians, the intensity of antislavery congressional rhetoric seemed to confirm the sanguine abolitionist outlook on the Proviso debates' transformative potential. Northern representatives and senators from both parties presented a sudden outburst of moral condemnations of slavery. Most commonly, antislavery lawmakers denounced slavery, as Wilmot himself did, as a "great moral and political evil." Almost as often though, they employed much harsher language, condemning slavery as a backwards, barbarous national embarrassment. Even rabidly partisan Democrats disparaged slavery as "a dark stain upon the institutions of the country" and "a curse to mankind." Vaguer denunciations of slavery as a "political evil" still made the case for non-extension by attacking the entire institution of slavery wherever it existed.[12]

A dramatic example of this sort of Christian moralizing, typically associated with abolitionists, or perhaps evangelical Whigs, appeared in a speech of Democrat Jacob Brinkerhoff (OH), one of the Proviso's architects (in fact, he claimed to be its true originator). Brinkerhoff appealed to Northern morality when he effusively praised the Wilmot Proviso, savaged Southerners who dubbed slavery a "positive good," and tried to shame wavering colleagues:

> I ask them to remember that not only political life, but natural life, ends; and that after death—I will not say what; but there *is* such a thing as right and wrong; and though I make no pretensions to extraordinary sanctity . . . there are some wrongs so great I cannot consent to commit them; some rights so sacred, that I cannot consent to be instrumental in their violation.

His denial of "pretensions to extraordinary sanctity" would appear to be the basis for differentiating himself from abolitionists, a common concern of many who hoped to retain the support of their still numerous anti-abolitionist constituents as they simultaneously appealed to anti–Slave Power sentiment. Brinkerhoff's disclaimer enabled him to present his position as part of a more broadly shared, less doctrinaire moral standard. Yet, his theatrical, combative homily concluded with a pious avowal that the "tribunal above" would vindicate his antislavery stance.[13]

Even when not denouncing slavery in its entirety, supporters of the Proviso raised decidedly moralistic objections to its extension. They sought to avoid implicating Congress, themselves, or their constituents, in *establishing* slavery. Since slavery was prohibited in all Mexican territory the United States might, and eventually did, acquire, many Northerners contended that this territory would remain free unless Congress positively established slavery. "An acquisition of territory for the purpose of establishing slavery where it has once been abolished," a Maine Whig opined, "would be turning backward in the march of civilization, and [would] be a national calamity." George Fries (D-OH) vowed "that no further territory shall come into this Union with the institution of slavery ingrafted upon it, unless it is found there when it comes in: not one single square foot." Wilmot's hometown Democratic paper similarly demanded that "the armies and navy, the treasure and the blood, the diplomacy and legislation of the whole Union" no longer "be devoted to the nefarious purpose of spreading that barbarous institution over regions now unpolluted by the footsteps of a slave."[14]

Moral aversion to the extension of slavery usually went hand in hand with attacks on Slave Power control of the government, as they long had for the Liberty Party. By the mid-1840s, numerous mainstream Northern congressmen had begun to espouse the Slave Power argument against aggressive Southern politicians and their doughface allies, although not the Liberty Party's full-blown condemnation of the cross-sectional parties. During debates over the Proviso, leading antislavery radicals like Giddings, New Hampshire Independent Democrat Amos Tuck, and new member John G. Palfrey (W-MA) rehearsed the old abolitionist litany of proslavery manipulations of the government, including the gag rule, the Second Seminole War, the executive branch's support of the Spanish claimants in the *Amistad* affair, and the annexation of Texas, to remind Northerners' of the Slave Power's national sway. More moderate Proviso supporters echoed abolitionist attacks on the Slave Power by cataloging disproportionate Southern representation in the nation's highest offices and blaming this inequity on the three-fifths clause.[15]

Proponents of the Wilmot Proviso repeatedly invoked the specter of a looming Slave Power hell-bent on extending slavery to enhance Southern political influence. Indeed, proslavery extremists openly affirmed their determination to preserve slaveholders' functional veto in the Senate through admission of new southwestern slave states. John C. Calhoun, slavery's preeminent sentinel, warned that if the institution did not expand, the South would "be at the entire mercy of the non-slaveholding States," a quandary made more acute by Iowa's recent admission and imminent statehood for the Wisconsin Territory. For many Northerners, however, the intimation that protecting Southern investments in human property should dictate federal territorial policy confirmed, and gave new weight to, abolitionists' familiar charges of a grasping Slave Power seeking to dominate the national government.[16]

More than ever before, Northern congressmen inveighed against Slave Power control of the government because they, and the constituents they represented, sought to avoid complicity with the evil of slavery. James Dixon (W-CT) insisted that his constituents would never willingly "steep their souls in the guilt of extending the dominion of slavery." Dixon warned fellow representatives that "the people of the North are watching, with anxious attention, the votes of their representatives on this floor." Connecticut's Democratic senator, John Niles, similarly insisted that Northerners would "resist . . . to the last" the efforts of the "slave power" to "extend slavery over the continent." Increasing Northern reluctance to shoulder the moral burden of supporting slavery induced free state congressmen to tenaciously contest the Slave Power's tightening grip on the federal government. Underscoring this shift in the electorate, and needling the many Northern Democrats who so jealously guarded their white male independence, the *Emancipator* confidently predicted that "there are thousands of the democratic rank and file" who would no longer allow their votes to be "sold to the man mongers of the South."[17]

Even given the moral force with which antislavery and anti–Slave Power arguments were broadcast, pro-Proviso speeches, as historians have widely noted, often coupled antislavery and anti–Slave Power rhetoric with paeans to free white labor. The Slave Power concept provided an ideal rhetorical framework through which major-party politicians, especially Democrats, could assail the prospect of slavery extension while maintaining their traditional exaltation of free white men's independence. Whigs and Democrats alike charged that slavery "discourages productive industry of every kind," a point consistent with arguments Liberty leaders had trumpeted for years. Wilmot and like-minded co-partisans, however, also went out of their way to couch their anti-extensionism as protecting industrious white settlers from unfair competition with "the degrading and servile labor of the Negro race." Accepting the racist premise of black men's inherent dependence on white elites (an argument long deployed to justify institutionalized racial inequality in the North), Democrats like Wilmot found that attacking the Slave Power allowed them to oppose slavery as "a great political and a great social evil" while simultaneously rejecting abolitionists' unmanly "morbid sympathy for the slave." While adopting anti–Slave Power rhetoric, Northern Democrats could maintain their longstanding celebration of white male supremacy and virtuous free labor while voting alongside an antislavery radical like Liberty ally Amos Tuck, who unflinchingly denounced the "iniquitous and hateful power for one man to hold another in bondage" as a "violation of the laws of God."[18]

Notwithstanding their resort to both prolabor and racist anti-extension rhetoric, Proviso Democrats broke sharply from Jacksonian tradition when they repeatedly prioritized sectional concerns over party unity. Designed initially to enable Northern Democrats to remain loyal on the key partisan issue of the day—the Mexican War—the Proviso offered a useful rejoinder to criticisms that they were supporting a proslavery war. A growing number of Northern Whigs who had been opponents (however hesitant in many cases) of the Mexican War argued that lust for slave territory had plunged the country into an unnecessary, unjustified "bloody war of conquest." Proviso Democrats' devotion to non-extension aimed to counter antiwar Whigs and reframe the ongoing war, which had grown unpopular in antislavery constituencies. Preston King, for example, wholeheartedly approved further operations against Mexico but insisted publicly and privately that the "Wilmot Proviso must be most rigidly adhered to" and its "agitation must set permanent perpetual barriers against the extension of slavery." Martin Grover (D-NY) acknowledged that "the northern mind was in doubt" but believed the Proviso would convince his constituents that the war sought to promote freedom and not slavery. But by resolutely demanding antislavery policy and deploying anti–Slave Power language resembling abolitionist claims that proslavery interests threatened Northern freedom, dissident Democrats challenged their party's core principle of fostering sectional harmony.[19]

Objecting to slavery on moral, political, and economic grounds, proponents of the Proviso proclaimed the utter impossibility of compromise. This stance resembled the inflexibility long expressed by political abolitionists and their small band of antislavery Whig coadjutors (like Giddings, Seth Gates, and William Slade) but rarely by mainstream Whig and Democratic politicians, who had so prized intersectional unity up until this point. Most Northern congressmen now cast any further compromise with slavery as cowardly, but slavery moderates from both sections held out hope of a new settlement based either on the old Missouri Compromise or a new "popular sovereignty" formula.[20]

The proposition of extending westward the Missouri Compromise line demarcating the northern boundary of slavery in the Louisiana Purchase at 36° 30′ north latitude quickly became many Southern congressmen's, and eventually the Polk administration's, preferred plan. Overwhelming Northern opposition defeated this proposal multiple times, including on the day that Wilmot first introduced the Proviso. The original Missouri Compromise, Northern congressmen noted, did not *establish* slavery, but rather allowed it to *persist* in part of the Louisiana Purchase. Mexican territory was different; slavery had already been abolished there—a distinction also never lost on Liberty partisans.[21]

Popular sovereignty posited that Congress either should not, or could not, decide the fate of slavery for territorial inhabitants. Instead, proponents argued, Congress should cede responsibility to the local determination of the territorial legislature, although when in the territorial process this should be decided was hazy. Antislavery critics warned that once slavery gained a foothold in a new territory, eradicating it would be difficult if not impossible. At this point in the sectional conflict, the popular sovereignty plan also received minimal Northern support.[22]

Developments in Oregon intensified the dispute over territorial slavery. Even though Southerners and Northerners both believed that Oregon's climate would not support slavery, and notwithstanding urgent pleas for a territorial government from settlers warring with local Native Americans, congressmen from both sections transformed Oregon's application for territorial status into a proxy debate over the Proviso. Southerners insisted that the federal government had no power to interfere with slavery, while Northerners called just as vociferously for organization of Oregon under the antislavery (although also antiblack) constitution its (white) inhabitants had already drafted. As Oregonians awaited their territorial government, Congress rehashed the arguments that had been articulated for and against the Wilmot Proviso. Would-be compromisers attempted to establish a precedent for either the Missouri Compromise or popular sovereignty formula, while antislavery men like Senator Hale used controversy over Oregon to advocate prohibition of slavery in all future American territories. The recently-established Washington Liberty paper the *National Era* denounced the "spectacle" of "the slave power doggedly forbidding the erection of a *free* government in Oregon," simply because Northerners would not "give the national sanction to a slave government in California and New Mexico."[23]

After both popular sovereignty and the Missouri Compromise line seemed doomed to fail, a Senate committee led by John Clayton (W-DE) devised a plan to organize Oregon and divest Congress of further responsibility for the fate of slavery in the territories. This proposal evaded explicit affirmation of congressional jurisdiction by entrusting the question of slavery in Oregon to its inhabitants (who would certainly prohibit slavery) and in California and New Mexico to the federal judiciary. Enduring a grueling twenty-one-hour session, a contentious Senate passed the Clayton Compromise long after sunrise on July 27, 1848. Unmoved by the upper chamber's labors, the House quickly tabled the bill. A leading Whig from each section dismissed this harebrained scheme as merely postponing sectional conflict until the courts reached a decision bound to offend the losing section. The tabling opened the door for a new round of sectional recriminations that persisted long after the Senate acquiesced in Oregon settlers' slavery prohibition.[24]

The emergence of Clayton's proposal in the Senate (not without substantial opposition) demonstrated that Congress had no confidence in either popular sovereignty or the Missouri Compromise line as solutions for the territorial slavery question. But the House's summary rebuff dispatched Clayton's bill as yet another untenable compromise. Ideological positions had advanced so far that the polarized rhetoric the Wilmot Proviso had generated easily overwhelmed, and nearly supplanted, pressing practical questions about territorial governance. The recurrent failure of these various compromise options illustrates the seeming impossibility of a territorial settlement that could win support from a significant number of Northern congressmen. Invested with moral absolutism, their stand in favor of the Proviso became one from which few seemed willing to retreat.

For many Democrats, rejection of intraparty compromise could also be framed as a masculine refusal to be bullied. At this moment of crisis and fracture, an appeal to while male self-defense rather than pusillanimous submission to the Slave Power offered a way to repurpose policy demands that were fundamentally consistent with those of Liberty Party radicals. Challenging "every craven heart" who might be cowed by Southern threats of disunion, Wilmot Proviso Democrats boldly insisted that the North must not be "deceived and betrayed" into extending slavery over free territory. Wilmot manfully proclaimed, "Sooner shall they draw this right shoulder from its socket, than I will yield." Confident that "we can appeal heartily to Men, and to manly feeling that our opponents dare not arouse," antislavery Democratic presses railed against the Southern "scheme" that threatened free white settlers with "a degradation with if not inferiority to, the black bondsman of the South." And when the Clayton Compromise tried to pawn the slavery extension question off on the courts, many Northern Democrats like Hannibal Hamlin fiercely "objected to the shuffling off, the skulking from, the shirking behind a political question which it was our duty to meet."[25]

When they sounded this call to arms, Northern Democrats reprised a familiar abolitionist tune about the danger of slaveholders' overweening political power, if in a slightly different key. Liberty partisans had long derided doughfaces of both parties who "manifested the guilty cowardice of voting in Congress on the side of oppression." Once the Proviso was introduced, Wisconsin Liberty leaders affirmed their joy that "what has so long been the tame, servile, all-confiding north, as regards the subject of slaveocratic domination, rapacity, and insolence, appears, though late and hesitatingly, to be rousing itself to a sense of its past and present degradation, and a determination no longer to acquiesce." As Proviso debates accelerated, Liberty voices continued to smear "fawning, cringing" Democratic and Whig luminaries alike as "miserable sycophants." After some Illinois Democrats' abortive effort to defeat their pro-Proviso congressman John Wentworth's renomination, the local Liberty paper mocked the anti-Proviso men as sporting "leather patches on their knees" to soften the impact of their genuflection to slaveholder superiors.[26]

And on the floor of Congress, Ohio's Joseph Root—an antislavery Whig far more comfortable with honestly recognizing that Southern aggressions had forced mainstream Northerners to approach the Liberty position—joined racist Democrats in attacking the very possibility of a new compromise, admonishing that any Northern "doughfaces" the South "could scare up" would be ostracized at home. "Any northern man whose vote should be given against the North," Root continued, "must make up his mind to brave the scorn and execration of his constituents; to hang his head before his old neighbors; nay, to make his wife ashamed for him." Not stopping at this challenge to Northern Proviso opponents' matrimonial bliss, Root also echoed extreme Liberty rhetoric that equated Northern compromisers to Southern slaves: "They [Southern congressmen] were very confident of their power to manage both their black and white slaves [doughfaces]. They certainly had managed their white slaves admirably well. If they were going to treat their black ones as despotically and oppressively, God pity them!" In short, the Slave Power's imperious claims on Northern Whigs and Democrats now bore too close a resemblance to the way Southerners dictated to their black dependents. No self-respecting Northern man, abolitionist or otherwise, could tolerate this.[27]

Political Abolitionists and Anti–Slave Power Constituents in the Proviso Debates

Critics of the Proviso impugned Northern representatives' repudiation of conventional legislative bargaining as evidence of non-extensionists' affiliation with, or desire to appease, fanatical abolitionists. Like the abolitionists themselves, proslavery expansionists viewed anti-extensionism as an outgrowth of abolitionism. A speech by Virginia Democrat Thomas Bayly traced the rising congressional antislavery agitation back to the 1830s abolitionist petition onslaught. Another Virginia Democrat complained that "the House seemed to have been converted into a magnificent abolition society." A Northern opponent of the Proviso similarly lamented that abolitionist sentiment had "become sufficiently formidable . . . to make it the *present* interest of politicians" to endorse such an incendiary measure.[28]

Abolitionists wholeheartedly concurred with these proslavery estimations of their influence, celebrating the dissension in the Whig and Democratic Parties as "owing primarily to the pressure of the Liberty Party." John Greenleaf Whittier viewed the Proviso as a direct response to the "complete triumph of Hale" and the "attitude of hostility to the Slave Power" that political abolitionists had worked so hard to foment. Liberty partisans did not fail to note that many of the most forcefully antislavery politicians "represent districts in which the pure doctrines of anti-slavery prevail, embodied in the liberty party." Illinois abolitionists crowed that the impressive Liberty vote (16 percent) for Owen Lovejoy had pushed "[Chicago Democrat John] Wentworth and the dominant influence of his party, to take a position ahead of the democratic party in any other section of the Union." Formerly a reluctant backer of the gag rule, Wentworth became a firm Proviso man, and initially the only Illinois Democrat to support it.[29]

Even Liberty partisans who criticized Proviso supporters for their unwillingness to go beyond this incomplete measure and adopt the full Liberty program still viewed it as "one of the strongest rays of hope" for reorienting national politics around slavery. Acknowledging the limits to Wilmot's antislavery, the *Philanthropist* nonetheless lauded his Proviso as signaling that the "power and the progress of the anti-slavery movement," along with the Polk administration's misdeeds, had "opened the eyes of the country." "Next to the abolition of slavery itself," the *Emancipator* declared, "we can conceive of nothing which will exert so controlling an influence upon the destiny of this country." A territorial slavery ban, the paper continued, would represent "the first important victory which liberty has won over slavery in this country during the last half-century."[30]

Although numerous Northern congressmen denied the Proviso's connection to abolitionism, their rhetoric clearly drew on antislavery polemics and articulated a view that slavery was immoral and unjust—perhaps only a step (if ultimately a very long one) away from the abolitionists' logical conclusion that it should be ended everywhere. Some of the Proviso's most inflexible supporters were quite explicit about this connection. In language that must have terrified Southern congressmen, their antislavery colleague Columbus Delano (W-OH) cautioned slaveholders: "If you will drive on this bloody war of conquest to annexation, we will establish a cordon of free States that shall surround you; and then we will light up the fires of liberty on every side, until they melt your present chains, and render all your people *free*."[31]

The obvious continuities between abolitionist ideology and the non-extensionist program put many Proviso advocates in the difficult position of trying to marginalize political abolitionists within an emerging antislavery consensus that drew extensively from their ideals and rhetoric. For example, George Ashmun (W-MA) explained that he spoke not for "ultra men" but for "the mass of sober-minded, reflecting, foreseeing people of the free States who" also demanded adoption of the Proviso. Race-baiting Proviso-supporter Allen Thurman (D-OH) considered allegations of abolitionism's connection to non-extensionism "ridiculous and preposterous." All Northerners, Thurman explained, shared "a belief that slavery is injurious to any community in which it exists," but avowing such sentiments did not make him an abolitionist. Wilmot, an especial target of Southern invective, responded angrily to critics who classed him with the abolitionists, whom he had "denounced . . . publicly upon all occasions." The fact remains, though, that Proviso Democrats like Wilmot and Thurman, previously so eager to ignore slavery, suddenly accepted many of the abolitionists' contentions about the Slave Power. Northern congressmen, especially racist Democrats, had never before insisted with such frequency "that slavery is injurious to any community in which it exists." Thurman was correct in distinguishing this position from abolitionism, but Southerners and Liberty men were equally astute in their recognition of a sea change in the congressional politics of the Second Party System.[32]

Northern Whigs opposed new territorial acquisitions. Northern Democrats lusted after western territory. Both concurred in the unanimity of Northern repugnance at the idea of extending slavery. One Democrat estimated that "nine-tenths of the people of the free States are in favor of the Wilmot proviso." A Whig similarly assured the House that the Proviso "embodied the universal sentiment of the North," and yet another averred that "there was no division of sentiment at the North. On this question the whole North went as one man."[33]

These emphases on Northern unity demonstrate a deep awareness that the rising antislavery sentiment across the free states compelled most Northern lawmakers to support the Wilmot Proviso. New York moderate Samuel Gordon (D), for example, initially worried that the Proviso had been prematurely introduced, but soon granted, "After what has taken place on this subject, I dare not, in reference to public opinion in the North, vote against it." Preston King, Congress's leading antislavery Democrat, praised Gordon's speech as evidence of the "development of public opinion." Committed antislavery Whigs remained deeply suspicious of Northern Democrats, but recognized that intense constituent pressure would preclude most of them from abandoning non-extension. Joseph Root confidently pronounced, in the same speech in which he invoked doughfaces' humiliated wives, that any Northern man who rejected the Proviso "destroyed his future hopes forever and a day."[34]

Notwithstanding numerous denials of abolitionists' influence, Northern congressmen from both sides of the aisle clearly acknowledged a need to shield themselves from abolitionist attacks. Representative Martin Grover (D-NY) rejoiced that "when we address abolitionists, or anybody else, [we can] tell them it is a question we have nothing to do with." Since the South, Root asserted, had recently "joined with this Liberty party in their doctrine that Congress had power over the subject," Northern congressmen now felt forced to side with the Liberty Party and demand that Congress contain rather than enlarge slavery. In these efforts to blame the South for inciting the rising anti–Slave Power fervor, New York Democrat Bradford Wood attacked slaveholders' earlier insistence on the gag rule and support for anti-abolitionist mob violence. Recognizing what Liberty partisans had for years, Wood predicted that "the violent speeches which have been made by some of you on the floor of this House" would "make more Abolitionists than the whole of the North could unmake."[35]

Underscoring the pervasiveness of Northern opposition to slavery extension, nearly every free state legislature sent non-extensionist resolutions to their congressional delegations—both to enter these states' positions into the record and to influence their representatives. Political abolitionists celebrated that most Northern legislatures passed these resolutions nearly unanimously. On the Senate floor, John Dix (D-NY) similarly touted "the unanimity with which the Legislatures of New York, Pennsylvania, Ohio, and other states have acted" as "an index to the universal [anti-extension] opinion which pervades the whole North and West."[36]

As most Northerners assumed this uncompromising posture, they elicited spirited replies from irate Southern colleagues. The most radical Southerners matched non-extensionists' moral absolutism with equal bluster and intransigence, once again demonstrating how public exchanges between antislavery activists and proslavery politicians, with both groups seemingly courting confrontation, could dramatically escalate the sectional conflict. Proslavery extremists denied Congress *any* right to legislate on slavery in the territories and jealously guarded proslavery prerogatives, pontificating on slavery's morality to horrified antislavery onlookers. Southern leaders repudiated Northern allegations that a Slave Power controlled the government with well-worn protestations of their defensive posture, and some menacingly alluded to the possibility of disunion. A prophetic North Carolinian announced, "When sectional grounds turn a presidential election, then the Union is truly at an end." A similarly clairvoyant (and ironic) anti-Proviso spokesman, Jefferson Davis (D-MS), implored, "Let not the battle-fields of our country be stained with the blood of brother fighting against brother."[37]

With the sections so polarized, moderate Southern Whigs sought to restore amity by renouncing territorial conquest. Championed by many national Whig leaders, including several Northerners who also supported the Proviso, this "No Territory" strategy aimed to avert an irreparable rift within the Whig Party—or even worse the Union—by circumventing the territorial question altogether. Meredith Gentry (W-TN), for example, decried any new acquisitions because the ensuing debate over slavery in the territories would threaten the Union. Gentry recognized early on that Northerners and Southerners would find little room for compromise once the question of extending slavery had been injected into national politics. Senator Reverdy Johnson (W-MD) similarly cautioned, "As you deprecate civil war and all the manifold calamities which ever follow in its train . . . Keep out this fearful element of eternal strife—KEEP OUT TERRITORY." The following session, Johnson clarified that, unlike many Whig colleagues, he harbored no principled objection to new territory, only to "the conflict to which such an acquisition would lead." Numerous conservative Northern Whigs who backed the Wilmot Proviso but preferred to avoid sectional tension, such as Massachusetts senator Daniel Webster, also heartily espoused No Territory.[38]

Southern Whigs recognized that the primary significance of the Proviso for many of its Whig supporters was symbolic, as it was for many Liberty men. The Proviso would establish an important antislavery precedent. Even though few Northern Whigs coveted this territory, they wanted to ensure that if acquired it would remain free. This was also the stance of Liberty men, most of whom condemned the Mexican War far more vociferously than leading Northern Whigs. Salmon Chase described the No Territory gambit as a "humbug" and "the most palpable deception in the world." Committed antislavery Whigs like Giddings joined Liberty partisans in balking at the No Territory strategy as a transparent effort "put forth [by] those who have strong affinities with the slave power" to evade the Proviso's anti-extensionist mandate. Ultimately, ratification of the Treaty of Guadelupe-Hidalgo in March 1848 foiled conservative Whigs' No Territory strategy by ceding to the United States California and most of the modern American Southwest. As Amy Greenberg has shown, though, this treaty's acceptance by a Polk administration that was growing ambitious for still vaster conquests reflected the influence of a broad, if amorphous, antiwar movement that included mainline Whigs from both sections along with more radical antislavery opponents.[39]

By early 1848, a growing circle of antislavery congressmen collaborated with Liberty allies to promote further congressional incursions. For example, Massachusetts abolitionists worked with Boston antislavery Whig Charles Sumner and Congressman Giddings to lobby famous education reformer and recently elected Whig congressman Horace Mann (who was chosen to replace John Quincy Adams after he died in the Capitol at age eighty) to speak out forcefully against slavery. Like Liberty lobbyists, Sumner, who had long maintained a cordial and productive relationship with Boston's activist black abolitionist community, recognized the importance of such congressional attacks on slavery: "every new voice against Slavery on the floor of the House helps mightily to create a Public Opinion." Giddings, by now long accustomed to private collaboration with abolitionists, eagerly awaited the arrival of Gamaliel Bailey in Washington in late 1846 to edit the new national Liberty Party paper, the *National Era*, just as controversy over the Proviso heated up. Bailey worked vigorously on the ground in Washington to pressure antislavery congressmen and regularly attended congressional debates, as Leavitt had in the past. Bailey's home became a gathering place for antislavery congressmen from both parties, and Bailey persuaded abolitionist friends like Salmon Chase to attend Congress when possible to aid in his lobbying.[40]

In a political climate increasingly dominated by argument over slavery, congressional antislavery voices grew more numerous and more strident. The radical speeches of leading antislavery representatives like Giddings and Tuck had become less widely viewed as impermissible intrusions, enabling them to more frequently render Congress a public forum for interrogating slavery's political power. Tuck, for example, paired nonextension with the longstanding abolitionist demand for emancipation in the District of Columbia as the two conditions necessary to prove the North's independence of the Slave Power. The most aggressive antislavery congressmen railed with equal vigor against the Fugitive Slave Act of 1793, combining moral denunciations with allusions to the Slave Power designed to elicit broad Northern support. The "heinous act," antislavery Whig John Palfrey argued, "insulted, if it did not endanger, the liberty of every white man in the land." While simultaneously appealing to this mounting fear of the Slave Power's threat to white male independence, Northern radicals also articulated militant antislavery beliefs, as with Senator (and former counsel to the *Amistad* Africans) Roger Baldwin's (W-CT) contention that *any* slave should be considered free *as soon as* he or she set foot on free state soil.[41]

Even more dramatic than their agitation of these old political abolitionist standbys, antislavery radicals exploited a failed April 1848 slave escape to further inflame Congress. In the *Pearl* affair, seventy-seven fugitive slaves and free black relatives (including slaves owned by Secretary of the Treasury Robert Walker and former first lady Dolley Madison) attempted to flee north from the District of Columbia on a boat named the *Pearl*, in a plot organized by William Chaplin, a radical political abolitionist closely affiliated with Gerrit Smith. Uncooperative winds slowed the vessel, and local slaveholders apprehended and imprisoned the slaves and their collaborators. This failed escape incited anger and consternation within the Washington community and induced a proslavery mob to gather outside the *National Era*'s office and harass its activist employees, who may or may not have been aware of Chaplin's scheme. In response, John Palfrey proposed a House committee to inquire whether the mob action in Washington threatened any congressmen. By broaching the *Pearl* affair, Palfrey set off a lengthy debate in which Southerners berated antislavery radicals, blamed Palfrey and Giddings for the escape attempt, accused them of promoting insurrection, and suggested they deserved to be hanged.[42]

In the Senate, Hale offered a municipal anti-rioting bill, which alluded only implicitly to the mob activity that followed the *Pearl* affair. Although the bill did not mention slavery, no fewer than six Southern senators immediately attacked the bill as incendiary and Hale as suggesting that "slaves should be permitted to cut the throats of their masters." Southern senators saw in Hale's action further evidence of abolitionist designs to destroy slavery by encouraging rebellion, and they spoke at length about the threat posed by rising antislavery sentiment. Henry Foote (D-MS) declared that if Hale ever came to Mississippi, "He would grace one of the tallest trees of the forest, with a rope around his neck, with the approbation of every virtuous and patriotic citizen; and that, if necessary, I should myself assist in the operation." Hale's response to the Southern assaults affirmed his abolitionist convictions, but focused on highlighting the paranoia of the slaveholding senators who so viciously denounced him for a bill that merely stipulated measures for protecting property in case of a riot. Hale mocked Southern belligerence in his sardonic reply to Foote, who had just threatened to lynch him. Inviting Foote to go "into some of the dark corners of New Hampshire," Hale assured Foote he "would find that the people" there "should be very happy to listen to his arguments and engage in an intellectual conflict with him, in which the truth might be elicited."[43]

Further vexing those who hoped to evade the slavery issue, antislavery congressmen seized on the 1848 French Revolution as yet another opportunity to embarrass the Slave Power and its minions. When Congress attempted to pass resolutions praising the successful rising of the French populace to overthrow the monarchy, Hale in the Senate and Ashmun in the House proposed amendments to also congratulate the new republic for abolishing slavery in French colonies. These resolutions incensed Southern congressmen who had grown "sick and tired of this continual thrusting of the subject of slavery" into legislative debate "upon every occasion." Though the resolutions failed, their proponents capitalized on the chance to enter further condemnations of slavery into the public record.[44]

As Northern congressmen distanced themselves from proslavery expansionism, they acknowledged, with varying degrees of enthusiasm, that sectional loyalty had overtaken partisanship on the territorial issue. The *Utica Democrat* asserted that "the time has now come for the North to unite," even as it explained that Northern partisans need not "abandon our support of or opposition to other prominent measures of national policy." Proviso Democrat Frederick Lahm (OH) responded to accusations that the Proviso was "calculated to divide the Democratic party of the country" by trying, unconvincingly, to bracket the slavery issue as an issue outside of, and having no bearing on, partisan politics:

> Whenever you make the question of slavery, in any shape, a political test, you do away with the old, well-defined party lines, and array the North against the South. This ought, and I have no doubt will be avoided. In our action here, every man must be governed by his own convictions of what is right and due to his constituents.

Giddings likewise, but less apprehensively, observed that "old party lines" were "becoming indistinct and uncertain" as congressmen increasingly "divided into the propagandists of slavery, and the advocates of freedom."[45]

Eager Northern Whig support for the Proviso underscores the degree to which sectional concerns had eclipsed partisanship in these debates. Antiexpansion Whigs' votes for not only the Wilmot Proviso, but also the territorial acquisition bills to which it had been attached especially revealed the overriding importance of the slavery question. Notwithstanding their Southern co-partisans' hopes for a No Territory strategy, nearly every antislavery Whig forsook opposition to expansion to capitalize on the precious opportunity to enact an anti-extensionist legislative promise. The Wilmot Proviso quickly became as much a standard for Northern Whigs as for Northern Democrats.

In the Democratic Party, the Proviso had opened a dramatic sectional cleavage. When faced with past antislavery pressures, proslavery politicians had relied on the cooperation of a large number of Northern Democrats. Southerners, it seemed, could now no longer count on Northern Democrats' support, nor even their reticence. Antislavery rhetoric had infiltrated the mainstream of American politics and threatened to expose and exacerbate the sectional tensions that party unity had previously suppressed. Democratic and Whig congressmen both felt palpable antislavery influences from their districts compelling them to act and speak forcefully against the threat of a growing Slave Power.

The moralistic antislavery and anti–Slave Power rhetoric used by the Proviso's supporters both demonstrated the inroads antislavery activists had made in the national political arena and suggested that increasing numbers of Northerners might soon be convinced to abandon their parties. The vast majority of Northern congressmen not only opposed the extension of slavery, but justified this stance with uncompromising denunciations of the institution's political influences and immorality. Northern congressmen refused further concessions to the Slave Power in large part because they believed their constituents simply would no longer tolerate them. This marked a new watershed for political abolitionists who had long believed Congress could be used to disseminate anti–Slave Power arguments to the Northern electorate. Whether or not Northern politicians ever admitted or even recognized their debts to political abolitionism mattered little to Liberty partisans. The anti–Slave Power rhetoric that abolitionists had voiced incessantly since the late 1830s had found its way into the political lexicon of most Northern congressmen.

Seeing this stunning progress, many Liberty men reasoned that numerous major-party politicians might now be persuaded to accept a more complete version of the abolitionists' Slave Power argument, with its insistence on independence from the proslavery Whig and Democratic parties. More sanguine than ever about prying antislavery Whigs and Democrats loose, political abolitionists across the North anticipated the 1848 presidential campaign as an unparalleled opportunity to expand the Liberty Party. It remained questionable, though, whether the Slave Power's new congressional adversaries would maintain their antislavery stances under the partisan strain of a presidential contest. Seizing on the Wilmot Proviso and the intensely antislavery rhetoric of its congressional adherents, many Liberty leaders believed they had finally found their chance to wrest antislavery Democrats and Whigs en masse from their proslavery national organizations.

* Interlude Three *

"Let the Lines Be Drawn":
Conscience Whig Insurgency and the 1847 Speakership Election

Despite the destabilizing influences of the Wilmot Proviso, most Northern congressmen remained committed to securing national power for their party organizations. The 1847 speakership contest, however, suggested that a small but vocal band of antislavery insurgents were making fast progress towards the Liberty position that resistance to the Slave Power required independence from Whig and Democratic power structures. In the short-lived revolt of three defiant antislavery congressmen, Liberty men further glimpsed the prospect of dislodging growing anti–Slave Power masses from the major parties.

The House that convened in late 1847 had been chosen in elections conducted in the fall of 1846 through early 1847, before the congressional controversy over slavery's extension had fully blossomed. With enthusiasm for Polk's expansionist war waning and the economy lagging, Whigs scored gains throughout the country. The Whig Party looked forward to controlling the incoming House in December 1847, but held only the narrowest majority, opening the door for new antislavery disruptions. During the months between congressional elections and the opening of the 30th Congress, bitter debates over the Proviso had sharply inflamed sectional tensions, and a few members now saw the upcoming speakership vote as a valuable opportunity to press for antislavery concessions.

Antislavery "Conscience Whigs" recognized that the speakership election offered a chance to publicly avow their principles, and Charles Sumner consequently advised Giddings, "Let the lines be drawn . . . in the organization of the House." Since most Northern Whigs opposed the Mexican War, or supported it hesitantly and unenthusiastically, many had successfully campaigned as opponents of Slave Power aggressions in the Southwest. Frustrated Liberty men meanwhile charged that hypocritical Whig posturing had denied the third party droves of potential converts. Despite Northern Whigs' *supposed opposition to slavery extension, few seemed ready to stake the organization of the House on this issue. In this sectionally charged atmosphere, Representatives Joshua Giddings, John G. Palfrey, and Amos Tuck cast controversial protest votes. In rejecting Whig nominee Robert Winthrop, Conscience Whigs Giddings and Palfrey demonstrated the deepening tensions within the Northern Whig Party.*[1]

While Winthrop had voted for the Wilmot Proviso, his action at the 1847 Massachusetts state Whig Convention had reassured Southern Whigs and severely antagonized Massachusetts Conscience men. A leading Boston "Cotton Whig" (a term used to characterize the larger Massachusetts Whig faction that privileged Southern business and party unity over the anti-extension program championed by Conscience Whigs), Winthrop had led the opposition to Palfrey's proposed resolution that the state party refuse support for any presidential candidate who did not pledge himself against the extension of slavery.[2]

Because Winthrop had opposed the Mexican War fairly feebly, Giddings did not trust him to appoint committees that would promote peace and favor antislavery legislation. Declining to attend the Whig caucus, Giddings instead awaited Palfrey's arrival at a Washington train station, while their ostensible co-partisans met to nominate Winthrop. On Giddings's suggestion, Palfrey sent Winthrop a note inquiring whether, if elected speaker, he would arrange key committees so as to promote antislavery legislation. Winthrop refused to offer "pledges of any sort," confirming Palfrey's and Giddings's inclination to vote against him. Amos Tuck, the New Hampshire ex-Democrat elected by an antislavery cross-party coalition of Liberty men, Whigs, and Independent Democrats, happily joined them, noting that "Mr. Giddings was in extacies [sic] of joy at the resolution which he found on the part of Palfrey and myself."[3]

On the first ballot, Winthrop, opposed by Giddings, Palfrey, Tuck, and two Southern Whigs, fell three votes short of a majority. On the next trial he failed by only one, as one of those Southerners switched his vote to Winthrop, and the other abstained. On the decisive third ballot, South Carolina's Isaac Holmes, "a rabid Calhoun Democrat," dramatically donned his coat and exited the chamber to help quell the antislavery interruption. When the single member from the anti-Catholic American Party then switched his vote to Winthrop, the Boston conservative eked out a bare majority after a nearly three-hour contest.[4]

The controversy over Winthrop's election aggravated festering acrimony between antislavery radicals like Giddings and more conservative Northern Whigs. Party leaders berated Palfrey and Giddings (and sometimes Tuck), even after Winthrop's ascension to the speaker's chair. Attacks from the Whig leadership were met in turn by both Conscience Whig and Liberty rebuttals praising the insurgents' "noble stand." Giddings proudly told Sumner, "It has been my object since I reached Washington to draw the Line of seperation [sic] between the men and the Doughfaces of the north. Our vote for speaker was the first important step."[5]

The votes of Giddings, Palfrey, and Tuck suggested that Liberty men might soon convince antislavery politicians to abandon their proslavery parties. To Giddings's regular Liberty challenger Edward Wade, the vote offered "cheering hopes that Mr G. may be redeemed from his vassalage to party." Henry B. Stanton similarly saw it as evidence that Liberty men and Conscience Whigs "agree in more points than we differ in," and Boston Liberty man Henry Bowditch was thrilled with the votes against Winthrop, whose election represented "one of the greatest disgraces that could happen to Boston." Bowditch continued, "I knew he could not be chosen without bowing down to Slave power," concluding from Winthrop's committee assignments, "It is evident that he did so." The Emancipator echoed those criticisms, smearing the new speaker as a "cringing suppliant and supple tool of the Slave Power," and praising Conscience Whigs back in Massachusetts who supported the rebellious congressmen.[6]

This 1847 speakership contest, though it only briefly delayed organization of the House, portended more momentous divisions in future choices of speaker. Even the nomination of a nonslaveholder was no longer sufficient to attract the votes of the most radical antislavery members. The 1847 contest demonstrated that antislavery members now demanded a speaker who would promise meaningful antislavery committee appointments. This contest drew new attention to the power of the House committees on Territories, Foreign Policy, the District of Columbia, and the Judiciary to promote policies that might relieve the federal government from support of slavery. The rebellion of Giddings and Palfrey also heartened Liberty men who hoped to further detach antislavery men from the major parties and thereby enable the Liberty Party or some new antislavery coalition to transform national politics.

* CHAPTER FIVE *

Liberty Men and the Creation of an Anti–Slave Power Coalition, 1846–1849

As controversy over the Wilmot Proviso fixed the nation's attention on slavery, the ongoing congressional rancor inspired added confidence that political abolitionists might soon reorganize national politics. With sectional tensions threatening to derail Whig and Democratic efforts to once again unite their partisans behind proslavery presidential tickets, the Liberty Party stood ready to exploit the upcoming campaign to further propagate anti–Slave Power politics. While many Liberty managers insisted that antislavery politics could be pursued only under Liberty auspices, a number of key third-party leaders suggested that a new, and implicitly moderated, anti–Slave Power coalition might better attract converts, challenge the major parties, and, they hoped, transform national politics. This coalitionist camp, including Gamaliel Bailey, Salmon Chase, Henry B. Stanton, and John Greenleaf Whittier, played a vital role in catalyzing the Free Soil Party. Through the long buildup to the 1848 presidential election, Liberty coalitionists made crucial strategic calculations that paved the way for a new and distinctly anti–Slave Power political coalition.

Conventional accounts of the Free Soil Party's founding concentrate on the revolt of disgruntled Barnburner Democrats, motivated as much by an intraparty feud (rooted in longstanding grievances unrelated to slavery) as by antislavery political ideals. In light of the Free Soil Party's 1848 Barnburner and Conscience Whig presidential and vice-presidential nominees and the larger Barnburner and Conscience Whig voting bases, the role of Liberty men has often been underemphasized. However, the Free Soil Party can be best understood as the product of a conscious effort by Liberty managers and a small group of dedicated Whig allies to expand the reach of anti–Slave Power politics. Undoubtedly, the numerical power of New York Barnburners gave them a powerful influence on the coalition they joined, but the origins of the Free Soil Party long predated the maturation of the Democratic schism in the Empire State.¹

The establishment of a national organization that could shape Northern politics beyond the 1848 election owed much to Liberty men who saw rising anti-extensionism as offering a valuable opportunity to reorient national politics around a contest between the Slave Power and its enemies. In the final run-up to the founding of the Free Soil Party, Joshua Leavitt (who came to support coalition later than many of his Liberty colleagues) highlighted this goal:

> *The Slave Power* is now indissolubly incorporated in the political nomenclature of this country, & will be inscribed indelibly upon the historic page. We must make the most of that word. It is not necessary that they who use it should ever know who taught it to them—the name & the thing—but the incessant use of the term will do much to open the eyes & arouse the energies of the people. *The Slave Power!* . . . We must keep our eyes upon this, & familiarize the people to the facts; and must not be drawn by any acts into a compromise with the Slave Power. We must rescue the government from the control of the Slave Power, as slavery has evidently fastened its death-grasp upon the political institutions of the country, we shall doubtless be compelled to pursue this controversy until slavery itself shall be no more.²

Liberty Strategic Debates and the Vision of Broadened Antislavery Politics

For many Liberty partisans, the years preceding the 1848 election occasioned both excitement and anxiety. The Hale movement's success had heightened aspirations for a new antislavery coalition, the Wilmot Proviso debates stirred dissension over slavery in both major parties, and the near defeat of Winthrop's speakership bid demonstrated how tenuously the Slave Power clung to its national prerogatives. But the third party's slowing rate of growth by 1846 proved disquieting, especially in parts of New York and the West, where plurality election rules made wielding a narrow balance of power a far less promising strategy than in majority-rule New England states (and even in some of these, legislators were working to revise rules that had facilitated Liberty obstructionism).³ At the same time, though, rising antislavery sentiment among Northern Whigs and Democrats heartened coalition-minded Liberty leaders who hoped to woo major-party dissidents into the anti–Slave Power movement. In these efforts they found a few eager allies among antislavery Conscience Whigs or Young Whigs, mostly in Massachusetts and northeastern Ohio. Leading Whig proponents of antislavery collaboration, Charles Sumner and Joshua Giddings had both already worked closely with abolitionists, and yet they still hoped to pursue antislavery politics as Whig partisans. Old loyalties died even harder for antislavery Democrats. Political abolitionists, however, patiently awaited the major parties' anticipated proslavery presidential nominations, expectant that frustrated antislavery partisans would then be ripe for the picking. Coalition-seeking Liberty men thus worked vigorously to channel broadening anti–Slave Power sentiment into a more formidable national political movement.

Even before the Wilmot Proviso had sowed discord in the major parties, some Liberty men, inspired by the Independent Democratic movement in New Hampshire, had begun strategizing to broaden the anti–Slave Power political coalition. Like its western neighbor, Maine had long been dominated by the Democratic Party, but Polk's proslavery war unsettled many Maine Democrats. Perceiving this, Maine Liberty men like Austin Willey hoped to extend "the great and auspicious reformation" that John P. Hale had initiated in New Hampshire. Willey, editor of the state's leading Liberty paper, the *Liberty Standard*, remained wary, however, of "even the appearance of any compacts with the proslavery parties." John Godfrey, who edited the Liberty *Bangor Gazette* aimed, with fewer reservations, to reorganize Maine politics along similar lines as in New Hampshire. Godfrey entreated Hale's direct support and assured Hale that though they were "not in name politicians of the same party," their shared desire for "the overthrow of the accursed slave power" gave him the "power to do in this state [Maine] what no other man can," especially by reaching out to Maine's Proviso Democrats.[4]

While Maine Liberty men ultimately failed to persuade Democratic leaders to join a new antislavery coalition for the 1846 election, Liberty gubernatorial candidate Samuel Fessenden won over many Democrats anyway. Increasing the Liberty vote by over 3,000 to 9,343, 13 percent of the total, Fessenden defeated the choice of a governor by popular election, winning by Liberty estimates two-thirds of the increase from former Democrats. Liberty men elsewhere celebrated that Maine antislavery men, like their New Hampshire counterparts, had "produced a schism which has prostrated the proslavery Democracy."[5]

The Hale movement's success in New Hampshire and the progress of Maine Liberty men in recruiting Democrats encouraged coalitionist national Liberty leaders like Whittier. Working together, Liberty men and their growing ranks of antislavery allies in New England could, Whittier hoped, make "Abolition of Slavery the leading & paramount political question" on the national stage. While such a "great *League of Freedom*" as Whittier envisioned might be a departure from Liberty partisanship, it would necessarily maintain the Liberty commitment to never "voting for Slave holders" or "men who are in political fellowship with Slave-holders."[6]

Coalition-seeking Ohio Liberty leaders like Chase similarly recognized antislavery Whigs like Giddings as potential partners, but Congressman Giddings preferred an attempt to rally Liberty men to the Whigs in hopes of refashioning his own party into an anti–Slave Power instrument. Giddings first proposed formal cooperation days before Wilmot introduced his Proviso, suggesting a meeting of Ohio Liberty leaders and antislavery Whigs to jointly advocate repeal of Ohio's discriminatory Black Laws. Giddings badgered Salmon Chase through the summer of 1846, couching this plan as an entering wedge for more comprehensive cooperation. Giddings underscored his sympathy for the Liberty anti–Slave Power program by expressing genuine enthusiasm for Gamaliel Bailey's planned Liberty paper in Washington: "*We* [emphasis added] ought to have had a paper there long since."[7]

Chase and fellow Ohio Liberty leaders seeking to broaden the reach of anti–Slave Power politics seriously considered such antislavery Whig overtures but ultimately rejected them. Former congressman Edward Hamlin, editor of the antislavery Whig Cleveland *True Democrat*, had offered a similar proposition at the June 1846 North-Western Liberty Convention held in Chicago. In response, Bailey praised the goal of uniting "Anti-slavery members of all parties, North and South," but criticized proposals "for a union between Liberty men and Whigs." Notwithstanding Giddings's and Hamlin's good will, Ohio Liberty men refused to participate in any conference that might appear Whig-controlled. Also, Chase sympathized with Democrats on issues unrelated to slavery (such as opposition to protective tariffs) and expressed some hope of joining antislavery Democrats in a new "True Democratic" party. It remained all too clear, though, that Democrats were even less ready than Whigs to renounce their Southern-dominated party. Reiterating well-worn Liberty analyses of the Slave Power's control over both major parties, Chase insisted that, among extant political parties, only the Liberty organization could be counted on for "uncompromising hostility to slavery & the Slave Power." Lamenting, however, that as soon as Liberty men managed to "bring public sentiment right" on some issue, Northern politicians adopted policy stances "sufficiently close" to Liberty demands as "to prevent any great accession to our numbers," Chase saw growing appeal in some sort of antislavery voting "League" or broadened anti–Slave Power third party.[8]

Gamaliel Bailey shared Chase's desire for collaboration with antislavery

Whigs and Democrats. And Bailey's voice reached thousands. Beginning publication of the Washington *National Era* on January 7, 1847, Bailey soon became the Liberty Party's preeminent opinion shaper. Controlling the first truly national Liberty paper, and with access to fast-moving political developments in Washington, Bailey played a vital role in promoting a new antislavery coalition. Bailey's paper developed a wide readership across the North and Border South and made him a powerful advocate for broadened antislavery politics.[9]

Still, most Liberty men were not ready to give up their organization. In many locales, they saw reason for optimism. In light of the Wilmot Proviso enthusiasm, Vermont abolitionists, for example, believed that "the foundation principles of the Liberty party are forcing themselves upon the whole people of the free States." Capitalizing on these developments and drawing on the persuasive testimony that formerly enslaved Liberty leaders could offer, Vermont activists held a "mass Convention of the friends of Liberty, & True, Independent Democracy" keynoted by Henry Bibb and urged an "energetic campaign against the pro-slavery parties in Vermont." Henry Highland Garnet traversed the state on behalf of the Liberty cause, and Vermonters rewarded these efforts with enough Liberty votes to elect nineteen state legislators (compared to twelve a year before) and prevent candidates for state executive office from winning a popular majority. Even in Chase's Ohio there were cheering signs. In 1846, the Ohio Liberty Party polled its highest vote ever, for gubernatorial candidate and Chase ally Samuel Lewis, at the same time that the state's total vote dropped off significantly from the 1844 presidential election. Liberty men especially gained on the Western Reserve, vindicating Liberty leaders' decision against a formal alliance with Giddings.[10]

Most importantly, though, the fiery anti–Slave Power rhetoric that had come to dominate congressional debate over the Wilmot Proviso signaled the potential for an expanded national antislavery politics. With the enticing defections in the Northern Whig and Democratic ranks, many Liberty leaders began working even harder to recruit the antislavery rank and file of all parties. By the summer of 1847, it had become patently clear to Liberty men that slaveholders would accept "no man [for president] but a determined friend of slavery, and sworn opponent of the Wilmot Proviso." Political abolitionists urged that antislavery Democrats, Whigs, and "Independent men of whatever name" together oppose any "*candidate belonging to a party that supports slaveholders for office.*"[11]

Convinced, even a year in advance, that the Whigs and Democrats would once again field proslavery presidential tickets, some coalition-minded Liberty men advocated postponing their party's nominating convention until after those of the major parties. Bailey's *Era* argued that awaiting the conclusion of the major-party conventions would enable Liberty men to choose a ticket best designed to attract disillusioned Whigs and Democrats. Chase worked similarly vigorously to postpone the nomination in hopes of building a national movement of antislavery "Independents" around Senator Hale. Other Liberty managers, however, insisted on the originally scheduled fall 1847 convention, and a clear majority of those who sat on the national committee reaffirmed the early convention date. Leavitt's *Emancipator* was especially vocal in defense of an early convention and in denouncing Liberty leaders who disagreed.[12]

At the root of this controversy over the timing of the party meeting was a smoldering dispute over how to channel the broadening antislavery impulse. Coalitionists like Chase and Bailey hoped Liberty men could remain available to join a new anti–Slave Power coalition. Leavitt, by contrast, accustomed to electoral battles with Massachusetts's formidable antislavery Whigs, insisted that political abolitionists could challenge proslavery control of the government only by maintaining the Liberty organization. To promote new accessions to the party, Leavitt wanted a presidential candidate in the field early. Leavitt and his allies feared that further stalling might pave the way for the collapse of abolitionist third-party politics.

Of course, *who* the convention nominated was at least as important as when, and many Liberty coalitionists had their eye on John P. Hale, the Senate's only antislavery independent. Tapping Senator Hale, a prominent officeholder allied but not officially affiliated with the Liberty Party, would clearly expand the Liberty appeal and encourage support from outside the party's ranks. The darling of the abolitionist lecture circuit since late 1846, Hale had been beset with requests from Liberty organizers to speak at rallies across New England. Some Liberty leaders expressed doubt about nominating such a recent convert, but most, including Leavitt by the summer of 1847, considered Hale firmly aligned with Liberty men in his opposition to the Slave Power and independence from the major parties. Stanton worked especially tirelessly to make the case for Hale as Stanton gradually took over many of Leavitt's responsibilities at the *Emancipator* after being brought on as an associate editor in August 1847.[13]

That month Stanton helped arrange a Boston tête-à-tête between several northeastern Liberty leaders and Hale and his key lieutenants, editor George Fogg and Congressman Amos Tuck. The sterling Liberty group Stanton assembled to vet Hale included the other members of the *Emancipator* editorial staff, Leavitt and Joseph C. Lovejoy (brother of murdered Elijah and Illinois Liberty politician Owen), along with John Greenleaf Whittier, Austin Willey, and Lewis Tappan. Their "friendly conference" fully won over the Liberty contingent. Party managers who had been on either side of the convention date fight made Hale their shared favorite for the nomination. Praising Hale's "hearty devotion to the principles and objects of the Liberty Party," and anticipating "great accessions from the Democratic and Whig ranks," Liberty leaders deemed Hale "the strongest man we can bring out."[14]

In the face of persistent Liberty assertions that his nomination would best unify opponents of the Slave Power, Hale, though clearly ambivalent about both a presidential run and formally binding himself to the abolitionist third party, promised not to "shrink from any post of duty, where I can by any possibility advance the interests of humanity." This was all the reassurance excited Liberty managers needed. Liberty papers enthusiastically promoted Hale, and supporters politicked aggressively on his behalf, few more so than Stanton and Whittier.[15]

By the approach of the party's nominating convention, the only organized challenge to this draft-Hale sentiment came from a splinter group centered in upstate New York. Since 1845 a small but growing number of Liberty men, especially in Michigan and upstate New York, had called for expansion of the Liberty platform beyond its antislavery "one idea." In 1847, William Goodell spearheaded a more formal effort to reposition the Liberty Party as a party of "universal reform." Goodell won a few prominent adherents from among the state's Liberty leadership, including Gerrit Smith, and then moved quickly to convene a new "Liberty League." At Macedon Lock, New York, these abolitionists adopted a radical constitutional interpretation that declared slavery unconstitutional everywhere and selected candidates and wrote a platform that they hoped to foist on the Liberty Party proper. The League's universal reform agenda included free trade, free (or nearly so) homesteads, and opposition to legalized monopolies, such as the postal system. This contradicted the one-idea strategy that had held the Liberty Party together by putting aside policy questions unrelated to slavery and the Slave Power. In addition to its new platform, the Macedon Lock convention also nominated Smith for president. Many among the most radical political abolitionists of upstate New York no longer trusted national Liberty Party leaders, who appeared "too anxious to adapt" to win over Whigs and Democrats.[16]

The Macedon Lock platform found sympathy in many quarters, but few were prepared to stake the national party on it. Wisconsin's Liberty paper lauded the League's issue stances and choice of Smith but refused to support a separate nomination that seemed likely to drive so many Liberty voters away. Vermont abolitionists, expressing disbelief that Smith had ceased to be "a firm and staunch friend of the One Idea," likewise dismissed the plan to add new issues to the Liberty creed. Alvan Stewart, who had originated the radical constitutional interpretation championed by the Macedon Lock convention, also criticized the movement as a dangerous distraction.[17]

With only Liberty Leaguers in open opposition, Stanton and Leavitt "left no stone unturned" in drumming up support for Hale's candidacy when the Liberty Party convened on October 20, 1847, in Buffalo. There the approximately 150 national Liberty delegates resoundingly voted down both Gerrit Smith's attempt to commit the party to the Liberty League's universal reform agenda and Chase's last-ditch effort to postpone the selection of candidates. Then on an informal ballot for the presidential nomination, Hale easily outpolled Smith. The convention enthusiastically resolved in favor of nominating Hale and selected for his running mate Ohio's Leicester King, a former Liberty gubernatorial candidate who had served as a Whig state senator and county judge before the Liberty Party's founding.[18]

Accepting the nomination, Hale embraced the Liberty platform, but also foresaw the emergence of a new coalition to replace the Liberty Party, noting his willingness, with Liberty leaders' consent, to withdraw if "unforeseen contingencies and emergencies" created new opportunities to unite "the good & true of every party." Relieved that Hale left the door open for a broader movement, Liberty coalitionists continued to prepare for the "unforeseen contingencies and emergencies" to which his acceptance letter alluded.[19]

Nevertheless, both coalitionists and purists among the Liberty leadership appreciated the opportunities that would grow out of having, for the first time, a prominent congressional politician as their standard-bearer. Long committed to inciting congressional controversy over slavery, Liberty men emphasized Hale's "most important position before the country." Illinois's leading Liberty journalist urged Hale to use his Senate seat to promote antislavery politics to the entire Northern electorate, and Stanton reminded Hale that he was in position to "lead the great anti slavery movement of the country." Although Hale was "not so thoroughly identified with the Liberty party as I might wish," Leavitt too conceded that Hale was "as fully and absolutely & irrevocably alienated from the old parties, as any man could desire." Hale's continual efforts to steer Senate debate towards slavery during the 1847–48 session confirmed Liberty hopes. Refusing to "be intimidated . . . from pressing this question [slavery] whenever he could," Hale repeatedly demanded prohibition of slavery extension; assailed the Polk administration's proslavery, prowar policies, including with his radical, solitary vote against formally thanking officers and men who had fought in Mexico; vocally defended the rights of abolitionist petitioners; pushed for federal protection of free black citizens; and deliberately goaded slaveholders into unwanted arguments, as in his previously discussed anti-rioting bill after the *Pearl* affair. Hale's stands in the Senate, "where no voice has been raised these many years in behalf of the stricken down principles of bleeding Liberty," gave political abolitionists reason to celebrate that "never before, since the commencement of the anti-slavery agitation, have we stood on such elevated vantage ground as at the present time."[20]

Major Party Schisms and Coalition Opportunity

Amidst the ongoing congressional wrangling, antislavery Whigs, especially in Massachusetts and northern Ohio, slowly warmed to Liberty coalitionists' suggestions of a national antislavery union, and New York Barnburner Democrats also seemed increasingly frustrated with conservative co-partisans. Gamaliel Bailey, on scene in Washington to monitor congressional debates and collaborate with antislavery congressmen as Leavitt had in prior years, especially appreciated the tensions within the major parties. Leading antislavery Whigs like Charles Francis Adams, Joshua Giddings, Edward Hamlin, and Charles Sumner appeared to be potentially receptive, if uncertain, allies for erecting a new national anti–Slave Power coalition. Already by late 1846, Sumner shared the Liberty view that "there is no *real* question now before the country except the Slave-Power" and wrote Chase of his desire for "a new chrystallization [sic] of parties, in which there shall be one grand Northern party of Freedom."[21]

Antislavery Whigs privately discussed abandoning their party, but remained constrained by their hope, however unrealistic, that the Whig Party might nominate a tolerable presidential ticket. Sill believing they might dissuade their party from nominating proslavery candidates, most antislavery Whigs would not commit to a new anti–Slave Power venture. Charles Francis Adams's Conscience organ the *Boston Daily Whig* insisted on a pro-Proviso Whig ticket as a condition for the paper's party loyalty. Adams at times sympathized with Liberty hopes for "general and combined action," but through 1847, he professed greater "confidence in the ultimate correctness of the course of the Whigs than in that of any other existing party." Indeed, for most of that year, Adams's *Whig* remained supportive of slave-owning Kentucky stalwart Henry Clay, who, of course, remained anathema to Liberty men even after a ballyhooed November 1847 antiwar address that forswore territorial acquisition aimed at expanding slavery. With Clay's speech having antagonized many Southern Whigs, though also censuring abolitionists, Adams fantasized that Clay might go further and boldly recast himself as a champion of the Wilmot Proviso. Meanwhile, antislavery congressional Whigs like Giddings, struggling to pass anti-extension legislation, lamented the added difficulties imposed by the "constant intrigues . . . in regard to the Presidential candidates." Liberty coalitionists, by contrast, saw the approaching presidential election as an ideal opportunity to force the hand of antislavery factions within the major parties.[22]

A unified antislavery political movement seemed increasingly likely to Liberty coalitionists once Louisiana planter and Mexican War general Zachary Taylor emerged as the Whig frontrunner. Whig interest in Taylor, a political novice first mentioned as a candidate for a possible Southern cross-party movement, seemed to indicate that Whig leaders would acquiesce in Southern demands and reject the Wilmot Proviso. As a "deeply grieved" Amos Tuck observed, "Taylor is brought out for the purpose of diverting or withstanding the anti-slavery spirit of the Country." Denying Taylor the nomination thus became the key condition for the continued party loyalty of Conscience men.[23]

As the Taylor movement strengthened, Giddings strove to "arouse and unite the north," believing he could do this best from within the Whig Party. More moderate antislavery Whigs voiced similar disgust at the Taylor groundswell. *New-York Tribune* editor Horace Greeley, for example, sought to avoid another slaveholding nominee by trying to steer the party towards Ohio's antiwar senator Thomas Corwin, but Corwin soon disappointed Conscience men by endorsing the "No Territory" gambit over the Proviso. Far more willing to compromise than insurgents like Sumner and Giddings, Greeley was representative of modestly antislavery Whig managers who wielded much greater power in the national party. Ultimately, though, the more tepidly antislavery Whigs would publicly swallow Taylor, as even Greeley did, reserving his condemnation of the Whig Party's "putrid corpse" for private correspondence.[24]

Proviso Democrats proved even more hesitant than antislavery Whigs. Jacob Brinkerhoff, one of the Proviso's chief architects and most uncompromising floor advocates, for example, roundly rebuffed Liberty efforts to pry him from the Democratic fold. The willingness of most Northern Democrats to incongruously combine anti-extensionism with Democratic partisanship was pointedly illustrated by the Democrat-dominated Michigan House of Representatives. On the very day that body resolved forcefully in support of the Wilmot Proviso, forty-four Democratic legislators also endorsed their home-state senator Lewis Cass, a doughfaced popular sovereignty proponent, "as their first and favorite candidate for the Presidency."[25]

In the New York Democracy, riddled with factionalism for years before the Wilmot Proviso debates, Liberty coalitionists saw more cause for optimism. By the start of 1847, an open split, partly over the Proviso, threatened to rend the party in the nation's largest state. The fissure within the New York Democracy, though, had deep roots in older disputes over patronage and state economic policy. New York Barnburners had been seething at the conservative wing of their party, known as "Hunkers" (because they hankered, or "hunkered" after patronage), since the 1844 election. After the Democrats had won both nationally and in New York, some Barnburners expressed concern about Texan slavery, and thirteen of twenty-three New York Democratic representatives voted against annexation. Once annexation was an accomplished fact, though, most Barnburners dedicated surprisingly little energy to further contesting slavery's expansion before late 1846. Until that point, Barnburner leaders seemed more concerned with patronage, though Polk disappointed them on that count too.[26]

As discord over the Wilmot Proviso was overlaid onto a muddled map of preexisting controversies among New York Democrats, the intraparty conflict gradually came to revolve around the politics of slavery. To Liberty partisans' delight, Barnburner sheets like the *Albany Atlas* and William Cullen Bryant's New York *Evening Post* extolled the Proviso and predicted that slavery would now shape all "the great political topics of the day." Representative Preston King similarly pushed slower-moving colleagues to avow the Wilmot Proviso as "an essential indispensable principle." Notwithstanding the antislavery zeal of key leaders like King and Bryant, most Barnburners persisted in couching their anti-extension posture as a defense of white Northern men. In championing non-extension, the *Atlas*, for example, not only demanded "that the new possessions shall be preserved for the free white laborers," but also at times descended into disturbingly racist polemics. The editors seemingly unselfconsciously lamented that the territories' current population was "composed of a mixed race, in which Indian and Negro blood predominates," and later the paper characterized the extreme Southern position that would introduce slavery into future northern acquisitions as "Niggerising the North." Though Liberty men could not condone Barnburner racism, the elasticity of the Slave Power argument provided a potential basis of alliance among a wide range of committed abolitionists, moralistic Conscience Whigs, and Barnburners who were at best ambivalent about, or more often outright opposed, the proposition of racial equality. The sentiments of the more radical Barnburners, like King, who had become convinced that "the time for the contest between freedom and slavery on this continent has come," further signaled the growing promise for a broadened anti–Slave Power coalition.[27]

Despite this rising anti-extensionist tide within the New York party, Hunkers seized control of the October 1847 state convention, selected the state ticket, and defeated a proposed resolution expressing "uncompromising hostility to the extension of slavery into free territory." Thoroughly frustrated with their conservative co-partisans, New York Barnburners gathered in protest the next week at Herkimer (southeast of Utica). Barnburners, representing by Liberty estimates at least half the New York Democracy, proclaimed non-extension "an inseparable element" of their "political creed," prefiguring the coming conflict over New York's delegates to the 1848 Democratic presidential nominating convention.[28]

Coalition-minded Liberty men greeted this widening strife with great enthusiasm. Chase waxed eloquent that he knew "of no event in the history of Parties in this Count[r]y, at all approaching, in sublimity & moment, the Herkimer convention." Henry Stanton, writing from New York State "in the midst of the Wilmot Proviso Barnburners," concluded that they had "passed the Rubicon." Based on his "best informal sources," Stanton adjudged that if the Democratic presidential candidate was "hostile to them & the Proviso, then they will lay open a wide field for us to enter & cultivate." Barnburner managers concurred: "a dough-face cannot get the vote of this state for President in 1848." Stanton conceded that a desire to avenge Hunker betrayals, especially of Martin Van Buren, motivated many Barnburners, but Stanton believed they would "stand their ground none the less firm for that." By March 1848, Stanton could see "no prospect of a healing of the breach" and consequently considered Barnburners as "Missionary ground" for Liberty men to convert.[29]

Liberty men, convinced that both national nominating conventions would ignore the Proviso and select proslavery candidates, worked assiduously to lay the foundation for a new movement. When increasingly discomfited antislavery Democrats and Whigs were finally ready to abandon their parties, preparations for a new coalition would be well underway. With this in mind, Stanton urged Hale to privately woo the Barnburners. More importantly, Chase, exultant at "the augury of approaching union, among the true & earnest lovers of freedom of all parties," began working to organize free territory meetings to convene shortly after the national nominating conventions.[30]

By late March, Chase was pre-circulating to potential allies a public call for a "People's Convention" to be held in Columbus in June, shortly after the major parties nominated. Joined by fellow Cincinnati Liberty leaders Samuel Lewis and Stanley Matthews, several prominent Cincinnati Whigs, and one Democrat, Chase beseeched antislavery men "to be ready, if need be, to suspend, for a time, ordinary party contentions, and unite." With both major parties apparently intent on selecting candidates who would "favor, either by active co-operation, or silent connivance, the designs of the Slave Power," the signers demanded that antislavery men prepare in advance. Piggybacking on the congressional proliferation of gendered anti-extension rhetoric, the announcement urged all antislavery patriots to "unite in one manful, earnest, and victorious effort for the holy cause of Freedom and Free Labor," and assailed the "prominent men in each of the two great parties" who seemed all too "ready to submit" to the Slave Power's "degrading demand." Assembled together, a convention of all "who prefer Freedom to Slavery and Free Territory to Slave Territory" could either bless a worthy major-party nomination, or, more likely, field a new ticket to challenge the Slave Power.[31]

Giddings showed interest, but, still hoping that the Whig Party would nominate an anti-extensionist, refused to sign Chase's formal call for the Columbus Convention. In the months before the Whig convention, Giddings still believed antislavery Whigs might secure the party's nomination for a cautiously antislavery aspirant like Supreme Court Justice John McLean. And in what can now only be seen as remarkable efforts at self-delusion, Charles Francis Adams privately maintained an unrealistic shred of hope (as late as April 1848!) that Clay would sustain the Proviso and receive the nomination. Sumner too encouraged Giddings that same month "to give Clay every opportunity of putting himself in a position [against slavery extension], which will take from us the necessity of organising an opposition." Perhaps even more shockingly, the *Ashtabula Sentinel*, now under the charge of Giddings's son, *publicly* suggested support for Clay if he would only come out in favor of the Proviso.[32]

As Chase planned the Columbus convention that would ultimately spearhead the movement for a national Free Soil Party, he also began feeling out Hale's willingness to step down if a "union of all Anti-slavery men" developed after the major-party nominations. Many other Liberty partisans, however, remained skeptical of cooperation with politicians who seemed so reluctant to leave their party folds. As late as April, Leavitt reiterated that he did not "in the slightest degree" share Chase's "anticipations of a union of effort among 'Free-Territory men' at the coming election," believing instead that the Liberty Party represented "the last hope of the country for the deliverance from slavery in our day or by peaceful means."[33]

The hesitating course of Conscience Whigs demonstrated that both sides of this internal Liberty debate had merit. In the months before the Whig nominating convention, Conscience Whigs seemed to despair of their party nominating a non-extensionist. Still, they waited. Many held out hope, however faint, that the Whigs might endorse the Proviso. The *Boston Daily Whig* made clear, however, that the Conscience faction would flee the party before supporting Taylor, who had skirted the territorial question by promising only to veto unconstitutional legislation without indicating what he considered constitutional. While antislavery Whigs experienced "nausea" as his nomination became increasingly likely, Liberty men, by contrast, watched excitedly for the long-anticipated rift in the Whig Party.[34]

Meanwhile, Chase also saw increased reason for hope of cooperation from antislavery Democrats. Democrats in Wisconsin's strongly antislavery First Congressional District rode to victory on their forceful local commitment to non-extension. Jacob Brinkerhoff also gave voice to Proviso Democrats' frustrations with their party establishment when he told Chase that "the Democratic [presidential] candidates now spoken of are all like rotten eggs—incapable of being made worse." Yet, Brinkerhoff, like Giddings, declined to sign Chase's call for a Free Territory Convention, and Wilmot, the face of Democratic anti-extension, too eschewed public support for the proposed Columbus Convention.[35]

Within the New York Democracy, the schism continued to simmer as the national party stood poised to nominate an anti-Proviso man, most likely Michigan's Lewis Cass, who was doubly anathema to Barnburners for helping defeat Van Buren's nomination in 1844. When Democrats convened in Baltimore in May, rival delegations claimed to represent New York. Martin Van Buren, who had ensconced himself in a Manhattan hotel to help coordinate Barnburner tactics, urged his son John and lieutenant Samuel Tilden to insist on full acceptance of only the Barnburner delegates. The acrimonious Baltimore convention first offered the state's seats to Barnburner delegates, but only if they pledged to wholeheartedly abide the national party's decisions. The Barnburners refused this apparent design to ram an anti-Proviso nominee down their throats. So in a self-evident ploy to weaken New York's influence, the convention instead sat both the Barnburner and Hunker delegates and allocated half of a vote to each. Already seething at this compromise, Barnburners angrily bolted the hall after Cass secured the presidential nomination.[36]

Liberty coalitionists were ecstatic. Seizing on the Barnburner defection, Bailey encouraged Massachusetts Conscience Whig leaders Sumner, Adams, and former congressman and Salem mayor Stephen C. Phillips to join Stanton in a strategy session with Preston King and Barnburner ex-congressman George Rathbun. This way the three groups could "agree, if possible, upon a certain declaration of principles and certain mode of action." Hale, Bailey assured Sumner, would be unlikely to stand in the way of any cross-party anti–Slave Power coalition.[37]

At the Whig convention a couple weeks later in Philadelphia, the Taylor forces triumphed, but some Northerners demanded resolutions requiring Taylor to endorse "Whig principles," including non-extensionism. The convention dismissed this proposal as out of order, and, as Liberty men had expected, Conscience Whigs revolted. Massachusetts delegate Charles Allen declared, over great clamor, his "belief that the Whig Party is here and this day dissolved," and Henry Wilson (also of Massachusetts) announced, "I will go home; and so help me God, I will do all I can to defeat the election of" the Whig ticket. The convention closed by nominating New York's Millard Fillmore for vice president and declining to draft a platform, thus evading the Proviso question.[38]

As delegates poured out of the convention hall, fifteen Northerners stayed behind to coordinate support for a new national anti-extension coalition. Led by Wilson, this group embraced the national antislavery union that Liberty coalitionists like Chase and Bailey had been advocating for months. The dissident Whigs appointed Allen, Giddings, and antislavery editor John C. Vaughan a committee to oversee the transition and deputed Vaughan and other Ohio men, including Liberty attendee Stanley Matthews, to urge the Columbus Free Territory Convention to call for a national nominating convention.[39]

Assembling the New Anti–Slave Power Party

Chase and the Columbus convention organizers, of course, had had a new national nomination in mind all along. Most crucial to ex-Liberty men would be that any broadened third party insist on comprehensive opposition to the Slave Power, and not merely to slavery in the territories. When New York Democrats pushed for the nomination of Martin Van Buren, Liberty leaders' careful management ensured that he could become a national candidate only by accepting a thorough anti–Slave Power platform.

Chase had prepared the ground well for these developments by scheduling the Free Territory Convention in advance of the major parties' nominations. To promote *national* cooperation, Chase and Giddings agreed that the convention should emphasize "*separation of the federal government*" from slavery as the best way to combat the Slave Power without scaring off new converts. Meeting in the hall of the Ohio House of Representatives, "filled to overflowing," the Ohio Free Territory Convention called for a national convention of the "Friends of Freedom, Free Territory, and Free Labor" to be held in Buffalo on August 9. Condemning both major-party nominations, Ohio's free territory men resolved "to resist inflexibly the aggressions of the Slave Power" and asserted their hope of cooperating with

New York Barnburners. This convention also specifically urged antislavery Ohioans to vote only for known anti–Slave Power candidates in congressional and state legislative elections that would precede the presidential vote. The next day, a preplanned Ohio Liberty convention met in the same hall to concur in support of a national convention as the best "means of uniting the People of the free states . . . for the final overthrow of the tyrant Slave Power."[40]

While Ohio Liberty men were meeting to ratify the Columbus Free Territory Convention, New York Barnburners gathered at Utica to chart their course. Disgusted with the Baltimore nominations, New York bolters had immediately called a state convention at which Barnburners might select their own ticket. In the intervening weeks, Barnburner managers persuaded a reluctant Martin Van Buren to lead their schismatic movement, but the ex-president privately advised close friend Benjamin F. Butler (his former attorney general) that the Barnburners should focus on New York State and avoid entangling themselves in a national movement. Addressing a letter to the Utica convention, Van Buren commended the Barnburner bolt, urged opposition to the Baltimore ticket, and asserted the importance of protecting free territory from slavery. To Liberty men's dismay, Van Buren's letter also defended his past course of opposing abolition in the District of Columbia. The ebullient New York Barnburners gathered at Utica, joined by a smaller contingent of Wilmot Proviso Democrats from other states, adopted anti-extension resolutions and unanimously nominated Martin Van Buren for president and Senator Henry Dodge (D-WI) for vice president. The Utica meeting authorized Barnburners to participate in a broader convention, but by nominating at this juncture, Barnburners clearly established their overriding interest in Van Buren's candidacy. The *Atlas* proudly affixed the names of Van Buren and Dodge to its masthead, even though it was not certain that either would accept (and indeed Dodge ultimately declined).[41]

Liberty coalitionists had been worried that an independent Barnburner nomination might undercut the movement to unite antislavery men from all three parties. Though he had anticipated the Barnburners' go-it-alone nomination, Chase found the move dispiriting and complained that Van Buren had "some sins to answer for." Nonetheless, Chase remained willing to consider backing Van Buren *if* he received a national Free Soil nomination on an acceptable platform. "If he is true to the Free States & Freedom," Chase wrote, "much in the past may be overlooked."[42]

Notwithstanding the hesitancy of the Utica convention, any lingering uncertainty about the prospects for assembling a national convention was dispelled by the June 28 People's Convention at Worcester, Massachusetts.

Outraged at the Taylor nomination, Bay State Conscience Whigs arranged a mass convention that drew from all three parties. The *Boston Daily Whig* urged, "Let Whigs, Democrats and Liberty men, all forget alike their vain party differences, and unite in support of that sacred *principle*, which will be violated by the election of Cass or Taylor—*Freedom in Free Territories.*" Though guided by Conscience Whigs like convention chair Stephen C. Phillips, Charles Francis Adams, and Sumner, the convention also featured prominent Liberty men like Leavitt and Joseph Lovejoy and Democrats such as Amasa Walker and New York City's John Bigelow. Although "it was generally taken for granted that the issue in the present contest was to be the non-extension of slavery," Liberty men were pleased to discover that "the feeling of the meeting . . . went far beyond this, embracing the whole scope of the Liberty movement." Drawing at least five thousand "men of all classes," with the "fire of Freedom burning in their bosoms," the Worcester convention's "enthusiasm was unmeasured, bordering, at times, even on wildness." Though Whigs numerically dominated, the Worcester attendees followed the precedent set in Columbus of appointing equal numbers of Whigs, Democrats, and Liberty men as delegates to the national meeting in Buffalo.[43]

Coalitionists like Chase, Bailey, and Stanton had prepared well for this anti-extension insurgence. Viewing the Columbus, Utica, and Worcester conventions as "fruit of the seed of our own sowing," Liberty leaders across the North now concluded that slavery's opponents "*all* better rally around one common standard" and predicted that the upcoming Buffalo Convention would "tell mightily against the Slave Power." "It is impossible to keep pace with the movements of the people," the *National Era* remarked, as it applauded Ohio Whig congressman Joseph Root's public denunciation of Taylor and catalogued dozens of Whig and Democratic presses that had abandoned their party nominations. In the strongest abolitionist state, Vermont's disgruntled Proviso Democrats called a state Free Soil convention at which they appointed longtime Liberty Party publisher Joseph Poland convention secretary and nominated Liberty man Oscar Shafter for governor. Even Leavitt, long fearful of compromising the Liberty Party's contest against the Slave Power, commended Chase's "superior sagacity" and welcomed bolting Whigs' and Democrats' newfound willingness "to look to 'the overthrow of the Slave Power' as the ultimate result of our movement."[44]

Despite the widespread antislavery enthusiasm, more than a few prominent Liberty partisans remained skeptical. Moreover, after the Utica Barnburner convention, many Liberty men grew particularly apprehensive about empowering a new coalition to replace Hale with Van Buren. Liberty stalwarts like Leavitt, Whittier, and Joseph Lovejoy all hoped Hale could be persuaded not to step down, and Lewis Tappan went so far as to argue that Liberty men shouldn't even attend the Buffalo convention.[45]

Most Liberty spokesmen were more open-minded than Tappan, but insisted firmly that any new antislavery organization adopt the Liberty Party's anti–Slave Power posture. Those who were willing to give up Hale's candidacy vowed that Van Buren would have to at least endorse a platform contravening his prior position on abolition in the District of Columbia. Liberty men would only join a movement dedicated to combating the Slave Power throughout the federal government. Even Whittier, a *National Era* contributor and coalition advocate, agreed that the Buffalo convention would "prove the greatest farce in which earnest and honest men ever engaged" if it committed Liberty men to a merely anti-extension platform. Whittier predicted, however, that Liberty partisans would "not contend about *men*" if the convention instead advocated "the entire divorce of the government of the United States from slavery."[46]

To secure their desired anti–Slave Power platform, Liberty coalitionist leaders like Chase were prepared to sacrifice Hale's candidacy. Furthermore, even before the Columbus convention, Chase had received letters from Hale expressing his willingness to be replaced. By mid-July, Hale had publicly announced that he would gladly withdraw with "the concurrence of his friends." Barnburner managers meanwhile had made Chase well aware that they intended to support only Van Buren for president, but that they would accept a Liberty or Whig vice presidential nominee. With their numerical power in the nation's largest state, Barnburners were well positioned to demand Van Buren's nomination, perhaps, some thought, even if he did not speak out against slavery in the District of Columbia. But Chase warned that "our contest is with the Slave Power . . . The People will not stop with the exclusion of slavery from territories: they will demand its complete denationalization;" and Chase felt confident that Liberty men could persuade Barnburners to support such a platform.[47]

Finally, after weeks of organizing, on August 9, 1848, twenty-thousand Liberty men, Whigs, and Democrats together descended on Buffalo. Gathering under an enormous tent because no building could hold the throng, this mass meeting developed into a two-day antislavery political rally with the fervor of a camp meeting. Charles Francis Adams, still publicly mourning his illustrious father (who had died in February after collapsing on the House floor), presided as dozens of speakers repeated that slavery had superseded the issues that had divided the old parties. Far too unwieldy to organize a new party, this mass meeting cheerfully accepted the proposal to allow the actual delegated convention to retire to a nearby church. There this "Committee of Conference" of nearly 500 would hammer out a platform and select candidates before returning to the masses for ratification. Following the precedent established by the Ohio and Massachusetts conventions, the committee allocated up to six at-large votes per state and three votes per congressional district so that all three parties could receive equal representation. Nine Southern delegates (from Delaware, Maryland, and Virginia) also joined.[48]

The evening before the convention commenced, backroom negotiations laid the foundation of the new Free Soil Party. Chase, Leavitt, and Stanton, convinced Hale could not win the nomination, promised to back Van Buren if Barnburners would accept "a thorough Liberty platform" and pledge the ex-president to support that platform. For Liberty coalitionists it had long been imperative that any new platform go beyond non-extension. The resolutions committee carefully balanced members from all three parties, including such Liberty luminaries as Chase, Leavitt, Owen Lovejoy, Poland, and Stanton. The resolutions ultimately drafted were primarily Chase's handiwork and resembled his long-articulated anti–Slave Power platform. At first, some conservative members, hoping "to adopt a narrower basis" of non-extension, balked at the anti–Slave Power draft platform. But with Preston King joining Liberty men in urging that "the General Government should rid itself of all responsibility for its [slavery's] existence under the action of national legislation," the conferees adopted Chase's resolutions unanimously.[49]

While focusing foremost on opposing slavery extension, the resolutions committee expressed a "determination to rescue the Government" from the "Slave Power." The key resolution for Liberty men declared, "That it is the duty of the federal government to relieve itself from all responsibility for the existence or continuance of slavery wherever that government possess constitutional power to legislate on that subject, and is thus responsible for its existence." This resolution, resembling Liberty calls for divorce of the federal government from slavery, implied, without explicitly mentioning, support for abolition in the District of Columbia. Of course, the platform was more direct in its demand for "no more slave territory and no more slave states." A full ten resolutions related to slavery, its extension, and the Slave Power; and the preamble explicitly condemned the major parties for bending to "slaveholding dictation."[50]

Liberty coalitionists applauded the Buffalo platform's opposition to the Slave Power, even if the resolutions did not quite match the idealism of former Liberty platforms. The platform Liberty men drafted in 1847, by contrast, had identified constitutional "abolition of slavery in the United States" as the party's ultimate aim and had demanded the abrogation of all racially discriminatory state legislation. The Free Soil platform, unsurprisingly given the open racism of many Barnburners, omitted longstanding Liberty calls for free black civil rights, though when Frederick Douglass and Henry Bibb were invited to address the mass convention at Buffalo, the assembled thousands greeted the black orators with "most deafening cheers." Many Liberty men also regarded the platform's invocation of the Declaration of Independence as implying the new party's commitment to "absolute and universal equality of human rights," although most Barnburners probably did not infer such a lofty subtext from that plank. Still, the anti–Slave Power platform testified to Liberty men's crucial role in creating the Free Soil Party, and Liberty men had long asserted that eliminating federal support for slavery would ultimately lead to emancipation. Political abolitionists' influence in promoting antislavery coalition and their power at the Buffalo Convention had impelled Barnburners to make antislavery concessions that went well beyond their Utica resolutions.[51]

Once the Buffalo platform had been enthusiastically ratified, the Conference Committee proceeded to select a presidential ticket. To present the appearance that the nomination was not predetermined, Barnburners agreed to allow Van Buren's and Hale's names to be placed before the convention for an "open" vote. (It had by this time become known that Conscience Whig favorite John McLean did not want the nomination.) Butler and Stanton withdrew Hale and Van Buren from their earlier nominations, and Butler read from a letter Van Buren had prepared to assure delegates that he trusted them to determine the best course for the free territory cause. As Butler eulogized the ex-president, he digressed into bucolic imagery of Van Buren happily tending his vegetable gardens, until an exasperated Ohioan interjected, "Damn his cabbages and turnips! What does he say about the Abolition of Slavery in the Deestrick of Columby?" Butler weathered the outburst by promising that Van Buren would accept the platform, regardless of his earlier position. This swayed enough Conscience Whigs to vote for the better-known Van Buren over Hale. With this Whig support and a few Liberty votes, including those of Chase, Leavitt, and Stanton, Van Buren won the nomination on the first informal ballot with 244 votes to Hale's 183.[52]

After this vote, Joshua Leavitt urged a motion of unanimity, calling it "the most solemn experience of my life." Claiming to "feel as if in the immediate presence of the Divine Spirit," Leavitt asserted that "the Liberty party is not dead, but translated." Ex-Whig George Julian reminisced that "there did not seem to be a dry eye in the Convention." With Liberty men having achieved an approximation of their desired platform, and the Barnburners getting the presidential choice, ex-Whigs were due the vice presidential nominee. The conference happily ratified Ohio Whigs' suggestion of Charles Francis Adams, the son, Chase reminded the mass convention, of "'old man eloquent'" John Quincy Adams. As the *Emancipator* explained: "The Barnburners have their choice for the Presidency, the Conscience Whigs theirs for the Vice Presidency, and the Liberty men have the principles—the platform. This is the union."[53]

The Free Soil Campaign and Its Fruits

Most Liberty men fell in behind the new party, and Liberty leaders exerted a disproportionate influence in shaping Free Soil Party strategy. Though Van Buren failed to seriously challenge the major-party candidates, Liberty partisans who had long concentrated on Congress soon celebrated when the Free Soil Party made possible a new anti–Slave Power congressional bloc.

As they returned home, former Hale supporters felt proud to "have secured a glorious platform" and "consolidated the forces of freedom." Liberty men like Leavitt were pleased to have "found the zeal & generosity of the Van Buren men, so far beyond what was deemed possible." Even Sherman Booth, whose Wisconsin Liberty paper had formerly protested vehemently against an anti-extension coalition, was persuaded by the enthusiastic convention that "the fires of freedom" had "united and burst forth into a mighty flame."[54]

Liberty coalitionists, of course, anticipated complaints about the nominee and worked to defuse misgivings:

> Mr. Van Buren was subservient to the Slave Power in 1836 [when he pledged to veto any bill abolishing slavery in the District of Columbia], you say—well, he is not, like Gen. Cass, a vassal of it, or, like Gen. Taylor, its embodiment, in 1848. On the contrary, he is its open direct antagonist. . . . He alone of all the principal candidates for the Presidency, represents the cause of Freedom, Free Labor, and Free Soil.

Van Buren's public acceptance letter also helped dispel lingering concerns. The Free Soil candidate lauded the Buffalo platform and promised that, if given the opportunity, he would sign legislation for abolition in the District of Columbia. Thoroughly persuaded, Liberty mainstays like John Greenleaf Whittier entered the campaign with alacrity. Leavitt too, after meeting with Van Buren, was convinced that the "glorious old man" was "with us, heart & soul."[55]

Certainly there remained cause for criticism, especially among black

Liberty leaders. Some supported the Free Soil Party, none more emphatically than Henry Bibb, but a significant portion of the black abolitionist leadership rebuked the new party's failure to protest racial discrimination. At the National Convention of Colored Freemen in Cleveland a month after the Buffalo gathering, Bibb encouraged colleagues to embrace Free Soil partisanship, but many did not share Bibb's enthusiasm for the broadened coalition. Convention president Frederick Douglass, although he briefly addressed the Free Soil Party in Buffalo, had not yet abandoned Garrison's nonvoting strategy. Moreover, the criticisms of Samuel Ward, who had also attended the Buffalo Convention, reflected the popular preference among New York's black political abolitionists for the radical moral high ground embodied in Gerrit Smith's Liberty League (which soon after nominated Ward for state representative). The Cleveland convention's formal resolution on the matter conveyed black activists' ambivalence: "That while we heartily engage in recommending to our people the Free Soil movement, and the support of the Buffalo Convention, nevertheless we claim and are determined to maintain the higher standard and more liberal views which have heretofore characterized us as abolitionists." This formulation did, however, leave latitude for men like Bibb, as well as other African American political abolitionists who supported the new coalition less full-throatedly, like biracial Ohio activist Charles Henry Langston and several prominent black Bostonians, to campaign on the moderated antislavery third party's behalf.[56]

Notwithstanding the doubts raised by these distinguished African American leaders, tens of thousands of antislavery Northerners embraced the new movement, and leaders from all the constituent parts of the Free Soil Party looked forward to the upcoming elections. Giddings whipped antislavery northern Ohioans into a fervor, even if many would have preferred an ex-Whig candidate. Leading Barnburner Preston King asserted, overconfidently, that he had "no doubt" Free Soilers would carry New York. He was on firmer ground when he predicted an overwhelming majority for Van Buren in King's own St. Lawrence County. In Massachusetts, Leavitt traversed the state speaking to promote "our glorious cause." Massachusetts Liberty men convened in September and urged former Liberty partisans to "carry the uncompromising and steadfast spirit of the Liberty party into the new movement."[57]

Despite their smaller voting base than Conscience Whigs or Barnburners, Liberty men played prominent roles on many Free Soil tickets. Liberty leader Chauncey Knapp, the former editor of the abolitionist Montpelier *Voice of Freedom*, ran as a Massachusetts Free Soil candidate for Congress and ultimately finished second in a three-way race, as did Ohio abolitionist lawyer John Joliffe. In one Wisconsin District, the Free Soil Party enthusiastically nominated the recent president of the state Liberty Association, Charles Durkee, for Congress. Though the Free Soil organization was weak in Rhode Island, both of its congressional nominees were ex-Liberty men. In Maine, too, Liberty men led the new coalition, and longtime Liberty candidate Samuel Fessenden ran as the party's gubernatorial nominee. Even in New York, where Barnburners dominated the party and handpicked John Dix as their gubernatorial candidate, Free Soilers tapped Seth Gates as his running mate.⁵⁸

Hosts of former Liberty leaders threw themselves into the campaign with unbounded enthusiasm. Austin Willey, who had previously opposed a Van Buren nomination, excitedly projected over 12,000 votes "for Liberty" in Maine, and Whittier predicted that "in view of the great moral revolution," the Free Soil Party could more than quadruple the last year's Liberty vote. Longtime abolitionist jurist William Jay gushed that "the *third or free soil party*, to which the abolitionists have almost unanimously attached themselves is making wonderful progress," while "the old parties are greatly disorganized & exhibit very little zeal." "The seed the abolitionists have been scattering for years," Jay waxed on, "is suddenly germinating." Even ex-Democrats like Connecticut senator John Niles acknowledged the Liberty Party's indispensable influence on the new coalition. Quickly establishing the *Era* as the leading national Free Soil paper, Gamaliel Bailey dedicated his fall editorials almost wholly to promoting the party as a culmination of Liberty anti–Slave Power politics. The *Era* worked hard to convince voters of the prospects of the Free Soil ticket, often exaggerating (probably knowingly) its chances.⁵⁹

For those who predicted a national victory for Van Buren, or imagined his candidacy might at least throw the election into the House of Representatives, the results were somewhat disappointing. Most who had spoken that confidently, though, had done so to coax undecided voters to sever party ties, rather than out of a genuine expectation Van Buren would win. The Free Soil ticket polled slightly fewer than 300,000 votes, approximately 10 percent of the national vote and 14 percent of the free state vote, far more than Birney's 62,000 in 1844. Van Buren did not carry a single state but probably was responsible for denying Cass the electoral votes of New York. Van Buren finished second, ahead of Cass, there (with 26.4 percent of the vote), as well as in Massachusetts (with 28.4 percent) and Vermont (with 28.9 percent). Impressively, Vermont Free Soilers also elected over a third of the lower house of the Vermont legislature. Wisconsin Free Soilers also ran well, with Van Buren garnering more than a quarter of the state's presidential vote. Though the 11 percent vote in Ohio was disappointing, the 35,354 Free Soil votes were enough to thwart Taylor there, since so many Ohio Free Soilers were Western Reserve ex-Whigs. Former Liberty men felt "satisfied that a great work has been done in the organization of the 'Free Soil party,'" and relished its disruptive effects, claiming that Free Soilers had "flogged both parties."[60]

Despite the 11 percent vote in Ohio, below the Free Soil average for the North, results there were particularly auspicious. In addition to electing Giddings and Joseph Root as Free Soil congressmen, the new party achieved a balance of power in the state legislature, enabling the election of Salmon Chase to the U.S. Senate and the repeal of a portion of the state's Black Laws. Chase won his narrow election with mostly Democratic votes only after a series of contentious political maneuvers through which two Western Reserve Free Soilers, Norton Strange Townshend (a former Liberty man) and John F. Morse (a former Whig), established Democratic control of the state house with their casting votes in a complicated apportionment dispute. In exchange, the Democrats supported Chase for senator and accepted Morse's bill (which Chase helped write) to repeal a portion of the state's ignominious Black Laws and to establish public schools (though segregated) for African American children. Whigs and many Free Soilers seethed at Townshend and Morse, since the ex-Whig majority of the Free Soil bloc had hoped to maintain their independence and force Whigs to help Free Soilers send Giddings to the Senate. Nevertheless, Townshend received resounding plaudits from former Liberty co-partisans.[61]

While many ex-Whig Free Soilers felt Chase, Townshend, and Morse had betrayed Giddings, and Western Reserve voters did not return Townshend or Morse to the next legislature, their bargain nonetheless gave the Free Soil Party its second senator and eliminated the worst of Ohio's Black Laws. In response Chase claimed, perhaps sincerely, that "Repeal of those laws is an object dearer to me than any political elevation whatever; and is worth more to us as a Party than the election of any man to any office in the gift of the Legislature." Even those who disliked Chase celebrated at least this result of his allies' arrangements. Free Soilers outside of Ohio excitedly anticipated Chase joining Hale as a potent anti–Slave Power voice in the Senate. Indeed, Leavitt considered "this one result as a full equivalent for the campaign of 1848."[62]

Perhaps even more exciting than the election of a new antislavery senator, Free Soilers won several House races across the North. Wisconsin Free Soilers hailed the election of former state Liberty Association president Charles Durkee to Congress as having "vindicated the honor of one two-hundred-and-thirtieth part of this Republic." In majority-rule Massachusetts, Charles Allen and John G. Palfrey both won pluralities on the initial ballot. The vigorous organization that followed elected Allen on the second trial, but Palfrey was less successful. Although he never served in Congress again, Palfrey's strong Free Soil support prevented either major party from filling the seat *for the entire next Congress*, as his district balloted unsuccessfully a dozen additional times. Wilmot and King were both returned by their Proviso Democrat–dominated districts. All told, Free Soilers won at least eight seats in a closely divided Congress, and were joined by several other committed non-extensionists who had won with Free Soil aid. In several locales where congressional elections were held in advance of the presidential election, Free Soilers and one of the major parties worked together to elect staunch Proviso advocates. Among these congressional victors with clear antislavery sympathies and ambiguous party loyalties, some, like Lewis Campbell (W-OH), would remain as loyal to their old party as before, but others, like Connecticut Proviso Democrats Walter Booth and Loren Waldo and Michigan free soil Whig William Sprague, soon privileged antislavery convictions. Estimates of expected Free Soil strength in the next House ranged from ten to eighteen men who would prioritize free territory over party allegiance. It seemed almost certain that Free Soilers would wield a balance of power in the next House. "The party of Freedom," political abolitionists optimistically forecast, would "henceforth give shape and character to the legislation of the country."[63]

Although it had not lived up to the hopes of its most sanguine supporters, the Free Soil Party transformed the national standing of antislavery politics. To old Liberty strategists who had long privileged congressional antislavery action, the influx of new congressmen severed from ties to the Slave Power parties offered a promise of new confrontations. From their congressional vantage point, Free Soil partisans would play a vital role in assuring continued attention to slavery and the Slave Power, despite the major parties' best efforts to quell sectional tensions that the 1848 election had laid bare.

* Interlude Four *

"Glorious Confusion in the Ranks": The Free Soil Balance of Power, 1849

The 1849 speakership contest represented a pivotal moment for political abolitionists. In the incoming House, Free Soilers achieved what the Liberty Party never could: a congressional balance of power. For three weeks in December 1849, the House repeatedly failed to organize. Ultimately it took sixty-three ballots over twenty days before the House gave up the time-honored majority rule and appointed a plurality winner unacceptable to more than half the members.

Over the weeks of stalemate, the deep divisions over slavery in the national legislature became ever clearer. Threats of disunion, physical violence, and general pandemonium characterized the proceedings. By repeatedly defeating the major parties' attempts to organize and insisting that any candidate meet certain basic antislavery demands to receive their votes, Free Soilers established the new national power of political antislavery and highlighted the old parties' inabilities to silence sectional conflict.[1]

With the major parties so closely divided and wracked with discord over slavery expansion, the new third party could "effect much by holding a whip over the old parties." Joshua Giddings especially recognized the attention that disputes over Winthrop's previous speakership election had drawn to key committee arrangements. Now, two years later the veteran congressional brawler was joined by a party of allies ready to renew that controversy in hopes of forcing the election of an antislavery speaker and guaranteeing themselves a voice on key committees out of which they could report antislavery legislation: a bill from the Committee on Territories incorporating the Wilmot Proviso, a bill from the Committee on the District of Columbia to abolish slavery in the capital, and a bill from the Judiciary Committee repealing the 1793 Fugitive Slave Act. If neither party's Southern wing would permit the election of a Proviso adherent, Free Soilers thought they might do one better, and precipitate a sectional organization. At minimum, they would further dramatize the Slave Power's control of both major parties.[2]

As representatives began arriving in Washington, it quickly became apparent that neither the Whigs nor the Democrats could control a House majority. On the eve of this 31st Congress, Giddings boasted to his wife of both major parties' "glorious confusion in the ranks." While Free Soilers could count on only nine sure votes, they identified a number of other potential antislavery Whig or Democratic defectors "who hang between heaven and he-ll," torn between anti-extensionism and old party loyalties. Both major-party delegations, caucusing simultaneously in separate areas of the Capitol building, nominated candidates who were entirely unacceptable to Free Soilers. Democrats tapped gifted floor leader Howell Cobb, a thirty-four-year-old Georgia planter considered a moderate among Deep South Democrats, and Whigs nominated the conservative incumbent Winthrop. Faced with one dogged opponent of the Proviso and another candidate only tepidly supporting it, Free Soilers and several fellow travelers huddled at an apartment in the National Hotel and, agreeing to support their own David Wilmot, hunkered down for a long battle.[3]

On the first ballot Cobb ran six votes ahead of Winthrop but fell nine shy of a majority, as Wilmot received eight votes, and himself voted for another Free Soiler, while five other Northerners cast antislavery protest votes. The results on the next several ballots were similar. Gamaliel Bailey's National Era excitedly reported:

> For the first time in the history of the Government, a distinct Anti-Slavery party held the balance of power between the old parties . . .
>
> It was apparent that there was a body of fourteen men determined to make opposition to Slavery in the Territories of the United States, just as the slaveholders had determined to make Opposition to Slavery-Restriction, a test.

Cobb himself likewise blamed antislavery sentiment, privately attributing his failure to "the Northern free-soil Democrats who would vote for no southern man."[4]

Free Soilers disputed aspersions that they were playing the part of mere obstructionists and promised to support any staunch Wilmot Proviso Whig or Democrat put in nomination by either major party. If neither party would do so, Free Soilers hoped they might, better yet, unify Proviso supporters without regard to party labels and organize the House around the slavery extension question, which the members' actions had effectively "admit[ted] to be of more controlling importance than any other." The Free Soilers, the National

Era explained, sought *"nothing for themselves"* and stood *"ready, at any moment, to vote for any candidate, Whig or Democrat, who would appoint the committees of the House so as to give a fair expression to the Public Sentiment of the country."* [5]

Aggravated members of the major parties soon tried their hands at devising some new method to resolve the impasse. Already by the second day (though after thirteen unsuccessful ballots), future president Andrew Johnson (D-TN) was sufficiently frustrated to propose a plurality rule. Johnson was willing to immediately accept either a Whig or Democrat so they could begin legislating. At this point few agreed. The House tabled Johnson's motion, 210–11. After several more days of inconclusive balloting, Democrats and Whigs began to yearn for any solution to the unseemly standoff. A Louisiana Democrat suggested leaving the organization of the House to chance by putting Cobb's and Winthrop's names in a box and drawing one for speaker, and Robert Schenck (W-OH) offered to eliminate the problem of accountability to one's constituents by resorting to a secret ballot.[6]

Free Soilers denounced these proposals as evidence of just how desperately the major parties sought to evade the slavery issue, by any method necessary, however antidemocratic. Joseph Root (FS-OH) expressed smug satisfaction with the Free Soilers' disruptive role but attacked the notion that they alone bore responsibility for the House's disarray—after all, the other 220 members also could not find a way to agree on an organization. Charles Durkee (FS-WI) similarly celebrated that the failure to organize had advanced the *"cause of freedom"* by making it *"obvious to the whole American people, that the great struggle is between the slavery propagandists and the slavery restrictionists."* [7]

Indiana Democrat William Brown came closest to a majority, failing by only two votes on December 12, after surprisingly receiving five Free Soil votes, including those of ex-Whigs Giddings and Charles Allen (MA), along with the vote of every anti-extension Democrat who had refused to support Cobb. Brown fell just short in part because three Free Soilers would not vote for him, but also because a few Southerners who had previously supported him quickly switched their votes after hearing Free Soilers call out Brown's name. With the Democratic near-victory, nervous Whig representatives insinuated that Democrats had struck a deal with the Free Soilers. And, as Whigs accused, Brown had indeed provided Wilmot with a written pledge that the Territorial, Judiciary, and District of Columbia Committees would not be controlled by Southern majorities that could easily stifle efforts to pass the Proviso, contest the Fugitive Slave Law, or promote abolition in the capital. This correspondence had given Wilmot *"reason to believe that a majority of these committees would be composed of fair northern men"* and that all three would include at least one Free Soiler. Once Brown came clean about this agreement, he lost all chance of election, and Free Soilers lost the committee power Brown had seemed to promise. The House returned to deadlock and tempers continued to escalate.[8]

In this unsuccessful maneuver, Giddings, King, and Wilmot verified their willingness to see the House organized. They had nearly crowned a Democratic speaker who provided written assurance that under his speakership they could have anticipated committees that would bring antislavery legislation to the floor for debate. Angry Northern Whigs assailed Free Soilers as having bargained with the South. From the Free Soilers' perspective, embittered Whigs missed the point. Free Soilers had been elected to combat the Slave Power. Ensuring committees that would report antislavery bills out to the House was one of the best ways to do this. This was why Free Soilers distrusted Winthrop. Under Winthrop's previous speakership, the House's "committees on the District, the Territories, & the Judiciary" had been, as Free Soil senator Salmon Chase put it, "constituted for inaction."[9]

Brown's defeat demonstrated that a congressional coalition between the Free Soilers and either of the major parties would be impossible. For days before, Free Soilers had suggested that if Democrats united behind William Strong, a Wilmot Proviso Democrat, or Whigs behind abolitionist Thaddeus Stevens (both Pennsylvanians), the Free Soil votes that would follow would organize the House for whichever party nominated a stalwart antiextensionist. Yet, as soon as Free Soilers were seen to be massing behind a Democrat with a far more ambiguous record, many slaveholding Democrats withdrew support. Clearly Southerners would never suffer the election of any man acceptable to Free Soilers. Instead they had to remain firm and hope to so immobilize the House that a partisan organization would be deemed hopeless and give way to a sectional one.[10]

If the old parties fragmented, the Free Soilers stood poised to spearhead the longtime Liberty goal of uniting all opponents of the Slave Power. The National Era argued that "non-slaveholders of the country, constituting the great majority of the citizens, demand that the committees of the House should represent the Sentiment of Liberty, and not that of Slavery." This of itself signified dramatic progress towards the goals for which abolitionists had left "their respective parties in 1840, and commenced the policy of voting for candidates pledged in favor of Human Liberty." The stalemate provided the most promising opportunity yet to confront the Slave Power: "Let the Slavery Men and Free Soil Men meet each other face to face, with no compromisers between them. The sooner Congress is brought to this point, admitting of no evasion, compromise, or postponement, the better." Representative Charles Allen concurred, declaring obsolete the "artificial division" between Whigs and Democrats; slavery now constituted the *"principle which divides the whole House into two, and but two parties."*[11]

The day after Brown's ignominious defeat, the House witnessed even greater unrest. Proslavery extremist Richard Meade (D-VA) suggested that *"those who are desirous of crushing this demon of discord"* resolve against the Wilmot Proviso and abolition in the District of Columbia. If that resolution were adopted, Meade magnanimously promised to *"take a Speaker from either side of the House,"* but he then truculently averred, *"If the organization of this House is to be followed by the passage of these bills—if these outrages are to be committed upon my people, I trust in God, sir, that my eyes have rested upon the last Speaker of the House."* Unsurprisingly, Meade failed to mollify the chamber. New York Whig William Duer reproached Meade and branded him a disunionist and, worse still, a liar, a dangerous insult to hurl at a Southern man of honor. Meade exploded and had to be physically restrained from assaulting the New Yorker.[12]

Free Soilers exulted in the disorganization and the attention it drew to the Slave Power's influence over both parties. *"The old parties,"* Giddings asserted, *"appear to be totally paralised [sic], and their leaders incapable of action."* He assured Sumner that *"separation between the northern and southern wings"* of both major parties was *"becoming daily wider and wider."* As the standstill persisted, Free Soilers grew increasingly sanguine about their efforts to unravel the major parties. The Free Soilers, consulting *"every evening except Sunday,"* stood, in Giddings's view, as the House's *"only organized party."* Durkee similarly reported to his constituents that *"the two old pro-slavery connexions are now pretty well broken up."* Though he foresaw *"a stormy session,"* Durkee remained confident that its attention to the slavery issue would *"tend greatly to hasten the time, and promote the cause of emancipation."*[13]

To Free Soilers' dismay, though, the House adopted a rule to eliminate debate the day after Meade and Duer's altercation, for the apparent purpose of expediting a decision and probably also to prevent a repeat of the previous day's embarrassing display. Over the next few days, members unsuccessfully advocated increasingly inventive, and ridiculous, methods for choosing a speaker, though now none were debatable. One called for the election of anyone who could win a plurality of 49/100 on the next ballot or 48/100 on the ballot after that, continuing successively until someone reached the incrementally declining benchmark. Even more convoluted was a proposal that one Whig and one Democrat be appointed a two-man *"committee"* that would compose two lists of ten suitable candidates (excluding themselves and two witnesses). Added to those twenty, one other representative would be chosen by lot from the remaining members. Then the original *"committee"* and witnesses would retire to the speaker's room with their list of twenty-one members and alternately strike out names until one remained. This glorified, and absurd, version of the plan to draw names out of a box made little headway but demonstrated the growing desperation to select a speaker by any method that would avert a sectional organization.[14]

Eventually a simpler anti-majoritarian plan succeeded, despite vociferous Free Soil resistance. The House appointed a private conference of six Whigs and six Democrats—three Southerners and three Northerners from each party. Giddings and Root loudly declaimed against the exclusion of Free Soilers, but were silenced by the rule proscribing debate. Two days later the committee reported back with a motion that after three more unsuccessful ballots, the fourth one would select a speaker by plurality vote. Despite the outrage of Free Soilers, this plurality rule passed 113 to 106, supported by some Southern Democrats but mostly by Whigs, who needed the House organized to enable any action from the Whig presidential administration and perhaps also believed that in a plurality contest Free Soilers would swallow Winthrop to defeat the slaveholder Cobb. Those Whigs were disappointed when the House called the roll for the 63rd time and Cobb won 102 votes compared to Winthrop's 99. Even the long-awaited appointment of a speaker, however, could not restore calm. It took dozens of ballots and two more weeks of similar sectional discord before the House managed to elect a clerk and sergeant-at-arms and then gave up entirely on the stalemated contest for a new doorkeeper.[15]

In so delaying the House's organization, Free Soilers had shown their potential to wield power on the national level. The Free Soil Party had incorporated thousands of Liberty Party abolitionists who saw the broader movement as offering a genuine opportunity for concrete power in Congress. Congressional Free Soilers' ability to obstruct legislation and sow chaos through both national political parties confirmed this Liberty hope and dramatized both major parties' deference to the Slave Power. With the House's abandonment of majority-rule selection for speaker, the Free Soilers' apparent control of the Congress abruptly ended. The depth of Free Soil commitment to pursuing antislavery policy at the national level and the determined evasion of Whigs and Democrats, however, had clearly demonstrated the potential for anti–Slave Power third-party politics to further undermine the Second Party System.

* CHAPTER SIX *

Free Soil Politics and the Twilight of the Second Party System, 1849–1853

In the years following the opening of Congress in December 1849, Free Soilers played an indispensable role in sustaining anti–Slave Power politics despite facing numerous, at times seemingly overwhelming, obstacles. Though the Free Soil Party never again matched the 1848 showing that had provided its balance of power in the 31st House, Free Soilers nonetheless persisted in their efforts to use Congress as an antislavery platform and ensured continued national attention to the Slave Power, even as major-party politicians worked vigorously to tamp down brewing sectional conflict. The Free Soil Party also created new opportunities for antislavery men to bargain for power in many Northern states. Free Soilers' complicated coalition strategies often ended in disappointment, but played vital roles in ensuring the continued antislavery congressional presence that political abolitionists so deeply prized. Maintaining their analysis of the Slave Power's inevitable control of cross-sectional parties, most Free Soilers who supported coalition tactics at the state and local levels remained aloof from the major parties on the *national* level. After the Whigs' 1852 electoral disaster, Free Soilers cheered that party's seemingly imminent demise, interpreting the election results through the lens of political abolitionists' long-established analysis of the Slave Power's reliance on the Second Party System.

Compromise and Resistance

The ultimate defeat of the Free Soil agitators in the 1849 speakership contest provided an ominous prelude to the coming session. Over the ensuing months, congressional compromisers engineered yet another unsatisfying sectional entente. The Wilmot Proviso debates had originated as hypothetical arguments over territory the United States did not yet own, but by the start of the 31st Congress, California, flooded with immigrants during the 1849 Gold Rush, demanded admission as a free state. With President Taylor endorsing California statehood, Congress could only procrastinate for so long. The disorderly territory had attracted a considerable population (exceeding that of some states) desperate to establish a civilian government and had consequently drafted a state constitution, which excluded slavery. Admitting California as a free state, however, would be impossible without some concession for slavery in the Southern-dominated Senate.

In the resulting Compromise of 1850 (the conventional, if not entirely accurate, name for this Congress's intertwined legislation pertaining to slavery), Northerners gained the free state of California and the nearly meaningless concession of an end to the public slave trade at the capital (commerce in human beings simply moved to nearby Alexandria, already a major slave-trading hub). Free Soilers, however, viewed the compromise measures as a bitter defeat. Congress disregarded the Wilmot Proviso, organizing the New Mexico and Utah territories under popular sovereignty rules, and resolved a charged boundary dispute between slaveholding Texas and the federal New Mexico territory by assuming $10 million of Texas state debt in exchange for the surrender of *some* of her dubious land claims. Worst of all, Congress passed a more stringent Fugitive Slave Act, authorizing federal commissioners to return alleged fugitives to slavery without jury trials or testimony from the accused. Among the most needlessly offensive provisions of that bill, commissioners received ten dollars for remanding an alleged fugitive, but only five for releasing him or her. Supposedly designed to compensate for extra paperwork, this pay scale's proslavery bias infuriated abolitionists. Perhaps more galling still, the bill criminalized humanitarian assistance to runaway slaves and empowered federal marshals to compel Northern citizens to join slave-hunting posses under the threat of hefty fines or incarceration.[1]

This famous so-called compromise originated in Senator Henry Clay's attempt "to settle and adjust amicably all the existing questions of controversy . . . arising out of the institution of slavery." President Taylor had tried to simply bypass the territorial question, and thus the Wilmot Proviso as well, by calling for the immediate admission of California and New Mexico as *states*, even with an antislavery constitution certain for the former and likely for the latter. Clay offered a more complicated solution that would temper acceptance of California's proposed free-state constitution with other provisions to mollify slaveholding senators. Even though Clay incorporated James Mason's (D-VA) onerous new fugitive slave bill, many Southern senators still saw Clay's proposals as rife with concessions to Northern fanaticism. Free Soilers found Clay's proposals similarly disturbing.[2]

In the closely watched debates over Clay's compromise, aging senatorial giants like Daniel Webster and John C. Calhoun further focused national political interest on the slavery question. In the most dramatic articulation of proslavery opposition to Clay's proposals, Calhoun, emaciated and dying (he passed away later that month), drafted a final "speech," which Mason read. Eulogizing slavery, Calhoun warned that without new protections, disunion would soon become necessary. Webster responded, "not as a Massachusetts man, nor a northern man, but as an American," with a famous and controversial endorsement of Clay's proposals, including the fugitive slave bill. Condemning abolitionist agitation, Webster opined that on the issue of Northern obstruction of fugitive slave rendition, "the South is right, and the North is wrong." In this renowned Seventh of March Speech, Webster established conservative Northern Whig support for compromise and drew forth angry rebukes from antislavery men across the North.[3]

Antislavery senators of course met Webster's challenge. New York Whig William Seward's response to Webster has long been the best-known retort because of its incendiary appeal to "a higher law than the Constitution." But Free Soil speeches went even further in opposing the proposed settlement. John P. Hale's two-day philippic attacked slaveholders' national political power and the fugitive bill's privileging of "the rights of slavery" over all other American rights by treating apprehended African American citizens as slaves until proven otherwise. Dismissing Southern pleas to "save this Union," Hale demanded that slaveholders "cease from representing the North as oppressive" and the Wilmot Proviso as unconstitutional. Hale echoed the manly resistance and defense of white male independence that had infused pro-Proviso speeches in previous Congresses as he proudly deprecated Southern secessionists' attempts to intimidate his Northern colleagues. "If you can only purchase peace with us by compelling us to surrender everything which exalts us above your slaves," Hale scoffed, "let disunion come." Salmon Chase's similarly lengthy attack on the compromise proposals reiterated his old Liberty legal analysis that "freedom is national; slavery only is local and sectional" and condemned the "equally obnoxious" efforts of both major parties to paper over sectional strife. Joining Hale in dismissing disunionist bluster, Chase challenged Northern senators' senses of "duty, honor, patriotism, [and] shame." Circulating widely, Chase's anti–Slave Power harangue seemed to be well-received by all three parties in Ohio.[4]

While radicals from both sections drew attention to the question of slavery's future in the American polity, Mississippi Democrat Henry Foote seized the compromise's parliamentary reins. An enigmatic Deep South moderate who had earned the epithet "Hangman Foote" for his 1848 threat to lynch Hale if he ever visited Mississippi, Foote aimed to push Clay's plan through in a single "omnibus bill," fearing that otherwise California might be admitted without any recompense for the South. Following Foote's tactical lead, Clay watched his plan go down to defeat from both sides. Most Northern Whigs refused to support a bill containing Mason's fugitive law, and most Deep South Democrats could not brook a free California or Texas's relinquishment of such extensive land claims. Though the omnibus failed in the summer of 1850, one of the main impediments to compromise disappeared when President Taylor died suddenly of a stomach ailment. His successor, Millard Fillmore of New York, widely assumed to favor Clay's proposals, signaled his support and, from Free Soilers' perspective, "insulted the whole North" by appointing Webster Secretary of State.[5]

As an exhausted Clay left Washington, Illinois Democrat Stephen Douglas, Clay's junior by thirty-six years, picked up the pieces of the discarded compromise and cobbled together majorities for each component individually. A hyper-ambitious westerner who maintained a personal financial stake in slavery as manager of his wife's inherited Mississippi plantation, Senator Douglas was also a master tactician. His labors ultimately convinced enough Northern Democrats and Upper South Whigs to compromise and join the large sectional blocs voting accordingly for the separate bills that benefited either the slave or the free states. Especially contentious was the Texas boundary issue, ultimately settled by a bill to augment Texas to its present size, with Texas abandoning more far-reaching claims in exchange for federal assumption of $10 million of its state debt. Free Soilers assailed this plan as a bribe to Texas, while Deep Southerners who had greater interest in Texas's size than its finances opposed potentially closing off thousands of acres to slavery. With a Texan military expedition looming against the U.S. Army in New Mexico, the boundary dispute threatened to derail the entire compromise in the House. The hospitality of Washington socialites who possessed substantial Texas bond holdings ultimately helped lubricate congressional deal making on this issue in which they held so vested an interest, and a "little omnibus" yoking New Mexico's admission under popular sovereignty rules to the Texas border agreement won a 108–97 victory in the House. Soon after, the House passed the remaining compromise bills with shifting coalitions resembling those Douglas had assembled in the Senate. When this legislation reached Fillmore's desk in September 1850, he quickly signed the bills into law.[6]

Leaders of both major parties congratulated themselves that their compromise would extinguish sectional conflict and return slavery to the margins of national politics, but anyone who had paid close attention to the preceding debates should have realized that harmony would likely prove fleeting. House Free Soilers had repeatedly called attention to the major parties' efforts "to convert the Government into an instrument for the protection and perpetuation of slavery." Well before any of the individual measures even came up for a House vote, New Hampshire's Amos Tuck blasted the proposed compromise as "odious to the whole people" of the North. John Quincy Adams's antislavery Whig successor (and famous Massachusetts education reformer) Horace Mann, who drifted from his party during these debates and soon after won reelection as a Free Soiler, published letters to his constituents smearing slavery extensionists as emasculated and lazy, in contrast to hardworking antislavery laborers:

> Fifty hardy gold diggers from the North will never stand all day knee-deep in water, shovel earth, rockwashers, &c., under a broiling sun, and see a man with his fifty slaves standing under the shade of a tree, or having an umbrella held over his head, with whip in hand, and without wetting his dainty glove, or soiling his japanned boot, pocket as much at night as the whole of them together.

As debates wore on, former Liberty men grew excited that after years of having "almost hopelessly labored to awaken the public mind to a sense of the wrong of slavery, and the danger of its subverting our free institutions," they now saw "not only the masses, but the Congress of the nation itself, engrossed, for a whole session, with none other than the 'one idea' they were ridiculed for entertaining." "Slavery and Freedom," Free Soilers celebrated, "have become almost the sole questions agitated here. Nothing else is discussed; nothing else is talked of."[7]

No matter how loudly leading politicians proclaimed the finality of the compromise, Northern frustration with the Fugitive Slave Act simmered under the surface of sectional truce. While indignant at the Texas boundary adjustment and rejection of the Proviso for New Mexico and Utah, Free Soilers especially directed their fury against the Fugitive Slave Law — the Compromise's most barefaced proslavery concession. Even Free Soilers who believed the Texas boundary to be of greater importance shrewdly concentrated their fire on the Fugitive Slave Act. The new law further corroborated the Slave Power argument and "waked up an intense excitement." "This fugitive law," Maine political abolitionist leader Austin Willey asserted, "is doing a great work and we ought I think to make the most of it." Men who had recently "been the apparent slaves of hunkerism" now denounced the Fugitive Slave Act.[8]

Within Congress, the Free Soil band fought futilely to repeal the law, knowing that they might at least use their public platform to underscore the major parties' complicity with the Slave Power. When the post-Compromise congressional session opened in December 1850 with a presidential message exhorting Congress to refrain from further sectional agitation and promising a veto in the unlikely case Congress attempted to repeal the Fugitive Slave Act, Joshua Giddings (FS-OH) responded by vowing that "agitation will never cease until the law ceases." True to his word, Giddings seized the opportunity to castigate President Fillmore, who had "so suddenly and so boldly abjured the cause of freedom, and, before the world, pledged fealty to the slave power." Giddings, however, appreciated that the hated new law would force "every public man, and every elector of the nation" to "take his position either for freedom or for slavery." "We shall soon have but two political parties," Giddings predicted—one "in favor of compelling the people of the North to become the catchers of southern slaves" and another committed to "emancipation of the free States and this Government from the control of the slave power." Voicing similar sentiments, Horace Mann, now firmly in the Free Soil camp, made a lengthy case for not only the immorality, but also the unconstitutionality of the Fugitive Slave Law. Emphasizing the threat to hundreds of thousands of free black Northerners, Mann encouraged free states to pass legislation guaranteeing jury trials for alleged fugitives and "inflicting condign punishment upon every man who directly or indirectly assists in sending any man into southern bondage, unless he can prove before a jury that the man so sent was a slave."[9]

In their responses to the Fugitive Slave Act, political abolitionists adopted ever more aggressive defenses of Northern rights, including an increasing comfort, at least rhetorically, with righteous violence in defense of freedom. On the House floor, Indiana Free Soiler George Julian, for example, promised resistance and denigrated Northern compromise supporters as slavishly obedient to Southern demands: "If I believed the people I represent were base enough to become the miserable flunkies of a God-forsaken southern slave hunter by joining him or his constable in the blood-hound chase of a panting slave, I would scorn to hold a seat on this floor by their suffrages, and I would denounce them as fit subjects themselves for the lash of the slave-driver." The Boston *Emancipator and Republican* likewise questioned the courage and manhood of Northern compromisers in its defiant warning that "if any southern blood hound or northern spaniel crosses our threshold in search" of a fugitive, "he will be kicked out as we would serve any dead dog."[10]

Free Soilers especially attacked Webster, the onetime Wilmot Proviso advocate whose defense of the Fugitive Slave Act could be used to highlight

Northern major-party politicians' servility. Upbraiding Webster as a "pliant tool of the slave power," Free Soilers exploited his sectional treachery to urge antislavery secessions from the Whig Party. The day after Webster spoke, Joshua Giddings instructed his editor son: "Don't fail to use the weapon which Webster has put into the hands of the free soilers to beat out the brains of the Whigs." Former Liberty man John Jay similarly appreciated that "the apostacy [sic] of Webster melancholy as it is, is so open, bare-faced, & palpably unprincipled that I trust it will not be without its good effect."[11]

If white Free Soil strategists saw the newest Slave Power usurpation as at least providing political capital, for African Americans the Fugitive Slave Act was an unmitigated disaster. This law directly threatened the tenuous freedom of all black Northerners—fugitives, freemen, and freedmen. Though perhaps only 300 were apprehended under the law (through 1860), the increased danger of legal recapture or illegal kidnapping forced constant fearful vigilance in Northern black communities. Thousands of fugitives felt compelled to flee to the safety of British Canada, including prominent Michigan Free Soil spokesman and former Liberty Leader Henry Bibb. The new law consequently reinvigorated the ongoing work of the New York State Vigilance Committee and similar, interconnected Underground Railroad organizations that relied on black activists like Philadelphia's William Still and New York's Charles B. Ray and Louis Napoleon, alongside white abolitionists, including both Garrisonians like Sydney Howard Gay and political abolitionists like Lewis Tappan and John Jay.[12]

Several episodes of conspicuous resistance further dramatized the Slave Power's threat to Northern freedom, accelerating the already heated, often violent, conflicts that had long swirled around Southern attempts to claim alleged fugitives on Northern soil. In response to the 1850 legislation, black Bostonians established a League of Freedom and pledged that enforcement in their city "would be a dangerous business." Plans for an African American community self-defense network dovetailed with a new Boston Vigilance Committee set up soon after in collaboration with prominent white abolitionists. These forces sprang into action in October 1850 when two Georgia slave catchers arrived in Boston to apprehend famous fugitives William and Ellen Craft, who had fled north in 1848 with fair-complexioned Ellen posing as a sickly master traveling north with "his" manservant. While William armed himself, the League organized white and black Boston abolitionists to protect the fugitives and intimidate the slave catchers. After a weeklong standoff, the Georgians left the city empty-handed to abolitionists' delight.[13]

A few months later, still more dramatic resistance in Boston garnered national popular attention, along with congressional and presidential attention. In February 1851, slave-hunting agents seized a fugitive known as Shadrach Minkins and carried him to the city's federal courthouse, where an angry, predominantly black crowd gathered. As Minkins's abolitionist allies exited the building, the crowd stormed the court house and rescued the prisoner, who soon escaped to Canada. Though the Fillmore administration insisted on indictments, the Boston jury refused to convict the eight men charged (four black and four white, including longtime Liberty activist Elizur Wright).[14]

In yet more violent resistance, on September 11, 1851, local black abolitionists killed a Maryland slaveholder attempting to recover escaped slaves in Christiana, Pennsylvania. Since anti-abolitionists preferred to blame white agitators rather than acknowledge black militancy, Castner Hanway, a white miller who refused to join the posse, was branded the instigator. Fillmore's district attorney charged thirty-eight men on 117 counts of levying war against the U.S. Government—the largest treason proceedings in American history. Southerners cast the trial as a test of the government's proslavery credibility, while Free Soilers saw yet another troubling but newsworthy example of federal officeholders "prostituting Northern independence before the Slave Power to win its favor and alliance." To Free Soilers' relief, jurors found Hanway innocent of treason after just fifteen minutes of deliberation. Realizing the futility of further trials, the federal government dropped the remaining treason charges.[15]

In October 1851, shortly after the Christiana incident and months before Hanway's acquittal, another dramatic slave rescue further aggravated Fillmore's efforts to proclaim sectional peace. While Gerrit Smith's radical remnant of the Liberty Party was holding an annual meeting in Syracuse, news spread that fugitive William Henry, known as "Jerry," had been taken into federal custody. Egged on by Smith and Samuel May, a leading Garrisonian who had grown increasingly comfortable working alongside political abolitionists, a massive biracial crowd broke Jerry free and sent him north to Canada and his shackles south to President Fillmore. Efforts to prosecute the ringleaders were again largely unavailing, though federal indictment forced black Liberty leader Jermain Loguen, who had escaped slavery himself seventeen years earlier, to flee temporarily to Canada.[16]

Congressional Free Soilers seized on these dramatic challenges to further advocate repeal of the fugitive legislation, while Southerners and Northern compromisers bemoaned abolitionist resistance. The Shadrach Minkins rescue, for example, incited days of bitter Senate debate, as slaveholding senators brazenly demanded that President Fillmore formally reaffirm his commitment to executing the law. In response to this Southern posturing, Hale ridiculed the cowardice of the fugitive law's defenders, playing on their belief in black inferiority as he derided "the idea of the President of the United States issuing a formal proclamation, calling upon all the naval and military force of the Government to hold themselves in readiness . . . to defend this great Republic against a handful of negroes in Boston!" Boston Free Soil leader Charles Sumner similarly remarked, "The excitement at Washington about the Fugitive case here is most ridiculous. A *very few unarmed negroes did it all.* Their success shews the little support the law has in our community." When the obliging chief executive complied with slaveholders' requests and sent the Senate a message on Fugitive Slave Law enforcement, it touched off another extended debate that Hale and Chase again used to call attention to the Slave Power. Free Soil journals mocked Fillmore's slavish deference to Southern leaders and confidently predicted the miserable failure of all the administration's labors to win respect for the "vile" Fugitive Slave Act: "the President and his Cabinet may as well attempt to restrain the eruptions of Vesuvius as to quell agitation."[17]

Congressional Free Soilers consistently exploited such opportunities to assail the Slave Power, once again using legislative debate to broadcast arguments designed to rouse Northern readers. As a new outpouring of petitions reached the Senate for repeal of the hated fugitive law, the question of their mere consideration generated heated debates that harked back to the early days of the House gag rule battle. As slavery continually crept in, Free Soilers repeatedly seized the initiative to expose how unevenly mainstream politicians applied their proscriptions on agitation that might upset the tenuous harmony supposedly instilled by the Compromise. For example, when Southerners revived efforts to reimburse the *Amistad* slave owners for the illegally enslaved Africans freed by the Supreme Court, Senator Hale loudly objected to the offensive proposition to indemnify foreigners who, had they been American, would have been hung for piracy as illegal slave traders. In doing so, Hale mocked Southerners who claimed that "there has been a great compromise and a great settlement; everybody is in love with everybody; there is no quarreling, no commotion, no agitation; the agitators are dead and buried," while at the same time raising ever more outlandish demands that the government prove its fidelity to slavery.[18]

Notwithstanding the continued antislavery incursions on Capitol Hill and the handful of dramatic fugitive rescue attempts, the sentimental fiction of Harriet Beecher Stowe provided the most potent means for further diffusion of anti–Slave Power opposition to the fugitive law. First serialized in Gamaliel Bailey's *National Era*, Stowe's *Uncle Tom's Cabin; or Life among the Lowly* was an instant sensation. Originally planning a short story that would run for only ten weeks, Stowe responded to popular acclaim by expanding it into a full-length novel. Bailey was all too pleased to print chapters of *Uncle Tom's Cabin* week after week for over nine months. Stowe's book personalized the horrors of the slave system by drawing especially on themes of domesticity to appeal to a white middle-class Christian readership of both genders.[19]

The novel was an immediate success, winning plaudits far beyond what Stowe or Bailey could have anticipated. Recognizing the sudden popularity of Stowe's serialized story, Gamaliel Bailey made a point of offering all new *National Era* subscribers the back issues they would need to catch up on *Uncle Tom's Cabin*. When the novel was completed in the *Era*'s pages, the initial print run of five thousand books sold out in under a week. The book sold perhaps as many as 100,000 copies in its first two months in print and 300,000 in one year, making it the most commercially successful nineteenth-century American novel (and it sold even better in Great Britain).[20]

Stowe's story enabled antislavery arguments to reach many who had previously seemed inured. *National Era* correspondents wrote to the paper of the serialized novel's great success in "enlisting" the "sympathies" and overcoming the "prejudices" of "many persons heretofore violently opposed to everything of an Anti-Slavery nature." John Jay celebrated that "'Uncle Toms Cabin' is revolutionizing public opinion in circles heretofore inaccessible." With Stowe's novel having "awakened a never ceasing-interest in behalf of the slave," Free Soilers challenged "can there be any finality to the compromise when there is no finality to Uncle Tom?" John Greenleaf Whittier even expressed "*Thanks* for the Fugitive Slave Law!" since it "gave occasion for 'Uncle Tom's Cabin'!"[21]

Uncle Tom's Cabin clearly sensitized new groups of Northerners to the horrors of the domestic slave trade and generated new ire against the Fugitive Slave Act. It was unclear, though, the degree to which this cultural phenomenon could translate into antislavery political gains, with so many Northern politicians hoping to maintain party unity by silencing divisions over slavery, and with such a large segment of the book's readership—middle-class Northern women—unable to vote. Though it is difficult to quantify the book's immediate political impact, John Brooke persuasively argues that the novel, along with a range of stage adaptations, exercised powerful antislavery influences that helped to unmoor a wide range of Northerners, but especially disillusioned evangelical Northern Whigs, from decaying party structures. And in the short term, at a minimum, the novel (and the expectation of future contributions from Stowe) had helped win the influential Free Soil *National Era* thousands of new subscribers.[22]

The Promises and Perils of Coalition Politics

Outside of Washington, Free Soilers in many Northern states attempted to improve the prospects of political antislavery through a series of experiments in coalition politics. In many of these efforts, Free Soilers attempted to trade state power for opportunities to elect antislavery men to Congress, where they could most directly contest the Slave Power. Many of these coalitions coupled Free Soilers with Democrats of questionable antislavery credentials, but in most places coalition with Whigs seemed ill-advised as long as they controlled the White House and oversaw proslavery federal policy. As both major parties' national commitments to the new compromise became harder and harder to overlook, coalition efforts eventually became difficult, or impossible, to sustain.

Preferring Democratic economic policies and the name Free Democrats, Senator Chase vigorously promoted coalition between Ohio Free Soilers and old-line Democrats. Now that antislavery men were electing a substantial number of officeholders, Chase argued, political abolitionists could no longer afford a one-idea strategy, since as legislators they would have to vote on other issues. After the controversial 1849 deal that sent Chase to the U.S. Senate and repealed many of the state's Black Laws, antislavery Democrats and some Free Soilers saw continued coalition as a chance to both promote antislavery political action and end Whig dominance on the Western Reserve. Other Free Soilers, however, disputed Chase's claim that Free Soilers' "natural sympathies are with the Democracy." Former Liberty man Edward Wade, for example, scorned the "depraved bastard called Democracy . . . as I would an imp from Hell." Friction between coalitionists and advocates of strict independence wracked the Ohio Free Soil Party, even as the two positions' leading exponents, Chase and Giddings, trusted and respected each other far more than did their rank-and-file enthusiasts.[23]

In early 1850 some Ohio Free Soilers grew optimistic about using coalition to again trade state office for congressional power, but the Democratic state convention surprisingly abandoned the Proviso. Frustrated Free Soil legislators consequently held the major parties hostage in the state House of Representatives, but Whigs and Democrats, shockingly, came together to overcome Free Soil obstruction. Disillusioned, coalitionist Free Soil editor Edward Hamlin graphically bewailed the treachery: "The Democratic party have . . . no *virtue*. They are quietly lying on their backs, with [anti-Proviso presidential hopeful Lewis] Cass holding their legs, while the Whig Party is ravishing them. The result will be the birth of a bastard, half hunker Whig & half hunker Democrat." Former coalitionists now conceded that Free Soilers would have to field an independent ticket, and though they polled only 5 percent of the 1850 gubernatorial vote (barely better than the best Liberty showing), the third party continued to play an influential disruptive role, and as Democratic opposition to the Fugitive Slave Act emerged in Ohio, prospects for coalition revived. Indeed, in late 1850, Chase's original allies in the 1849 legislature, John F. Morse and Norton Townshend (a former Liberty man) respectively won the speakership of the Ohio House and a seat in Congress running as Free Soil–Democratic coalition candidates. Chase was especially pleased that Townshend's election would provide another congressional "colaborer, devoted to our great cause." Chase, perhaps prematurely, claimed Townshend's victory as "complete vindication" of the coalition strategy.[24]

Democratic state legislators, however, refused to support another Free Soil senator. Instead, with the help of some ex-Whig Free Soilers, the Whigs elected Judge Benjamin Wade (Edward's brother), a Whig Party loyalist whom Giddings nonetheless considered a sincere "hater of slavery." With the continued instability of Ohio politics, Free Soilers remained influential and experienced occasional successes, like the 1852 election of Edward Wade to Congress, but they clearly could not control the state as Chase desired. So in 1851, to the dismay of more resolute third-party men, Chase backed a Democratic gubernatorial candidate over Free Soiler Samuel Lewis, Chase's old Cincinnati Liberty ally. Chase's interest in working with Ohio Democrats increased tension within the state's largely ex-Whig Free Soil ranks, but Chase sat securely in the Senate with a term that ran into 1855. From that chamber his speeches could forcefully promote opposition to the Slave Power, and Free Soil allies rightly celebrated that they could at least be "sure of one reliable advocate of Liberty" in the Senate "for the next six years." A contingent of Chase backers, like Hamlin and Townshend, praised Ohio Democrats for declining to endorse the 1850 Compromise, but most Free Soilers shared Giddings's commitment to third-party independence as the 1852 election approached and both parties' *national* leaders committed themselves to the congressional settlement.[25]

Free Soilers elsewhere pursued similar, if usually less sustained, coalition strategies. Though it dissolved after the 1849 elections, a Connecticut Free Soil–Democratic coalition elected three anti-extensionist congressmen who spurned Cobb's candidacy in the speakership battle. Democratic leaders in Hartford, however, refused to continue working with the "few miserable free soilers" who controlled a balance of power in their state legislature.[26] In Democratic-dominated Michigan, Free Soilers formed a rare alliance with the Whigs after Proviso Democrats made peace with the state party's Cass wing. Working together, Michigan Free Soilers and Whigs defeated Cass lieutenant and Fugitive Slave Law supporter Alexander Buel and elected two coalition congressmen. In Wisconsin, efforts to unite Free Soilers and Democrats at first seemed promising, but ended in disaster as Democrats outmaneuvered the once potent Wisconsin Free Soilers, and many returned to their pre-1848 allegiances. Still, in 1850 Free Soilers instead combined with Whigs to reelect antislavery congressmen Free Soiler Charles Durkee and James Doty, an anti-extension Democrat (and a scatterer in the 1849 speakership contest) who had been jettisoned by local party bosses.[27]

In New York, the well-chronicled failure of coalition was most dispiriting. Even the staunchest Barnburners receded into the Democratic Party, vainly believing they could transform it from within. While Free Soilers had outpolled Cass Democrats in 1848, the election had also demonstrated the futility of a go-it-alone approach in the Empire State. Though only winning a plurality statewide, Whigs controlled thirty-two of thirty-four congressional seats and won nearly as daunting majorities in the state legislative elections. To prevent a long period of Whig dominance, Barnburners returned to the Democratic fold. At first, ex–Free Soilers insisted on the 1848 Buffalo platform. "There is no doubt in my opinion," Preston King claimed, "that the whole party will fight together the battle of freedom." Even Seth Gates (the former Whig congressman who became a Liberty man and then the Free Soil lieutenant gubernatorial candidate) praised "the Union," since "nine tenths of the hunkers have come in cordially & done well." A year later, though, Gates complained about "how shabbily the Democracy have acted in this state," and "how nearly they ignored the glorious Buffalo Platform." When New York Democrats upheld the 1850 Compromise, most Barnburners grudgingly toed the party line. Even Henry Stanton, a former Liberty leader and once an immediatist abolitionist lecturing agent but now a Barnburner state senator, acquiesced, evincing how far his escalating political ambition had eclipsed his commitment to moral reform. The New York Democracy soon descended into complicated factional struggles among Barnburners, "Soft Shells" who welcomed the 1848 bolters back, and embittered "Hard Shells" who opposed reunion.[28]

Vermont Free Soilers, by contrast, found the Democratic Party courting *them* as early as 1849. The resulting Vermont Free Democratic coalition forcefully advocated the Wilmot Proviso and abolition in the District of Columbia. Abolitionist Democrats like Edward Barber enthusiastically championed the alliance, but many of his co-partisans reluctantly rejoined those who had deserted in 1848, and expressed discomfort at "fighting shoulder to shoulder with the party of '*one idea*.'" The coalition nonetheless gave its first gubernatorial nomination to a former Liberty man, and Barber, at least, appreciated that "the Liberty men have been acting independent of both of us for years & have been fighting the Whigs as hard as they have the democrats." Clearly, Vermont Free Soilers recognized the new anti–Slave Power third-party's deep debts to its Liberty predecessor. After the Compromise, though, dissension within the coalition mounted as many Vermont Democratic leaders deemed the Wilmot Proviso "dead," and grew frustrated with "ultra Free Soilers" who demanded repeal of the Fugitive Slave Act. Although Vermont Free Democrats never defeated the dominant Whig Party in a state or congressional contest, they consistently ran well ahead of recalcitrant Hunker Democrats through 1851. As elsewhere, though, the 1852 presidential election would unravel the alliance.[29]

In Massachusetts, coalition bore its most valuable fruit—the election of Charles Sumner to the U. S. Senate. In 1850 with the albatross of Webster's Seventh of March Speech around Whig necks, prospects for a Free Soil–Democratic collaboration appeared especially promising. Despite skepticism from some ex-Whigs, several young Free Soil managers, led by former shoemaker and savvy political operator Henry Wilson, worked hard to promote coalition, a strategy that seemed especially tantalizing in the 1850 state elections, since the next legislature would elect a new senator. Free Soilers eagerly anticipated an opportunity to barter state offices for the post in Washington, and during a summer 1850 meeting, John Greenleaf Whittier persuaded state committee chairman Charles Sumner to make himself available for a coalition nomination. Democrats and Free Soilers fielded their own tickets, but both recognized that majority-rule electoral laws would allow them to work together in the legislature to direct state politics. Although Whigs ultimately won seven of ten congressional races, voters reelected Free Soilers Horace Mann and Charles Allen, and the increasingly antislavery Democrat Robert Rantoul won in a runoff after Free Soiler (and former perennial Liberty gubernatorial candidate) Samuel Sewall withdrew. In state-level elections, Whigs won their expected plurality, but if Democrats and Free Soilers could cooperate, they would control the state government—and the senatorial selection.[30]

National Free Soil leaders like Chase, Giddings, and Bailey giddily interpreted these results as heralding the coming of a Massachusetts Free Soiler to join Chase and Hale in the senate. Even Joshua Leavitt, once zealous for Liberty independence, expressed excitement about Sumner's prospects. In Boston, Wilson thus led Free Soil legislators to support Democrat Francis Boutwell for governor in exchange for a Democratic pledge to elect Sumner. This bargain highlights Free Soilers' continued prioritization of congressional over state power; though Free Soil legislators outnumbered Democrats, the latter party was given nearly all the state offices in exchange for the Senate seat. After Free Soilers helped elect Boutwell, though, about thirty "Indomitable" Massachusetts House Democrats, led by the onetime anti-gag Whig but now doughface Democrat Caleb Cushing, balked. Though Sumner led on ballot after ballot, he consistently fell short of a majority. Respected physician, reformer, and noted advocate for the blind, Samuel Gridley Howe (who also had won fame in the 1820s for his heroism as a volunteer fighter in the Greek Revolution) worked the lobbies vigorously on Sumner's behalf, noting that many Whig representatives "in their souls" preferred Sumner, but "their souls are not their own." Free Soil legislators faced further setbacks as they failed to pass either a new personal liberty law or resolutions condemning the Fugitive Slave Act. But they finally reaped the coalition's crucial harvest when a bare majority broke the four-month stalemate and elected Sumner.[31]

Antislavery politicians who privileged congressional agitation viewed Sumner's election as a momentous, "inspiring" victory. Whittier asserted, overoptimistically, that Sumner's triumph would spell the "certain [d]oom of the wicked Slave Laws." Even New York Barnburners supported Sumner's Senate bid, notwithstanding the tentative course they pursued in their own state. And perhaps no one relished Sumner's entrance into the Senate more than Chase, who looked forward to consulting regularly with a new antislavery colleague.[32]

As months passed, though, supporters at home grew "much perplexed at the utter silence" of Senator Sumner. Finally resolving, after seven months in Washington, to speak out against what he still referred to as the "Fugitive Slave *Bill*" (since calling it an "Act" implied accepting its legality), Sumner struggled to gain the floor. When Sumner proposed his motion for repeal, now ready to deliver a long-rehearsed antislavery tour-de-force, his colleagues refused to grant him the customary privilege of speaking on his motion. Stunned and exasperated, Sumner staked all on a risky strategy of bringing in his speech collaterally during appropriation debates slated for the session's final week. Appearing resigned to save the oration for the next session, Sumner cleared his desk and sat patiently, engaging in the sort of stagecraft that John Quincy Adams had used so fruitfully a decade earlier in the other house to goad Southerners into discussion of slavery. On August 26, Virginia Democrat Robert M. T. Hunter (the former speaker of the 26th House) gave Sumner an opening with an amendment designed to defray the costs of enforcing the Fugitive Slave Act by reimbursing "extraordinary expenses" of federal officers. Sumner quickly moved his own amendment demanding that no additional monies be allocated towards executing the Fugitive Slave Act and also, he added casually, the repeal of "said act." Sumner then commenced the tirade he had been planning for months.[33]

Sumner's speech, later titled *Slavery Sectional, Freedom National*, condemned as "absurd" the major-party claims "that there is a final settlement, in principle and substance, of the question of slavery, and that all discussion of it is closed." Trying to prevent discussion of slavery had become as futile as an "attempt to check the tides of the ocean, the currents of the Mississippi, or the rushing waters of Niagara." Moving into learned legal disquisitions on the Constitution and on alleged fugitives' rights to a jury trial, Sumner concluded "that the Constitution nowhere recognizes property in man, and that, according to its true interpretation, freedom and not slavery is national, while slavery and not freedom is sectional." Sumner's nearly four-hour-long harangue touched off a debate in which over a dozen senators spoke at length. While Sumner's amendment failed 47–4, his speech further energized Free Soil assaults on the Fugitive Slave Law and the parties that supported it. A longer version of Sumner's speech became a widely circulated Free Soil pamphlet, and antislavery Northerners as diverse as Harriet Beecher Stowe and Barnburner Bradford Wood passed on their plaudits. Even Garrisonian David Child told Sumner that, "with the exception of Uncle Tom's cabin, nothing has occurred in the whole history of the slave question in the United States, that has consoled me so much under the sting and the shame of Southern usurpations and Northern treachery."[34]

The Election of 1852 and Its Aftermath: The Final Battle of the Slave Power Parties

Notwithstanding the excitement over Sumner's oratory, the approaching presidential contest looked far less auspicious than had the 1848 election. This time Free Soilers, or Free Democrats as they widely called themselves now, offered no overwrought predictions of third-party victory. (From this point forward, the terms "Free Soiler" and "Free Democrat" are used roughly interchangeably.) As it would turn out, the most important result of the 1852 election was its foreshadowing of the Whig Party's coming decline. Torn by sectional dissension over the compromise measures, the Whig Party was also further undermined by heightened popular political emphasis on temperance and anti-immigrant nativism. Many Free Democrats approached this enthusiasm for prohibitionist and nativist politics warily, but they strove nonetheless to help further break down the Whigs as the more vulnerable of the two Slave Power parties. Then, as Free Democrats observed the Whig Party's apparent disintegration in the wake of the 1852 election, antislavery men eagerly awaited new opportunities to further consolidate enemies of the Slave Power.

During the preceding year, Free Democrats had harbored diverse opinions about how to best pursue anti–Slave Power politics in the next election. Thinking selectively of the positive results of coalition, some Democratic-leaning leaders like Bailey, Chase, and Vermont's Edward Barber hoped for a new antislavery Democratic party and even fantasized that the national Democrats might nominate an acceptable candidate on a platform recapitulating the 1848 Buffalo resolutions.[35]

Those who preferred an independent third-party strategy spearheaded a September 1851 national gathering of the Friends of Freedom "for the purpose of consulting together as to the next Presidential canvass, and to harmonize and unite all the sentiment of the nation opposed to the slave power." Meeting in Cleveland and guided by Giddings, the assembled Free Democrats aimed to establish that they would once again be a disruptive antislavery force in presidential politics. A diverse antislavery group, including such radicals as Lewis Tappan and Francis LeMoyne, enthusiastically condemned the fugitive "bill of abominations," the Slave Power, and both major parties. The Cleveland attendees also appointed a formal committee to arrange the next year's third-party nominating convention. This group ultimately selected Pittsburgh for the meeting and scheduled it for after the major parties had nominated, placating Free Soilers who still eyed a broadened coalition.[36]

As the presidential campaign approached, it seemed evident to Free Soilers at least that the most pressing issue should be "opposition to the slave-catching law." It was unclear, however, if the Northern electorate shared this view. It was painfully obvious that Whig and Democratic leaders did not. First the Democrats nominated New Hampshire doughface Franklin Pierce for president. Adopting a platform endorsing the compromise measures, the assembled Democrats pledged to "resist all attempts at renewing, in congress or out of it, the agitation of the slavery question."[37]

The Whig Party offered antislavery voters little more. Once again Whig leaders attempted to straddle the concerns of Northern and Southern constituents and this time satisfied neither. President Fillmore entered his party's nominating convention as the pro-Compromise Southern favorite, while Mexican War hero Winfield Scott attracted the support of anti-Compromise Northerners allied with William Seward. Recognizing Scott's Northern strength on the convention floor, Southern delegates insisted that the party draft a pro-Compromise platform before choosing candidates. The resulting platform, much like the Democrats', explicitly denounced further antislavery "agitation." Only after Scott's managers promised his approval of these resolutions could he beat out Fillmore and a small bloc of Webster supporters in a bitter fifty-three-ballot contest.[38]

Free Democrats concluded that both parties had "deliberately sold their followers to the Slave Power." In their twin pro-Compromise platforms, the parties' convergence seemed to echo the brief flirtations of some major-party leaders the year before with a Southern-centered "Union party" movement. Though that impulse had ultimately petered out, it further indicated to Free Soilers that the major parties stood united in an effort to kill the Free Soil threat and "maintain the Union by *nationalizing slavery*." Consequently, with the 1852 major party conventions' "complete surrender to the slave Power" and ridiculous proscription on "talking against" the Fugitive Slave Act, Free Soilers became ever more convinced that "on the Free Democracy, alone, now rest the last hopes of Freedom." The Vermont Free Democratic Convention asserted that there had "ceased to be any distinguishing principles and measures of public policy between the self styled National Whigs and National Democrats . . . both having placed themselves upon sectional pro-slavery platforms." Indiana Free Soilers similarly proclaimed that the major parties had "outlived the questions which called them into life." With both the Whig and Democratic parties controlled by "ambitious and mercenary leaders" seeking "place and power" in exchange for "unqualified and bare-faced submission to the behests of slavery," the "friends of Freedom" were compelled to "vigorously maintain their separate political organization." After the major-party conventions, even Senator Chase agreed on the necessity of third-party independence.[39]

Meanwhile, as this season of "president-making" proceeded, Free Soilers looked to Congress for new demonstrations that could direct national attention to the Slave Power. In the wake of the major-party nominations, Austin Willey instructed Senator Hale, "The ear of freemen is now turned to Washington to hear the word *advance*." Free Democratic activists praised antislavery congressmen "for their fearlessness and fidelity in the support of the interests of freedom against the encroachments and domination of the slave power" and urged the circulation of antislavery congressional speeches as their best campaign literature against Pierce and Scott. Wisconsin's Free Democratic congressman (and former Liberty man) Charles Durkee, for example, responded with forceful condemnations of the "nearly identical" Whig and Democratic platforms. Durkee again reiterated Free Soilers' rejection of the "cruel and barbarous" Fugitive Slave Act as illegitimate: "While I am forbidden by law of Congress to give a cup of water or a crust of bread to the hungry and thirsty fugitive, or commanded to lay violent hands on his person for the purpose of returning him into a life-long bondage, rest assured sir, I shall treat all such laws with contempt. I shall trample them under my feet, as an outrage on humanity, and an insult to God." Attributing the "disgraceful condition" of national politics to "*African slavery at the South, and party slavery at the North*,"

Durkee noted, however, that "the friends of freedom have gained something; nay, a vast deal, in that they have driven the leaders of party slavery to avow, openly and boldly, what the third party has charged upon them for years, but which has always, till now, been denied, viz: that they love offices and honors more than great principles of right and humanity." Referring back to the previous session's speakership battle, Durkee explained, "that the little band of Free Soilers, during the organization of the Thirty-first Congress, by their integrity and firmness, drove the two old parties into an alliance" in defense of slavery.[40]

Given the attention being drawn to congressional Free Soil agitation, Senators Chase and Hale emerged as clear favorites for the Free Democratic presidential nomination, although neither seemed particularly desirous of the honor. Chase, seeking to avoid the nomination, urged Hale, not entirely disingenuously, that "the spontaneous impulses of the antislavery men every where designate you as the nominee." Hale's closest advisors counseled him to also disavow interest, thinking the nomination might ruin his political future and help elect Pierce by weakening Scott. Even after news leaked that Hale had penned a letter declining to run in the days before the Pittsburgh Convention, Free Democrats, lacking another candidate who could similarly unite the party, nominated Hale anyway in hopes he would feel compelled to accept.[41]

The Pittsburgh Convention incorporated an array of antislavery luminaries, and its leadership was characterized by a deeper moral antislavery impulse than that of the 1848 Buffalo Convention. Though no less a politician than Henry Wilson was chosen to preside, many far more radical abolitionists received prominent roles. The convention even appointed Frederick Douglass, now a radical political abolitionist ally of Gerrit Smith, as one of its secretaries. The resolutions, crafted mainly by Giddings, replicated much of the 1848 platform, with added attacks on the "repugnant" Fugitive Slave Act and "the Whig" and "Democratic wing[s] of the great Slave Compromise party." The convention then tapped Hale with overwhelming support, and nominated George Julian for vice president. Even though it was smaller than the 1848 convention, Free Soilers celebrated that "in every element of real moral force, in dignity, sober, earnestness, ability and *principle*, Pittsburg [sic] far exceeded Buffalo." Most Free Democrats left Pittsburgh eager to campaign against the Slave Power, even knowing they had virtually no chance of winning a single state. With the Pittsburgh Convention nominating Hale in spite of his letter, supporters from all sides beseeched him to run, declaring that only he could unite Free Democratic support. After deliberating for nearly a month, Hale finally penned a brief letter announcing that he did not feel "at liberty" to decline. True to his obligations once he accepted, Hale campaigned vigorously, stumping across the West at a torrid pace.[42]

At first even Gerrit Smith encouraged Hale, but Smith soon wavered, and his rump Liberty Party ultimately erected its own ticket headed by William Goodell. Goodell received only minimal support, concentrated overwhelmingly among a small community of upstate New York radicals. Even Frederick Douglass, who closely associated with this radical Liberty Party remnant, affixed the Hale ticket to his Rochester newspaper's masthead, though Douglass's true preferences remain ambiguous. For much of the campaign, Douglass committed his energies to a far more fervent promotion of Gerrit Smith's bid for Congress, which did not face a Free Soil challenge. At the opposite end of New York's antislavery political spectrum, Barnburners held fast to their reunion with the Democratic Party. Even radical Barnburner Preston King opposed a third-party campaign. Free Democrats lamented this "desertion of friends" and were especially disappointed that John Van Buren and former immediatist Henry Stanton, "the two most powerful Free Soil speakers in the State of New York, in the campaign of 1848" gave their support four years later "to the National Democratic Party, and consequently to the Slave Power."[43]

With their ranks reduced from 1848, Free Soilers knew not to expect victory, but throughout the 1852 campaign season they remained confident that they were working towards a transformation of national politics. "When the fight is over," former Free Soil congressman Joseph Root foretold, "the Northern Whigs will be convinced that it was their truckling to the slave power that broke them down and when the new president makes his appointments and avows his policy the democrats of the free states will find they have been sold. Then perhaps something effective may be *begun* for freedom." Austin Willey similarly predicted, "We can break down the defeated party, then the other falls of necessity. They stand and fall together." Hale lieutenant George Fogg likewise prognosticated that "with the end of the present campaign, one party is destined to be dissolved. Not again, during this generation, will two great national organizations go through the farce of running two candidates upon a common platform" dedicated to "the sustentation of human slavery, and resistance to free discussion."[44]

These enthusiastic Free Democratic analyses notwithstanding, the 1852 presidential campaign more generally was one of the dullest in decades, and turnout dropped to its lowest level since 1836. Both major parties avoided the slavery issue as much as possible, and Franklin Pierce won in a landslide. Winfield Scott won a meager four states as his candidacy disgruntled many Southern Whigs, while the pro-Compromise platform cost him antislavery Whig votes as well. Hale, meanwhile, polled only about 5 percent of the national total.[45]

In many places a resurgent nativism and movement for alcohol prohibition had powerfully weakened the Northern Whig Party. These traditionally Whig issues held widening appeal in the early 1850s and threatened to further destabilize the alliances of the Second Party System. A cross-party groundswell championed the 1851 "Maine Law" prohibiting the sale of alcohol as a model to be emulated across the North. Though these disputes seemed to bear little on the politics of slavery, Free Soilers would soon benefit from their own ability to attract temperance voters. New contention over naturalization and Catholic challenges to Protestant-dominated public schools also weakened party ties in many Northern cities, and the liquor issue dovetailed with nativist opposition to Catholic immigrant cultures that many sober Protestants associated with imbibing. During the 1852 campaign, meanwhile, Scott's ill-conceived attempt to attract support from the growing population of traditionally Democratic Catholic voters backfired and repelled many Whig nativists. The increasing centrality of temperance and nativist politics in many Northern states combined with antislavery Whig dissatisfaction to raise questions about whether the Whig Party could ever again contend for national power.[46]

On the slavery issue, though, most Democrats and many Whigs interpreted Pierce's victory as evidence of popular support for the Compromise of 1850. Free Democratic analysts took different lessons from their second national defeat. Free Democrats explained away the party's decrease from 1848 by arguing that the New York Barnburners who had inflated the earlier total were never truly part of the anti–Slave Power movement. Free Democrats preferred to compare Hale's 150,000 votes to the much smaller 1844 Liberty vote. Free Democrats disputed major-party commentators who claimed "that the Free Democracy is dead, perhaps because Mr. Hale is not elected President." Antislavery men predicted that "great events will soon take place, which cannot fail to test the strength of our free institutions, and Northern men must take their stand." Never before, Free Soilers asserted, had both major parties so unequivocally succumbed to the Slave Power, and as the old economic issues that had differentiated them grew obsolescent, party ties further frayed.[47]

In congressional races too, Free Soilers came up short of their 1848 successes but still celebrated that a persistent third-party bloc could continue to exploit Congress as a national platform for antislavery stand-taking. Free Soilers found reason for optimism in the ongoing presence of Sumner and Chase in the Senate and the election of a new, if small, group of Free Soil Representatives. Back once again was Joshua Giddings, who won a plurality in spite of a gerrymander designed to defeat him. Moreover, Free Democrats elected abolitionist Edward Wade, Giddings's former Liberty challenger, in the district carved partly out of Giddings's old one. In central Massachusetts, another Free Democrat, Alexander De Witt, won election from the region previously represented by Charles Allen. The most exciting result, though, was the victory of Gerrit Smith as an independent abolitionist candidate supported by the Free Democratic Party. In the weeks leading up to the election, Henry Wilson had told Smith, "The cause of Liberty would gain more by your election than by the election of any man in the country."[48]

Gamaliel Bailey provided this small band of committed antislavery congressmen a gathering place where they could caucus, work to convert sympathizers, or simply unwind and develop camaraderie with like-minded members. Bailey and his accomplished abolitionist wife Margaret consciously transformed their home (unlike most congressmen, the Baileys lived in a family household rather than a boarding house) into an antislavery salon. There Free Soilers and potentially sympathetic members like William Seward, Hannibal Hamlin (D-ME), Kinsley Bingham (D-MI), and Thaddeus Stevens (W-PA) were often joined by abolitionist activists like Leavitt, Tappan, and Whittier and noted literary figures, especially the female contributors to Bailey's newspaper, including on rare occasions Harriet Beecher Stowe. By 1851, Bailey opened his house "every Saturday night" to Free Soil congressmen for a "talk and a cup of coffee" (the Baileys did not drink or serve alcohol). George Julian reminisced later that Bailey recognized the "political value" of these soirees and made a point of inviting major-party men "who were tending" in an antislavery "direction" and "were evidently helped forward by the influence of these meetings." Such efforts at antislavery persuasion became ever more promising as the Whig Party continued to splinter.[49]

Within months of the election, some antislavery Whig newspapers began to dissent from their party's "obnoxious" platform and advocate unity among all "honestly opposed to the . . . slave power." With the presidential campaign passed, the losing party seemed on the brink of disintegration, and when it finally crumbled, national politics would be ripe for reorganization. Watching the Whig Party teeter, Free Soilers tried wherever possible to speed its collapse, confident that they might soon reorder politics around a fundamental division over slavery. Giddings asserted: "Let the Whigs disband, and the slave-democracy cannot keep up their organization.—Take from them the outside pressure and they will fall to pieces of their own weight." "For more than twenty years," the *Green Mountain Freeman* reminded readers, "those parties have been constantly assailing, ridiculing and denouncing the Anti Slavery organization, under whatever party name they may have acted, as the one idea party," but now, the Vermont Free Democratic organ explained with intended irony, the Whigs and Democrats, "forgetting all their distinctive principles," had "virtually become one, and that too on the one single idea of upholding Slavery." "The destruction of the Whig party," the paper enthusiastically concluded, "must involve the destruction of the Democratic party also." Then national politics could be transformed into a contest between the "party of Liberty and the party of Slavery." In celebrating the coming "abolition of the Whig Party," Leavitt, the longtime Liberty stalwart, forecast that as "the National Democracy succeeds I suppose, to the position of general conservatism & panic-making, from which the Whigs have been routed . . . the Free Democracy now comes to the position of the radical party, & will carry the country in eight years."[50]

Additionally, as partisan disputes over old economic issues like banking and tariffs were receding, unintended sectional political economic tensions were beginning to emerge around the federal government's role in promoting agricultural improvement. Strict constructionist Deep South Democrats repeatedly defeated reformers' efforts in the late 1840s and early 1850s to establish a federal agricultural bureau and opposed, albeit unsuccessfully, the subsidization and extensive circulation of the Patent Office's detailed agricultural reports. Even though there seemed to be little that was overtly sectional in these proposals, Northern agricultural reformers saw their pet projects impeded by Southern paranoia over expansion of federal bureaucratic capacity and thus found new merit in abolitionist warnings about slaveholders' disproportionate congressional sway.[51]

Whig electoral setbacks in 1853 seemed to offer new promises of furthering Free Soilers' goal of breaking down the old parties and reorienting national politics around slavery. Giddings's Ohio organ exulted that elections in early 1853 "appear to have pretty much annihilated the Whig party" in Connecticut and Rhode Island and predicted that Northern Pierce Democrats would soon face similar electoral retribution. New Hampshire Free Soilers improved dramatically on their previous results and predicted that Hunker Democrats' "God-blaspheming, man-enslaving tyrant worship" would soon "come to an end."[52]

Many of these results, however, are perhaps better attributed to resurgent nativism and the movement for alcohol prohibition than strictly to antislavery mobilization. While most Free Soilers preferred to focus on slavery, disputes regarding the Maine Law provided a potent reagent that further dissolved traditional party loyalties, often to the benefit of antislavery men, most of whom supported temperance anyway, as did "at least nineteen-twentieths of the Free Soil voters" in Connecticut according to one (probably exaggerated) estimate. Furthermore, Free Soilers, and Liberty men before them, had long believed that breaking down the Second Party System in the North would end the Slave Power's ascendancy in national politics. Though many antislavery men distrusted nativism and considered the Maine Law secondary to the slavery issue, they saw much promise in the Whig Party's further disintegration.[53]

Even where anti-liquor politics dominated the political reorganization, as in Maine and Connecticut, for example, pro-temperance Free Soilers formally emphasized the liquor issue as a way to break down the old parties. In Vermont, where the Maine Law cause was also influential, Free Soilers secured a balance of power in the legislature, with which they hoped to elect a Free Democratic senator. While the state legislature deadlocked and never selected a senator, Free Soilers used their power in Montpelier to make ex-Liberty man Horatio Needham speaker of the state House, and this apparent "prostration" of Vermont's long-dominant Whig Party seemed to mark the beginning of a "political revolution."[54]

Nowhere, though, were signs of the times so propitious as in Ohio and Wisconsin. Throughout 1853, Ohio Free Soilers asserted that "the fallow ground of party is better broken up now than ever before." Many antislavery Ohio Whigs despaired at their party's pro-Compromise leadership, and by the summer of 1853, the Ohio Whig Party appeared "to be perishing of atrophy." Even when the Ohio Democrats swamped their opponents, Free Soilers cheered gubernatorial candidate Samuel Lewis's (a former Liberty man) impressive gain over Ohio's 1852 Free Democratic presidential vote—Lewis winning over 17 percent of the vote compared to Hale's 8.8 percent the year before. The Whig share in the gubernatorial contest dropped to barely 30 percent. As the only pro-temperance candidate, Lewis's impressive gain stemmed partly from his appeal for anti-liquor voters, but if Free Democrats' goal was to promote the destruction of one of the two major parties, in Ohio at least, they seemed well on their way. In Wisconsin, they seemed to be all but there. Free Democrats absorbed nearly all of the state's reeling Whig Party on a new People's ticket, and their ex-Liberty gubernatorial nominee polled about 40 percent of the state vote. Across much of the North, it seemed to Free Soilers that, given the major parties' deepening struggles to offer compelling competing stances on the most important issues of the day, the Second Party System might well be facing imminent implosion.[55]

By the time the Democratic Congress elected on Pierce's coattails convened in late 1853, many Free Soilers were optimistic that they were witnessing the calm before a massive sectional storm. While alcohol and nativism had played prominent and disruptive roles in state politics, several national issues loomed that might reignite conflict over slavery. The Fugitive Slave Act, for one, remained deeply unpopular among many Northerners, owing not least to the continued dispersion of *Uncle Tom's Cabin*. Moreover, the expansionist agenda of President Pierce and congressional Democrats portended revived strife over slavery extension.

* CHAPTER SEVEN *

The Nebraska Outrage and the Advent of the Republican Party, 1853–1855

Notwithstanding the presumed sectional harmony established by the Compromise of 1850 and seemingly confirmed by Franklin Pierce's overwhelming victory, most Free Soilers foresaw that the coming presidential term would force new fights over slavery. With the Whig Party in precipitous decline, prospects seemed increasingly bright for reorienting national politics around a fundamental divide between slavery's supporters and opponents. When the Kansas-Nebraska Act returned slavery to the center of mainstream political debate, Free Soil congressmen deftly managed the fallout to help mobilize a new anti–Slave Power coalition built on the Whig Party's ruins. Though antislavery organizers had to first confront the shocking success of the anti-immigrant "Know Nothing" Party, most political abolitionists maintained their longstanding conviction of cross-sectional parties' inherent proslavery biases and trusted that the nativist party would necessarily prove ephemeral. As conflict over slavery in Kansas became the dominant national issue in the mid-1850s, political abolitionists worked to ensure that Northern politics would soon be controlled by a Republican Party committed to their longstanding goal of divorcing the federal government from slavery.

The Kansas-Nebraska Act and the Independent Democrats' Response

When President Pierce entered the White House as a landslide victor, many Americans touted the end of sectional conflict. More knowing observers understood that, as long as slavery remained, discord would inevitably resurface. To most antislavery analysts, it seemed that new agitation would concentrate primarily on Spanish Cuba, after which many Southern Democrats had lusted for some time. From the get-go, President Pierce signaled his designs on slaveholding Cuba by appointing "notorious" Louisiana expansionist Pierre Soulé to represent American interests in Madrid. Pierce's hopes of acquiring Cuba as a new slave state made it painfully obvious to Free Soilers that he would acquiesce in "whatever the Slave Power asks." Many Free Democrats, instead of fearing the new aggressions, emphasized the absurdity of staking national politics, and potentially international war, on the goal of annexing the Spanish sugar island. In the spring of 1854, the Cuba issue further fueled anti–Slave Power fires when news leaked of the Ostend Manifesto, a diplomatic memorandum averring support for purchasing Cuba if possible, and invading if necessary to protect slavery.[1]

But it was primarily domestic territorial policy that once again made slavery the controlling issue in national politics. In this case, manifest destiny had already become further entwined with sectionalism in the competition for federal railroad support. For many Americans, North and South, the most pressing national policy questions revolved around the proposed construction of a transcontinental railroad to better link eastern American commercial centers to Pacific coastal ports that were ideally situated to enhance the nation's position in the lucrative China trade. Southern boosters sought to establish a route from New Orleans across Texas, both to advantage Gulf commerce and to facilitate slavery's southwestern extension. Consequently, Pierce's minister to Mexico, South Carolinian James Gadsden, negotiated the expensive purchase of barren land that now comprises southern Arizona to ensure a passable southern right of way to the West Coast; abolitionists, of course, derided Gadsden's treaty as yet another concession to "the Slave Power, whose behest is little less than law at Washington." Expansionists further north argued that a road to the San Francisco Bay with a terminus at Chicago or St. Louis made far more sense. To enable either the central or northern route, though, Congress would have to again venture into the sensitive business of creating new federal territories, this time out of the large remaining northern portion of the Louisiana Purchase (bounded by the state of Missouri and the Missouri River on the east and the Continental Divide on the west).[2]

By 1853 Stephen Douglas, an ambitious expansionist and not coincidentally an owner of property whose value seemed sure to skyrocket if Chicago became the Pacific route's starting point, determined that he could wait no longer. Senator Douglas had already proposed bills to organize the remainder of the Louisiana Purchase as the Nebraska Territory as early as 1845 in the House and 1848 in the Senate, but neither had been taken up for debate. As American settlers trickled into Nebraska, they dispatched a delegate to Washington, further prodding Douglas and his "Representative Shadow"

William Richardson (D-IL), conveniently the chairmen of the two congressional committees on territories. Signs of a coming controversy appeared in the winter of 1853, when Richardson introduced a bill to establish the Nebraska Territory. This proposed "increase of free power" was, Joshua Giddings wrote, "ominous to the downfall of slavery," as demonstrated by the bitter Southern opposition when a highly sectionalized (and poorly attended) House passed Richardson's bill, 98–43. Free Soilers then watched closely as Southern senators, balking at a new territory where slavery was already barred by the 1820 Missouri Compromise, defeated the 1853 Nebraska bill on the session's final day.[3]

Observing these developments, Free Soilers anxiously predicted that the next Congress would attempt to open Nebraska to slavery. Aware that "one of the first measures likely to come before Congress, will be the Nebraska Territory Bill," Free Soilers fully expected Senate President Pro Tempore David Atchison, a western Missouri slaveholder, to press for repeal of the Missouri Compromise as a condition for the new bill's passage. Atchison had reluctantly supported the 1853 Nebraska bill to avoid antagonizing expansionist constituents and St. Louis railway boosters, but the rough-and-tumble planter made clear during the intervening summer that he would now demand slavery's admission into the new territory.[4]

After the New Year's holiday concluded, Congress stood poised for its greatest sectional conflict in years as Douglas prepared to introduce a modified Nebraska bill. The "friends of liberty," Giddings asserted, welcomed the opportunity to "drive members to take their positions either for or against slavery." The *Green Mountain Freeman* echoed Giddings:

> We are gratified nonetheless that this bold step has been taken; for it drops a large portion of the disguise, which the Slave Power has ever assumed to conceal her settled design of complete supremacy, and which has prevented the North from believing what, during the last three years, has become undeniable, that the question of Liberty or Slavery is now a national issue, and the next one to be settled by the American people.[5]

Douglas introduced the finalized version of his bill to organize Nebraska on January 23, 1854, after extensive consultation with Atchison and his powerful Southern Democratic messmates (known as the F Street Mess). Douglas would concede much to slaveholding powerbrokers to ensure that the Senate passed his bill to organize Nebraska under "popular sovereignty" rules allowing local settlers to dictate the fate of territorial slavery. The new bill thus abolished the slavery restriction of the Missouri Compromise and, for the first time, proposed to create two territories, setting off the southern part bordering Missouri as the Kansas Territory to increase the likelihood of settlers establishing slavery in at least that portion.[6]

Senators Chase and Sumner immediately requested a postponement, ostensibly to evaluate Douglas's adjusted bill. In fact, they had something else up their sleeves. These Free Soilers, or Independent Democrats as they now sometimes described themselves, sought the delay to alert the Northern public by disseminating a formal address written primarily by Chase, with the aid of Sumner, Giddings, and Gerrit Smith. On January 24, those four and Representatives Alexander De Witt and Edward Wade issued the already prepared "Address of the Independent Democrats in Congress to the People of the United States," or as it came to be known, "Appeal of the Independent Democrats," in both the *National Era* and the more moderate *New-York Daily Times*.[7]

The arguments and the form of the Appeal, as a public document penned and signed by a small group of issue-oriented antislavery congressmen, reflected the decades-old history of political agitation against Slave Power influences in Congress. The Appeal, which Eric Foner aptly describes as "one of the most effective pieces of political propaganda in our history," strove to rouse the Northern electorate against Douglas's Nebraska bill by framing it as a new extreme in the Slave Power's efforts to control federal policymaking. These antislavery propagandists also recast the Missouri Compromise as a "sacred pledge," of which the Nebraska bill was a "criminal betrayal" (notwithstanding years of abolitionist attacks on the 1820 legislation). For decades the South had reaped its benefits, and now, with the people of the free states finally ready to settle Nebraska, Southerners wanted to renege. Much of the Appeal then concentrated on debunking Douglas's canard that the Compromise of 1850 somehow overrode the Missouri Compromise in spirit, if not in law.[8]

As political abolitionists had done for nearly two decades, the Independent Democrats beseeched "the People to come to the rescue of the country from the domination of slavery." In directing attention to the aggressive designs of a "Federal government controlled by the slave power," they drew on the established antislavery discourse about how slaveholders' power presented an "imminent danger" to "the Freedom of our Institutions." Also emphasizing slavery's threat to the dignity of free labor, the Appeal charged that Douglas's bill would transform Nebraska into "a dreary region of despotism, inhabited [only] by masters and slaves," instead of by a "free, industrious, and enlightened population." The Independent Democrats promised, even if they failed in Congress, to "go home to our constituents" and "erect anew the standard of Freedom."

In addition to repeating arguments made originally by Liberty partisans, the Appeal's use of Congress as a forum from which to educate the nation about the Slave Power drew on established third-party antislavery tactics. The Appeal succeeded in enabling the Independent Democrats to use their congressional platform to shape the debate over the Kansas-Nebraska bill. With its extensive publication in antislavery-leaning papers of all party affiliations, the Appeal quickly reached a broad audience. Political abolitionists consequently urged that the "important document" be read widely to galvanize grassroots opposition to Douglas's bill:

> Gather the family around the cabin fireside, put the bright light on the stand, and read that document to every member of your family, and give one evening to the subject of that appeal, and make every one of the household familiar with the principles of freedom, that they may properly execrate the authors of this project to enslave the broad regions of the West. . . . Assemble the people together in every school district, and let every school house erected for the education of the young hear the reading of that appeal to the children and their parents, and then from the school district gathering of the people, let a voice of rebuke go up to Washington.[9]

When the Senate debate resumed on January 30, Douglas responded directly to the Appeal and won it even greater attention. Acting aghast at its attacks, the pugnacious Illinoisan complained that after he had allowed Chase and Sumner the week's postponement, these "Abolition confederates" abused his "act of courtesy" to publish the offensive, incendiary call to arms they had concocted in "secret conclave." In rebuttal, Chase characteristically asserted the political abolitionists' well-established anti–Slave Power policy program: "All that we have ever insisted upon is, that the Territories of this Union shall be preserved from slavery; and that where the General Government exercises the exclusive jurisdiction, its legislations shall be on the side of liberty." Keenly aware of this congressional conflict's political value, Chase thanked Douglas "for having brought it [the Appeal] so prominently before the country. It will now reach thousands and tens of thousands who would not have read it but for the discussion which has taken place here to-day."[10]

The Independent Democrats embraced this intense interest, and Sumner beseeched political abolitionists to petition both houses of Congress to ensure constant discussion of the Kansas-Nebraska bill, much in the way earlier abolitionist petitions had repeatedly reinserted slavery into congressional debate. Sumner urged abolitionist John Jay that congressional Independent Democrats must receive at least one petition for each day and predicted that Jay's prodigious organizational efforts in New York would "tell strongly here." The ensuing antislavery uproar was so dramatic that Giddings, a congressional fixture for fifteen years, reported home, "We are in as great excitement here as I have ever seen and the prospect is that it will increase." The *New-York Tribune*'s correspondent similarly observed, "There is nothing talked of now but Nebraska." A vast array of Northerners responded heartily to the call for anti-Nebraska petitions. One Brooklyn petition measured one hundred feet in length! Another, from the women of the much smaller community of Northampton, Massachusetts, reached nineteen feet. A petition from three thousand New England clergymen and professors, the vast majority of the region's clergy, protested the bill as "a great moral wrong" and touched off another lengthy Senate debate in which Douglas denounced the eminent petitioners and again blamed the Appeal for inciting continued agitation.[11]

The Independent Democrats meanwhile happily exploited this controversy as a flashpoint for the creation of an anti–Slave Power party that could aspire to control the national government. As Senate debate progressed, Chase and Sumner both asserted their expectation of "an inevitable reorganization of parties." "The old matters which have divided" political parties, Sumner averred, "have lost their importance." Slavery could "never be withdrawn from national politics," Sumner continued, until the federal government "erase[d] the blot of Slavery from our national brow." Numerous seasoned abolitionists analogized Sumner's Senate stand against the Kansas-Nebraska bill to John Quincy Adams's famous battles against the Slave Power in the House of Representatives, and Frederick Douglass proudly told Sumner that "all the friends of freedom, in every State, and of every color, may claim you, just now, as their representative."[12]

Free Soil allies across the North appreciated that "the proposition of Douglas to prostitute the Free Territory of Nebraska to slavery" might be used to reenergize antislavery politics and "secure a future Northern delegation of Congress, who will resist to the death the future aggressions of this insatiate monster," the Slave Power. "Clenched fists and set teeth everywhere" demonstrated the intensity of the "hatred that this last, crowning outrage has created toward the Slave power." If the "Nebraska iniquity" passed, it would enable Independent Democrats to rally Northerners of all parties, "Free Democrats, old line Democrats, Whigs," to "beat out the brains of that infernal slave power." "Douglas," Jay asserted, was "doing what no abolitionist could do — arousing the Country to a sense of its danger — & a remembrance of its duty." The more conservative *New-York Daily Times*'s Washington correspondent similarly recognized, although less enthusiastically, that "moderate men fear . . . that the passage of the bill would arouse a storm of indignation in the North, the effect of which would be to give that section completely into the hands of GIDDINGS, GERRIT SMITH, CHASE, SUMNER, and their political friends." Some former Whig outlets, though, like the *Springfield Republican*, "calmly" anticipated the emergence of "new and important arrangements of parties," with every intention of standing for "freedom and liberty, and against slavery and oppression."[13]

At 3:30 in the morning on March 4, Douglas forced a vote and won the support of nearly half the Northern senators voting and all but two Southerners. Notwithstanding the powerful efforts of Chase and Sumner, aided by Seward, Benjamin Wade, and a handful of other Northern Whigs, the Senate passed the Kansas-Nebraska bill, 37-14. Douglas's bill, however, faced a stiffer challenge in the House. Richardson tried to fast-track the Senate bill by referring it to his Committee on Territories, from which it could then be introduced into the House "at an auspicious moment" and "forced through" without debate. Instead, a House majority stymied Richardson and fellow "conspirators" by referring the bill to the Committee of the Whole on the State of the Union, where it would languish behind dozens of other bills and then be subject to a full-dress debate when it finally came up. This antislavery procedural victory put "the bill so far off on the roll of bills to be taken up in order, as to give ample time for the people, through their Legislatures, State Conventions and primary meetings to give their expressions on this new and stupendous aggression of the Slave Power." However, this delay did not dispel fears that presidential patronage could whip enough Northern Democrats into line, as Pierce had clearly staked the "political destiny" of his "depraved administration" on "the policy of extending slavery over Nebraska."[14]

By May 8, Douglas's allies were satisfied they had the votes to get his bill through the House. In Committee of the Whole, Richardson and Georgia's Alexander Stephens (a Whig who would soon switch parties and later would serve as the Confederate vice president) maneuvered vote after vote to postpone each preceding bill on the committee's calendar. When formal debates commenced, antislavery Northerners from all three parties savaged the "iniquitous larceny of freedom's birthright," as Edward Wade dubbed the bill. Giddings delivered an abolitionist tirade condemning the immorality of slavery but thanking the bill's proponents for bringing to a head the "long-pending contest between slavery and freedom." Prefiguring Abraham Lincoln's famous 1858 House Divided speech, Giddings declared it now "obvious to all" that "freedom and slavery" were as incompatible as "Heaven and Hell." Consequently, Giddings cautioned, "this Federal Government must be either separated from the support of slavery," or given over entirely to "the control of the slave power." Even "an earnest and devoted friend of the Democratic party" like Galusha Grow (PA) warned colleagues that if they passed the bill, "you will have destroyed the last breakwater that stands between your rights and the surges of northern Abolitionism."[15]

Notwithstanding widespread Northern outrage at the repeal of the Missouri Compromise, concert in opposition strategy proved elusive. Gamaliel Bailey and ex-congressman Preston King worked the lobbies to organize cross-party cooperation, but old loyalties died hard. Not until May 20 did Bailey succeed in assembling several leading anti-Nebraska men, among them future speaker candidates Nathaniel Banks (D-MA) and Lewis Campbell (W-OH), in a private cross-party caucus, and the bill passed before they could reconvene. On May 22, through a little-used parliamentary gambit, Richardson and Stephens succeeded in discharging the bill from committee to bring it before the House for a final vote. With half the Northern Democrats joining nearly every Southerner, the bill passed 113–100, as the sounds of both "hissing" and "prolonged clapping" rang across the galleries and the House floor.[16]

Unsuccessful as Bailey and King had been in outmaneuvering the Slave Power, their efforts helped lay the groundwork for a cross-party anti-Nebraska union. The thirty anti-Nebraska members who reconvened after the bill's passage discussed plans for founding a new "Republican" fusion party, but took no definitive public action. Instead a much larger meeting of anti-Nebraska members assembled to issue an "Address to the People of the United States," which asserted a commitment to restoring the Missouri Compromise and blocking all "further aggressions of Slavery." The meeting, however, voted down Lewis Campbell's more radical draft and declined to advocate a new anti-Nebraska party. Though Free Soilers found the address too circumspect, they nonetheless lauded the apparent unanimity of antislavery sentiment among those who had opposed Douglas's bill.[17]

Most Free Soilers, though disgusted at the new law, saw real promise in this unprecedented Slave Power aggressiveness. Free Soilers vigorously fanned the conflagration of anti–Slave Power sentiment in response to the Kansas-Nebraska Act. Within weeks of the bill's passage, Giddings could celebrate overwhelming Northern outrage, even among supporters of the 1850 compromise. Familiar barbs demeaned the forty-three Northern representatives who had voted for Douglas's bill and "marched into the field under the crack of the slave-driver's whip" as "chattels" in the "Congressional slave market." So great was the ire against Douglas, that he famously quipped that he "could travel from Boston to Chicago by the light of my own [burning] effigy." In Giddings's Ashtabula County, the Friends of Freedom wryly objected that this wave of effigy construction represented "the greatest indignity and insult" to the straw.[18]

Anti-Nebraska Fusion: Opportunities, Challenges, and Promise

Free Soilers, or Independent Democrats, immediately recognized that the Kansas-Nebraska Act might provide the fulcrum for the national realignment political antislavery men had so long desired. From the outset, congressional Free Soilers had structured the legislative debate as a conflict over the Slave Power. By the time Douglas's bill passed, Independent Democrats had become fierce advocates of an anti-Nebraska fusion movement uniting the new law's diverse opponents. With the Whig Party already in shambles in many Northern states, the Kansas-Nebraska Act sounded that party's death knell *and* offered the potential for recruiting Northern Democrats to a winning anti–Slave Power coalition. Urging, "Agitation is the right arm of Liberty," former Free Soilers worked vigorously at the Capitol, on the lecture circuit, and in the press to keep the Slave Power argument front and center before the voting public. As calls for cross-party anti-Nebraska fusion multiplied, sanguine political antislavery veterans like Giddings could "begin to feel confident of a majority of anti-slavery members in the next House of Representatives." Willing to join any "practical combination" committed to the "casting off of all party trammels," political abolitionists aimed to foment a new "revolution" against the "slave power of this nation."[19]

Amid the furor over Douglas's Nebraska bill, two sensational fugitive slave rescue attempts, one successful and one not, further fueled antislavery anger at the Democratic Party. In May 1854, just days after proslavery Democrats' congressional triumph had "deepened the abhorrence with which every attempt to enforce the Fugitive Slave act is regarded in Boston," a federal marshal apprehended Virginia runaway Anthony Burns. Thousands "without distinction of Party" gathered at Faneuil Hall to protest Burns's arrest, while a smaller, more militant, and mostly black group determined to rescue the prisoner. Led by the radical white abolitionist Thomas Wentworth Higginson (who later commanded the first official black regiment in the Union Army), they broke down the jailhouse door but were pushed back by the armed guard. In the melee, shots were fired and a deputy was stabbed to death. Burns meanwhile remained incarcerated. President Pierce, anxious to defend federal law, deployed marines, cavalry, and artillery to Boston, along with a ship to transport Burns to Virginia. The administration also reputedly deterred Burns's master from selling his freedom to abolitionists, so that Pierce could showcase his commitment to the Fugitive Slave Act. With perhaps fifty-thousand Massachusetts men and women observing mournfully, federal troops marched Burns to the vessel that would carry him back to slavery. Dovetailing with the

Kansas-Nebraska Act's "flagrant outrage against Freedom and Free Labor," Burns's rendition stimulated Bay State citizens' anti–Slave Power resentments to new heights.[20]

The rescue a couple months prior of Joshua Glover had attracted similar national attention. Upon receiving news that Glover, a Missouri fugitive, had been apprehended in Racine, Wisconsin, and imprisoned in Milwaukee, longtime political abolitionist editor Sherman Booth rode through the Milwaukee streets supposedly shouting, "To the Rescue!" At an ensuing rally, Booth roused the crowd of over five thousand, a portion of whom then battered down the jail door and freed Glover, who was ultimately escorted to safety in Canada. Four days later Booth was arrested for inciting the jailbreak. The Wisconsin Supreme Court, however, freed Booth from federal authorities by granting a writ of habeas corpus and, more astoundingly, in an extreme formulation of the "freedom national" doctrine, ruled the Fugitive Slave Act an unconstitutional violation of Wisconsin's state rights and therefore inoperable in the state. Abolitionists elsewhere cheered Wisconsin as "the first to nullify that detestable spawn of the Slave Power, the infamous Fugitive Slave Law."[21]

Against the backdrop of the Wisconsin Republican Party's rapid emergence, the Glover rescue and subsequent legal battle surrounding Booth, one of the new party's most prominent and radical leaders, took on added significance. In the weeks before the jailbreak, a February 28 cross-party meeting at a Ripon, Wisconsin, church had called for a new "Republican" Party if the Kansas-Nebraska bill passed. By summer, Free Soilers and Whigs were working together to orchestrate an impressive Republican state convention, of which Booth, though still facing federal charges, was a key organizer. With over a thousand delegates descending on the state capitol grounds, the July 1854 meeting enthusiastically established the new party and adopted resolutions resembling previous Free Soil platforms. District conventions conveniently selected a Free Soiler, a Whig, and an anti-Nebraska Democrat to run as Republicans for Wisconsin's three congressional seats, and the new party elected two of the three and controlled the state legislature, which sent former Liberty man Charles Durkee to the U.S. Senate.[22]

Michigan advocates of anti-Nebraska fusion achieved similar early success. A February 22 fusion meeting in Jackson plausibly challenges Ripon for the symbolic honor of hosting the anti-Nebraska party's founding, although attendees at the first Jackson meeting did not yet call themselves "Republicans." That assemblage proposed a cross-party ticket headed by anti-extensionist Democrat Kinsley Bingham, and five months later, a mass convention in the same town confirmed Bingham's nomination, drafted an anti–Slave Power platform, and inaugurated the Republican Party's first formal state organization. The incipient Michigan Republican Party swept the state elections and elected three of four congressmen.[23]

In antislavery Vermont, Free Soilers especially shaped the new fusion party, as the state's largely antislavery Whig Party joined with third-party men and a smattering of antislavery Democrats. Though Free Democrats had to accept gubernatorial and congressional candidates who simultaneously ran as Whigs, the Whigs adopted the fusionists' antislavery platform and united in support of a Free Soiler for lieutenant governor. When the Whig-Republican ticket won overwhelmingly, Vermont Whigs, an out-of-state antislavery paper observed, were "candid enough to acknowledge the death of their party." "In view of the fact that the aggressions of Slavery through the instrumentalities of the Administration and otherwise, were the only issues," the "friends of freedom" could "safely claim it as an Anti-Slavery victory."[24]

Across the North, pro-Nebraska Democrats suffered defeat after defeat, even in former strongholds like Iowa and New Hampshire. But in many Northern states, the political calculus facing antislavery politicians was complicated by the meteoric rise of the American, or Know Nothing, Party. This imposing new political force arose out of the nativist and anti-Catholic secret society, the Order of the Star Spangled Banner, whose members had received the sobriquet Know Nothings for their practice of claiming to "know nothing" when questioned about the order. Since the beginning of the decade, liquor prohibition and proscription of foreigners had grown increasingly popular among Northern voters. In the post-Nebraska political chaos of 1854, Know Nothings adeptly capitalized on these sentiments, along with a rising antipartisan climate generally, to take advantage of Northern Whiggery's decline at least as effectively as early Republican fusionists did.[25]

Indiana Know Nothings, for example, handpicked the state's anti-Nebraska ticket. In Pennsylvania, an anti-Nebraska Whig won the governorship, while a pro-Nebraska Democrat was chosen canal commissioner — both on the strength of Know Nothing endorsements. Across the Keystone State, Know Nothings scored unprecedented victories. Know Nothing success in the central and western parts of the state, where foreigners were few, though, can be attributed to the movement's emphasis there on temperance and opposition to the Kansas-Nebraska Act.[26]

Nowhere was the Know Nothing triumph as dramatic as in Massachusetts, where the movement incorporated a strong antislavery appeal. With the collapse of the state's Free Soil–Democratic coalition and the weakening of the once-dominant Boston Whig establishment, a political vacuum emerged in the Bay State. Free Soilers attempted to erect a Republican organization to capitalize on welling discontent over the Kansas-Nebraska Act and the rendition of Anthony Burns. In September 1854 they nominated Henry Wilson for governor, but he instead cast his lot with the Know Nothings in exchange for a promise of support for his election to the Senate. The state's demoralized Republicans were "stunned and overwhelmed" by the magnitude of the Know Nothing victory. Winning every state senate seat and all but three in the lower house, Know Nothings ushered in an astonishing political revolution. Nonetheless, the new movement's Republican opponents still looked favorably on "the 'eternal sunset' into which" the Know Nothings had "brought the two corrupt old parties in Massachusetts."[27]

The Know Nothing movement succeeded in its banner state only by coupling a fierce anti–Slave Power program with its antiforeign and anti-Catholic posture. The Know Nothing legislature thus resolved against the Kansas-Nebraska Act, passed a robust personal liberty law, and desegregated the Massachusetts common schools. By appealing to *both* antislavery and antiforeign sentiments, Know Nothings stalled the emergence of the Republican Party as a serious power in state politics. Ultimately, however, national politics would force Massachusetts Know Nothings to choose between nativism and antislavery, and then the Republican Party there would stand poised to emerge from the shadows. In fact, in 1856, antislavery Republicans agreed not to challenge the relatively conservative Know Nothing governor's reelection bid in exchange for the nativist organization's support for the Republican presidential ticket; yet again, when the opportunity presented itself, antislavery men bartered state office for national power.[28]

In other New England states, antislavery Know Nothings similarly prefigured their ultimate prioritization of the slavery issue through their adoption of forceful anti-Nebraska stances and collaboration with antislavery radicals. In the early months of 1855, Know Nothing–led coalitions achieved sweeping wins in Connecticut, Rhode Island, and New Hampshire, but these results could be attributed in large part to reactions against continued "slave rule of the nation" by the "sham democracy." In New Hampshire in particular, anti–Slave Power convictions united the Pierce Democracy's multiple opponents. Free Soilers in that state, which still employed a majority-rule electoral system, thus did not quibble about party labels, reminding voters that "in the multiplicity of parties, candidates, and organizations it should not be forgotten, for a moment, that there is in the field but one party and one set of candidates [Democratic], who are committed to the Nebraska villainy . . . For or against this gigantic conspiracy for the overthrow of Liberty and the eternal supremacy of the Slave power in America, every man in New Hampshire will vote at the coming election." And while in early 1855, Granite State Whigs, Independent Democrats, and Know Nothings ran separate state-level tickets, the three groups shared congressional nominees, all of whom won, including former senator John P. Hale's close ally Mason Tappan. Know Nothings secured a legislative plurality and the governorship, but Independent Democrats nonetheless crowed that "the victory is not of the American organization alone but of all the friends of Freedom, Temperance, and Reform, acting shoulder to shoulder for a common object—the overthrow of the Administration Slavery power in this State, and the establishment of a Freedom and Reform power in its stead." In the new legislature, moreover, Congressman-elect Tappan, who was identified with both the Know Nothings and the Independent Democrats, maneuvered skillfully to ensure Hale's return to the U.S. Senate, even though Hale was not a member of the nativist order.[29]

While the Know Nothing movement clearly captured substantial support from anti-Nebraska insurgents, its core emphasis on nativism and anti-Catholicism raised questions about its ability to endure as a meaningful antislavery protest vehicle. The unpredictable political landscape of New York (with Hard and Soft Shell Democrats still at odds) created unique conditions that particularly foreshadowed the future character of the *national* Know Nothing movement. In the nation's most populous state, Know Nothingism was hardly an antislavery enterprise. Ex-president Fillmore's conservative allies dominated the new party and played down slavery as they challenged William Seward and the antislavery wing that now controlled New York Whiggery. *New-York Tribune* editor Horace Greeley commented that in the Empire State, "Know Nothingism is notoriously a conspiracy to overthrow 'Seward, Weed and Greeley,' and particularly to defeat Gov. Seward's reelection to the Senate." Through 1854, Seward and Albany kingmaker Thurlow Weed remained loyal Whigs, fearful that joining a new fusion party would jeopardize Seward's reelection. Once the 1855 legislature returned Seward to the Senate, many old Whigs followed him, finally, into the burgeoning Republican Party, but conservative Know Nothings remained a formidable force in New York's political cacophony.[30]

The disparate Know Nothing movement so powerfully shaped Northern election outcomes that analysts often had little idea what to make of them. Some Free Soilers distrusted the Know Nothings for their anti-immigrant bigotry and the threat they posed of diverting frustrations against the old parties into issues unrelated to slavery. But a great many confronted the movement with equanimity, viewing it as a mere way station along voters' migrations from the Whig and Democratic parties to anti–Slave Power fusion. The Know Nothing groundswell, Vermont abolitionists appreciated, had at least "become a perfect flaming sword to the old parties." Former Free Soilers rejoiced in the overwhelming defeat of the Kansas-Nebraska Act's supporters, the complexity of the election results notwithstanding. Most auspicious was the anti-Nebraska commitment of what seemed like nearly every Northern congressman elected. Over 70 percent of Northern Democrats who ran for reelection lost. In Ohio, for example, anti-Nebraska candidates, running on a mix of Know Nothing and "People's Party" fusion tickets, won all twenty-one of the state's 1854 congressional elections. Even in New York, where fusionists failed in 1854 to absorb the old Whig Party, antislavery men celebrated that they would have a "strong Anti Nebraska delegation in the next Congress." The former Liberty editor of the Chicago *Free West* thus concluded, "Slavery will now be chained down to its own place. It will be surrounded by an atmosphere of freedom which will suffocate it.... There is now a North and a Freedom Power."[31]

Modern scholars have long debated the extent to which nativist politics decisively shaped the collapse of the Second Party System or simply benefited from the turmoil catalyzed by the Nebraska bill. In many of the Northern states where Know Nothingism was most potent, it clearly capitalized on antislavery sentiment by presenting itself as another anti-Nebraska alternative to the Democratic Party. But despite the Know Nothing movement's astounding success, antislavery men outside the order largely remained convinced that the nativist political upsurge would prove transitory. Early anti-Nebraska fusionists maintained that in approaching *national* contests their antislavery party would necessarily surpass the Know Nothings, as the American Party would fracture along sectional lines much like its Whig predecessor had. Once the pressures of national decision making confronted the nativist party, few American partisans North or South would be able to ignore their section's position on slavery in Kansas, still the most contentious national political issue.[32]

Already by late 1854 there were indications that Know Nothing managers would be forced to look "southward" in choosing a presidential nominee who was either a slaveholder or a "desperately conservative and slavish" doughface like ex-president Fillmore. While the movement recorded its greatest successes in antislavery New England, sizable Know Nothing parties had also emerged in Louisiana and several Upper South states as important landing places for ex-Whigs who sought to protect slavery and union by avoiding sectional conflict and limiting the Northern electorate's growth through immigration. Given early Republicans' anticipations that Southern Know Nothings would seek "to control their brethren at the North, and as heretofore in the old parties, draw them directly or indirectly into subservience to the Slave Power," antislavery spokesmen urged

Northern Know Nothings "to be on their guard." Convinced that "the main element" of Know Nothing "success at the North is to be found in their antagonism to the old pro-slavery parties," political abolitionists remained confident "that on the first step which the Order should take towards favoring slavery, its triumphs would be at an end, and its organization fall to pieces."[33]

In seeding a splinter group called the Know Somethings, antislavery politicos further exposed fissures over slavery in the Know Nothing movement. Early in 1855, Cleveland *Leader* (formerly the Free Soil *True Democrat*) editors Joseph Medill and John Vaughan created the Independent Order of the Friends of Equal Rights, or Know Somethings, as a stratagem for maneuvering Know Nothings more generally into the Republican ranks. Shunning the Know Nothing movement's secrecy and welcoming Protestant immigrants, Know Somethings combined anti-Catholicism with enhanced emphasis on "Resistance to the aggressions of the Slave Power." This new organization developed a potent, though short-lived, presence in northern Ohio and more limited followings in other strong antislavery locales, including parts of Massachusetts and New York. As Salmon Chase prepared to bid for an anti-Nebraska gubernatorial nomination in 1855, he lauded the "bold stand" of the Know Somethings as signaling that Republicans would soon overwhelm Ohio Know Nothings. This Know Something movement also presaged the difficulty that Know Nothings would face when organizing nationally forced them to address slavery. By the summer of 1855, New York Know Somethings demonstrated their progress towards Republican partisanship in a platform asserting that the "issue before the American people is whether Freedom shall be limited to the Free States, or Slavery shall be limited to the Slave States," along with the group's willingness to "unite with all men, under whatever name or organization," to preserve the "Nationality of Freedom."[34]

The votes of Northern Know Nothing legislators for U.S. senators further demonstrated the degree to which antislavery concerns in national politics could supersede Know Nothing partisanship. The election by Know Nothing–dominated legislatures of radicals like Wilson, "that fearless and unbending foe of Slavery," and Hale, not even an avowed Know Nothing, powerfully underscored this point, as did the decision of thirty New York Know Nothing legislators to buck conservative party bosses and reelect antislavery Whig, and soon to be Republican, Senator Seward (though Weed's power over state patronage also helped). Bailey's *Era* lauded Seward's reelection "as a triumph over the combined forces of the Pro-Slavery and Know Nothing parties," pointing out that his victory had hinged on his anti-Nebraska stand. Wilson's win was similarly interpreted as evidence that the "true spirit of freedom controls" the Massachusetts legislature, "whatever may be said of" its "Know Nothing name." In Pennsylvania, the Know Nothing–controlled legislature's inability to agree on a choice of senator also laid bare the tensions over slavery within the nativist party. Washington politicians, outgoing senator Chase gleefully reported, viewed Seward and Wilson, along with newly elected Republican senators Charles Durkee (a Wisconsin former Liberty man) and James Harlan (an Iowa ex-Whig) from states where nativism was weaker, as "hot shot from abolition cannon."[35]

With the House speakership election and presidential campaign approaching in the next year, continued debates over slavery figured to further compel Northern Know Nothings to establish their priorities. Despite his strong personal misgivings about the order, Gamaliel Bailey reassured *National Era* readers that once the Know Nothings began "openly aspiring to the control of the Federal Government," the American Party would have to enunciate a position "either for Slavery or against it." "The fact that the order exists in all the Southern cities, and that it seeks to assume a National form, is very conclusive evidence," the *Ashtabula Sentinel* inferred, "that the Anti-Slavery cause has but little to expect from it." Thus antislavery men looked forward to upcoming contests for the White House and the speaker's chair as opportunities to force antislavery Know Nothings into the budding Republican Party.[36]

Developments over the intervening year made these expectations seem all the more likely. By 1855, Southern Know Nothings complained that Northern nativists' antislavery records were costing their party votes. Abolitionist Republicans recognized a familiar pattern:

> Let the records of the past teach politicians and all concerned, lessons for the future. The Whig party is prostrated and dismembered. The so called Democratic Party was beaten in fifteen States in this Union by over 300,000 popular majority. The anti-slavery sentiment of the country uttering itself at the polls has achieved this. These parties have attempted to evade the American question, the question of slavery, and they are in ruins. The so called American party, (alias Know Nothing.) is striving to ignore, avoid, repudiate, the slavery question, and it too is beginning to be dismembered, and beginning to die.

As political abolitionists surmised, Southern Know Nothings had no intention of tolerating the anti–Slave Power sentiments so prevalent among their co-partisans from the Upper North. The Know Nothing National Council meeting scheduled for June of 1855 in Philadelphia to devise a national platform thus loomed large.[37]

When the Know Nothings convened, Southerners determined to challenge radical delegates like Henry Wilson and the Massachusetts "Abolition" men. Meanwhile, Northern moderates hoped to simply submerge the slavery issue and allow tacit disagreement, much as the Whigs once had. Wilson and his radical cronies, though, were as eager for confrontation as the proslavery men. Indeed, Wilson apparently hoped to foment a schism that would enable him to steer antislavery Know Nothings into the Republican coalition. Southerners insisted on, and ultimately secured, a platform resolution "to abide by and maintain the existing laws upon the subject of Slavery," including the Kansas-Nebraska Act, "as a final and conclusive settlement of that subject." Channeling the frustration of most Northern delegates, Wilson declared, "The adoption of this Platform commits the American party unconditionally to the policy of Slavery—to the iron domination of the Black Power. I tell you, sir, I tell this convention, that we cannot stand upon this platform in a single free State of the North. The people of the North will repudiate it, spurn it, spit upon it." While many antislavery Know Nothings continued to maintain local and state-level American Party organizations, Republicans seized on the Philadelphia meeting to argue ever more convincingly that the national Know Nothing movement was beholden to the Slave Power. Chase commented to Sumner that the result, consequently, had done "great good."[38]

Across much of the North, Know Nothings rebelled against this Philadelphia platform. The Vermont state council formally broke with the national party, founded a state organization committed against slavery extension and the Fugitive Slave Act, and chose to forgo any separate challenge to Vermont Republicans. Maine Know Nothings similarly began to advocate "open nominations in connection with the Republican Party." The contentious Pennsylvania state party conclave held in Reading repudiated the pro-Nebraska plank of the national platform but narrowly declined to adopt stronger antislavery resolutions calling for Fugitive Slave Law repeal.[39]

While conservative Northern nativists still vainly hoped to redirect the party "to let the slavery question alone," it had become increasingly obvious to antislavery Republicans that "the schism in the Nativist organization is likely to be permanent." Like the old parties before it, the Know Nothing attempt "to build up a great national party, outside the question of slavery" was doomed to "utter and most disastrous failure." No longer was it possible to "avoid the struggle, sectional if you please to call it, between the slave-holding and the non-slave-holding interests." Sectional parties would now organize the conflict "between the forces of Liberty and the forces of slavery." Projecting the imminent "End of the Know Nothings," Chicago abolitionists concluded that the party had "been ruined as every other leading party has been by an embrace with Slavery." Henry Wilson, who had done as much to break down the American Party as any member of the Know Nothing order, emphatically pronounced that the party had "received its death-blow at Philadelphia" when it submitted there to "the chiefs of the slave power."[40]

Effectively managing the fallout from the national Know Nothing schism, Chase secured election as governor of Ohio, a bellwether Republican victory. For several months, Chase had pursued a strategy of "keeping the Anti-slavery idea paramount" while prudently avoiding direct attacks on the state's numerous antislavery nativists. Having sufficiently placated most Ohio Know Nothings (and Know Somethings) while still eschewing nativist platform concessions, Chase's 1855 fusion gubernatorial nomination was widely understood as a Republican coup. Though members of the Know Nothing order filled the lesser slots on his ticket, Chase ran on an exclusively antislavery platform and successfully wooed both nativist and antislavery immigrant voters (mostly Protestant Germans). On the hustings, the former Liberty leader reiterated his longstanding conviction that "outside the state limits there was no power to establish slavery." Appealing to themes of unionism and masculinity that coursed through antebellum political discourse, Chase asserted, "Danger to the Union did not lie in manly opposition to slavery, but in submission to that galling yoke, which would grow so intolerable that it could not be borne." For years, "while others were contending about finance and trade," Chase recounted immodestly, "he had thought chiefly of this question, and had regulated his political conduct by it." In response to the nativist movement, Chase explained, "As if by magic then grew up the American party. It arrayed itself in the free states on the side of freedom—in the South it could do nothing but array itself for slavery." Thus, after the Philadelphia Convention, Ohio Know Nothings showed their "back-bone" and joined with anti-Nebraska fusionists like himself. Chase won the race comfortably, even though his refusal to join the nativist order made him anathema to some conservative Know Nothing holdouts. The Republican governor-elect and Congressman Lewis Campbell, Ohio's leading antislavery Know Nothing, alike exulted at the "glorious and complete" victory. Allies across the North applauded the election of so well-known an antislavery radical to preside over the nation's third largest state. Turning "more purely" on "Freedom or Slavery" than other Northern elections, Chase's victory neutralized the Ohio Know Nothing movement and broadcast a powerful signal of the Republican Party's rising fortunes.[41]

The intensifying "great battle" in Kansas further improved Republican prospects by ensuring slavery's continued centrality in national politics. Making a mockery of the Kansas-Nebraska Act's "popular sovereignty," thousands of proslavery Missourians descended on Kansas for the congressional delegate election in November 1854 and the territorial legislature election in March 1855. These "Border Ruffians," incited by Senator David Atchison, waged a concerted intimidation campaign against pro–free state settlers and controlled the election of a territorial legislature that the *Green Mountain Freeman* derided as "Atchinson's [*sic*] bowie-knife and revolver legislature." This assembly, fraudulently elected by Missouri's "mad minions of the Slave Power," quickly moved to criminalize antislavery agitation with a raft of restrictive ordinances rivaling those of any Deep South state. Moreover, the Democratic administration in Washington seemed too "afraid of offending the South" to intervene. By late 1855, a bloody civil war on the Kansas frontier seemed alarmingly probable. Tensions on the ground in Kansas over slavery and slave escapes were heightened by conflicting Northern and Southern gender ideologies about the appropriate roles to be played by women and men in the political, and increasingly militarized, contest for the fate of the Kansas territory. Focusing more on long-term national political consequences, political abolitionists further east warned that "to give up Kansas to the rule of slave-holding despotism" meant augmenting Southern power to establish national "laws more odious and stringent than the execrable Fugitive Slave Act." Events in Kansas thus combined with the Know Nothings' stance at Philadelphia to strengthen the case for a Republican-led assault on the Slave Power.[42]

Though the fledgling anti-Nebraska party as yet lacked an operational national organization, the Republican cause had made impressive progress by the end of 1855. The new party undoubtedly originated from diverse frustrations with the old party system, but none was more significant than the heightening conflict over the place of slavery and slaveholders' power in American politics. Third-party veterans embraced collaboration with more moderate antislavery politicians precisely because the Republican Party offered the most promising opportunity yet to achieve their longstanding goal of a major national party independent of the Slave Power and pledged "to make *Liberty national and Slavery sectional*."[43]

Political abolitionists thus excitedly awaited the next year's presidential contest and before that the arrival of the Congress elected amidst the anti-Nebraska groundswell. Regardless of the disparate partisan tickets on which they had been elected, the vast majority of incoming Northern congressmen had been chosen in 1854 or early 1855 expressly for their opposition to the Kansas-Nebraska Act. For the swelling Republican ranks, this represented a crucial payoff from the ensuing political tumult. Antislavery men controlling even the lower house of Congress could constitute the vital first step towards regeneration of national politics and defeat of the Slave

Power. As the *National Era* issued a prospectus for its tenth volume in late 1855, it knowingly predicted that organization of the House would provide the "first national struggle" between "the Republican and the Pro-Slavery" parties. "On no occasion, perhaps within the present generation," another Republican paper similarly asserted, "has this question of the organization of Congress loomed up in so much significance." The outcome would provide a telling "sign of the future" and dictate political "divisions and combinations of the next year," including in the presidential campaign. The likelihood of an anti-Nebraska triumph in the coming winter's highly anticipated speakership contest augured well for the future of political antislavery, which had come so very far since the initial enunciations of opposition to the "slaveholding power" in the 1830s.[44]

* Interlude Five *

"A New Era in Our History": The Longest Speakership Contest in American History and the First Republican National Victory, 1855–1856

Like so many antislavery political initiatives, the move to consolidate the Republican Party centered first on Congress. After watching slaveholders occupy the speaker's chair for thirty-one of the previous thirty-five years, antislavery men anxiously awaited the organization of the new House with hopes of finally electing an anti–Slave Power speaker. Doing so, they understood, would powerfully cement the Republican Party and establish its supremacy over Know Nothings in antislavery constituencies.

After the wave of indignation at the Kansas-Nebraska Act, Democratic congressional candidates had been routed across the North. Pro-Nebraska Democrats made up less than a third of the House that convened in December 1855, but it remained unclear how, or whether, the diverse opposition would coalesce. When elected in 1854 or early 1855—before Southern Know Nothings had secured a proslavery national platform at the June 1855 Philadelphia party conclave—almost two-thirds of the anti-Nebraska members were also affiliated with the Know Nothing movement; still others had run as candidates of the now all but defunct Whig Party. By the time Northern representatives arrived in Washington, only a fraction of those elected as members of the American Party seemed likely to act with Southern co-partisans. By one historian's estimates, the incoming House included about 121 members who had been elected as Know Nothings and 115 elected as anti-Nebraska candidates, but with only 92 sharing both affiliations. To assemble an anti-Democratic majority, either nativism or antislavery would have to be submerged. Facing even greater confusion than in the 1849 contest, the 34th House voted for speaker into February, balloting 133 times before selecting Massachusetts's Nathaniel Banks by plurality. This time, though, it was the burgeoning antislavery forces who benefited from a plurality election. This struggle and ultimate victory of Banks's anti-Nebraska coalition played a vital role in estab-

lishing anti–Slave Power Republicans, and not the nativist American Party, as the leading party in the North.¹

When the House opened on December 3, amidst packed galleries and unseasonably pleasant weather, only the Democrats stood behind a single candidate: Illinois's William Richardson, the representative most closely identified with the Kansas-Nebraska Act. In choosing "perhaps the most audacious of the whole set of traitors from the North who sold the interests and peace of the Union to the slaveholders of the South," the Democrats intentionally rebuked the anti-Nebraska movement. The Democratic nominating caucus, however, in what would prove a crucial mistake, also passed a unanimous resolution condemning the Know Nothing movement.²

For the Republican and American Parties, unified nominations were impossible. Initial Republican efforts to unite the anti-Nebraska forces had foundered, when only twenty-five members showed up at a November 30 caucus. Two days later, though, seventy anti-Nebraska men unanimously adopted Joshua Giddings's resolution "that we will support no man for Speaker who is not pledged . . . to organize the standing committees of the House by placing on each a majority of the friends of freedom." This, to antislavery veterans, was far more pressing than agreeing at the outset on any particular nominee.³

Three anti-Nebraska frontrunners emerged, all with ties to both the fledgling Republican Party and the Know Nothing movement. Among them, Ohio ex-Whig Lewis Campbell was initially considered the most antislavery but was also the most committed nativist. Massachusetts ex-Democrat Nathaniel Banks had opportunistically used the Know Nothing movement to help him win election on an anti-Nebraska platform, and this disingenuousness actually made him appealing to antislavery Republicans seeking to downplay nativism and focus on combating the Slave Power. If Campbell and Banks both failed, many in the anti-Nebraska ranks planned to try New Jersey's more conservative Alexander Pennington. Elected as a Whig, Pennington seemed to stand the best chance of attracting hesitant Know Nothing conservatives.⁴

When balloting commenced, Campbell led all anti-Nebraska candidates with 53 votes, but it quickly became evident that he could never approach a majority of the 220-some votes being cast. Antislavery men like Giddings led a trickle of support towards Banks, which soon became a flood. By the end of the first week, Banks had reached 100 votes, just 11 shy of a majority. The next Monday, Banks picked up several more and attained his high of 107. He led uninterrupted for the remainder of the contest, consistently within 12 votes, and often as few as 6 or 7, of a majority. Meanwhile, up to forty-one Know Nothings concentrated on Henry Fuller of Pennsylvania. Fuller further intensified the cross-pressures on conservative anti-Nebraska men clinging to the

American organization by announcing his preference for leaving the Kansas-Nebraska Act alone so as to avoid "agitation of the subject of slavery." With Fuller's declaration as added verification, Republicans hammered Northern Know Nothings' submission to the Slave Power. Indeed, once the speakership contest turned into a three-way race between Banks, Fuller, and Richardson, ideological stances on slavery almost completely dictated members' votes.[5]

With Banks so close to victory, antislavery Republicans designated him "as the Republican candidate." Republican managers feared that if they retreated to Pennington, the American Party would claim his election as a victory for nativism rather than for the anti-Nebraska Republican cause, a fear borne out in the correspondence of Fuller voter Solomon Haven, the lieutenant and former law partner of ex-president and American Party presidential hopeful Millard Fillmore. Haven and his allies stood "ready to help elect Pennington" as "a good American" with "no such thing as republicanism in him." A resolute Ohio Republican thus affirmed: "It is a point of honor with us who have thus sustained Mr. Banks, and identified him as the Anti-Nebraska candidate for speaker, not to yield." A Banks steering committee met almost nightly to coordinate strategy. Identifying potential backsliders and lobbying hesitant Northern Know Nothings, the committee even sent out letters to wavering congressmen's constituents, beseeching telegrams instructing their representatives to "Stick to Banks." This steering committee of Republican managers found the more radical Giddings an especially eager collaborator in their efforts to promote Banks at all costs. After "eighteen years" in the "business" of "struggling with Slavery and the Slave Power," Giddings exulted at the "good prospects of success" for an antislavery speakership. Thanking God that he could "witness some fruits of my labor," Giddings marveled to "see 100 men standing firmly on the very doctrines for which I was expelled fourteen years since."[6]

The stalemate persisted past Christmas, and then New Year's, and then heavy snows began to fall, but the House remained deadlocked. Debates grew bitter, and Washington cough drop ("hoarhound candy") sellers did brisk business soothing throats parched with bombast. As in 1849, the House's struggles to organize became a spectacle that magnified rising sectional conflict. For two months, Southerners, seeing a long-held bastion of their power slipping away, regularly threatened disunion. Republicans responded with ridicule, making "the House ring with laughter." Among proposed solutions to the impasse, the most obvious was election by plurality. Antislavery politicians, including veterans of the 1849 battle, now championed plurality election and unsuccessfully urged it on the House at least a dozen times. Banks's opponents, meanwhile, proposed a range of less conventional, often preposterous, alternatives including: organizing the House without a speaker by simply appointing Ways and Means and Foreign Policy committees; voting up or down on each member in alphabetical order until one received a majority; banning "meat, drink, fire, or other refreshments" to expedite the winter debates; and having every member of the House resign (to which Republican congressman and former Liberty man Edward Wade wryly replied that President Pierce should then also resign).[7]

Most dramatic was an all-night session in which Democrats, anxious to open Congress for Pierce, experimented for twenty-one hours with refusing to adjourn until a speaker was chosen, hoping to force pro-Nebraska Know Nothings to elect Richardson. Republicans accepted the Democratic challenge and joined in voting against adjournment as the January 9 session dragged on into the night, and then into the early morning, and then the not-so-early morning of January 10. Republican members won praise for their endurance and "orderly" conduct, and one participant boasted in a letter drafted at 8:15 AM that "not one" of the Banks voters was "in the least intoxicated," whereas "not less than a dozen of our opponents have been & are still as drunk as owls." Republicans cheered the "constant battle and confusion" as Democrats and Banks men together defeated the numerous Know Nothing-led attempts to adjourn. By daybreak, Democratic resolve began to waver, and around 8:30 or 9:00 AM the House finally voted to adjourn. Giddings proudly concluded that the overnight session had fortified the Republican ranks and would provide "a spectacle of moral sublimity" for the American people.[8]

Antislavery men recognized that the protracted contest would further bind the Republican Party together, and, as with previous speakership fights, focus national attention on the Slave Power. Veterans of antislavery third-party politics thus celebrated the "most exciting contest," believing that "the Election of Banks will . . . consolidate the union of our friends." Political abolitionists praised Banks votes as "strong testimonies against the Slave Power" and recognized that "even the struggle is a triumph—& should constitute a band of union for those Engaged in it." "The more votes [meaning separate roll calls] for speaker the better," an antislavery correspondent assured Banks, as "the lines between the Parties" would only become "more firmly consolidated." The contest, Giddings likewise observed, "got our party founded, consolidated and established," which was "of far more importance than the election of a Speaker."[9]

On February 2, 1856, the House finally adopted a plurality rule with the support of several Southern Democrats who believed they had found in South Carolina's William Aiken a Democratic candidate that pro-Nebraska Know Nothings would accept. By eliminating Fuller's chances and making the vote a referendum on "this anti-slavery monster, so horrid that he makes gentlemen shudder," Southern Democrats believed they could attract sufficient Know

Nothing support to defeat Banks. Instead, on the final, 133rd ballot, Banks was elected with a plurality of 103 votes over Aiken's 100, with several Northern Know Nothings scattering to avoid their constituents' ire at voting for a slaveholding South Carolina Democrat.[10]

When Banks won, old Free Soil stalwarts Charles Sumner and Joshua Giddings waxed eloquent that the "proud historic moment" was akin to arrival "in the promised land which flowed with milk & honey." "Never," wrote another Banks voter, "was there such a triumph gained by freemen for freedom over the Slave breeders & Slave Power." Hardnosed party managers, like Albany wirepuller Thurlow Weed, similarly crowed that "for once the North has been faithful" and calculated that "the Republican Party is now Inaugurated." When the House declared Banks victorious, his supporters both on the floor and in the galleries unleashed "vociferous cheers," cried, and waved handkerchiefs triumphantly, while many of Aiken's backers hissed and "swore like pirates." Banks's hometown of Waltham fired a one-hundred-gun salute, and Republican celebrants in New York, Chicago, and Bangor all commemorated the winning plurality with hundred-and-three-gun salutes. Even so uncompromising an abolitionist as Lewis Tappan exulted at this "first victory freedom has had in Congress for many years."[11]

Veterans of antislavery politics understood this election of a speaker independent of the Slave Power as a momentous turning point. Political abolitionists who had long fought the Slave Power's control of Congress hailed the "anti-Slavery party['s]" triumph over the "Administration and American factions of the pro-Slavery party" as the "First Victory of the North!," sharing Republican editor Horace Greeley's optimism that it marked "the commencement of a new era in our history." Banks's election and the lengthy contest beforehand had played crucial roles in solidifying the Republican coalition, such that of the seventy-two final-ballot Banks voters who ran for reelection, sixty-nine ran on Republican tickets. By uniting opponents of the Slave Power in advance of the 1856 presidential campaign, the contest had thus established the Republicans, rather than the Know Nothings, as the Democrats' main competitor in the North, ensuring that the slavery question would henceforth organize national political debate. At long last, former Free Soilers and Liberty men could rally behind a major national party independent of the Slave Power and dedicated to the longstanding abolitionist goal of divorcing the federal government from slavery.[12]

Conclusion

Seven years after he swore in Nathaniel Banks to conclude the famous speakership battle of 1855–56, Joshua Giddings received a letter from former constituent Ralph Plumb. A middle-aged Ohio lawyer, businessman, and Republican former state legislator, Plumb had long been a staunch abolitionist, and was previously an active local Liberty Party leader in northern Ohio. Plumb had also been indicted and incarcerated (but released before trial) for abetting the famous 1858 Oberlin-Wellington slave rescue, and he later helped defray travel expenses for two free black men who joined John Brown's notorious Harpers Ferry raid. Now a Union army quartermaster ranking as a captain, in late 1862 Plumb proudly surveyed the recent triumphs for which political abolitionists like himself had so long strove: "Within this year Slavery has been abolished in the National Capital, and what is better still the Proclamation of Freedom pronounced by President Lincoln has gone forth by which the legal status of millions of slaves is to be changed to freemen." Anticipating the New Year's Day Emancipation Proclamation, Plumb rejoiced "that in one short month the fetters are to be broken from millions of slaves upon American soil." "To be sure," he acknowledged, "the conquering army must follow the fiat, and by the power of arms, enable the slave to cast from himself forever the chains which the President's word has broken." Nonetheless, "at all events," the Ohio abolitionist predicted, "the slave is soon to be free!"[1]

From our twenty-first-century vantage point, political abolitionists' ultimate success can seem unsurprising or even inevitable. But if we look from the perspective of antebellum America, political abolitionists' incredible achievement comes more clearly into focus. Few in number, and marginalized by popular Northern racism, indifference, and anxieties for the Union, political abolitionist trailblazers confronted a formidable two-party system constructed to suppress disputes over slavery. Yet through assiduous agitation and organization, political abolitionists transformed national debate and expanded the arsenal of federal policies that could be pursued to undermine Southern slavery.

Conceding the constitutional constraints on congressional abolition in the states, antislavery activists carefully devised and vigorously pursued a policy program targeting slavery everywhere it *was* under federal jurisdiction. This book has described how efforts to eliminate slavery in the District of Columbia, bar its expansion into new federal territories, and circumscribe the fugitive slave rendition process all became central to abolitionist politics, as did efforts to resist proslavery foreign policy at particular moments of diplomatic and military controversy. Political abolitionists argued that "shorn of political power, slavery would fall by its own weight" once the federal government stood pledged to implement the abolitionist policy agenda, including, eventually, more politically delicate proposals to ban interstate slave trading, prohibit slave labor at all federal installations, and deploy patronage to stimulate homegrown Southern antislavery protest. Moving "first for the annihilation of the slavocratic control over the national politics," political abolitionists would follow their anticipated electoral success by implementing "all wise and lawful measures to accelerate the extinction of slavery itself." The bellicose Southern opposition that political abolitionist proposals consistently engendered made manifest the perceived danger that piecemeal federal inroads posed to slavery's long-term vitality.[2]

By the late 1830s, most abolitionists insisted that the national malady could be treated only with a *political* prescription. At its core, slavery relied on the legal fiction of property in man. Moral appeals to consciences North and South remained essential to any antislavery reform program, but they would be impotent without an effort to wield political power as well. This would be no easy task. Slaveholders represented perhaps the most powerful economic interest group in American political history, exerting disproportionate sway over federal policymaking and possessing nearly a fifth of all American wealth in just their enslaved human property. *Northern* political elites at best paid lip service to abolitionist pleas and at worst actively scourged and endeavored to silence them. In addition to this formidable proslavery political establishment, abolitionist insurgents also encountered substantial structural impediments that the American political system has always presented to upstart third parties—such as wide usage of single-member-district plurality electoral rules and emphasis on winner-take-all prizes like governorships, party control over Congress, and most importantly, the presidency (and the executive appointments it controls).[3]

And yet political abolitionists achieved a stunning degree of influence, especially given their third-party project's inauspicious beginnings (about seven thousand votes in the 1840 presidential election). This book has elucidated several reasons for political abolitionists' atypical third-party success. Credit is due first to the intensity of their convictions that American slavery both perpetrated intolerable injustices for enslaved African Americans and fostered concentrations of wealth and power detrimental to American democracy. Deep-seated moral motives, secular and religious, inspired political abolitionists to persevere in spite of the daunting barriers to upending such an entrenched political system.

But moral principle alone is rarely enough to effect sweeping political change. Equally importantly, antislavery partisans developed and popularized a highly persuasive and politically critical Slave Power argument. Abolitionists' anti–Slave Power rhetoric derived its analytic potency from their incisive institutional appraisal of the Second Party System's complicity in securing proslavery control of the American government. With national politics oriented around competition for the White House, and to a lesser extent control of Congress, both the Whig and Democratic parties sidestepped slavery when feasible and accommodated the South when evasion proved impossible. Making an increasingly convincing case that these cross-sectional major parties constituted the cornerstone of the Slave Power edifice, political abolitionists' commitment to third-party politics appears as logical in hindsight as it was bold at the time.

With their aspirations of withdrawing federal sanction from slavery, political abolitionists focused on infiltrating the national political arena, which they also exploited as a public venue for disseminating anti–Slave Power arguments. Third-party activists, however, also diligently scrutinized the gamut of American political institutions for openings that could allow them to wield influence beyond their numbers. Rare majoritarian electoral systems (most of which have since vanished from the American political scene, often amidst major-party efforts to crush later third-party movements) proved especially valuable for disruptive antislavery third parties. Manipulating majority-rule (as opposed to plurality-rule) electoral procedures in U.S. House speakership contests, within state legislatures for election of U.S. senators, and more routinely in numerous New England local, state, and congressional races, political abolitionists achieved outsized influence and frequently obstructed major-party attempts to mute antislavery dissent. And in the elections of John P. Hale, Salmon Chase, Charles Sumner, and later a host of anti-Nebraska senators, antislavery parties cannily mobilized balances of power in state legislatures and the rules for indirect election of U.S. senators to negotiate bargains that secured antislavery radicals another invaluable platform in national politics.[4]

Political abolitionists, and antislavery politicians more generally, also demonstrated a keen awareness that the institution's most extreme defenders could be made to serve as indispensable allies. Slaveholders' strenuous efforts to expand Southern power and muzzle antislavery petitions, mailings, and congressional speech powerfully corroborated abolitionist arguments that slavery threatened the liberty of all Americans. Antislavery political activists, when lacking the numbers to dictate the terms of national debate, became expert practitioners of reactive politics. Routinely goading defensive Southern politicians and fanning Northern outrage after each new outlandish Southern ultimatum, political abolitionists shrewdly capitalized on proslavery overreach to arouse ever more widespread and sustained anti–Slave Power agitation.

Abolitionist efforts to lobby sympathetic major-party politicians further kindled congressional controversies that reinforced abolitionists' anti–Slave Power message before a national audience. With ever-intensifying Southern demands, especially for slavery's westward expansion, ambivalent alliances between political abolitionists and more mainstream antislavery politicians matured into sustained cooperation. First in the Free Soil Party and then as Republicans, political abolitionists gained opportunities to vastly expand the reach of anti–Slave Power politics. Participation in these more moderate antislavery parties often meant working alongside politicos who did not always share abolitionists' loftiest goals of eradicating slavery everywhere and eliminating Northern racial discrimination. But political abolitionist veterans enthusiastically helped orchestrate these broadened antislavery coalitions precisely because they appreciated the larger parties' potentials for overcoming Slave Power misrule and advancing the abolitionist agenda for divorcing the federal government from slavery.

When the Banks speakership contest solidified the national Republican Party, many abolitionists felt themselves to be on the cusp of the political revolution for which they had so fiercely fought. It was certainly no foregone conclusion in 1856 that the Republican Party's emergence would eventuate in universal emancipation in under a decade. But political abolitionists' optimism reflected their established anti–Slave Power framework, which had long maintained that the ascendance of a political party committed to withdrawing federal support from slavery would pave the way for its ultimate destruction. With the budding Republican Party representing the first viable vehicle for achieving this longstanding goal, political abolitionists brimmed with confidence.

On Christmas Day 1855, with the raging speakership battle on a holiday hiatus, Salmon Chase, Charles Sumner, Gamaliel Bailey, Preston King, and soon-to-be Speaker Nathaniel Banks traveled north to Silver Spring, the Maryland estate of Francis P. Blair, a former advisor to President Jackson and powerful Democratic journalist who had broken with his party over the Kansas-Nebraska Act. Together these men adopted Bailey's plan for a preliminary informal Republican national convention in early 1856. Following their lead, five state-party chairmen jointly called a national gathering of all "Republicans of the United States" to be held in Pittsburgh on February 22.[5]

Meeting just weeks after the Republican speakership triumph, convention goers could confidently establish the national antislavery party organization political abolitionists had long sought and plan for the next presidential campaign. Assembling Republicans from across the antislavery spectrum, the convention afforded prominent roles to radicals like Giddings and former Liberty men Owen Lovejoy of Illinois and Lawrence Brainerd of Vermont but also evinced a surprising cautiousness geared towards persuading conservatives, Know Nothings, and some border state Southerners to throw in with the anti–Slave Power party. Nonetheless, resolutions calling for the "overthrow" of the Democratic administration, "identified" as it was "with the progress of the slave power to national supremacy," sufficiently satisfied Bailey's *National Era* that the meeting had "placed the Party in a position, in which it accepts the issue forced upon it by the Slavery and Administration Party." More important still was the upcoming June 1856 Philadelphia Convention, where Republicans would select a presidential ticket and draft a party platform.[6]

During the spring of 1856, bloodshed out west and the famous assault on Charles Sumner in Washington further confirmed political abolitionists' familiar warnings about the Slave Power's ruthlessness and the Democratic Party's complicity. Amid heightening Kansas guerilla warfare, Sumner's "Crime Against Kansas" speech condemned the Slave Power's "rape of a virgin territory" and personally besmirched South Carolina senator Andrew Butler. Seething, Butler's cousin Congressman Preston Brooks accosted Sumner at his Senate desk and mercilessly bludgeoned the defenseless senator with a gutta-percha cane. More galling still, South Carolinians feted Brooks as a Southern hero and defiantly returned the assailant to Congress. Convinced that Northern voters would now "awake," Chase predicted, "Sumner's grievous wrong will do more to open men's eyes to the true character of the men that Slavery makes than ten thousand [antislavery] speeches." "And the vileness perpetrated in Kansas" would similarly "expose" the "thorough recklessness" of the Slave Power.[7]

Now with a major political party at their back, political abolitionists trumpeted "Bleeding Kansas and Bleeding Sumner" as the freshest evidence supporting their Slave Power argument. Republican campaigners urged, as political abolitionists had since 1840, the necessity of electing a president disentangled from the Slave Power. Meeting in Philadelphia, the first Republican presidential nominating convention tapped the acclaimed "Pathfinder of the West" John C. Frémont, a political neophyte more renowned for his western exploration and elopement with former senator Thomas Hart Benton's (D-MO) daughter Jessie than for his brief and unremarkable Senate term. Radicals would have preferred an established antislavery luminary, but, as in 1848, they concentrated more on the platform, which demanded congressional prohibition of territorial slavery and castigated the Democratic administration for the disaster in Bleeding Kansas.[8]

Even though they did not win the presidency, the 1856 canvass ensconced the Republicans as the North's leading party, vindicating the long political abolitionist campaign to erect a major party independent of the Slave Power. Frémont won eleven of sixteen free states and a 45 percent plurality of the Northern popular vote in a three-way race with Pennsylvania doughface Democrat James Buchanan and ex-president Millard Fillmore, the Know Nothing candidate. Though Buchanan won, the results confirmed the promise that anti-Nebraska men espied in Banks's election for speaker. A new and powerful Republican Party had clearly eclipsed the conservative American Party across the North. Indeed, Frémont could have been elected by moving only Pennsylvania and either Illinois or Indiana into his column. For veteran antislavery activists, the long-pined-for advent of Northern majority rule now seemed imminent.[9]

Republican charges that the Slave Power would rule the national government as long as Democrats controlled the White House were persuasively corroborated within days of Buchanan's inauguration. In the infamous *Dred Scott v. Sandford* decision, the Supreme Court sweepingly denied black citizenship and established a federal property right in slaves, all, it turned out, with the new president's covert blessing. The case itself involved Scott suing for freedom by virtue of having resided in free territory before being returned to Missouri slavery. Writing for a seven-to-two majority, Chief Justice Roger Taney concluded that Scott should never have been permitted to sue, as the Constitution granted "the black man ... no rights that the white man is bound to respect." This finding, so grating to modern ears, could by itself have disposed of Scott's case, but the Taney court also ruled that Congress could not constitutionally prohibit Southerners from bringing slave property into federal territories. Effectively, Taney had declared the Republican platform unconstitutional. Republicans responded by denying the full scope of Taney's decision, and national debate now largely rehashed the Wilmot Proviso dispute, but in a radically transformed political landscape. While Taney and most Southern Democrats espoused the once extreme Calhounite position that the government could never bar slavery from any federal jurisdiction, and Northern (and some Southern) Democrats adhered to the hazy middle ground of popular sovereignty, Republicans ran on the longtime Liberty program of denationalizing slavery.[10]

Sectional recriminations continued to escalate through a series of controversies that Republicans interpreted as substantiating the Slave Power argument and Southerners saw as exposing Republicans' abolitionist proclivities. President Buchanan's support for both the Dred Scott decision and proslavery Kansans' fraudulent Lecompton Constitution further convinced many Northerners, including some from his own party, that the Slave Power controlled the national administration. Moreover, proslavery extremists advanced increasingly audacious demands for Cuban annexation, reopening of the African slave trade, and congressional authority to develop a federal territorial slave code (and on this last issue, the Democratic Party ultimately fractured in the run-up to the 1860 election). Republicans also harbored realistic fears that Taney might seize on a case winding its way through the New York courts to proclaim that free states could not bar Southerners from taking slaves into the North. Southerners meanwhile continued to bristle at resistance to the Fugitive Slave Act.[11]

In this climate of elevated sectional animosity, yet another contentious election for speaker of the House amplified the widening divide and further drove home Republican anti–Slave Power forebodings. In the months preceding the opening of the 36th Congress, John Brown, a pious abolitionist vigilante and the Kansas frontier violence's most notorious outlaw, had briefly captured the federal armory at Harpers Ferry, Virginia, in a failed attempt to raise a slave insurrectionary force. In Brown's October 1859 raid, Southern politicians saw evidence that Republican antislavery pronouncements encouraged slave rebellion. Northern abolitionist tributes honoring the convicted murderer as a martyr for freedom further aggravated the sectional unrest as the new Congress convened on the heels of Brown's execution. Republicans held a clear plurality in the incoming House, but they could not elect a speaker without overcoming opposition from a collection of minor parties including Know Nothing diehards, anti-Lecompton Democrats, and an Upper South–dominated Opposition Party. Republicans agreed to stand resolutely behind Ohio moderate John Sherman, much as they had Banks four years earlier, and Sherman came within three votes of a majority, but Southerners and Democrats refused to budge. In the second-lengthiest speakership contest in American history (by duration, not number of ballots), the shrill debates descended into a heated rehearsal of Southern arguments for disunion and Republican rebukes. Congressman Sherman had made himself particularly unacceptable to slaveholders by endorsing the *Compendium of the Impending Crisis of the*

South, a Republican campaign pamphlet that abridged North Carolinian Hinton R. Helper's inflammatory 1857 antislavery book appealing to nonslaveholding Southern whites. Deadlock in the House persisted for nearly eight weeks before Sherman, fearing the "national calamity" of a Democratic speaker controlling congressional committee assignments, backed out after negotiating to ensure the election of a more conservative Republican replacement, who, critically, had not endorsed the *Compendium*.[12]

Yet again, Congress, and the speakership election specifically, provided a pivotal venue that antislavery activists could use to further polarize national politics around slavery. Southern pretensions to stand in judgment over Republican endorsements provided another alarming manifestation of the Slave Power's intolerance of free speech, even, or perhaps especially, in the halls of Congress. Southerners meanwhile viewed Republicans' support for Sherman as indicating their intention to meddle with slavery in the states by enlisting the aid of nonslaveholding Southern whites; and political abolitionists had, in fact, long claimed that access to federal patronage would enable a victorious anti–Slave Power party to cultivate Southern antislavery grassroots. Helper's book, Brown's raid, and the acrimonious speakership fight dovetailed to convince a growing number of Southerners that slavery was more gravely imperiled than ever.[13]

In this tense political atmosphere, Republicans maintained their unbending opposition to territorial slavery and composed a party platform that gestured at abolitionists' "freedom national" doctrine, asserting "that the normal condition of all the [federal] territory of the United States is freedom." Recognizing the need for a candidate who could win the Northern swing states Frémont had lost, the party's heterogeneous 1860 nominating convention deemed Illinois moderate Abraham Lincoln the most universally acceptable choice. The party's anti-extensionist platform drew on anti–Slave Power polemics as it condemned Democrats' "measureless subserviency to the exactions of a sectional interest" and acceptance of "an unqualified property in person." Running on these firm, if measured, antislavery principles, as well as an activist federal economic program, Lincoln won the four-way race without a single Southern electoral vote and just under 40 percent of the national popular vote. Liberty abolitionists' vision of a federal government freed from the Slave Power seemed palpably close at hand. As Salmon Chase had confidently predicted on Election Day, "Mr. Lincoln will be President & the Slave Power will be overthrown." Even so radical a political abolitionist as Gerrit Smith (who could not bring himself to cast a Republican vote in 1860) praised Lincoln's outspoken commitment to the Declaration of Independence as evidence that he was "in his heart an abolitionist."[14]

As Smith had also forecast, Lincoln's victory was "regarded by the South as an Abolition victory." Seven Deep South states seceded in the months *before* Lincoln's inauguration. Republican plans to steer the federal government on an antislavery course drew on decades of earlier abolitionist political activism and terrified Southern secessionists. From the perspective of leading politicians in both sections, Republican governance portended a shift in federal policy so titanic that slavery might ultimately become untenable. A bloody Civil War consequently loomed as the final resolution to the sectional rift.[15]

Few Republican politicians, whether radical or moderate, seemed to doubt that if secessionists persisted in their course, the ensuing war would necessarily challenge, and if it lasted long enough, end American slavery. For many Republican leaders, and especially for a former Liberty man like Salmon Chase (who became Lincoln's secretary of the treasury), it was axiomatic that disunion would mean "abolition through civil and servile war." A month after South Carolina opened the fighting in April 1861 by bombarding Fort Sumter, former Free Soil congressman Amos Tuck matter-of-factly reiterated the common Republican conviction that if the South chose to "prosecute this rebellion as they threaten for years, then, Slavery will be over thrown."[16]

As Chase, Tuck, and their many peers had expected, the intensification of hostilities triggered an unprecedented assault on American slavery. Though the drama of wartime emancipation was notoriously complex — with an extensive and diverse cast of actors, Northern and Southern, black and white, civilian and military, all playing vital roles — for political abolitionists, the rapid dismantling of American slavery represented a logical outcome of their decades-long campaign to uproot the Slave Power. From the outset, Republican politicians acknowledged that international law authorized emancipation to aid the war effort. When, as many Republicans had anticipated, Southern slaves seized opportunities for self-emancipation and flooded into Union military camps, the Republican Congress responded with a partial emancipation policy ensuring that slaves who freed themselves would remain free. The legislation known as the First Confiscation Act emancipated thousands of slaves entering Union lines, even though the law technically only embraced slaves employed "in hostile service against the Government of the United States." Given the absurdity of tasking soldiers in the field with ascertaining the allegiance of each individual fugitive's former owner, Lincoln's War Department immediately expanded the confiscation policy to guarantee freedom for all slaves coming under Union control.[17]

For political abolitionists, it was equally important that Congress begin to implement their well-established peacetime program for divorcing the federal government from slavery. Republican legislators made abolition in the District of Columbia, the issue around which the political abolitionist mobilization had crystallized in the gag rule controversy, a key policy objective in the wartime Congress's first regular session (the emergency session that produced the confiscation legislation having been confined to war measures). Sumner urged that "slavery, which is a barbarous anomaly and an anachronism here, must be made to disappear from the national capital," recalling his address to the Senate a decade prior, declaring "*freedom and not slavery is national.*" Now though, Sumner found a supportive chamber, eager, as Henry Wilson put it, "to blot out slavery forever" in Washington, D.C. In April 1862, resounding Republican majorities abolished slavery in the District. Given congressional jurisdiction over the capital, radical Republicans soon transformed Washington into a laboratory for antislavery and antiracist policy experiments.[18]

Congress next banned slavery in the territories, fulfilling the Republican platform's central policy demand. Congressman Owen Lovejoy, a former Liberty activist and Underground Railroad operative, led the way in championing Isaac Arnold's (R-IL) bill to "render freedom national and slavery local" by illegalizing bondage everywhere under federal authority, including federal territories, as well as on the high seas and at Southern forts, arsenals, and dockyards. A fierce radical who had recently insisted on "an abolition war" and characterized John Brown as a "saint, hero, and martyr," Lovejoy ultimately accepted the necessity of a temporary compromise and pared down the legislation to simply "prohibit the crime of slavery in the Territories." With overwhelming Republican support, Congress achieved yet another longstanding Liberty goal and enacted what was effectively the old Wilmot Proviso, barring slavery from all current and future federal territories.[19]

Over the course of the war, Republican congressmen also secured other ancillary elements of the Liberty program, such as adopting an antislavery foreign policy, with measures like an Anglo-American treaty to better police the illegal transatlantic slave trade and long-denied diplomatic recognition for the independent black nations of Haiti and Liberia. And though the Republican Congress did not formally repeal the 1850 Fugitive Slave Act until 1864, the Republican administration had practically vacated the law through the policies of military emancipation in the rebelling slave states and of leaving fugitive slave rendition to local authorities in the loyal ones.[20]

Political abolitionists devised their program for divorcing the federal government from slavery as a strategy bounded by constitutional limits on federal emancipation; these same political abolitionists were quick to recognize that the exigencies of war, including the growing tide of self-liberating slaves, had vastly expanded federal authority. Antislavery radicals thus stood in the vanguard as the Republican congressional majority and President Lincoln adopted a groundbreaking, if legally complex, mass emancipation policy in the summer of 1862. Advocating an energetic new military "liberation" strategy, former Free Soiler George Julian opined in the House that "the mere suppression of this rebellion will be an empty mockery of our sufferings and sacrifices, if slavery shall be spared to canker the heart of this nation anew." In less fiery, more legalistic prose, Congress's confiscation and emancipation legislation, known today as the Second Confiscation Act, immediately freed all disloyal owners' slaves who had come under Union military authority, either in the occupied regions of the Confederacy, or by escape to a loyal state or Union military post. The law also encouraged the army to employ African Americans in any capacity that would assist the war effort.[21]

Moreover, the Second Confiscation Act made way for even more sweeping military emancipations, authorizing and prodding the president to offer freedom prospectively to *all* slaves in the vast yet-unconquered regions of the Confederacy. In the ensuing months, Lincoln responded with a September 22, 1862, Preliminary Emancipation Proclamation extending freedom to slaves in all areas still in rebellion at year's end, and as promised, on January 1, 1863, the commander-in-chief issued his now iconic Emancipation Proclamation. Soon welcoming former slaves into the Union ranks, federal policy proclaimed legal freedom for the vast majority of American slaves and scrapped old bans on soldiers enticing slaves away from their masters. Henceforth the Union army would actively spread liberty.[22]

Less than two years into Lincoln's presidency, it was clear that political abolitionists had achieved the reversal of the Slave Power's dominance in Washington. The national government now privileged freedom over slavery in nearly all cases where they came into conflict under federal jurisdiction, military or civil. And in the loyal states where slavery did not fall clearly under the wartime federal government's control, Lincoln and Republican policymakers attempted to use offers of compensation to induce voluntarily state abolition. By war's end Maryland, Missouri, and Union-occupied Arkansas and Louisiana would acquiesce, and West Virginia too adopted a gradual abolition program as a condition to gain statehood.

Yet slavery proved more resilient than many Republicans had anticipated. The old Liberty analysis of eliminating federal support for slavery had promised the institution's eventual demise, but the upheaval of war excited expectations of a much accelerated abolition timeline. Slavery, however, remained entrenched in many of the unoccupied regions of the Confederacy with the seemingly ineluctable Union victory fast approaching.

For all the radical legal and political transformations that had come with wartime antislavery policy, slaves who had actually achieved practical freedom under federal authority represented only a fraction, perhaps less than 15 percent, of the four million African Americans enslaved at the outbreak of fighting. And once Confederate surrender terminated the war powers born of military necessity, some feared that the courts, or future state governments, might reinstate Southern slave laws and leave in bondage the millions who had been legally but not practically freed (along with their posterity). Additionally, the loyal slave states of Kentucky and Delaware had still, as the war was drawing to a close, refused to adopt abolition.[23]

Well aware of the Slave Power's tenacity, Union policymakers identified a genuine danger that slavery might survive the war, an eventuality that neither congressional Republicans nor the Lincoln White House were willing to tolerate by 1864. Only a constitutional amendment could irrevocably extinguish American slavery. While celebrating antislavery legislative milestones that had once seemed like Liberty Party pipe dreams, Republican policymakers like Henry Wilson also demanded one more "crowning act in this series of acts for the restriction and extinction of slavery in America." An abolitionist constitutional amendment, Wilson asserted, would finally "obliterate the last lingering vestiges of the slave system" and "make impossible forevermore" the reemergence of both Southern slavery and the Slave Power's "despotism." The proposed thirteenth amendment, Sumner echoed, would "give completeness and permanence to emancipation." Despite substantial political obstacles, Lincoln's triumphant reelection and shrewd Republican floor management forced the amendment through in early 1865. Abolition thus became the essential, irreversible precondition for peace and union when Confederate troops laid down their arms that spring. Though none could have foreseen the precise twists and turns on the nation's winding, complicated, and bloody road from slavery to freedom, abolitionists' extended campaign to develop a winning anti–Slave Power political party concluded, as they had prophesied, in the ultimate eradication of American slavery.[24]

With the rebellion subdued and slavery forever outlawed, many leading Republicans, especially antislavery radicals with Liberty or Free Soil backgrounds like Senators Hale, Sumner, and Wilson, Representative Julian, and new Supreme Court Chief Justice Chase, held high hopes for not only vanquishing the Slave Power and emancipating the enslaved, but also for reshaping Southern society to establish a free labor economy and legal and political racial equality surpassing what existed in most of the North. Though radical Republicans, relying heavily on support from the Union

Army, experienced short-lived success in legislating dramatic changes in Southern society, the North writ large, plagued by creeping apathy and ingrained racism, soon abandoned its most ambitious designs. For nearly a century, the federal government would abdicate enforcement of legal and political guarantees promised in the Fourteenth and Fifteenth Amendments, a sad coda to the remarkable rise of antislavery politics. For all of the earthshattering changes the political abolitionist campaign against the Slave Power had wrought, the power of racism remained an obstacle that nineteenth-century America could not surmount with abolition alone. Political abolitionists may have succeeded in building a "Liberty Power," but a lasting "Equality Power" remained out of reach. It would take many decades and a Civil Rights Movement mirroring the unheralded political sophistication of its abolitionist forerunners to implement a Second Reconstruction aimed at overcoming the political power of racial discrimination, which long outlived its cousin the Slave Power.[25]

Perhaps partly because of the ultimate failure of the postwar radical Republican program, or perhaps because of the long shadow that Southern apologias and post-Reconstruction national (white) reconciliation have cast on our historical memory, political and abolitionist historians have together overlooked the incredible success of political abolitionists in catalyzing by the mid-1850s a nationally viable, if moderate, anti–Slave Power party. This Republican Party would have been inconceivable to nearly every prominent politician just a decade and a half earlier when a small group of committed abolitionists made the fateful decision to found the Liberty Party. Against the starkest of odds, political abolitionists worked with surprising effectiveness to challenge the Second Party System. Attacking Whigs and Democrats as vital auxiliaries of an insidious Slave Power and yet sometimes collaborating with sympathetic well-placed members of those major parties, political abolitionists used the institutions of a political system stacked against them to popularize this Slave Power argument to the point that it became the central appeal of the victorious Republican Party.[26]

Reintegrating the oft-disconnected histories of antebellum abolitionism and of the sectional political conflict that produced the Republican Party helps us understand both histories far better. With a fuller appreciation of political abolitionist influences, we can see that those two histories are, in truth, much the same story—the story of the most important third-party movement in American history. Through that movement, political abolitionists forced the nation to confront the power of American slavery and begin a long, perhaps still ongoing, rethinking of the meaning of American freedom.

Acknowledgments

This book began years ago as a collection of ideas about antislavery activism and third-party politics. The relationships I have built, and strengthened, over these years have made *Liberty Power* a better book and the research, writing, and revision process one of the most rewarding experiences of my life. I am excited now to finally, formally thank colleagues, friends, and family who have so enthusiastically shared their advice and encouragement along the way.

Since this project's beginning at Berkeley, Robin Einhorn and David Henkin, both brilliant and generous, have been my most important scholarly guides. This book owes much to their dedicated counsel. Incisive and demanding but caring and genuine, Robin exemplifies the kind of advisor from whom all young historians should have the good fortune to learn. David has been my most patient and creative writing critic, continually offering distinctive insights on the craft of historical composition, always with a smile. A kind and thoughtful commenter, Eric Schickler helped me appreciate and incorporate alternative ways to understand the political development of nineteenth-century America. My late undergraduate mentor Robert Engs was a model of a big-hearted and rigorous scholar-teacher. I will long be trying to emulate Bob's example. It is a source of great sadness that I am unable to share this book with him.

A few good friends from Berkeley read large swaths of this manuscript. I am indebted to Ariel Ron and Padraig Riley for their many insights on the histories of slavery, antislavery, and nineteenth-century politics, and I am particularly grateful to Miriam Kingsberg, a wise confidant and careful reader who constructively critiqued a very lengthy draft in exceptionally good cheer. Many others, including Candace Chen, Kathryn Eigen, Peter Fishman, Daniel Lee, Karen Lucas, Sarah Munchel, Robert Nelson, Caroline Shaw, and Ryan Shultzaberger, also provided important intellectual camaraderie as I commenced my research.

Various portions of this project were floated first as conference presentations and have been improved through many discerning formal comments, especially those from John Craig Hammond, Stanley Harrold, Elizabeth Varon, Jon Wells, and Eva Sheppard Wolf. Many more informal exchanges over a drink or meal have immeasurably enriched this work. James Brewer Stewart has been a crucial interlocutor, inspiration, and champion for my work, and Amy Greenberg has become a valued advisor. Conversations with James Oakes and Richard Bensel also helped shape my approach to key issues addressed in these pages, as have chats with Randall Miller, Gautham Rao, Joseph Murphy, Nicholas Wood, Stacey Robertson, Matthew Mason, Paul Polgar, Joshua Greenberg, Andrew Diemer, James Huston, Richard John, Matthew Karp, Cathy Rodabaugh, Thomas Sheeler, and many other members of the SHEAR community. I thank John Brooke, Sarah L. H. Gronningsater, Michael Todd Landis, and Dael Norwood for sharing their work in advance of publication. I also received much helpful feedback from members of the Baltimore History Writing Group; thanks are due in particular to its organizer Elizabeth Kelly Gray.

At York College of Pennsylvania, I have repeatedly benefitted from the support of the Academic Senate Faculty Development Committee, former Dean of Academic Affairs Dominic DelliCarpini, and the Department of History and Political Science. I am very grateful for the warmth and collaborative spirit of my departmental colleagues, and I thank chair John Altman and previous chair Peter Levy for being consistent and earnest advocates. Peter's good humor and patient advice, in particular, smoothed my transition to faculty life as I moved this manuscript toward publication.

Several other institutions supplied funding that made the research and writing of this book possible. Research fellowships were provided by the Library Company of Philadelphia and the Albert M. Greenfield Foundation, the Friends of the Princeton University Library, the Gilder Lehrman Foundation, the Institute for Political History, and the Graduate Division, Institute of Governmental Studies, and Department of History at the University of California Berkeley. My work has also been aided by attentive assistance from librarians and archivists too numerous to name. But I must specifically acknowledge the exceptional staffs at the American Philosophical Society, the Clements Library at the University of Michigan, the Library Company of Philadelphia (especially Connie King and Phil Lapsansky), the New York Historical Society, and the Vermont Historical Society, and also Orson Kingsley, formerly of the Henry Sheldon Museum in Middlebury, Vermont. During my many stretches conducting this work from my hometown of Philadelphia, the McNeil Center for Early American Studies (thanks in large part to director Daniel Richter) provided both stimulating discussion and access to the Penn library. The Interlibrary Loan offices there and at Berkeley made a good bit of my research feasible. I also owe special thanks to the dedicated staff of York College's Schmidt Library, and particularly to Interlibrary Loan specialist CaseyAnn Salanova.

Throughout the publication process, I have had the privilege of working with an excellent group of editors at the University of Chicago Press. Timothy Mennel has been supportive and expeditious, and before him Robert Devens went out of his way to carefully shepherd this project's acquisition and identify peer reviewers who offered astute suggestions for revision. Series editor Stephen Mihm brought my work to the attention of this press, and he continued to provide thoughtful and timely advice throughout the revision process. Thanks also to the other series editors, Edward Gray and Mark Peterson, and to promotions manager Ashley Pierce, senior manuscript editor Michael Koplow, and the editorial staff at University of Chicago Press more broadly. A portion of this work was included in my 2013 article "Stoking the 'Abolition Fire in the Capitol': Liberty Lobbying and Antislavery in Congress." I thank the *Journal of the Early Republic* for allowing republication of this material, much of which appears in chapter 2 here.

I could not have completed this book without the extraordinary love and support of my parents Marlene and Ronald Brooks. They have consistently nurtured my intellectual curiosity, work ethic, and sense of self. My father has also critiqued my writing thoroughly, speedily, and charitably for nearly two decades. Thanks also to my always supportive in-laws Ronda and Leonard Karp, sister and brother-in-law Meredith and Brandon Podel, and uncle and dearly missed aunt Arnold and Caren Toren, whose guest bedroom became my home away from home during many extended research trips to New York City.

Finally, I can hardly begin to express sufficient gratitude to my incredible wife Lauren Karp Brooks. She is my most enthusiastic cheerleader, my most trusted sounding board, my most important and honest critic, and my very best friend. I love her more deeply than sometimes seems possible. I cannot imagine dedicating this book, or my life, to anyone else.

Abbreviations

AAP	Amos A. Phelps
AAP Papers	Amos Augustus Phelps Papers, Anti-Slavery Collection, Rare Books and Manuscripts Department, Boston Public Library
AS	Alvan Stewart
BDW	*Boston Daily Whig*
CFA	Charles Francis Adams
CG	*Congressional Globe*
CG Appendix	*Appendix to the Congressional Globe*
CS	Charles Sumner
CS Papers	*The Papers of Charles Sumner* (microform ed.), ed. Beverly Wilson Palmer (Alexandria, VA: Chadwyck-Healey, 1988), originals from Houghton Library, Harvard University.
EWJ	Elizur Wright, Jr.
EWJ Papers	Papers of Elizur Wright, Library of Congress
GB	Gamaliel Bailey
G-J Papers	Giddings-Julian Papers, microform, Library of Congress
GMF	*Green Mountain Freeman*, Montpelier, VT
GS	Gerrit Smith
GS Papers	*Microfilm Edition of the Gerrit Smith Papers* (Glen Rock, NJ: Microfilming Corp. of America), originals from Gerrit Smith Papers, Syracuse University Library
JG	Joshua Giddings
JG Papers	Joshua R. Giddings Papers, microform, Ohio Historical Society, Columbus
JGP	John G. Palfrey
JGW	John Greenleaf Whittier
Jn Jay	John Jay
JL	Joshua Leavitt
JL Papers	Joshua Leavitt Family Papers, Library of Congress
JPH	John P. Hale
JPH Papers	John Parker Hale Papers, New Hampshire Historical Society, Concord
JQA	John Quincy Adams

LC	Library of Congress
LMG	Lura Maria Giddings
LT	Lewis Tappan
LT Papers	Lewis Tappan Papers, microform, Library of Congress
MVB	Martin Van Buren
NHHS	New Hampshire Historical Society, Concord
NST	Norton Strange Townshend
NYHS	New York Historical Society, New York City
NYPL	New York Public Library, Manuscripts and Archives Division, New York City
SPC	Salmon P. Chase
SPC Papers	Salmon P. Chase Papers, Historical Society of Pennsylvania, Philadelphia
TDW	Theodore Dwight Weld
VHS	Vermont Historical Society, Barre
WHS	William H. Seward
WHS Papers	William H. Seward Papers, Microfilmed by Research Publications, Woodbridge, CT, from the Holdings of the Rush Rhees Library, Department of Rare Books, Manuscripts and Archives, University of Rochester
WLG	William Lloyd Garrison
WJ	William Jay
WS	William Slade

Notes

Introduction

1. Revere House, menu for Feb. 28, 1856 dinner, Robert Carter Letters from Various Correspondents, Houghton Library, Harvard University, Cambridge, MA.

2. In addition to the further discussion of this contest later in this book, the 1855–56 speakership election is described in Jeffery A. Jenkins and Timothy P. Nokken, "The Institutional Origins of the Republican Party: Spatial Voting and the House Speakership Election of 1855–56," *Legislative Studies Quarterly* 25 (Feb. 2000): 101–130, Jenkins and Charles Stewart III, *Fighting for the Speakership: The House and the Rise of Party Government* (Princeton: Princeton University Press, 2013), 177–192, and Fred Harvey Harrington, "The First Northern Victory," *Journal of Southern History* 5 (May 1939): 186–205; *CG*, 34th Congress, 1st Session, 27, 72, 149.

3. JG to LMG, Feb. 3, 1856, G-J Papers.

4. SPC to Nathaniel P. Banks, Feb. 4, 1856, Papers of Nathaniel P. Banks, LC.

5. A note on terminology: "abolitionist" here refers to those who participated in the organized movement to end American slavery. "Antislavery" refers to a wider range of viewpoints, including those of many who were far more moderate in condemning slavery and less willing to take action against it. "Political abolitionist" here describes those whose abolitionist beliefs dictated their political affiliations and led them to reject proslavery party organizations. This term also distinguishes abolitionists who embraced an electoral strategy (through the Liberty Party beginning in 1840) from nonvoting "Garrisonian" abolitionists.

6. For examples of broad syntheses that give little weight to political abolitionist influence, see Michael F. Holt, *The Political Crisis of the 1850s* (New York: W. W. Norton & Company, 1978), and *The Fate of Their Country: Politicians, Slavery Extension, and the Coming of the Civil War* (New York: Hill and Wang, 2004); Daniel Walker Howe, *What Hath God Wrought: The Transformation of America, 1815–1848* (New York: Oxford University Press, 2007); and the latter chapters of Harry L. Watson, *Liberty and Power: The Politics of Jacksonian America* (New York: Farrar, Straus and Giroux, 1990). Even Elizabeth R. Varon's impressive, pluralistic *Disunion!: The Coming of the American Civil War, 1789–1859* (Chapel Hill: University of North Carolina Press, 2008) often privileges Garrisonian rhetoric over Liberty tactics. Aileen S. Kraditor, *Means and Ends in American Abolitionism: Garrison and His Critics on Strategy and Tactics, 1834–1850* (Chicago: Ivan R. Dee, Inc., 1989[1967]), exemplifies the pro-Garrisonian interpretive bias; W. Caleb McDaniel, *The Problem of Slavery in the Age of Democracy: Garri-*

sonian Abolitionists & Transatlantic Reform (Baton Rouge: Louisiana State University Press, 2013), enriches the older scholarship on Garrison and his associates by demonstrating that they were sophisticated democratic thinkers enmeshed in a complex international network of cosmopolitan reformers. Though they shunned institutionalized politics, their "agitation," aimed at swaying public opinion, reflected their political awareness, however unconventional.

7. For a sampling of this important work on African-American and women abolitionists, see John Stauffer, *The Black Hearts of Men: Radical Abolitionists and the Transformation of Race* (Cambridge, MA: Harvard University Press, 2002); Patrick Rael, *Black Identity and Black Protest in the Antebellum North* (Chapel Hill: University of North Carolina Press, 2002); Richard S. Newman, *The Transformation of American Abolitionism: Fighting Slavery in the Early Republic* (Chapel Hill: University of North Carolina Press, 2002); Julie Roy Jeffrey, *The Great Silent Army of American Abolitionism: Ordinary Women in the Antislavery Movement* (Chapel Hill: University of North Carolina Press, 1998); Stacey Robertson, *Hearts Beating for Liberty: Women Abolitionists in the Old Northwest* (Chapel Hill: University of North Carolina Press, 2010); Deborah Bingham Van Broekhoven, *The Devotion of these Women: Rhode Island in the Antislavery Network* (Amherst: University of Massachusetts Press, 2002); and Susan Zaeske, *Signatures of Citizenship: Petitioning, Antislavery & Women's Political Identity* (Chapel Hill: University of North Carolina Press, 2003).

8. James B. Stewart, "Reconsidering the Abolitionists in an Age of Fundamentalist Politics," *Journal of the Early Republic* 26 (Spring 2006): 1–24, quote on 5; For examples of recent work on political abolitionism, see Frederick J. Blue, *No Taint of Compromise: Crusaders in Antislavery Politics* (Baton Rouge: Louisiana State University Press, 2005); Stanley Harrold, *Subversives: Antislavery Community in Washington, D.C., 1828–1865* (Baton Rouge: Louisiana State University Press, 2003); Bruce Laurie, *Beyond Garrison: Antislavery and Social Reform* (New York: Cambridge University Press, 2005), and *Rebels in Paradise: Sketches of Northampton Abolitionists* (Amherst: University of Massachusetts Press, 2015); Reinhard O. Johnson, *The Liberty Party, 1840–1848: Antislavery Third-Party Politics in the United States* (Baton Rouge: Louisiana State University Press, 2009); Robertson, *Hearts Beating for Liberty*, ch. 2; and Michael D. Pierson, *Free Hearts and Free Homes: Gender and American Antislavery Politics* (Chapel Hill: University of North Carolina Press, 2003). Much of this excellent work concentrates on illuminating underappreciated leaders, state- and local-level antislavery political networks, and antislavery gender ideologies; Richard H. Sewell, *Ballots for Freedom: Antislavery Politics in the United States, 1837–1860* (New York: Oxford University Press, 1976), remains the best comprehensive discussion of abolitionists' national political contributions. See also James Oakes, *Freedom National: The Destruction of Slavery in the United States, 1861–1865* (New York: W. W. Norton & Company, 2013), ch. 1, which traces the origins of the wartime Republican Party's antislavery policymaking to antebellum political abolitionists.

9. Eric Foner, *Free Soil, Free Labor, Free Men: The Ideology of the Republican Party Before the Civil War* (1970; rep. Oxford: Oxford University Press, 1995) established the emphasis on free labor ideology, but does acknowledge political abolitionist contributions; Louis S. Gerteis, *Morality and Utility in American Antislavery Reform* (Chapel Hill: University of North Carolina Press, 1987), argues that antislavery reform also focused on free labor republicanism. For a revision of Foner's argument that focuses on Republican valorization of wage labor, see John Ashworth, "Free Labor, Wage Labor, and the Slave Power," in *The Market Revolution in America: Social, Political, and Religious Expressions*, ed. Melvyn Stokes and Stephen Conway (Charlottesville: University of Virginia Press, 1996), 128–146. Ashworth presents similar arguments about the abolitionist movement in his Marxist *Slavery, Capitalism, and Politics in the Antebellum Republic*, vol. 1, *Commerce and Compromise, 1820–1850* (Cambridge: Cambridge

University Press, 1996), 125–191. For scholarship emphasizing Democratic antislavery impulses, Jonathan H. Earle, *Jacksonian Antislavery & the Politics of Free Soil, 1824–1854* (Chapel Hill: University of North Carolina Press, 2004), quote from 7, is the leading work. See also Arthur M. Schlesinger, Jr., *The Age of Jackson* (Boston: Little, Brown and Company, 1945), especially 432–433; Yonatan Eyal, *The Young America Movement and the Transformation of the Democratic Party, 1828–1861* (Cambridge: Cambridge University Press, 2007), ch. 7; and Sean Wilentz, "Slavery, Antislavery, and Jacksonian Democracy," in *The Market Revolution in America*, ed. Stokes and Conway, 202–223. Wilentz's subsequent *The Rise of American Democracy: Jefferson to Lincoln* (New York: W. W. Norton & Company, 2005) more fully addresses the significance of political abolitionist activism. "New political histories" led by Lee Benson, *The Concept of Jacksonian Democracy: New York as a Test Case* (Princeton: Princeton University Press, 1961), concluded (using social science methodologies) that "ethnocultural" issues exerted decisive influence on antebellum political allegiances as voters divided based on reference groups dictated by religion and ethnicity. See also Ronald P. Formisano, *The Birth of Mass Political Parties: Michigan, 1827–1861* (Princeton: Princeton University Press, 1971); William E. Gienapp, *The Origins of the Republican Party, 1852–1856* (New York: Oxford University Press, 1987); and Joel H. Silbey, *The Partisan Imperative: The Dynamics of American Politics before the Civil War* (New York: Oxford University Press, 1985). Among the most influential ethnoculturalists, Holt, *Political Crisis*, argues that the antebellum parties had been designed to squelch conflict over slavery by creating trans-sectional alliances and focusing politics on other economic issues; once those parties ceased to embody substantive policy differences, they began to crumble. Political abolitionists figure minimally in Holt's analysis, notwithstanding its striking resemblance to their critiques of the Second Party System. Michael Morrison, *Slavery and the American West: The Eclipse of Manifest Destiny and the Coming of the Civil War* (Chapel Hill: University of North Carolina Press, 1997), emphatically rejects the ethnocultural approach but otherwise shares with Holt an emphasis on conflicting understandings of the American Revolution's republican legacies. Morrison, like Holt, largely ignores antislavery third parties. Also downplaying political abolitionist influences, Marc Egnal, *Clash of Extremes: The Economic Origins of the Civil War* (New York: Hill and Wang, 2009), offers a controversial economic explanation of Civil War causation, focusing on the emergence of a "Lake Economy" in the Upper Midwest. For a more nuanced analysis of economic influences on the Republican Party's emergence, see Ariel Ron, "Developing the Country: 'Scientific Agriculture' and the Roots of Republican Party" (Ph.D. diss., University of California, Berkeley, 2012).

10. For a good overview of historiographical trends in Civil War interpretation through the mid-twentieth century, see Thomas J. Pressley, *Americans Interpret Their Civil War* (Princeton: Princeton University Press, 1954). An excellent summary of recent work on Civil War causation is provided in Michael E. Woods, "What Twenty-First-Century Historians Have Said about the Causes of Disunion: A Civil War Sesquicentennial Review of the Recent Literature," *Journal of American History* 99 (Sept. 2012): 415–439.

11. JG, *History of the Rebellion: Its Authors and Causes* (New York: Follet, Foster & Co., 1864); Henry Wilson, *History of the Rise and Fall of the Slave Power in America* (Boston: J. R. Osgood and Co., 1872–1877). Late nineteenth- and early twentieth-century historians' absorption of this interpretation is exemplified in James Ford Rhodes, *History of the United States from the Compromise of 1850* (New York: Harper, 1892–1906), and *Lectures on the American Civil War* (New York: MacMillan, 1913).

12. Avery Craven, "Coming of the War Between the States: An Interpretation," *Journal of Southern History* 2 (August 1936): 1–20; Craven, *The Repressible Conflict, 1831–1860* (Baton

Rouge: Louisiana State University Press, 1939); Craven, *The Coming of the Civil War* (New York: Charles Scribner's Sons: 1942); Charles W. Ramsdell, "The Changing Interpretation of the Civil War," *Journal of Southern History* 3 (Feb. 1937): 3–27; J. G. Randall, "The Blundering Generation," *Mississippi Valley Historical Review* 27 (June 1940): 3–28. Frank Owsley, "The Fundamental Cause of the Civil War: Egocentric Sectionalism," *Journal of Southern History* 7 (Feb. 1941): 3–18, asserted, "Indeed as far as I have been able to ascertain, neither Dr. Goebbels nor Virginio Gayda nor Stalin's propaganda agents have as yet been able to plumb the depths of vulgarity and obscenity reached and maintained by George Bourne, Stephen Foster, Wendell Phillips, Charles Sumner, and other abolitionists of note," 16. Revisionists' distaste for radicalism that eroded sectional harmony has been incorporated into later, more judicious arguments, as in David M. Potter, *The Impending Crisis, 1848–1861*, ed. Don E. Fehrenbacher (New York: Harper & Row, 1976), and Roy F. Nichols, *The Disruption of American Democracy* (New York: Free Press, 1948). More recently, Rachel Shelden's illuminating analysis of national politicians' collegial cross-sectional relationships rejects older revisionists' tendencies to blame "blundering" politicians for sectional antagonism. If they blundered at all, in Shelden's telling, they did so through misplaced faith in their ability to transcend the electorate's sectional polarization. Shelden's book, however, seems to share revisionists' sympathy for the compromising impulses that the insular Washington community nourished. Rachel A. Shelden, *Washington Brotherhood: Politics, Social Life, and the Coming of the Civil War* (Chapel Hill: University of North Carolina Press, 2013).

13. David Donald, "Toward a Reconsideration of Abolitionists," in *Lincoln Reconsidered* (New York: Alfred A. Knopf, 1956), 19–36, fixed the parameters of this debate by depicting antislavery leaders as conservative elites misusing abolitionism to restore lost social status. Discrediting arguments like Donald's thus became a major interpretive thrust of abolitionist scholarship inspired by the civil rights movement. See Betty Fladeland, "Who Were the Abolitionists?" *Journal of Negro History* 49 (Apr. 1964): 99–115; Martin Duberman, "The Abolitionists and Psychology," *Journal of Negro History* 47 (June 1962): 183–191; and most of the essays within *The Antislavery Vanguard: New Essays on the Abolitionists*, ed. Duberman (Princeton: Princeton University Press, 1965). Gerald Sorin, *The New York Abolitionists: A Case Study of Political Radicalism* (Westport, CT: Greenwood Publishing Corporation, 1971), directly rebutted Donald, showing that most abolitionist organizers were moderately prosperous community leaders embedded in economic modernization; John W. Quist, "'The Great Majority of Our Subscribers Are Farmers': The Michigan Abolitionist Constituency in the 1840s," *Journal of the Early Republic* 14 (Autumn 1994): 325–358, further undercuts Donald's argument. Related scholarship also worked to assess abolitionists' relationship to American society and the role of antislavery in the rise of Western capitalism. For example, Ronald G. Walters, *The Antislavery Appeal: American Abolitionism after 1830* (Baltimore: Johns Hopkins University Press, 1976), grounds abolitionists in the middle-class culture of their era. See also Lawrence Friedman, *Gregarious Saints: Self and Community in American Abolitionism, 1830–1870* (Cambridge: Cambridge University Press, 1982); David Brion Davis, "The Emergence of Immediatism in British and American Antislavery Thought," *Mississippi Valley Historical Review* 49 (Sept. 1962): 209–230, connects the evangelical impetus to immediatist abolitionism to a new modern worldview emphasizing individuals' capacity to transform the world. In *The Problem of Slavery in the Age of Revolution, 1770–1823* (Ithaca, NY: Cornell University Press, 1975), Davis, focusing mainly on British abolitionism, attributes the movement's spread to a subconscious quest to legitimate wage labor. In contrast to Davis's (and Donald's) view, Edward Magdol, *The Antislavery Rank and File: A Social Profile of the Abolitionists' Constituency* (New York: Greenwood Press, 1985) locates the abolitionist constituency in the emergent working

class in several industrializing Northern towns. Mark Voss-Hubbard, "Slavery, Capitalism, and the Middling Sorts: The Rank and File of Political Abolitionism," *American Nineteenth Century History* 4 (Summer 2003): 53–76, and Laurie, *Beyond Garrison*, reinforce Magdol's conclusions. Andrew Delbanco, "The Abolitionist Imagination," in *The Abolitionist Imagination* (Cambridge, MA: Harvard University Press, 2012), 1–55, returns to this old question, "Who were the abolitionists?" Construing the "abolitionist imagination" broadly as a potentially problematic mode of political thought, Delbanco seeks to redeem the ambivalent centrism manifested in the writings of antebellum novelists Nathaniel Hawthorne and Herman Melville. In the same volume, John Stauffer, "Fighting the Devil with His Own Fire," 57–79, and Manisha Sinha, "Did the Abolitionists Cause the Civil War?" 81–133, offer fierce rejoinders (which accord more closely with interpretations presented in *Liberty Power*) celebrating radical antebellum abolitionists' inspiration, struggles, and successes.

14. On the origins of the antebellum abolitionist movement, see Newman, *Transformation of American Abolitionism*, and Paul Goodman, *Of One Blood: Abolitionism and the Origins of Racial Equality* (Berkeley: University of California Press, 1998). For more on the impacts of British abolitionism and British emancipation on American antislavery and proslavery thought, see Edward Bartlett Rugemer, *The Problem of Emancipation: The Caribbean Roots of the American Civil War* (Baton Rouge: Louisiana State University Press, 2008). For a compelling argument on the progressivity of Early National abolitionism in its temporal context, see Paul J. Polgar, "'To Raise them to an Equal Participation': Early National Abolitionism, Gradual Emancipation, and the Promise of African American Citizenship," *Journal of the Early Republic* 31 (Summer, 2011): 229–258. For more on Early National antislavery activism as an interracial project with important implications for antebellum abolitionism, see Sarah Levine-Gronningsater, "Delivering Freedom: Gradual Emancipation, Black Legal Culture, and the Origins of Sectional Crisis in New York, 1759–1870" (Ph.D. diss., University of Chicago, 2014). This dissertation deftly explicates the lasting influence of alliances forged among, and lessons learned by, New York's "children of gradual emancipation" in the early decades of the nineteenth century.

15. Michael R. Haines, "Population by Sex and Race, 1790–1990," table Aa145–84, in *Historical Statistics of the United States: Earliest Times to the Present, Millennial Edition*, ed. Susan B. Carter et al. (New York: Cambridge University Press, 2006), 1:48. For 1860 census statistics on the immense wealth held in slave property, see James L. Huston, *Calculating the Value of the Union: Slavery, Property Rights, and the Economic Origins of the Civil War* (Chapel Hill: University of North Carolina Press, 2003), 28, table 2.3. For more on the South's, and the nation's, enormous investment in slavery and its ongoing expansion, see Edward E. Baptist, *The Half Has Never Been Told: Slavery and the Making of American Capitalism* (New York: Basic Books, 2014). On racism in the antebellum North, see Leon F. Litwack, *North of Slavery: The Negro in the Free States* (Chicago: University of Chicago Press, 1961), David R. Roediger, *The Wages of Whiteness: Race and the Making of the American Working Class* (New York: Verso, 1991), and James B. Stewart, "The Emergence of Racial Modernity and the Rise of the White North, 1790–1840," *Journal of the Early Republic* 18 (Summer 1998): 181–217. On (largely unsuccessful) efforts to "abolitionize" national denominational organizations, see John R. McKivigan, *The War against Proslavery Religion: Abolitionism and the Northern Churches, 1830–1865* (Ithaca, NY: Cornell University Press, 1984). Useful starting points on slavery's national political influence include Leonard L. Richards, *The Slave Power: The Free North and Southern Domination, 1780–1860* (Baton Rouge: Louisiana State University Press, 2000); and Don E. Fehrenbacher, *The Slaveholding Republic: An Account of the United States Government's Relations to Slavery*, ed. Ward M. McAfee (New York: Oxford University Press, 2002). See also David F. Ericson,

Slavery and the American Republic: Developing the Federal Government, 1791–1861 (Lawrence: University of Kansas Press, 2011), as well as Robin L. Einhorn, *American Taxation, American Slavery* (Chicago: University of Chicago Press, 2008) on tax policy; Matthew Jason Karp, "'This Vast Southern Empire': The South and the Foreign Policy of Slavery, 1833–1861" (Ph.D. diss., University of Pennsylvania, 2011) on foreign policy; and Michael Todd Landis, *Northern Men with Southern Loyalties: The Democratic Party and the Sectional Crisis* (Ithaca, NY: Cornell University Press, 2014), which offers a forceful, if sometimes overly polemical, argument about the proslavery orientation of leading Northern Democrats.

16. The most important latecomer to the northern emancipation trend was New York, which passed its gradual emancipation law in 1799 at least partly in response to the fierce campaign of black activists and their white benefactors in the New York Manumission Society. Levine-Gronningsater, "Delivering Freedom," 71–87. Richard S. Newman, "Prelude to the Gag Rule: Southern Reaction to Antislavery Petitions in the First Federal Congress," *Journal of the Early Republic* 16 (Winter 1996): 571–599.

17. Stanley Harrold, *Border War: Fighting over Slavery before the Civil War* (Chapel Hill: University of North Carolina Press, 2010), 21–34.

18. Padraig Riley, *Slavery and the Democratic Conscience: Political Life in Jeffersonian America* (Philadelphia: University of Pennsylvania Press, 2016).

19. Richard H. Brown, "The Missouri Crisis, Slavery, and the Politics of Jacksonianism," *South Atlantic Quarterly* 65 (Winter 1966): 55–72, MVB quoted on 69–70; Holt, *Political Crisis*, 17–38. See also Robert Pierce Forbes, *The Missouri Compromise and its Aftermath: Slavery & the Meaning of America* (Chapel Hill: University of North Carolina Press, 2007). For a somewhat alternative take on the trajectory of antislavery politics in the years following the Missouri crisis, see Donald Ratcliffe, "The Decline of Antislavery Politics, 1815–1840," in *Contesting Slavery: The Politics of Bondage and Freedom in the New American Nation*, ed. John Craig Hammond and Matthew Mason (Charlottesville: University of Virginia Press, 2011): 267–290.

20. James Oakes, *Freedom National: The Destruction of Slavery in the United States, 1861–1865* (New York: W. W. Norton & Company, 2013), ch. 1; Oakes, *The Scorpion's Sting: Antislavery and the Coming of the Civil War* (New York: W. W. Norton & Company, 2014).

21. Shelden, *Washington Brotherhood*, esp. ch. 1.

22. William W. Freehling persuasively describes how slaveholders' anxieties and accelerating demands heightened sectional enmity in *The Road to Disunion*, vol. 1, *Secessionists at Bay, 1776–1854* (New York: Oxford University Press, 1990) and vol. 2, *Secessionists Triumphant, 1854–1861* (New York: Oxford University Press, 2007). A version of Freehling's argument about proslavery loyalty politics was proposed earlier by Lee Benson, "Explanations of American Civil War Causation: A Critical Assessment and a Modest Proposal to Reorient and Reorganize the Social Sciences," in *Toward the Scientific Study of History* (Philadelphia: J. B. Lippincott Company, 1972), 225–340.

Chapter One

1. David Brion Davis, *The Slave Power Conspiracy and the Paranoid Style* (Baton Rouge: Louisiana State University Press, 1969). Also see James Huston, "The Origins of 'The Paranoid Style in American Politics,'" in *Saints and Revolutionaries*, ed. David Hall, John Murrin, and Thad Tate (New York: W. W. Norton & Company, 1984), 332–372, specifically 366–369, and William Gienapp, "The Republican Party and the Slave Power," in *New Perspectives on Race and Slavery in America*, ed. Robert Abzug and Stephen Maizlish (Lexington: University Press of Kentucky, 1986), 51–78.

2. Jonathan H. Earle, *Jacksonian Antislavery & the Politics of Free Soil, 1824–1854* (Chapel

Hill: University of North Carolina Press, 2004). For an older interpretation of the Slave Power concept as Democratic in origin, see Arthur M. Schlesinger, Jr., *The Age of Jackson* (Boston: Little & Brown, 1945), 432–433.

3. For example, Michael F. Holt, *The Political Crisis of the 1850s* (New York: W. W. Norton & Co, 1978), 28–29, 39, 51, 151–154, 191–199, 209–212, presents the Slave Power idea as central to "the political crisis of the 1850s," but marginalizes abolitionists' contributions to the argument; Larry Gara, "Slavery and the Slave Power: A Crucial Distinction," *Civil War History* (March 1969): 5–18, also distances anti–Slave Power rhetoric from abolitionism. While Leonard L. Richards, *The Slave Power: The Free North and Southern Domination, 1780–1860* (Baton Rouge: Louisiana State University Press, 2000), demonstrates the validity of the Slave Power idea, he too gives political abolitionists short shrift in his brief genealogy of the argument, 23–25.

4. The most detailed analysis of abolitionists' development of this argument in response to assaults on their civil liberties remains Russel B. Nye, *Fettered Freedom: Civil Liberties and the Slavery Controversy, 1830–1860* (1949; rev. ed, East Lansing: Michigan State University Press, 1963). Nye credits abolitionists with originating the "Great Slave Power Conspiracy" idea, but focuses on the period after 1845, 217–249. See also Richard H. Sewell, *Ballots for Freedom: Antislavery Politics in the United States, 1837–1860* (New York: Oxford University Press, 1976), 6–9, 86–89, 102–106; Reinhard O. Johnson, *The Liberty Party, 1840–1848: Antislavery Third-Party Politics in the United States* (Baton Rouge: Louisiana State University Press, 2009), 24–25, 53–54, 227–230; and Merton L. Dillon, *Abolitionists: The Growth of a Dissenting Minority* (DeKalb: Northern Illinois University Press, 1974), ch. 5. Eric Foner, *Free Soil, Free Labor, Free Men: The Ideology of the Republican Party Before the Civil War* (1970; rep., Oxford: Oxford University Press, 1995), ch. 3, explores how Liberty partisan Salmon Chase articulated the legal doctrines that came to undergird the argument, but primarily depicts the Slave Power argument as a subcomponent of Republican free labor ideology. For an updated analysis that looks forward to Civil War Republican policies, see James Oakes, *Freedom National: The Destruction of Slavery in the United States, 1861–1865* (New York: W. W. Norton & Company, 2013), esp. 15–34.

5. On the earlier period, see Matthew Mason, *Slavery and Politics in the Early American Republic* (Chapel Hill: University of North Carolina Press, 2006), and Padraig Riley, *Slavery and the Democratic Conscience: Political Life in Jeffersonian America* (Philadelphia: University of Pennsylvania Press, 2016). For a broader overview of cutting-edge work on slavery and antislavery in Early National politics, see the excellent essays included in *Contesting Slavery: The Politics of Bondage and Freedom in the New American Nation*, ed. John Craig Hammond and Matthew Mason (Charlottesville: University of Virginia Press, 2011).

6. Boston *Liberator*, Jan. 1, 1831; "Declaration of the National Anti-Slavery Convention," in ibid., Dec. 14, 1833.

7. Although completely discounting Garrison's role, Gilbert Hobbs Barnes, *The Antislavery Impulse, 1830–1844* (New York: D. Appleton Century Company, 1933), remains an otherwise useful account of the moral suasion strategy. For a more balanced discussion, see James B. Stewart, *Holy Warriors: Abolitionists and American Slavery* (New York: Hill & Wang, 1976), 50–64. A related tactic, employed especially by Garrisonians, aimed to stir public shame by mobilizing international criticism of American hypocrisy. See W. Caleb McDaniel, *The Problem of Democracy in the Age of Slavery: Garrisonian Abolitionists & Transatlantic Reform* (Baton Rouge: Louisiana State University Press, 2013).

8. On the controversy over the abolitionist postal campaign, see Nye, *Fettered Freedom*, 67–85, and Richard R. John, *Spreading the News: The American Postal System from Franklin to Morse* (Cambridge, MA: Harvard University Press, 1995), ch. 7.

9. Nye, *Fettered Freedom*, 70; EWJ to Samuel L. Gouverneur, Aug. 8, 1835, Samuel L. Gou-

verneur Correspondence, microform, NYPL; Gouverneur to Gentlemen [president and directors of the American Anti-Slavery Society], Aug. 6[?], 1835, copy, included in Gouverneur to Amos Kendall, Aug. 7, 1835, ibid.; Gouverneur to Gentlemen, Aug. 1835, ibid.; William Goodell, "Common Cause," in New York *Emancipator*, Oct. 20, 1835.

10. "Governor McDuffie's Message to the Legislature of South Carolina," in *Liberator*, Dec. 12, 1835; Goodell, *Slavery and Antislavery: A History of the Great Struggle in Both Hemispheres; with a view of the Slavery Question in the United States* (New York: William Harned, 1852), 413–420; James Birney to LT, Jan. 7, 1836, in *Letters of James Gillespie Birney, 1831–1857*, ed. Dwight L. Dumond (1938; rep. Gloucester, MA: Peter Smith, 1966), 1:297.

11. AS, "Mr. Stewart's Remarks Before the Vermont Legislative Committee (Concluded)," in Utica *Friend of Man*, Dec. 19, 1838. On the complicated federal jurisprudence surrounding the interstate slave trade, and on abolitionist hopes for abolishing the trade, see David L. Lightner, *Slavery and the Commerce Power: How the Struggle against the Interstate Slave Trade Led to the Civil War* (New Haven: Yale University Press, 2006), 65–139.

12. On the politics of the gag, see William W. Freehling, *The Road to Disunion*, vol. 1, *Secessionists at Bay, 1776–1854* (New York: Oxford University Press, 1990), 308–352; Scott R. Meinke, "Slavery, Partisanship, and Procedure in the U.S. House: The Gag Rule, 1836–1845," *Legislative Studies Quarterly* 32 (Feb. 2007): 33–57; William Lee Miller, *Arguing about Slavery: John Quincy Adams and the Great Battle in the United States Congress* (New York: Vintage Books, 1995); and Nye, *Fettered Freedom*, 47–69. Barnes, *Antislavery Impulse*, esp. 109–152, presents an impressive discussion of the petition campaign, but does not adequately connect it to subsequent abolitionist political action.

13. Freehling, *Road to Disunion*, 1:308, 310–321. On the petition controversy in the First Congress, see Richard S. Newman, "Prelude to the Gag Rule: Southern Reaction to Antislavery Petitions in the First Federal Congress," *Journal of the Early Republic* 16 (Winter, 1996): 571–599. Miller, *Arguing about Slavery*, 107–108, 111–112, notes that the Massachusetts Anti-Slavery Society regarded the count of 34,000, made by the Pinckney Committee, of which more below, as a gross underestimate. See also Barnes, *Antislavery Impulse*, 131; *CG*, 24th Congress, 1st Session, December 16, 1835, 27–29; Drew Faust, *James Henry Hammond and the Old South: A Design for Mastery* (Baton Rouge: Louisiana State University Press, 1982), 169.

14. *CG*, 24th Congress, 1st Session, 170–171. For the lengthy debates preceding this temporary denouement, see ibid., 29–165, passim; ibid., 498–499, 505–506. Though the first gag was technically a resolution applicable only for the session and not yet a standing rule, Richards, *The Slave Power*, 132, notes that it was "known from the beginning as the 'gag rule.'"

15. The Senate "rule" continually tabled the *question* of whether particular antislavery petitions should be received. This procedure, while theoretically less restrictive than the House gag, attracted less attention and was thus ironically more effective. Daniel Wirls, "'The Only Mode of Avoiding Everlasting Debate': The Overlooked Senate Gag Rule for Antislavery Petitions," *Journal of the Early Republic* 27 (Spring, 2007): 115–138; *Emancipator*, Apr. 23, 1836; EWJ, *Third Annual Report of the American Anti-Slavery Society* (New York: William S. Dorr, 1836), 84–85; *Emancipator Extra*, June 1836. On doughface Democrats, see Richards, *The Slave Power*. On the term's origin, see 85–88. For an alternative interpretation of Randolph's meaning, see Nicholas Wood, "John Randolph of Roanoke and the Politics of Slavery in the Early Republic," *Virginia Magazine of History and Biography* 120 (2012): 129–130.

16. EWJ, *Third Annual Report of the American Anti-Slavery Society*, 46; letter of AS to the Pennsylvania Anti-Slavery Convention, Jan. 22, 1837, in *Emancipator*, Feb. 9, 1837.

17. Address of Henry B. Stanton to the New England Anti-Slavery Convention, in *Emancipator*, July 21, 1836.

18. SPC to Cincinnati *Gazette*, Nov. 1836, SPC Papers. For more on Birney, see Betty Fladeland, *James Gillespie Birney: Slaveholder to Abolitionist* (Ithaca, NY: Cornell University Press, 1955). Nye, *Fettered Freedom*, 193–217, discusses the impact of anti-abolitionist mob violence on public opinion. Abolitionists' understanding of political elites' instigation of anti-abolitionist riots anticipated Leonard Richards, *Gentlemen of Property and Standing: Anti-Abolition Mobs in Jacksonian America* (New York: Oxford University Press, 1970).

19. For a good account of the "Alton tragedy," see Nye, *Fettered Freedom*, 115–121; resolutions of Massachusetts Anti-Slavery Society, quoted in *Emancipator*, Nov. 30, 1837; editorial, ibid.

20. *Quarterly Anti-Slavery Magazine* II, ed. EWJ (New York: American Anti-Slavery Society, July 1837): 345; "New Hampshire Anti-Slavery Anniversary," from the *Herald of Freedom*, in *Philanthropist*, June 30, 1837; "Indiana—Decatur Co. Society—Call for a State Convention," *Philanthropist*, Feb. 20, 1838; *Philanthropist*, Oct. 9, 1838. Also see WJ to JQA, July 9, 1839, John Jay Collection, Rare Books and Manuscripts Library, Columbia University, New York.

21. *CG*, 24th Congress, 2nd Session, 51–52, 79–81, 106; Miller, *Arguing about Slavery*, 301–305; Nye, *Fettered Freedom*, 46–47; Barnes, *Antislavery Impulse*, 74–87, 104–105, 133–145; American Anti-Slavery Society's Directions to County Anti-Slavery Societies, 1837, in *Letters of Theodore Dwight Weld, Angelina Grimké Weld and Sarah Grimké*, ed. Gilbert H. Barnes and Dwight L. Dumond (1934; rep., Gloucester, MA: Peter Smith, 1965), 1:403–405. On the women's petition campaign, see Susan Zaeske, *Signatures of Citizenship: Petitioning, Antislavery & Women's Political Identity* (Chapel Hill: University of North Carolina Press, 2003), and Julie Roy Jeffrey, *The Great and Silent Army of American Abolitionism* (Chapel Hill: University of North Carolina Press, 1998), 86–94.

22. *Emancipator*, Dec. 14, 1837, Jan. 11, 1838; Dillon, *Abolitionists*, 101–102.

23. For examples of abolitionists' hopes for state legislative action, see "Petitions to the Legislature," from the *Haverhill Gazette*, reprinted in *Liberator*, Dec. 10, 1836, and Montpelier *Voice of Freedom*, Sept. 21, 1839; Stanton, *Remarks of Henry B. Stanton in the Representatives' Hall, on the 23nd [sic] and 24th of February* (Boston: Isaac Knapp, 1837), 40, 55, 42.

24. Birney to JL, Oct. 30, 1837, in *Letters of James Birney*, ed. Dumond, 1:428–432; JGW to Edward Davis, February 26, 1837, in *The Letters of John Greenleaf Whittier*, ed. John B. Pickard (Cambridge, MA: Belknap Press of Harvard University Press, 1975), 1:223; Massachusetts General Court, House of Representatives, *Report and resolves relating to slavery in the District of Columbia* (Boston: 1837); "M W C" [Maria Weston Chapman], "Angelina E. Grimké," *Liberator*, Mar. 2, 1838; E. W. Goodwin, "New York Legislature. Light and Shadows of Abolition," *Liberator*, Mar. 29, 1839.

25. For examples of abolitionists' efforts to influence Massachusetts state civil rights policy, see Bruce Laurie, *Beyond Garrison: Antislavery and Social Reform* (New York: Cambridge University Press, 2005), 108–124; "The third annual meeting of the Washington County [Vermont] Anti-Slavery Society," Resolutions, in *Voice of Freedom*, Feb. 9, 1839; Pittsburgh *Christian Witness*, July 18, 1838.

26. Joel H. Silbey, *Storm over Texas: The Annexation Controversy and the Road to Civil War* (Oxford: Oxford University Press, 2005), 6–15. Randolph B. Campbell, *An Empire for Slavery: The Peculiar Institution in Texas, 1821–1865* (Baton Rouge: Louisiana State University Press, 1989), ch. 2, concludes that slavery was an "underlying" but "not the primary cause of the Texas Revolution," 48–49. Andrés Reséndez, *Changing National Identities at the Frontier: Texas and New Mexico, 1800–1850* (Cambridge: Cambridge University Press, 2005), also complicates abolitionists' analyses by showing how Tejanos and Anglo-Texans alike struggled to negotiate the conflicting forces of the American market and the Mexican state, but Reséndez

acknowledges that "efforts to preserve slavery contributed at least to some extent to the independentist impulse," 161–162. See also Birney, EWJ, and Stanton, *Fifth Annual Report of the Executive Committee of the American Anti-Slavery Society* (1838; rep., New York: Kraus Reprint Co., 1972), 72; *Philanthropist*, July 7, 1837.

27. Benjamin Lundy [Columbus, pseud.], *The Origin and True Causes of the Texas Insurrection, commenced in the year 1835* (Philadelphia, May 1836); Lundy [A Citizen of the United States, pseud.], *War in Texas; Instigated by Slaveholders, Land Speculators, &c. For the Re-Establishment of Slavery and the Slave Trade in the Republic of Mexico* (Philadelphia: Merrihew and Gunn, 1836), 47. Lundy dedicated most of his life to the twin projects of fighting slavery and advocating colonies for freed blacks to show that they were capable of prosperity and respectability. See Merton L. Dillon, *Benjamin Lundy and the Struggle for Negro Freedom* (Urbana: University of Illinois Press, 1966).

28. "Letter from the Senior Editor [Birney]," *Philanthropist*, June 16, 1837; "Washington County [Pa.] Anti-Slavery Meeting," from *Washington Reporter*, in *Christian Witness*, Sept. 6, 1837; *Friend of Man*, June 28, 1837.

29. *Philanthropist*, Sept. 8, 1837; *Quarterly Antislavery Magazine* II, ed. EWJ, 345.

30. Massachusetts General Court, Joint Committee on the Annexation of Texas, *Report on the Annexation of Texas to the United States* (Boston, 1838), 32; Birney, EWJ, and Stanton, *Fifth Annual Report of the American Anti-Slavery Society*, 72; Silbey, *Storm over Texas*, 13–17; *CG*, 24th Congress, 2nd Session, 213–214; *Emancipator*, Aug. 23, 1838; WJ, *A View of the Action of the Federal Government in Behalf of Slavery* (1839; rep., Miami: Mnemosyne Publishing, 1969), 158–159.

31. WJ, *View of the Action of the Federal Government*, quotes from 18–20. On Jay's life and background, see Stephen P. Budney, *William Jay: Abolitionist and Anticolonialist* (Westport, CT: Praeger, 2005).

32. *CG Appendix*, 25th Congress, 3rd Session, 167–175.

33. *Gales and Seaton's Register of Debates in Congress*, 24th Congress, 1st Session, 1165–1171; "Clermont Co. Anti-Slavery Society," Cincinnati *Philanthropist*, Dec. 9, 1836; Earle, *Jacksonian Antislavery*, 18, 37–48. On conflicts over "race-based kidnapping" in the sectional borderlands, including Morris's response, see Stanley Harrold, *Border War: Fighting over Slavery before the Civil War* (Chapel Hill: University of North Carolina Press, 2010), 57–61.

34. AS, quoted from speech to the Vermont Legislature, in *Friend of Man*, Dec. 12, 1838; *Emancipator*, Oct. 8, 15, 1840; quoted from Utica *Anti-Slavery Lecturer*, in *Emancipator*, Dec. 12, 1839.

35. "Address to the People of the United States, from the Executive Committee of the American Anti-Slavery Society," printed in the *Liberator*, July 9, 1836; GS to AAP, December 28, 1838, AAP Papers.

36. JGW to Abijah Wyman Thayer, January 10, 1836, in *Letters of JGW*, ed. Pickard, 1:185–187; JGW to Caleb Cushing, February 10, 1836, in ibid., 1:188–189. Whittier, given his experience as a National Republican and Whig journalist, had long viewed politics as central to antislavery tactics. Frederick Blue, "To Mitigate the Suffering of Our Countrymen: John Greenleaf Whittier, Abolitionist Poet," *No Taint of Compromise: Crusaders in Antislavery Politics* (Baton Rouge: Louisiana State University Press, 2005), 37–46; JGW to Rantoul, Mar. 13, 1837, in *Letters of JGW*, ed. Pickard, 1:226–227.

37. On the role of mass mobilization in British abolitionism, see Seymour Drescher, *Capitalism and Antislavery: British Popular Mobilization in Comparative Perspective* (New York: Oxford University, 1987), 70–96; *Emancipator*, Oct. 25, 1838; WJ to Samuel Webb (draft), Jan. 3, 1838, John Jay Collection.

38. WJ to Samuel Webb (draft), Jan. 3, 1838, John Jay Collection. On the "inherent flaws in the interrogation system," see Sewell, *Ballots for Freedom*, 14–17.

39. JGW to an unidentified correspondent, Nov. 8, 1838, in *Letters of JGW*, ed. Pickard, 1:312–313; JGW to Cushing, Nov. 9, 1838, in ibid., 1:313–314; JGW to Cushing, Jan. 17, 1839, in ibid., 1:317. Cushing and Whittier's exchanges leading up to this election are discussed in Sewell, *Ballots for Freedom*, 13–14, and John M. Belohavek, *Broken Glass: Caleb Cushing & the Shattering of the Union* (Kent, OH: Kent State University Press, 2005), 99–101. In light of Cushing's later political career as a doughface Democrat, Cushing's antislavery positions were likely motivated by electoral considerations.

40. *Emancipator*, May 31, Sept. 6, 1838; EWJ, Birney, and Stanton on behalf of the American Anti-Slavery Society Executive Committee, in ibid., Sept. 20, 1838; ibid., Oct. 25, 1838.

41. JGW to H. B. Stanton, January 12, 1839, in *Letters of JGW*, ed. Pickard, 1:316; *Emancipator*, Mar. 21, 1839; Philadelphia *Pennsylvania Freeman*, Apr. 11, 1839; *Voice of Freedom*, Jan. 26, 1839; Michael J. Dubin, *United States Congressional Elections, 1788–1997: The Official Results of the Elections of the 1st through 105th Congresses* (Jefferson, NC: McFarland, 1998), 124; Laurie, *Beyond Garrison*, 41–47.

42. GB to Birney, October 14, 1837, in *Letters of James Birney*, ed. Dumond, 1:426–428; *Philanthropist*, Sept. 4, 1838; GB to Birney, October 28, 1838, in *Letters of James Birney*, ed. Dumond, 1:472–476; GB to Birney, Oct. 14, 1837, in ibid., 426–428.

43. "Political Action in Belmont," *Philanthropist*, Nov. 6, 1838; GB to Birney, October 28, 1838, in *Letters of James Birney*, ed. Dumond, 1:472–476; Stanley Harrold, *Gamaliel Bailey and Antislavery Union* (Kent, OH: Kent State University Press, 1986), 28–29; Sewell, *Ballots for Freedom*, 18–19; *Philanthropist*, Oct. 2, 1838; *Emancipator*, Nov. 1, 1838; *Philanthropist*, Nov. 20, 1838; "Election of Senator," ibid., Jan. 1, 1839; Jan. 29, 1839. For more on the controversy over this extradition, see Harrold, *Border War*, 79–82.

44. WJ and GS to WHS, Oct. 1, 1838, WHS Papers; WJ and GS to Bradish, Oct. 1, 1838, Luther Bradish Papers, NYHS; John C. Spencer to Bradish, Oct. 8, 1838, ibid.; James Watson Webb to Bradish, Oct. 10, 1838, ibid.

45. Thurlow Weed to WHS, Oct. 28, 1838, WHS Papers; WHS to Bradish, Oct. 27, 1838, Bradish Papers; Bradish to WJ and GS, Oct. 13, 1838, in *Emancipator*, Oct. 25, 1838; LT to Bradish, Oct. 25, 1838, Bradish Papers; Bradish to WHS, Nov. 16, 1838, WHS papers.

46. Sewell, *Ballots for Freedom*, 17–18; *Emancipator*, Oct. 25, 1838, Nov. 1, 1838; GS, "Letter to the Abolitionists of Madison County," Nov. 8, 1838, from *Cazenovia Union Herald*, in *Friend of Man*, Nov. 14, 1838; "Vote for Bradish and Against Seward, Extract of a Letter from Henry B. Stanton," Oct. 26, 1838, in *Friend of Man*, Nov. 7, 1838; Thurlow Weed to WHS, Nov. 4, 1838, WHS Papers; Weed to Bradish, Oct. 28, 1838, Bradish Papers; James Watson Webb to Bradish, Nov. 1, [1838], ibid.; Nathaniel P. Tallmadge to WHS, Nov. 25, 1838, WHS Papers.

47. *Emancipator*, Nov. 15, 1838; EWJ, "The Human Rights Party," from Boston *Massachusetts Abolitionist*, in *Friend of Man*, Dec. 11, 1839; AS to Samuel Webb, Nov. 22, 1838, Alvan Stewart Papers, NYHS; Blue, "A Self-sharpening Plow: Alvan Stewart's Challenge to Slavery," *No Taint of Compromise*, esp. 24–27, 29–31; Sewell, *Ballots for Freedom*, 49–51.

48. GS to Myron Holley, Jan. 17, 1839, Gerrit Smith Miscellaneous Manuscripts, NYHS; Sewell, *Ballots for Freedom*, 55–56.

49. *Emancipator*, Aug. 15, 1839; JGW to Moses Cartland, Aug. 6, 1839, in *Pennsylvania Freeman*, Aug. 15, 1839.

50. AS to Edwin Clark[e], Sept. 14, 1839, Clark(e) Family Miscellaneous Manuscripts, NYHS; *Emancipator*, Oct. 10, 1839. Goodell openly supported a third-party strategy by the end of the year. See, for example, *Friend of Man*, Dec. 4, 1839. Laurie, *Beyond Garrison*, 45–48;

EWJ to Beriah Green, Oct. 10, 1839, EWJ Papers; EWJ, "The Human Rights Party," from *Massachusetts Abolitionist*, in *Friend of Man*, Dec. 11, 1839.

51. Stewart argued that the Fifth Amendment had made slavery unconstitutional, since the enslaved were deprived of life, liberty, and property without due process of law. Blue, *No Taint of Compromise*, 20–21; EWJ to Beriah Green, Apr. 11, 1838, EWJ to parents, Aug. 9, 1837, EWJ to AAP, Sept. 5, 1837, EWJ Papers; GB to AAP, Nov. 2, 1837, AAP Papers; EWJ to AAP, July 11, 1838, EWJ Papers. For more on Wright's fascinating, varied, and lengthy reform career, see Lawrence B. Goodheart, *Abolitionist, Actuary, Atheist: Elizur Wright and the Reform Impulse* (Kent, OH: Kent State University Press, 1990). Lori D. Ginzberg, *Elizabeth Cady Stanton: An American Life* (New York: Hill and Wang, 2009), 31–38.

52. On the abolitionist infighting discussed in this paragraph and the next few below, Sewell, *Ballots for Freedom*, 24–47, 74–76, explains the movement's divisions over political action, and Laurie, *Beyond Garrison*, 32–48, closely examines the conflict in Massachusetts. Also see Laurie, *Rebels in Paradise: Sketches of Northampton Abolitionists* (Amherst: University of Massachusetts Press, 2015), esp. 25–27, 67–70, for insightful discussion of how some local political abolitionist organizers navigated this division; For the pro-Garrisonian view, see Aileen Kraditor, *Means and Ends in American Abolitionism: Garrison and His Critics, 1834-1850* (Chicago: Ivan R. Dee, Inc., 1989 [1967]), ch. 3 on the importance of the woman question, and ch. 5 on divisions over political action.

53. EWJ to Maria Weston Chapman, Feb. 5, 1839, Letters written by EWJ, Boston Public Library; Julie Roy Jeffrey, "The Liberty Women of Boston: Evangelicalism and Antislavery Politics," *New England Quarterly* 85 (Mar. 2012): 38–77; EWJ to Stanton, Oct. 12, 1839, EWJ Papers; William Goodell to Henry B. Stanton (to be forwarded by AAP), Feb. 5, 1839, AAP Papers; Appleton Howe to AAP, June 25, 1839, ibid.

54. For a good, brief account of the *Amistad* rebellion and trials, see Bertram Wyatt-Brown, *Lewis Tappan and the Evangelical War against Slavery* (New York: Atheneum, 1971), 205–220. For more detail, see Howard Jones, *Mutiny on the Amistad: The Saga of a Slave Revolt and Its Impact on American Abolition, Law, and Diplomacy* (New York: Oxford University Press, 1987). On the Second Seminole War, see John K. Mahon, *History of the Second Seminole War, 1835-1842*, rev. ed. (Gainesville: University Press of Florida, 2010), and Daniel Scallet, "This Inglorious War: The Second Seminole War, the Ad Hoc Origins of American Imperialism, and the Silence of Slavery" (Ph.D. diss., Washington University in St. Louis, 2011).

55. Edwin Clarke to Thomas Meacham, Oct. 26, 1839, Clark(e) Family Miscellaneous Manuscripts; *Emancipator*, Dec. 26, 1839; AS to Edwin Clark[e], Sept. 14, 1839, Clark(e) Family Miscellaneous Manuscripts; AS, "Mr. Stewart's Remarks Before the Vermont Legislative Committee (Concluded)," in *Friend of Man*, Dec. 19, 1838.

56. *Emancipator*, Aug. 13, 1840; LT to JG, Feb. 17, 1840, LT Papers; D. Pierce to Erastus Fairbanks, May 20, 1839, Fairbanks Papers, VHS.

57. Daniel Walker Howe, *What Hath God Wrought: The Transformation of America, 1815-1848* (New York: Oxford University Press, 2007), 586; "Speech of Hon. Henry Clay, of Kentucky, in the Senate, February 7, 1839," *CG Appendix*, 25th Congress, 3rd Session, 354–358; *Philanthropist*, Apr. 30, 1839; Michael F. Holt, *Rise and Fall of the American Whig Party: Jacksonian Politics and the Onset of Civil War* (New York: Oxford University Press, 1999), 99–100; *Emancipator*, Feb. 21, 1839, Mar. 7, 1839; letter from Albert L. Post, editor of the Montrose *Spectator*, May 28, 1839, in *Pennsylvania Freeman*, June 6, 1839; WS to JG, July 25, 1839, JG Papers; Gates to WHS, Nov. 23, 1839, WHS Papers; E. H. Prentiss to Erastus Fairbanks, May 23, 1839, Fairbanks Papers.

58. Holley to Birney, Nov. 16, 1839, Miscellaneous Manuscripts, Myron Holley, NYHS;

Emancipator, Nov. 7, 1839; Henry B. Stanton to EWJ, EWJ Papers; *Friend of Man*, Nov. 13, 1839; Birney to Myron Holley, Joshua H. Darling, and Josiah Andrews, Dec. 17, 1839, in *Letters of James Birney*, ed. Dumond, 1:514–516; Birney to Holley, Dec. 26, 1839, in ibid., 1:516–517. On the Warsaw convention, see also Sewell, *Ballots for Freedom*, 61–62.

59. LT to Joseph Sturge, Dec. 14, 1839, LT Papers; *Emancipator*, Dec. 12, 1839, Mar. 12, 1840; Augustus Sawyer to Goodell, May 26, 1840, in *Friend of Man*, June 10, 1840. See also ibid., Dec. 18, 1839.

60. *CG*, 26th Congress, 1st Session, 150–151; *Pennsylvania Freeman*, Feb. 6, 1840.

61. *CG Appendix*, 26th Congress, 1st Session, 906–907; WS to William (son) Slade, Jan. 19, 1840, Jan. 20, 1840, Slade Family Papers, Henry Sheldon Museum, Stewart-Swift Research Center, Middlebury, VT, vol. 1: William Slade Letters (Domestic Correspondence Scrapbook).

62. "Address to the Freemen of Oswego County," in *Emancipator*, Nov. 14, 1839; "Ascendancy of the Slave Power," *Friend of Man*, Sept. 2, 1840.

63. *Friend of Man*, Apr. 8, 1840. For an example of meetings endorsing the nominations, see *Friend of Man*, May 20, 1840; Birney to Holley, JL, EWJ, May 11, 1840, in *Friend of Man*, July 8, 1840; Sewell, *Ballots for Freedom*, 69–72; EWJ, *Myron Holley: And What he did for Liberty and True Religion* (Boston: Printed for the Author, 1882), 258–268.

64. *Friend of Man*, June 3, 17, 1840; *Philanthropist*, June 16, 1840; Austin Willey, *The History of the Antislavery Cause in State and Nation* (Portland, ME: Brown, Thurston, and Hoyt, Fogg & Donham, 1886), 134.

65. *Emancipator*, Nov. 14, 1839. See also LT to Birney, Dec. 6, 1839, in ibid., Dec. 12, 1839, and LT to Francis Gillette, P. Canfield, S. J. Cowles, Com. of Arrangements for a Special Meeting of the Connecticut Anti-Slavery Society, Dec. 5, 1839, LT Papers; LT to GS, Mar. 14, 1841, GS Papers; LT to Samuel D. Hastings, Apr. 15, 1840, LT Papers. See also Bertram Wyatt-Brown's excellent biography, *Lewis Tappan and the Evangelical War against Slavery*.

66. JGW to the Anti-Slavery Convention at Albany, Mar. 22, 1840, in *Letters of JGW*, ed. Pickard, 1:398–399; JGW to EWJ, Mar. 25, 1840, in ibid., 1:400–401; Stanton to Birney, Mar. 21, 1840, in *Letters of James Birney*, ed. Dumond, 1:541–543.

67. WJ to GS (draft), July 25, 1840, John Jay Collection; Andrew S. Barker, "Chauncey Langdon Knapp and Political Abolitionism in Vermont, 1833–1841," *New England Quarterly* 73 (Sept. 2000): 457–459; GB to Birney, Mar. 3, 1840, in *Letters of James Birney*, ed. Dumond, 1:535–538; GB to Birney, Nov. 28, 1839, in ibid., 1:508–510; GB to Birney, Apr. 18, 1840, in ibid., 1:556–558; *Emancipator*, July 2, Aug. 13, 1840; *Philanthropist*, Sept. 8, 1840; Harrold, *Gamaliel Bailey and Antislavery Union*, 33–36; Edward Wade to GB, July 9, 1840, in *Philanthropist*, Oct. 13, 1840; SPC to Charles Cleveland, Aug. 29, 1840, in *The Salmon P. Chase Papers*, ed. John Niven (Kent, OH: Kent State University Press, 1993), 2:69–71.

68. *Pennsylvania Freeman*, Oct. 29, 1840; JGW to GS, Aug. 30, 1840, in *Letters of JGW*, ed. Pickard, 1:438; *Emancipator*, Aug. 13, 1840; "Address to the Abolitionists of Oneida County," *Friend of Man*, July 29, 1840; New York *Colored American*, Oct. 10, 1840.

69. For work focusing on the moral imperative to third-party action, see Douglas M. Strong, *Perfectionist Politics: Abolitionism and the Religious Tensions of American Democracy* (Syracuse, NY: Syracuse University Press, 2002), 66–76, and Alan Kraut, "Partisanship and Principles: The Liberty Party in Antebellum Political Culture," in *Crusaders and Compromisers: Essays on the Relationship of the Antislavery Struggle to the Antebellum Party System*, ed. Kraut (Westport, CT: Greenwood Press, 1983), 71–100; *Emancipator*, Mar. 12, 1840; ibid., Jan. 9, 1840.

70. *Massachusetts Abolitionist*, Apr. 16, 1840; *Emancipator*, Jan. 9, 1840, Oct. 1, 1840; *Colored American*, Oct. 3, 1840 (also see Sept. 12, 1840).

71. *Pennsylvania Freeman*, Oct. 29, 1840; *Emancipator*, May 29, Aug. 13, 1840. Also see ibid., Aug. 20, 1840, which catalogues Harrison's long career of opposition to abolition; "Address to the Abolitionists of Oneida County," *Friend of Man*, July 29, 1840.

72. *Emancipator*, Oct. 1, 1840. Leavitt explicated slavery's detrimental effect on American political economy most comprehensively in an Ohio speech on "The Financial Power of Slavery," first published in ibid., Oct. 22, 1840, and later as a pamphlet; ibid., Oct. 29, 1840. For further detail on the "one-idea" strategy, see chapter 3 below.

73. Stanton to Birney, Mar. 21, 1840, in *Letters of James Birney*, ed. Dumond, 1:541–543; Willey, *History of the Antislavery Cause*, 134–135; Stephen J. Rosenstone, Roy L. Behr, and Edward H. Lazarus, *Third Parties in America: Citizen Response to Major Party Failure* (Princeton: Princeton University Press, 1996), 49–50.

74. *Colored American*, Aug. 29, Dec. 5, 1840; National Committee of Correspondence, quoted in *Emancipator*, Dec. 17, 1840; JL to Birney, Oct. 1, 1840, in *Letters of James Birney*, ed. Dumond, 2:603–604; Sewell, *Ballots for Freedom*, 71–73.

75. *Emancipator*, Dec. 31, 1840.

Interlude One

1. For more on the institutional history and political significance of nineteenth-century speakership elections, see Jeffery A. Jenkins and Charles Stewart III, *Fighting for the Speakership: The House and the Rise of Party Government* (Princeton: Princeton University Press, 2013). JQA, *Memoirs of John Quincy Adams, Comprising Portions of his Diary from 1795 to 1848*, ed. CFA (Philadelphia: J. B. Lippincott & Co., 1874–1877), 10:142–162, provides a good account of the proceedings regarding the disputed seats. Also see *CG*, 1–52, passim.

2. John C. Calhoun to A[nna] M[aria Calhoun] Clemson, Dec. 18, 1839, in *The Papers of John C. Calhoun*, ed. Clyde N. Wilson (Columbia: University of South Carolina Press, 1959), 15:20; JQA, *Memoirs*, 10:144.

3. New York *Emancipator*, Oct. 10, 1839.

4. *CG*, 26th Congress, 1st Session, 52–54; JQA, *Memoirs*, ed. CFA, 10:163–164. Though twenty Southern scattering votes were cast on the initial roll call, two came from Bell and Jones, who followed the custom of not voting for oneself.

5. *CG*, 26th Congress, 1st Session, 55–56. The *CG*'s final tally contains ten Whig names—seven of them Northerners, including Gates—appended to the end of the list of Hunter votes, not in alphabetical order with the other ninety-nine, suggesting that these ten either voted late or changed their vote at the end of the count to secure Hunter's election; JQA, *Memoirs*, ed. CFA, 10:164–65.

6. Boston *Massachusetts Abolitionist*, Feb. 20, 1840; *Emancipator*, Dec. 26, 1839; Washington, D.C. *Globe*, quoted in New York *Evening Post*, Dec. 18, 1839.

7. AS, quoted in *Emancipator*, Feb. 6, 1840; "The Fifth Annual Report of the New York State Anti-Slavery Society," in *Friend of Man*, Sept. 23, 1840.

8. George Fitzhugh to R. M. T. Hunter, Dec. 17, 1839, in *Correspondence of Robert M. T. Hunter, 1826–1876*, ed. Charles Henry Ambler (Washington: Annual Report of the American Historical Association for 1916, vol. 2, 1918), 31; John C. Calhoun to Orestes Brownson, Dec. 30, 1839, in *The Papers of John C. Calhoun*, ed. Wilson, 15:25.

9. *Emancipator*, Dec. 26, 1839.

10. LT to Seth Gates, Jan. 31, 1840, LT Papers; LT to JG, Feb. 7, 1840, G-J Papers; JG to [Anon.], Dec. 28, 1839, JG Papers.

Chapter Two

1. On antebellum lobbying at the state level, and its emphasis on special legislation, see Douglas E. Bowers, "From Logrolling to Corruption: The Development of Lobbying in Pennsylvania, 1815–1861," *Journal of the Early Republic* 3 (Winter 1983): 439–474. For an example of how lobbying by specific private interests could influence federal legislation, see Phillip W. Magness, "Morrill and the Missing Industries: Strategic Lobbying Behavior and the Tariff, 1858–1861," *Journal of the Early Republic* 29 (Summer 2009): 287–329. Also see Mark W. Summers, *The Plundering Generation: Corruption and the Crisis of the Union, 1849–1861* (New York: Oxford University Press, 1987), 85–112; Ariel Ron, "Developing the Country: 'Scientific Agriculture' and the Roots of Republican Party" (Ph.D. diss., University of California, Berkeley, 2012), esp. ch. 5, highlights another instance of underappreciated antebellum congressional lobbying. Unlike intentionally disruptive abolitionists, however, agricultural reform lobbyists attempted (though largely failed) to sidestep sectional contention that might jeopardize their agenda. William DiGiacomantonio, "'For the Gratification of a Volunteering Society': Antislavery and Pressure Group Politics in the First Federal Congress," *Journal of the Early Republic* 15 (Summer 1995): 169–197, depicts Philadelphia Quakers attending the First Congress in New York as the original modern lobby. On the Sabbatarian movement see Bertram Wyatt-Brown, "Prelude to Abolitionism: Sabbatarian Politics and the Rise of the Second Party System," *Journal of American History* 58 (Sept. 1971): 316–341, and Richard R. John, *Spreading the News: The American Postal System from Franklin to Morse* (Cambridge, MA: Harvard University Press, 1995), 179–189.

2. David R. Mayhew's unique canvass of congressional history (and historiography) suggests that many of the most influential actions of individual congressmen have had more to do with "taking stands" than directly with legislating. Mayhew, *America's Congress: Actions in the Public Sphere, James Madison through Newt Gingrich* (New Haven: Yale University Press, 2000), esp. 90–102. Although Rachel A. Shelden's discussion of slightly later congresses, *Washington Brotherhood: Politics, Social Life, and the Coming of the Civil War* (Chapel Hill: University of North Carolina Press, 2013), downplays the significance of floor debates, she shares abolitionists' assessment that the most important audiences for congressional oratory were constituents at home. Shelden's dismissal of polarized congressional rhetoric as theater performed to appease restive voters, however, risks diminishing the real sectional pressures that were reshaping antebellum politics and eliciting such hostile speeches. On news coverage of Congress in this period, see Thomas C. Leonard, *The Power of the Press: The Birth of American Political Reporting* (New York: Oxford University Press, 1986), 63–96.

3. Paula Baker, "The Domestication of Politics: Women and American Political Society, 1780–1920," *Journal of American History* 89 (June, 1984): 620–647, explicates how contemporary gender ideologies both provided and circumscribed opportunities for women to exert political influence in nineteenth-century America, often by emphasizing claims to motherly virtue. Evidence of (some) women's active roles in antebellum politics can be seen in Elizabeth R. Varon, *We Mean to be Counted: White Women and Politics in Antebellum Virginia* (Chapel Hill: University of North Carolina Press, 1998), and Ronald J. Zboray and Mary Saracino Zboray, *Voices Without Votes: Women and Politics in Antebellum New England* (Durham, NH: University Press of New England, 2010); Stacey M. Robertson, *Hearts Beating for Liberty: Women Abolitionists in the Old Northwest* (Chapel Hill: University of North Carolina Press, 2010), ch. 2, provides an excellent description of western women's in some ways analogous political abolitionist activism. On women's use of petitions, as well as on the uniquely politicizing effect of abolitionist petitioning, see Alisse Portnoy, *Their Right to Speak: Women's Activ-*

ism in the Indian and Slave Debates (Cambridge, MA: Harvard University Press, 2005), and Susan Zaeske: *Signatures of Citizenship: Petitioning, Antislavery, and Women's Political Identity* (Chapel Hill: University of North Carolina Press, 2003).

4. On Adams's role in the contest against the gag rule, see William Lee Miller, *Arguing about Slavery: John Quincy Adams and the Great Battle in the United States Congress* (New York: Vintage Books, 1995), passim; Leonard Richards, *The Life and Times of Congressman John Quincy Adams* (New York: Oxford University Press, 1986), 117–131, 135–139; and William W. Freehling, *The Road to Disunion*, vol. 1, *Secessionists at Bay, 1776-1854* (New York: Oxford University Press, 1990), 343–352. Utica *Friend of Man*, May 31, 1837. Also see examples included in WLG to JQA, Apr. 10, 1837, and Francis Jackson and AAP in behalf of the Massachusetts Anti-Slavery Society to JQA, Feb. 3, 1838, Adams Family Papers, Microfilm Edition, Massachusetts Historical Society, Boston. JQA to JGW, Jan. 26, 1837, Adams Family Papers; JGW to JQA, Jan. 23, 1837, ibid.; Sarah Grimké to JQA, May 8, 1837, ibid.; Cincinnati *Philanthropist*, Nov. 14, 1837. Deeming immediate abolition at the capital impractical and dangerous to the union, Adams preferred a gradual process similar to that used earlier in Pennsylvania and New York. JQA to JGW, Apr. 19, 1837, JQA to JL and Henry B. Stanton, July 11, 1839, and JQA to LT, July 15, 1841, Adams Family Papers.

5. JQA to GS, July 31, 1839, Letterbooks, Adams Family Papers; JQA, *Memoirs of John Quincy Adams, Comprising Portions of his Diary from 1795 to 1848*, ed. CFA (Philadelphia: J. B. Lippincott & Co., 1874–1877), 9:365, 9:349–350.

6. JQA, *Memoirs*, ed. CFA, 9:365; *CG*, 24th Congress, 2nd Session, 162–175. Since the House did not permit the petition to be read, Adams never explicitly identified its request, but a Kentuckian suggested that it, in fact, called for Adams's expulsion from the House: *Gales and Seaton's Register of Debates in Congress*, 24th Congress, 2nd Session, 1627–1631. On the petition's questionable provenance, see Abijah Mann's (D-NY) speech suggesting that "some mischievous persons [had] trifled" with Adams: ibid., 1597–1598; Resolutions of Feb. 6, 1837, Adams Family Papers.

7. WJ to JQA, July 9, 1839, John Jay Collection, Rare Books and Manuscripts Library, Columbia University, New York; *Letters from John Quincy Adams to His Constituents of the Twelfth Congressional District in Massachusetts, To which is Added his Speech in Congress Delivered February 9, 1837* (Boston: Isaac Knapp, 1837), 3–4; New York *Emancipator*, June 15, 1837.

8. LT to JQA, May 13, 1837, Adams Family Papers; TDW to LT, Dec. 14, 1841, in *Letters of Theodore Dwight Weld, Angelina Grimké Weld and Sarah Grimké*, ed. Gilbert H. Barnes and Dwight L. Dumond (1934; rep., Gloucester, MA: Peter Smith, 1965), 2:879–882; Address of the Massachusetts Anti-Slavery Society Board of Managers to the Abolitionists of Massachusetts, in *Emancipator*, Aug. 23, 1838.

9. *Emancipator*, Jan. 19, 1837; WJ to Richard Wylly Habersham (draft), Feb. 24, 1840, John Jay Collection; *Emancipator*, Feb. 9, 1837.

10. JQA to Lundy, May 12, 20, 1836, Adams Family Papers; Benjamin Lundy [A Citizen of the United States, pseud.], *War in Texas* (Philadelphia: Merrihew and Gunn, 1836), 47; JQA to Benjamin Lundy, May 12, 1836, Adams Family Papers; Richards, *Life and Times of Congressman JQA*, 154–172; JQA to Lundy, May 20, 1836, Adams Family Papers. In the speech mentioned here, Adams also pronounced the doctrine of emancipation by war powers, suggesting a war on the southern border could give Congress reason, and constitutional justification, for freeing Southern slaves. For more on antebellum endorsements of emancipation under extraordinary war powers, see James Oakes, *Freedom National: The Destruction of Slavery in the United States, 1861-1865* (New York: W. W. Norton & Company, 2013), 34–42.

11. Lundy to JQA, June 9, 1836, Adams Family Papers; *Emancipator*, Oct. 14, 1837; Lundy to JQA, Dec. 15, 1837, Adams Family Papers.

12. JL to TDW, Nov. 16, 1837, in *Letters of TDW, Angelina Grimké Weld and Sarah Grimké*, ed. Barnes and Dumond, 1:478; Henry B. Stanton, *Random Recollections* (New York: Harper & Brothers, 1887), 59–61; JGW to Joseph Healy, Jan. 28, 1840, in *The Letters of John Greenleaf Whittier*, ed. John B. Pickard (Cambridge, MA: Belknap Press of Harvard University Press, 1975), 1:381; LT to Seth Gates, Feb. 29, 1840, Mar. 10, 1840, LT Papers.

13. LT to Seth Gates, Mar. 10, 1840, LT Papers; *Emancipator*, Sept. 14, 1837; JL to Roger Hooker Leavitt, Nov. 9, 1841, JL Papers; *Philanthropist*, Jan. 6, 1837; WS to AAP, Jan. 12, 1839, AAP Papers. Unfortunately the list is no longer preserved with Slade's letter; JL to WJ, Feb. 6, 1840, John Jay Collection. On Jay's 1839 book-length indictment of the Slave Power, see chapter 1 above.

14. Thomas Morris to GB, in *Philanthropist*, Oct. 28, 1840. The best accounts of Leavitt's lobbying work can be found in James McPherson, "Joshua Leavitt and the Antislavery Insurgency in the Whig Party, 1839–1842," *Journal of Negro History* 43 (July 1963): 177–195; James B. Stewart, *Joshua R. Giddings and the Tactics of Radical Politics* (Cleveland: Press of Case Western Reserve University, 1970), 52–53, 66–71, 87–90; and Hugh Davis, *Joshua Leavitt: Evangelical Abolitionist* (Baton Rouge: Louisiana State University Press, 1990), 176–200. Still, Leavitt's important place in American political history has eluded many antebellum political historians. Michael F. Holt's encyclopedic *Rise and Fall of the American Whig Party: Jacksonian Politics and the Onset of Civil War* (New York: Oxford University Press, 1999), for example, fails to note Leavitt's efforts to lobby Whig legislators.

15. Stanley Harrold, *Subversives: Antislavery Community in Washington, D.C., 1828–1865* (Baton Rouge: Louisiana State University Press, 2003). On Torrey, see 64–93.

16. Whitney R. Cross, *The Burned-over District: The Social and Intellectual History of Enthusiastic Religion in Western New York State, 1800–1850* (Ithaca, NY: Cornell University Press, 1950), 217–226, situates abolitionism in the small towns and cities of this mostly rural but decidedly commercial region. Many of these were, not coincidentally, areas of Whig electoral strength, as noted in James B. Stewart, "Abolitionists, Insurgents, and Third Parties: Sectionalism and Partisan Politics in Northern Whiggery, 1836–1844," in *Crusaders and Compromisers*, ed. Kraut, 26–27; Edward Magdol, *The Antislavery Rank and File: A Social Profile of the Abolitionists' Constituency* (Westport, CT: Greenwood Press, 1986), esp. ch. 4, 5. Also see Bruce Laurie, *Beyond Garrison: Antislavery and Social Reform* (New York: Cambridge University Press, 2005), esp. ch. 4; JG, "Diary of *Three months* During the Second session of the twenty fifth congress of the United States," Entry for Jan. 29, 1839, JG Papers. Some of the other Whig representatives allied with Gates, Giddings, and Slade and who at times collaborated with abolitionists include Sherlock Andrews of Ohio, Nathaniel Borden, William Calhoun, William Jackson (who became a staunch Liberty man in the 1840s, after serving as a Whig congressman in the mid-1830s), and Stephen C. Phillips of Massachusetts, Francis James of Pennsylvania, and Heman Allen and John Mattocks of Vermont.

17. For example see *Philanthropist*, Feb. 19, 1836, New York *Colored American*, July 21, 1838, and Anti-Slavery Convention of American Women, *Address to the Senators and Representatives of the Free States, in the Congress of the United States* (Philadelphia: Merrihew and Gunn, 1838); WS to Abel Libolt, Jan. 25, 1839, in *Voice of Freedom*, Mar. 30, 1839; WS to James Slade, Jan. 28, 1836, WS to William (son) Slade, Mar. 27, 1836, WS to Abigail Slade, Dec. 22, 1837, Slade Family Papers, Henry Sheldon Museum, Stewart-Swift Research Center, Middlebury, VT, vol. 1: William Slade Letters (Domestic Correspondence Scrapbook); WS to William (son) Slade, Dec. 31, 1837, ibid.

18. WS to Abigail Slade, Dec. 22, 1837, Slade Family Papers; WS to William (son) Slade, Dec. 31, 1837, ibid.; WS to Dr. Isaac Parrish, Mar. 18, 1836, in *Emancipator*, July 14, 1836; WS to James Slade, Dec. 20, 1838. Also see WS to Abigail Slade, Dec. 26, 1838; LT journal entry for

Dec. 9, 1838, LT Papers; WS to William (son) Slade, Dec. 31, 1837; WS to JG, July 25, 1839, JG papers; letter from WS, in *Emancipator*, May 6, 1841.

19. Uri Seeley to JG, Nov. 28, 1838, JG Papers; JG diary, entry for Dec. 14, 1838, ibid.; JG to "Sir," Feb. 26, 1839, Joshua R. Giddings Miscellaneous Manuscripts, NYHS.

20. For examples of the abolitionist constituent letters Giddings received, see Uri Seeley to JG, Nov. 28, 1838, and Edward Wade to JG, January 29, 1839, JG Papers. GB to JG, February 7, 1839, G-J Papers; *CG*, 25th Congress, 3rd Session, 181; "Remarks of Mr. Giddings (of Ohio,) Wednesday, February 13, 1839," *Liberator*, Mar. 22, 1839; Stewart, *Joshua Giddings*, 41–43.

21. Philadelphia *Pennsylvania Freeman*, Jan. 16, 1840; letter from JL, Feb. 8, 1841, in *Emancipator*, Feb. 18, 1841; JG, "The Florida War," in *Speeches in Congress* (Cambridge, MA: John P. Jewett & Company, 1853), 10; Edward Wade to JG, Apr. 3, 1841, JG Papers; *Colored American*, Feb. 27, 1841; SPC to JG, Dec. 30, 1841, in *The Salmon P. Chase Papers*, ed. John Niven (Kent, OH: Kent State University Press, 1993), 2:81–83; E. D. Moore to AAP, Jan. 10, 1842, AAP Papers.

22. JQA, *Memoirs*, ed. CFA, 10:287; Howard Jones, *Mutiny on the Amistad: The Saga of a Slave Revolt and Its Impact on American Abolition, Law, and Diplomacy* (New York: Oxford University Press, 1987), 144–148.

23. Jones, *Mutiny on the Amistad*, 153–55; LT to WJ, Oct. 29, 1840, John Jay Collection; Gates to GS, Feb. 1, 1841, GS Papers; JQA to JL, Mar. 15, 1841, Adams Family Papers.

24. JGW to Abijah Wyman Thayer, Jan. 10, 1836, in *Letters of JGW*, ed. Pickard, 1:185–187; JGW to EWJ, Feb. 25, 1834, in ibid., 1:142; JGW to Rantoul, March 13, 1837, in ibid., 1:226–227.

25. *Emancipator*, Mar. 22, Apr. 26, Oct. 25, 1838, Oct. 17, 1839; *Liberator*, Apr. 20, 1838; "Abstract of Sixth Annual Report of the Executive Committee of the American Anti-Slavery Society," in *Philanthropist*, May 21, 1839.

26. Jonathan Blanchard to AAP, May 5, 1837, in *Emancipator*, May 18, 1837; letter from Jonathan Blanchard, Sept. 18, 1837, in *Emancipator*, Sept. 28, 1837. Stevens had established his antislavery credentials both in the legislature and by defending fugitive slaves in court. Hans Louis Trefousse, *Thaddeus Stevens: Nineteenth-century Egalitarian* (Chapel Hill: University of North Carolina Press, 1997), 46–47, 50–51; *Pennsylvania Freeman*, Jan. 25, Feb. 22, 1838; letter from Thaddeus Stevens, July 15, 1839, in *Emancipator*, Aug. 29, 1839. This was the Albany convention that pledged the abolitionist movement to political action, but not yet to forming an independent party.

27. Robert Purvis, *Appeal of Forty Thousand Citizens, Threatened with Disfranchisement, to the People of Pennsylvania* (Philadelphia: Merrihew and Gunn, 1838); *Proceedings of the State Convention of the Colored Freemen of Pennsylvania* (Pittsburgh: Matthew M. Grant, 1841), 4–5, 12–13. On Michigan, see for example, *Minutes of the State Convention of the Colored Citizens of the State of Michigan* (Detroit: William Harsha, 1843). On Midwestern Black Laws and activism against them, see Robertson, *Hearts Beating for Liberty*, 6–7, 59–66, and Dana Elizabeth Weiner, *Race and Rights: Fighting Slavery and Prejudice in the Old Northwest, 1830–1870* (DeKalb: Northern Illinois University Press, 2013), 34–75.

28. *Colored American*, June 16, 23, July 14, 1838, July 27, 1839; "Proceedings of the New York State Convention held in the city of Troy, August 25th, 26th, and 27th, 1841," in *Colored American*, Sept. 11, 1841; *Pennsylvania Freeman*, Mar. 17, 1841; Jane H. Pease and William H. Pease, *They Who Would be Free: Blacks Search for Freedom, 1830–1861* (New York: Atheneum, 1974), 183–184, and Jane H. Pease and William H. Pease, *Bound with Them in Chains: A Biographical History of the Antislavery Movement* (Westport, CT: Greenwood Press, 1972), 169–173. On Garnet's contributions to the Liberty Party and his fight for equal suffrage in New York, see Joel Schor, *Henry Highland Garnet: A Voice of Black Radicalism in the Nineteenth Century*

(Westport, CT: Greenwood Press, 1977), 33–44; For more on this black-led suffrage campaign and its roots in the rising generation of freeborn black New Yorkers' longstanding equal citizenship demands, see Sarah Levine-Gronningsater, "Delivering Freedom: Gradual Emancipation, Black Legal Culture, and the Origins of Sectional Crisis in New York, 1759–1870" (Ph.D. diss., University of Chicago, 2014), esp. 294–302.

29. Laurie, *Beyond Garrison*, 84, 106–124; James Oliver Horton and Lois E. Horton, *Black Bostonians: Family Life and Community Struggle in the Antebellum North* (New York: Holmes and Meier, 1979), 15–25, 48–49, 73–74; Stephen Kantrowitz, *More Than Freedom: Fighting for Black Citizenship in a White Republic* (New York: Penguin Press, 2012), 158–163.

30. For an example of Camp's abolitionist sentiments, see *Voice of Freedom*, Feb. 9, Feb. 16, 1839. Barber's three unsuccessful runs for lieutenant governor are noted in Office of the Vermont Secretary of State, Vermont State Archives and Records Administration, General Election Results, Lieutenant Governor, 1813–2012, accessed June 18, 2014. https://www.sec.state.vt.us/media/308156/stoff2ltgov.pdf. Andrew S. Barker, "Chauncey Langdon Knapp and Political Abolitionism in Vermont," *New England Quarterly* 73 (Sept. 2000): 452–462. *Fourth Annual Report of the Vermont Anti-Slavery Society* (Brandon: Telegraph Office, 1838); *Fifth Annual Report of the Vermont Anti-Slavery Society* (Montpelier: Allen & Poland, 1839); *Emancipator*, June 25, 1840.

31. This brief background on Leavitt draws mainly on Davis, *Joshua Leavitt*.

32. The best, although still sparse, discussions of Gates can be found in Stewart, *Joshua Giddings*, and Davis, *Joshua Leavitt*. *Le Roy Gazette*, July 24, Sept. 19, Dec. 26, 1838. On the 1838 New York election, see chapter 1 above. Gates won abolitionists' endorsement by averring support for abolition in the District of Columbia and opposing admission of new slave states and the annexation of Texas. He also suggested that he was inclined to support banning the interstate slave trade, but that the issue warranted further investigation. Gates to C. O. Shepard, Oct. 26, 1838, in *Emancipator*, Nov. 15, 1838; ibid., Oct. 25, Dec. 13, 1838.

33. F. C. D. McKay to GS, Nov. 18, 1839, GS Papers. The partnership of Gates and McKay is advertised in Rochester *American Citizen*, Dec. 7, 1841; Gates to GS, Aug. 28, 1839, GS Papers.

34. *Le Roy Gazette*, Oct. 9, 1839; "Letter from Gerrit Smith to Hon. Seth M. Gates," Oct. 22, 1839, in *Friend of Man*, Oct. 30, 1839; *Le Roy Gazette*, Dec. 11, 1839; Gates to GS, Nov. 4, 1839, GS Papers; "Answer of Seth Gates to Letter of Gerrit Smith," Oct. 29, 1839, in *Le Roy Gazette*, Nov. 6, 1839; GS to Gates, Dec. 21, 1839, Letterbooks, GS Papers; *Emancipator*, Dec. 12, 1839.

35. *Emancipator*, Jan. 30, 1840; *CG Appendix*, 26th Congress, 1st Session, 142–144; *CG*, 26th Congress, 1st Session, 150–151; *Pennsylvania Freeman*, Feb. 6, 1840; JQA, *Memoirs*, ed. CFA, 10:206. The Johnson Gag and the surrounding debates are also discussed, in a slightly different context, above in chapter 1.

36. *CG Appendix*, 26th Congress, 1st Session, 906–907. For more on Slade's speech, see chapter 1; Edwin Clarke to Thomas Meacham, Aug. 14, 1840, Clark(e) Family Miscellaneous Manuscripts, NYHS.

37. *Emancipator*, Oct. 1, 1840; JL, "Sketch of a Speech" delivered at the first anniversary of the Massachusetts Abolition Society, May 29, 1840, in *Emancipator*, June 25, 1840; JG to [Anon.], Dec. 28, 1839, JG Papers.

38. James B. Stewart, *Holy Warriors: Abolitionists and American Slavery* (New York: Hill & Wang, 1976), 106–107; Davis, *Joshua Leavitt*, 176–180; McPherson, "Joshua Leavitt and the Antislavery Insurgency," 182–184; JL to Roger Hooker Leavitt, Dec. 10, 1841, JL Papers; Boston *Emancipator and Weekly Chronicle*, Nov. 27, 1844. From March 1844 through October 1845, the *Emancipator*'s name was changed to *Emancipator and Weekly Chronicle* before being changed back to simply *Emancipator*. In the notes that follow the citation is abbreviated as *Emanci-*

pator for issues throughout this period. *Emancipator*, May 5, 1842; JL to JG, Apr. 22, 1842, JG Papers; *Emancipator*, Jan. 21, 1841; Jn Jay to WJ, May 26, 1838, John Jay Collection. This is John Jay (1817–1894), sometimes known as John Jay II or John Jay, Jr., to distinguish him from his namesake and grandfather John Jay (1745–1829), the Revolutionary-era politician and first U.S. Supreme Court chief justice.

39. Quoted from *Ohio Free Press*, in *Emancipator*, May 13, 1841; WS to Abigail Slade, Jan. 3, 1841, Slade Family Papers; letter from WS, in *Emancipator*, May 6, 1841; Gates to GS, Feb. 1, 25, 1841, GS Papers.

40. JL to JG, Mar. 31, Oct. 29, 1841, JG Papers; SPC to JG, Dec. 30, 1841, in *SPC Papers*, ed. Niven, 2:81–83.

41. *Emancipator*, Apr. 8, May 6, June 10, 1841; WS to *Voice of Freedom*, Apr. 28, 1841, in *Emancipator*, May 13, 1841; JL to JG, Oct. 29, 1841, JG papers. On the Republican Party's roots in Whig political economy, see Ariel Ron, "Developing the Country: 'Scientific Agriculture' and the Roots of Republican Party" (Ph.D. diss., University of California, Berkeley, 2012).

42. On the tension over the rules, see *Pennsylvania Freeman*, July 7, 1841, and McPherson, "Joshua Leavitt and the Antislavery Insurgency," 184–185. Leavitt's analysis of these complicated proceedings can be found in *Emancipator*, June 24, July 1, 8, 1841. Gates defended the rule in his letter to the *Albany Evening Journal*, in *Le Roy Gazette*, July 14, 1841. For similar arguments see the letters of Slade and Giddings in *Emancipator*, July 15, 1841; ibid., July 8, 15, 1841. Also, Leavitt thought ignoring slavery to focus on the country's financial woes an exercise in futility, since they stemmed primarily, in Leavitt's view, from the instability of the slave-based sector of the American economy. See Leavitt's speech "The Financial Power of Slavery," in *Emancipator*, Oct. 22, 1840; Arthur Tappan and JL, For the Executive Committee of the American and Foreign Anti-Slavery Society, "Appeal to the Abolitionists, and the Friends of the Constitutional Right of Petition, Throughout the United States," Sept. 1, 1841, from the *Anti-Slavery Reporter*, in *Philanthropist*, Nov. 3, 1841.

43. Arthur Tappan and JL, For the Executive Committee of the American and Foreign Anti-Slavery Society, "Appeal to the Abolitionists, and the Friends of the Constitutional Right of Petition, Throughout the United States," Sept. 1, 1841, from the *Anti-Slavery Reporter*, in *Philanthropist*, Nov. 3, 1841; *CG*, 27th Congress, 2nd Session, 172.

44. JL to JG, Oct. 29, 1841, JG Papers; Miller, *Arguing about Slavery*, 403–408, provides a brief account of the antislavery "select committee" and the important role played by Leavitt and Weld, but slights Leavitt's tactical sophistication by dismissively describing him as "a pure reformer" guided by "abstract idealism". On the antislavery lobby, see also Gilbert Hobbs Barnes, *The Antislavery Impulse, 1830–1844* (New York: D. Appleton Century Company, 1933), 177–184. Barnes, however, downplays the lobby's links to the Liberty Party, as part of his more general denigration of the third-party strategy. For an informative discussion of congressional boarding house life, see Rachel A. Shelden, "Messmates' Union: Friendship, Politics, and Living Arrangements in the Capital City, 1845–1861," *Journal of the Civil War Era* 1 (Dec. 2011): 453–480. Shelden focuses on fraternal feelings nurtured in cross-sectional living arrangements far more common than the scattered hives of sectional agitators like this "abolition house." Shelden also shows that Sprigg's clientele had shifted somewhat by the late 1840s (after the gag rule had been repealed and Leavitt had gone, though Giddings remained).

45. JL to Birney, Oct. 12, 1841, in *Letters of James Gillespie Birney, 1831–1857*, ed. Dwight L. Dumond (1938; rep., Gloucester, MA: Peter Smith, 1966), 2:638–640; *Emancipator*, Oct. 14, 1841; letter from JL in ibid., Dec. 10, 1841.

46. JG to Laura Waters Giddings, Jan. 1, 1843, JG Papers; TDW to LT, Dec. 14, 1841, in *Letters of TDW, Angelina Grimké Weld and Sarah Grimké*, ed. Barnes and Dumond, 2:881;

LT to GS, Feb. 7, 1842, GS Papers; Angelina Grimké Weld and Sarah Grimké to TDW, Feb. 1842, Weld-Grimké Collection, William L. Clements Library, University of Michigan, Ann Arbor; Robert H. Abzug, *Passionate Liberator: Theodore Dwight Weld and the Dilemma of Reform* (New York: Oxford University Press, 1980), 225–238, explains that Weld rejected Liberty partisanship as part of a broader withdrawal from organized reform associations. On Weld's lobbying, see also Barnes, *Antislavery Impulse*, 180–195, though Barnes excessively privileges Weld over Leavitt.

47. McPherson, "Joshua Leavitt and the Antislavery Insurgency," 190–91; Barnes, *Antislavery Impulse*, 183–87.

48. JQA, *Memoirs*, ed. CFA, 11:75, 79; JG, *History of the Rebellion: Its Authors and Causes* (New York: Follett, Foster & Co., 1864), 161–172; McPherson, "Joshua Leavitt and the Antislavery Insurgency," 191; Barnes, *Antislavery Impulse*, 183–187; Miller, *Arguing about Slavery*, 429–444; *CG Appendix*, 27th Congress, 2nd Session, 975; Gates to GS, Jan. 24, 1842, GS Papers. Leavitt also related his memories of Adams's "trial" in *Emancipator*, Mar. 7, 1844. *CG*, 27th Congress, 2nd Session, 214; JL to Roger Hooker Leavitt, Feb. 9, 1842, JL Papers.

49. McPherson, "Joshua Leavitt and the Antislavery Insurgency," 192; *CG*, 27th Congress, 2nd Session, 215; JG to SPC, Feb. 5, 1842, SPC Papers; JG to Laura Waters Giddings, Feb. 6, 1842, JG Papers. Also see Stewart, *Joshua Giddings*, 71–73. On the *Courier* and its longtime editor Joseph Buckingham, see Laurie, *Beyond Garrison*, 54–55.

50. WJ to JQA, Feb. 11, 1842, Adams Family Papers; Edward Wade to JG, Jan. 26, 1842, JG Papers; *Emancipator*, Mar. 31, 1842.

51. Weld explained this concept in *The Power of Congress over the District of Columbia* (New York: John F. Trow, 1838). For more on the legal reasoning employed in debating the fate of the *Creole* slaves, see Oakes, *Freedom National*, 22–26; Barnes, *Antislavery Impulse*, 183–189; *CG*, 27th Congress, 2nd Session, 342–346.

52. Gates to JG, Mar. 25, Apr. 4, 1842, JG Papers; Stewart, *Joshua Giddings*, 71–76; JL to JG, Apr. 22, 1842, JG Papers.

53. GS to W. M. Clarke and Chas. Wheaton, Apr. 7, 1842, Letterbooks, GS Papers; WS to JG, Mar. 26, 1842, JG Papers.

54. *Philanthropist*, Apr. 6, 13, 1842. On King's efforts, see JG to Gates, Apr. 1, 1842, GS Papers; SPC to JG, May 19, 1842, JG Papers; AAP to Joseph Sturge, Apr. 30, 1842, Amos August Phelps Copybooks, Anti-Slavery Collection, Boston Public Library; Miller, *Arguing about Slavery*, 467, 472; JG, *History of the Rebellion*, 197; Scott R. Meinke, "Slavery, Partisanship, and Procedure in the U.S. House: The Gag Rule, 1836–1845," *Legislative Studies Quarterly* 32 (Feb. 2007): 33–57, affirms this contemporary assessment that antislavery constituent pressure helped defeat the gag. As many districts grew increasingly anti–Slave Power, Northern Democrats became less willing to sustain the gag, a phenomenon, though, that operated primarily through inter-term replacement of gag supporters with gag opponents, as shown by Jeffery A. Jenkins and Charles Stewart III, "The Gag Rule, Congressional Politics, and the Growth of Anti-Slavery Popular Politics," unpublished paper, draft of Apr. 16, 2005, http://web.mit.edu/cstewart/www/gag_rule_v12.pdf.

55. JQA, "Address to his Constituents, delivered at Braintree, September 17," in *Quincy Patriot*, Oct. 29, 1842; LT to JL, Dec. 29, 1843, LT Papers. On the proslavery motives behind Tyler's efforts to secure Texas, see Matthew Jason Karp, "'This Vast Southern Empire': The South and the Foreign Policy of Slavery, 1833–1861" (Ph.D. diss., University of Pennsylvania, 2011), 170–216.

56. Gates to GS, Mar. 14, 1842, Feb. 9, 1843, Apr. 8, 1842, GS Papers; Boston *Emancipator and Free American*, May 11, 1843. From December 1841 through March 1844, the *Emancipator*'s

name was changed to *Emancipator and Free American*. In the notes that follow, the citation is abbreviated as *Emancipator* for issues throughout this period; ibid., May 25, 1843.

57. Gates to GS, Jan. 24, Feb. 4, 1842, GS Papers. Gates had also battled illness while in Congress. At one point in 1841, Gates was so sick that a Liberty paper praised him for "almost risking his life" when he "came out of his sick room" to vote for a bankruptcy bill. Rochester *American Citizen*, Aug. 31, 1841; Gates to JG, July 31, Dec. 5, 1843, Oct. 2, 1844, JG Papers; Gates to GS, Sept. 18, 26, Oct. 10, 1843, GS Papers. Gates never again served in elected office, although he later became one of western New York's leading Free Soilers and ran for lieutenant governor in both 1848 and 1852. Washington (DC) *National Era*, July 13, 27, 1848, Oct. 7, 1852.

58. JGW to JQA, Feb. 10, 1841, in *Letters of JGW*, ed. Pickard, 1:492–493; *Emancipator*, Mar. 7, 1844. For counterexamples critical of Adams, see Birney to Leicester King, Jan. 1, 1844, and EWJ to Birney, Feb. 6, 1844, in *Letters of James Birney*, ed. Dumond, 2:766–773, 777; *Quincy Patriot*, Dec. 9, 1843.

59. On the Prigg decision and its implications, see Don E. Fehrenbacher, *The Slaveholding Republic: An Account of the United States Government's Relations to Slavery*, ed. Ward M. McAfee (New York: Oxford University Press, 2002), 219–225, and Paul Finkelman, "Story Telling on the Supreme Court: Prigg v Pennsylvania and Justice Joseph Story's Judicial Nationalism," *Supreme Court Review* 1994 (1994): 247–294. On personal liberty laws, see Thomas D. Morris, *Free Men All: The Personal Liberty Laws of the North, 1780-1861* (Baltimore: Johns Hopkins University Press, 1974). On those proposed in response to *Prigg*, see 107–126.

60. William F. Channing to JQA, Jan. 31, 1843, Adams Family Papers; Boston *Latimer Journal, and North Star*, Nov. 14, 23, 1842, in Papers related to the George Latimer Case, Massachusetts Historical Society; Louis Filler, *The Crusade against Slavery* (New York: Harper & Brothers, 1960), 171; Laurie, *Beyond Garrison*, 78–80, 116–118; Wm. F. Channing and Henry I. Bowditch to JQA, Feb. 12, 1843, Adams Family Papers; Washington *National Intelligencer*, quoted in *Emancipator*, Mar. 9, 1843; *Latimer Journal*, May 10, 1843; JG to TDW, Feb. 21, 1843, in *Letters of Theodore Dwight Weld, Angelina Grimké Weld and Sarah Grimké*, ed. Barnes and Dumond, 2:975–977; *U.S. Gazette*, quoted in *Emancipator*, Mar. 9, 1843.

61. LT to JL, Jan. 9, 1844, LT Papers; JG to TDW, Jan. 28, 1844, in *Letters of Theodore Dwight Weld, Angelina Grimké Weld and Sarah Grimké*, ed. Barnes and Dumond, 2:990–991; LT to GB, Jan. 18, 1844, LT Papers; Davis, *Joshua Leavitt*, 222-224; *Emancipator*, Dec. 11, 1844; William L. Chaplin Correspondence, in *Albany Patriot*, Dec. 18, 1844.

62. *CG*, 28th Congress, 2nd Session, 7; Gates to JG, Oct. 2, 1844, JG Papers. For more on how this 1844 presidential campaign shaped political abolitionists' relationships with antislavery Whigs, see chapter 3 below; *Albany Patriot*, Dec. 18, 1844, Jan. 8, Feb. 12, 1845. On the *National Era*'s founding, and its connection to earlier lobbying, see more below, and also Harrold, *Gamaliel Bailey and Antislavery Union*, 81–84, 127–128, and Harrold, "Gamaliel Bailey, Antislavery Journalist and Lobbyist," in *In the Shadow of Freedom: The Politics of Slavery in the National Capital*, ed. Paul Finkelman and Donald R. Kennon (Athens, OH: Ohio University Press, 2011), 58–82.

Interlude Two

1. New York *Emancipator*, May 27, 1841; *Le Roy Gazette*, May 12, June 2, 1841. Fillmore fully expected to win, having already lined up support from most of New York's large Whig delegation. Robert J. Rayback, *Millard Fillmore: Biography of a President* (Buffalo: Buffalo Historical Society, 1959), 117–118.

2. Seth Gates to GS, June 7, 1841, GS Papers. On White see William Henry Smith, *Speakers*

of the House of Representatives of the United States (1928; rep., New York: AMS Press, 1971), 111–113; Seth Gates to James Birney, June 7, 1841, in *Letters of James Gillespie Birney, 1831–1857*, ed. Dwight L. Dumond (1938; rep., Gloucester, MA: Peter Smith, 1966), 2:630; JQA, *Memoirs of John Quincy Adams, Comprising Portions of his Diary from 1795 to 1848*, ed. CFA (Philadelphia: J. B. Lippincott & Co., 1874–1877), 10:470; *CG*, 27th Congress, 1st Session, 2.

3. *Emancipator*, June 3, 10, 1841; Gates to GS, June 7, 1841, GS Papers.

4. Cincinnati *Philanthropist*, June 10, 1841; Gates to GS, June 7, 1841, GS Papers; Gates to Birney, June 7, 1841, in *Letters of James Birney*, ed. Dumond, 2:630–631; *Emancipator*, June 10, 1841.

5. Kings County Liberty Party Meeting, Resolutions, in *Emancipator*, Oct. 14, 1841; ibid., July 15, 1841.

Chapter Three

1. On nineteenth-century party tickets, see Richard Franklin Bensel, *The American Ballot Box in the Mid-Nineteenth Century* (New York: Cambridge University Press, 2004), 14–18.

2. On the "party period," see, for example, Joel Silbey, *The American Political Nation, 1838–1893* (Stanford, CA: Stanford University Press, 1991), and Ronald P. Formisano, "The 'Party Period' Revisited," *Journal of American History* 86 (June 1999): 93–120. Even historians that take seriously the third-party tradition in nineteenth-century America often depict the Liberty Party as emblematic of antipartisan third-party thought. See, for example, Mark Voss-Hubbard, "The Third Party Tradition Reconsidered: Parties and American Public Life, 1830–1900," *Journal of American History* 86 (June 1999): 121–150, esp. p. 130.

3. Henry Mayer's adulatory biography of William Lloyd Garrison derides Liberty men as naively striving for the "fantasy of an abolitionist political takeover," *All on Fire, William Lloyd Garrison and the Abolition of Slavery* (New York: W. W. Norton & Company, 1998), 383. See also Aileen S. Kraditor, *Means and Ends in American Abolitionism: Garrison and His Critics on Strategy and Tactics, 1834–1850* (Chicago: Ivan R. Dee, Inc., 1989 [1967]), esp. ch. 6; Lewis Perry, *Radical Abolitionism: Anarchy and the Government of the God in the Antislavery Thought* (Knoxville: University of Tennessee Press, 1973), 170, presents the Liberty Party as "antipolitical, . . . moralistic, . . . and individualistic."

4. Gilbert Hobbs Barnes, *The Antislavery Impulse* (New York: D. Appleton Century Company, 1933), 176, for example, characterizes the Liberty Party as "the most pathetic residue of antislavery organization." See also Alan M. Kraut, "Partisanship and Principles: The Liberty Party in Antebellum Political Culture," in Kraut, ed. *Crusaders and Compromiser: Essays on the Relationship of the Antislavery Struggle to the Antebellum Party System* (Westport, CT: Greenwood Press, 1983), 71–100, and Kraut, "The Forgotten Reformers: A Profile of Third Party Abolitionists in Antebellum New York," in *Antislavery Reconsidered: New Perspectives on the Abolitionists*, ed. Lewis Perry and Michael Fellman (Baton Rouge: Louisiana State University Press, 1979), 119–145; Douglas M. Strong, *Perfectionist Politics: Abolitionism and the Religious Tensions of American Democracy* (Syracuse, NY: Syracuse University Press, 1999), esp. 81–83, suggests that Liberty men (at least in upstate New York) aimed primarily to assert moral authority and transform politics by example, rather than by manipulating political institutions with the purpose and effectiveness that I describe. Similar themes figure prominently in Vernon L. Volpe, *Forlorn Hope of Freedom: The Liberty Party in the Old Northwest* (Kent, OH: Kent State University Press, 1990).

5. Samuel Sewall (on behalf of the state Central Committee) to EWJ, Sept. 9, 1840, EWJ Papers; Henry B. Stanton to EWJ, July 4, 1843, ibid.; AS to Samuel Webb, Nov. 13, 1841, Alvan

Stewart Papers, NYHS. Utica *Friend of Man*, June 1, Aug. 24, 1841; Hallowell (ME) *Liberty Standard*, Dec. 8, 1841. By 1844, New York Liberty men expressed grander ambitions of creating precinct-level rolls listing every Liberty voter, *Albany Patriot*, Dec. 11, 1844. For a modern analysis of how individual local leaders operated as key political abolitionist organizers, see Bruce Laurie, *Rebels in Paradise: Sketches of Northampton Abolitionists* (Amherst: University of Massachusetts Press, 2015).

 6. Stacey M. Robertson, *Hearts Beating for Liberty: Women Abolitionists in the Old Northwest* (Chapel Hill: University of North Carolina Press, 2010), ch. 2; Julie Roy Jeffrey, "The Liberty Women of Boston: Evangelicalism and Antislavery Politics," *New England Quarterly* 85 (Mar. 2012): 38–77; Alice Taylor, "From Petitions to Partyism: Antislavery and the Domestication of Maine Politics in the 1840s and 1850s," *New England Quarterly* 77 (Mar. 2004): 70–88; Michael D. Pierson, *Free Hearts and Free Homes: Gender and American Antislavery Politics* (Chapel Hill: University of North Carolina Press, 2003), 34–37; Frederick J. Blue, "Free Men, Free Soil, and Free Homes: Jane Swisshelm's Search," *No Taint of Compromise: Crusaders in Antislavery Politics* (Baton Rouge: Louisiana State University Press, 2005), esp. 142–145.

 7. James Birney, "Letter No. 1," in Cincinnati *Weekly Herald and Philanthropist*, Sept. 25, 1844; Eric Foner, *Free Soil, Free Labor, Free Men: The Ideology of the Republican Party Before the Civil War* (1970; rep., Oxford: Oxford University Press, 1995), 120–123.

 8. Boston *Emancipator and Free American*, Mar. 30, 1843. From December 1841 through March 1844, the *Emancipator*'s name was changed to *Emancipator and Free American*. In the notes that follow, the citation is abbreviated as *Emancipator* for issues throughout this period.

 9. GS to Charles King, Mar. 18, 1842, Letterbooks, GS Papers. Also see Richard H. Sewell, *Ballots for Freedom: Antislavery Politics in the United States, 1837–1860* (New York: Oxford University Press, 1976), 86–88; SPC to LT, Feb. 15, 1843, in *The Salmon P. Chase Papers*, ed. John Niven (Kent, OH: Kent State University Press, 1993), 2:101–102; SPC to William Ellery Channing, May 3, 1842, in ibid., 2:94–96. On abolitionist activity in the Border South, see Stanley Harrold, *Subversives: Anti-Slavery Community in Washington D.C., 1828–1865* (Baton Rouge: Louisiana State University Press, 2003), and *Abolitionists and the South, 1831–1861* (Lexington: University of Kentucky Press, 1995). On Chase and Bailey's ideas about Southern abolitionism see ibid., 135–139.

 10. On arguments over the meaning and validity of the one-idea principle, see Sewell, *Ballots for Freedom*, 88–90; Philadelphia *Pennsylvania Freeman*, Aug. 4, 1841.

 11. Reinhard O. Johnson, *The Liberty Party, 1840–1848: Antislavery Third-Party Politics in the United States* (Baton Rouge: Louisiana State University Press, 2009), 242–259. For more on Liberty efforts to promote racial equality, see Sewell, *Ballots for Freedom*, 95–101. For a counterargument that casts Liberty men as abandoning their antiracist principles, see Kraditor, *Means and Ends in American Abolitionism*. Bruce Laurie's adaptation of the notion of paternalism to explain the Liberty Party's improvement over the overt racism of Massachusetts's major-party politicians offers a historiographical compromise. Laurie, *Beyond Garrison: Antislavery and Social Reform* (New York: Cambridge University Press, 2005), esp. ch. 3. Harrold, *Subversives*, argues that the most radical political abolitionists maintained a deep commitment to egalitarian interracial cooperation that was diminished among more mainstream Liberty men and later Free Soilers in the late 1840s. Omar H. Ali, *In the Balance of Power: Independent Black Politics and Third-Party Movements in the United States* (Athens: Ohio University Press, 2008), 32–41, notes the role of black Liberty Party leaders but questions the degree of support the party received from black voters. See also Benjamin Quarles, *Black Abolitionists* (New York: Oxford University Press, 1969), 183–185, and Howard H. Bell, "National Negro Conventions of the Middle 1840's: Moral Suasion v. Political Action," *Jour-

nal of Negro History 42 (Oct. 1957): 247–260. Also see ch. 2 above on black activism aimed at lobbying antislavery politicians to repeal discriminatory state laws.

12. Lowell (IL) *Genius of Liberty*, Apr. 2, 1842; The Liberty Party [JL], *The Right Sort of Politics*, Liberty Party Tract. no. 2 (Boston: J. W. Alden, 1843); Austin Willey, *The History of the Antislavery Cause in State and Nation* (Portland, ME: Brown, Thurston, and Hoyt, Fogg & Donham, 1886), 227; Albany *Tocsin of Liberty*, Nov. 24, 1841; Lee Benson, *The Concept of Jacksonian Democracy: New York as a Test Case* (Princeton: Princeton University Press, 1961), 113; Office of the Vermont Secretary of State, Vermont State Archives, General Election Results, Governor, 1789–2012, accessed June 18, 2014, https://www.sec.state.vt.us/media/308153/stofflgov.pdf; *Emancipator*, Mar. 16, 1842, Apr. 27, 1843; JGW to Samuel Edmund Sewall, Mar. 16, 1842, *The Letters of John Greenleaf Whittier*, ed. John B. Pickard (Cambridge, MA: Belknap Press of Harvard University Press, 1975), 1:549–550; Albany *Tocsin of Liberty*, Nov. 10, 1842.

13. *Emancipator*, Mar. 4, 1842, Feb. 2, 1843; GS to John Scoble, Jan. 1, 1843, GS Papers; *Emancipator*, Dec. 28, 1843; *Tocsin of Liberty*, Nov. 24, 1841.

14. JL, *The Financial Power of Slavery, The Substance of an Address Delivered in Ohio in September, 1840* (n.p., [1841?]); Edward E. Baptist, *The Half Has Never Been Told: Slavery and the Making of American Capitalism* (New York: Basic Books, 2014), esp., 261-292, and also, 326, on Leavitt's economic analysis. Charles D. Cleveland, "Address of the Liberty Party of Pennsylvania to the People of the State," in *Anti-Slavery Addresses of 1844 and 1845* (1867; rep., New York: Negro Universities Press, 1969), 40–43. See also, for example, copy of Leicester King response to J. W. Piatt, Aug. 22, 1842, SPC Papers; *Pennsylvania Freeman*, Aug. 4, 1841; and *Emancipator*, Mar. 4, 1842. James C. Jackson, *The Condition of Living* (Utica, NY: N.Y. S. A. S. Society, Monthly Tract no. 8, 1844), 7. On this facet of the Slave Power argument, see also Sewell, *Ballots for Freedom*, 103–106; Foner, *Free Soil, Free Labor, Free Men*.

15. Proceedings of the New York State Anti-Slavery Society, in *Emancipator*, Oct. 1, 1840, ibid. Dec. 17, 1840; Cincinnati *Philanthropist*, Oct. 4, 1843; *Weekly Herald and Philanthropist*, Sept. 18, Oct. 2, 1844; Henry B. Stanton to GS, GS Papers Nov. 23, 1844; AS to Samuel Webb, Feb. 7, 1843, Alvan Stewart Papers, NYHS; James C. Jackson, *The Duties and Dignities of American Freemen* (Utica: Liberty Press—Extra, 1843).

16. Thomas Morris, William Birney, Gamaliel Bailey, and William H. Brisbane to Boston Liberty Convention, Feb. 9, 1842, in *Emancipator*, June 16, 1842. This brief background on Bailey is based mostly on Stanley Harrold's excellent biography, *Gamaliel Bailey and Antislavery Union* (Kent, OH: Kent State University Press, 1986). Bailey's commitment to individual rights incorporated both opposition to racial discrimination, as well as a Democratic-leaning distrust of centralized power and affinity for working men. Stephen E. Maizlish, "Salmon P. Chase: The Roots of Ambition and the Origins of Reform," *Journal of the Early Republic* 18 (Spring, 1998): 47–70.

17. Frederick J. Blue, *Salmon P. Chase: A Life in Politics* (Kent, OH: Kent State University Press, 1987), 31–40; Foner, *Free Soil, Free Labor, Free Men*, 74–77; James Oakes, *Freedom National: The Destruction of Slavery in the United States, 1861-1865* (New York: W. W. Norton & Company, 2013), 15–18.

18. Johnson, *Liberty Party*, 259–263; Eric Foner, *Gateway to Freedom: The Hidden History of the Underground Railroad* (New York: W. W. Norton & Company, 2015), 63-189, passim, illuminates the contributions of Loguen, Ray, Pennington, Smith, Tappan, and many others to Underground Railroad operations in New York City and State; Frederick J. Blue, "The Barbarism of Slavery: Owen Lovejoy and the Congressional Assault on Slavery," *No Taint of Compromise: Crusaders in Antislavery Politics* (Baton Rouge: Louisiana State University Press, 2005), 94–96.

19. Sewell, *Ballots for Freedom*, 90–92; SPC to GS, May 14, 1842, GS Papers; SPC to JG, Jan. 21, 1842, G-J Papers; Thomas Morris, William Birney, Gamaliel Bailey, and William H. Brisbane to Boston Liberty Convention, Feb. 9, 1842, in *Emancipator*, June 16, 1842; Blue, *Salmon P. Chase*, 46–47; "Address of the Liberty Convention to the People of Ohio," in *Philanthropist*, Jan. 5, 1842.

20. JL to SPC, May 20, 1842, SPC Papers; LT to WJ, Mar. [date mutilated], 1843, LT Papers; LT to SPC, June 7, 1842, SPC Papers.

21. Albert G. Riddle to JG, June 7, 1842, JG Papers.

22. Leonard Richards, *The Slave Power: The Free North and Southern Domination* (Baton Rouge: Louisiana State University Press, 2000), 137, notes that "abolitionists made their heaviest inroads in districts represented by Whigs," since antislavery societies, the Liberty Party, and the Whig Party were all likely to be strong in the same districts. For further discussion of the relationship between antislavery and Northern Whig partisanship see James B. Stewart, "Reconsidering the Abolitionists in an Age of Fundamentalist Politics," *Journal of the Early Republic* 26 (Spring 2006): 1–24, and "Abolitionists, Insurgents, and Third Parties: Sectionalism and Partisan Politics in Northern Whiggery, 1836–1844," in *Crusaders and Compromisers*, ed. Kraut, 26–43. On antislavery Democrats see Jonathan H. Earle, *Jacksonian Antislavery & the Politics of Free Soil, 1824-1854* (Chapel Hill: University of North Carolina Press, 2004); Boston *Daily Atlas*, Nov. 9, 1842; William F. Ainsworth to EWJ, Nov. 26, 1845, EWJ Papers.

23. *Emancipator*, July 20, 1843; "Appeal to the Anti-Slavery Whigs of Monroe, and New York Generally," Rochester *American Citizen*, Oct. 19, 1841.

24. "Letter from John Mattocks," July 29, 1843, in Montpelier *Voice of Freedom*, Aug. 10, 1843; *Emancipator*, Oct. 5, 1843. For more on Baldwin's antislavery candidacy and Liberty Party politics in Connecticut, see Johnson, *Liberty Party*, 131–134; Edward Wade to SPC, Oct. 24, 1843, SPC Papers. On Liberty electoral challenges to Giddings, see also James B. Stewart, *Joshua Giddings and the Tactics of Radical Politics* (Cleveland: Press of Case Western Reserve University, 1970), 84–87, 95–98.

25. *Weekly Herald and Philanthropist*, Oct. 2, 1844, Sept. 25, 1844; Slade to JG, June 6, 1844, JG Papers.

26. *Weekly Herald and Philanthropist*, Oct. 2, 1844; Ann Arbor *Signal of Liberty*, Oct. 21, 1844.

27. The most significant speech to this effect was Clay's speech against abolitionist petitioning on Feb. 7, 1839, *CG*, 25th Congress, 3rd Session, 167, which touched off the debate with Thomas Morris that helped popularize the phrase "Slave Power." See chapter 1 above; *Friend of Man*, Mar. 20, 1841; *Weekly Herald and Philanthropist*, Mar. 16, 1844; *Emancipator*, Sept. 15, 1842; Albany *Tocsin of Liberty*, Nov. 11, 1842.

28. *Emancipator*, Jan. 28, 1841.

29. *Emancipator*, Dec. 7, 1843; ibid., Feb. 9, 1843; *Pennsylvania Freeman*, Apr. 25, 1844; *Emancipator*, Mar. 16, 1843.

30. *Emancipator*, July 20, 1843. See LT to Slade, Nov. 18, 1843, LT Papers; Boston *Emancipator and Weekly Chronicle*, July 31, 1844. From March of 1844 through October of 1845, the *Emancipator*'s name was changed to *Emancipator and Weekly Chronicle* before being changed back to simply *Emancipator*. In the notes that follow, the citation is abbreviated as *Emancipator* for issues throughout this period; ibid., Mar. 7, 1844; Charles Davis to Erastus Fairbanks, Apr. 21, 1840, Fairbanks Papers, VHS; Erastus Fairbanks to Albert G. Whittemore, Oct. 27, 1843, Misc. 437, VHS.

31. "Henry Clay and Thomas Corwin," *Philanthropist*, Sept. 17, 1842; GB to James Birney, Nov. 16, 1842, in *Letters of James Gillespie Birney, 1831-1857*, ed. Dwight L. Dumond (1938; rep.,

Gloucester, MA: Peter Smith, 1966), 2:709–712; *Emancipator* Oct. 5, 1843; James A. Briggs to Oran Follett, July 26, 1843, quoted in James Stewart, "Abolitionists, Insurgents and Third Parties: Sectionalism and Partisan Politics in Northern Whiggery, 1836–1844," in *Crusaders and Compromisers*, ed. Kraut, 34.

32. Johnson, *Liberty Party*, ch. 5, provides the best extant illustration of how majority-rule systems created electoral opportunities for New England Liberty men, but focuses on Liberty influence in state politics, rather than on connecting these contested local and state races to national Liberty strategy or congressional politics.

33. For an excellent discussion of dilatory legislative strategies (and of attempts at using procedural change to limit them), see Douglas Dion, *Turning the Thumbscrew: Minority Rights and Procedural Change in Legislative Politics* (Ann Arbor: University of Michigan Press, 1997).

34. In the other two Vermont gubernatorial contests, Liberty men also came close to denying the victor a popular majority, with Whig Charles Paine winning 50.9 percent of the vote in 1842, and William Slade winning 51.5 percent in 1844. Office of the Vermont Secretary of State, Vermont State Archives, General Election Results, Governor, 1789–2012, accessed June 18, 2014, https://www.sec.state.vt.us/media/308153/stofflgov.pdf.

35. Laurie, *Beyond Garrison*, 74–76, 80–81.

36. *Emancipator*, Dec. 10, 1841; "LEGISLATIVE ELECTIONS," ibid., Sept. 8, 1842.

37. *Emancipator*, Nov. 4, 1841; Sewell, *Ballots for Freedom*, 85–86; *Emancipator*, Nov. 25, 1841, Dec. 10, 1841. On fugitive slaves in New Bedford, see Kathryn Grover, *The Fugitive's Gibraltar: Escaping Slaves and Abolitionism in New Bedford, Massachusetts* (Amherst: University of Massachusetts Press, 2001). Grover, however, barely mentions the Liberty Party.

38. *Emancipator*, January 5, 1843; Johnson, *Liberty Party*, 93; Boston *Daily Atlas*, Nov. 22, 1842. Before the legislature could choose the governor, the lower house had to organize for business. After four unsuccessful ballots for speaker, both Whigs and Democrats abandoned their caucus candidates and divided between Daniel P. King, a Whig with abolitionist sympathies, and Lewis Williams, the Liberty choice and a former Democrat. When King won with a mix of Whig and ex-Whig Liberty votes, some Liberty voices assailed third-party men who voted for King, while others celebrated that the major parties had been forced to accept speaker candidates with notable antislavery reputations. For more on these developments, see *Emancipator*, Jan. 12, 19, 1843, and Reinhard Johnson, "The Liberty Party in Massachusetts, 1840–1848: Antislavery Third Party Politics in the Bay State," *Civil War History* 28 (1982): 238–265, esp. 250–252, which focuses on Liberty debates about under which circumstances support for major-party politicians could be acceptable.

39. *Emancipator*, Jan. 12, 19, 1843; Nina Moore Tiffany, *Samuel E. Sewall: A Memoir* (Boston: Houghton Mifflin, 1898), 94–95; *Emancipator*, Feb. 9, 1843.

40. Michael J. Dubin, *United States Congressional Elections, 1788–1997: The Official Results of the Elections of the 1st through 105th Congresses* (Jefferson, NC: McFarland, 1998), 136–137.

41. *Emancipator*, Feb. 2, 23, Apr. 13, 1843; Dubin, *United States Congressional Elections*, 132–133, 136–137; Laurie, *Beyond Garrison*, 75–76.

42. *Emancipator*, May, 8, 1844; *Letter of The Honorable William Jay to Hon. Theo. Frelinghuysen* (New York: 1844); William W. Freehling, *The Road to Disunion*, vol. 1, *Secessionists at Bay, 1776–1854* (New York: Oxford University Press, 1990), 429–430; David M. Potter, *The Impending Crisis, 1848–1861*, ed. Don E. Fehrenbacher (New York: Harper & Row, 1976), 23–24.

43. Sewell, *Ballots for Freedom*, 121–125; SPC to James Birney, Jan. 21, 1842, in *Letters of James Birney*, ed. Dumond, 2:661–662. Another drawback of Birney's candidacy was his aversion to universal manhood suffrage. For example, see GB to Birney, Mar. 31, 1843, ibid., 725–728. For Birney's explanation of his views see Birney to Samuel Lewis, July 13, 1843, ibid.,

743–748; SPC to JG, Jan. 21, Feb. 9, 1842, G-J Papers. For an overview of Chase's role in these efforts, see Blue, *Salmon P. Chase*, 47-50; "LIBERTY" to GB, Aug. 22, 1842, in *Philanthropist*, Sept. 10, 1842; Birney to SPC, Feb. 2, 1842, in *Letters of James Birney*, ed. Dumond, 2:670–672; JL to Birney, Feb. 14, 1842, ibid., 673–674; JL to SPC, Feb. 16, 1843, SPC Papers.

44. GB to Birney, Mar. 31, 1843, in *Letters of James Birney*, ed. Dumond, 2:725–728; Bertram Wyatt-Brown, *Lewis Tappan and the Evangelical War against Slavery* (Cleveland: Press of Case Western Reserve University, 1969), 269, 274–276; LT to SPC, Mar. 20, 1843, LT Papers; Chase to LT, Feb. 15, 1843, in *SPC Papers*, ed. Niven, 2:101–102; H. B. Stanton to GS, Aug. 4, 1843, GS to H. B. Stanton, Aug. 9, 1843, GS Papers; SPC to JG, Feb. 9, 1842, G-J Papers; Birney to Charles H. Stewart and JL, Aug. 17, 1843, in *Letters of James Birney*, ed. Dumond, 2:754–758. On Leavitt's response to Chase and Bailey's efforts, see Hugh Davis, *Joshua Leavitt: Evangelical Abolitionist* (Baton Rouge: Louisiana State University Press, 1990), 207–211.

45. Freehling, *Road to Disunion*, 1:426–430, 433–437; Amy S. Greenberg, *A Wicked War: Polk, Clay, Lincoln, and the 1846 U.S. Invasion of Mexico* (New York: Knopf, 2012), 17–20, 33–37, 55–58; Michael F. Holt, *Rise and Fall of the American Whig Party: Jacksonian Politics and the Onset of the Civil War* (New York: Oxford University Press, 1999), 178–186; *Voice of Freedom*, July 4, Aug. 15, 1844; *Pennsylvania Freeman*, Apr. 25, 1844; Utica *Liberty Press*, Aug. 6, 1844; letter of WS, July 10, 1844, in *New-York Daily Tribune*, July 27, 1844.

46. *Bangor Gazette*, quoted in *Emancipator*, July 10, 1844; LT to Benjamin Tappan, Oct. 14, 1844, LT Papers.

47. While 62,000 is the standard estimate of Birney's total (see for example Johnson, *Liberty Party*, 45), Sewell, *Ballots for Freedom*, 110, puts Birney's 1844 tally at 65,608. It is worth noting that Birney further hurt his cause by giving public expression to his doubts about universal manhood suffrage. Ibid., 109–111, 120–124. Benson, *Concept of Jacksonian Democracy*, 134–136, demonstrates that, although New York Whigs seem to have lost far more votes to the Liberty Party than Democrats did, the Liberty Party's gains had been made primarily in the 1843 state elections. In fact, the New York Liberty vote dropped off slightly from 1843 to 1844; *Emancipator*, Nov. 13, 1844; *New-York Daily Tribune*, Nov. 9, 1844; *Emancipator*, Oct. 30, 1844; EWJ to Wife, [Nov. 1844], EWJ Papers.

48. Utica *Liberty Press*, July 19, 1845; Gerrit Smith, "William H. Seward, Esquire: Peterboro, January 1, 1845" (Peterboro[?], NY, 1845), GS Papers.

49. Henry B. Stanton to GS, Nov. 12, 1844, GS Papers; Dubin, *United States Congressional Elections*, 142–143.

50. Theodore Sedgwick III [Veto, pseud.], *Thoughts on the Proposed Annexation of Texas to the United States* (New York: D. Fanshaw, 1844), quote on 45. On Tappan's efforts to coordinate the pamphlet's distribution, see, in LT Papers, LT to Sedgwick, Mar. 22, 24, May 14, 1844, LT to JG, Apr. 30, June 10, 1844, and LT to Luther Severance, July 18, 1844; Earle, *Jacksonian Antislavery*, 54, 63–65; Richards, *Slave Power*, 144–148, For more on this "diffusion" theory, articulated most prominently by Mississippi Democratic senator Robert Walker, see Thomas Hietala, *Manifest Design: American Exceptionalism and Empire* (Ithaca: Cornell University Press, 1985), 30–34; Lemuel Stetson to A. C. Flagg, Dec. 31, 1844, Azariah Cutting Flagg Papers, NYPL.

51. *Letter from John P. Hale, Of New Hampshire, to his constituents, on the Proposed Annexation of Texas* (Washington: Blair & Rives, 1845), in Hale-Chandler Papers, Rauner Special Collections Library, Dartmouth College Library, Hanover, NH; Franklin Pierce to JPH, Jan. 24, 1845, ibid.; Richard H. Sewell, *John P. Hale and the Politics of Abolition* (Cambridge, MA: Harvard University Press, 1965), 52–58.

52. JGW to JPH, Jan. 24, 1845, in *Letters of JGW*, ed. Pickard, 2:654–655; Jacob H. Ela to

JPH, Jan. 15, 1845, JPH Papers; Wm. M. Claggett to JPH, Jan. 21, 1845, ibid.; John G. Parkman to JPH, Jan. 14, 1845, ibid.; Amos Tuck to JPH, Jan. 15, 1845, ibid.; Preston King to Azariah Flagg, Jan. 11, 1845, Azariah Cutting Flagg Papers, NYPL; Ela to JPH, Jan. 29, 1845, JPH Papers.

53. Sewell, *John P. Hale*, 67–76; Tuck, *Autobiographical Memoir of Amos Tuck* (n.p., 1902); G. W. Wendell to JPH, Feb. 20, 1845, JPH Papers; *Weekly Herald and Philanthropist*, Apr. 9, 1845.

54. Sewell, *John P. Hale*, 76–85; JG to JPH, Mar. 11, 1846, Hale-Chandler Papers; *Weekly Herald and Philanthropist*, June 17, 1846. Hale's old house seat, meanwhile, remained vacant for the duration of the 28th Congress. Dubin, *United States Congressional Elections*, 144n20.

55. "Letter from G[eorge]. W. Clark," June 16, 1845, in Utica *Liberty Press*, June 28, 1845, put the attendance at over 3,000. Blue, *Salmon P. Chase*, 50, estimates that it was closer to 2,000. *Weekly Herald and Philanthropist* Apr. 23, June 18, 25, 1845; Salmon P. Chase, "The Address of the Southern And Western Liberty Convention, Held at Cincinnati, June 11 and 12, 1845, To the People of the United States," in *Anti-Slavery Addresses of 1844 and 1845* (1867; rep., New York: Negro Universities Press, 1969), quotes on 111, 124; Earle, *Jacksonian Antislavery*, 154–155, with some merit, presents Chase's address as evincing Chase's interest in eventual coalition with Democrats, but Earle overstates his case. Chase's main arguments attacked the Slave Power's perversion of the Constitution and control of *both* major parties.

56. *Proceedings of the Great Convention of the Friends of Freedom in the Eastern and Middle States, Held in Boston, Oct. 1, 2, & 3, 1845* (Lowell: Pillsbury and Knapp, 1845), Quotes from 4, 15, 19. Also see Johnson, *Liberty Party*, 54–61, on this convention and on internal debates about antislavery interpretations of the U.S. Constitution.

57. *Signal of Liberty*, Mar. 30, July 4, 1846; Prairieville (WI) *American Freeman*, Aug. 11, 1846. See also Johnson, *Liberty Party*, 55.

58. JGW to the Liberty Voters of District no. 3, Jan. 1, 1844 (originally published in *Essex Transcript*), in *Letters of JGW*, ed. Pickard, 1:623–624; Martin Mitchel, "To the friends of Freedom," Oct. 25, 1844, in *Liberty Press*, Nov. 9, 1844; ibid., Nov. 1, 1845.

Chapter Four

1. *CG*, 29th Congress, 1st Session, 1214–1217; JGW to Joseph Sturge, Aug. 28, 1846, in *The Letters of John Greenleaf Whittier*, ed. John B. Pickard (Cambridge, MA: Belknap Press of Harvard University Press, 1975), 2:30.

2. A brief filibuster by Massachusetts Whig John Davis prevented a vote before the mandatory adjournment time. Davis later asserted that he had intended to delay the vote just long enough that the Senate would not have sufficient time to amend the bill and return it to the House. Davis's ploy failed when the House adjourned eight minutes before the Senate, because of a discrepancy between the chambers' clocks. While Davis was criticized for defeating the Proviso, it seems unlikely that it would have passed the Senate anyway. David M. Potter, *The Impending Crisis, 1848–1861*, ed. Don E. Fehrenbacher (New York: Harper & Row, 1976), 22–23; *CG*, 29th Congress, 2nd Session, 509.

3. SPC, "The Address of the Southern And Western Liberty Convention, Held at Cincinnati, June 11 and 12, 1845, To the People of the United States," in *Anti-Slavery Addresses of 1844 and 1845* (1867; rep., New York: Negro Universities Press, 1969), 79–83. On Chase's interpretation of the founders' antislavery views, see also Eric Foner, *Free Soil, Free Labor, Free Men: The Ideology of the Republican Party Before the Civil War* (1970; rep., Oxford: Oxford University Press, 1995), 75–77; Preston King to SPC, Aug. 16, 1847, SPC Papers; Cincinnati *Weekly Herald and Philanthropist*, Aug. 19, 1846; Washington (DC) *National Era*, Apr. 1, 1847. This slanted

history served a valuable political purpose but overlooked both the proslavery Southwest Ordinance of 1790 and the actual incursions of slavery into the Old Northwest. See John Craig Hammond, *Slavery, Freedom, and Expansion in the American West* (Charlottesville: University of Virginia Press, 2007), 1–4, 9–11.

4. Chaplain Morrison, *Democratic Politics and Sectionalism: The Wilmot Proviso Controversy* (Chapel Hill: University of North Carolina Press, 1967), cites the frustration of Van Burenite Democrats, or Barnburners, with Polk for his role in denying Van Buren the 1844 presidential nomination, distribution of patronage, 1846 veto of legislation for river and harbor improvements popular in the Northwest, and willingness to compromise with Great Britain on Oregon's territorial boundaries. Eric Foner, "The Wilmot Proviso Revisited," *Journal of American History* 56 (Sept. 1969): 262–279; Charles Buxton Going, *David Wilmot, Free-Soiler: A Biography of the Great Advocate of the Wilmot Proviso* (New York: D. Appleton and Company, 1924), which remains the only book-length biography of Wilmot, insists that Wilmot's opposition to slavery extension stemmed from genuine "ethical" motives and not crass "political calculations," 117. Frederick J. Blue's more recent biographical treatment, "Neither Slavery Nor Involuntary Servitude: David Wilmot and the Containment of Slavery," *No Taint of Compromise: Crusaders in Antislavery Politics* (Baton Rouge: Louisiana State University Press, 2005), 184–212, emphasizes free labor ideology and racism among Proviso supporters and focuses on Wilmot's construction of the Slave Power as a "landed aristocracy" (Blue's words), 193.

5. Charles G. Sellers, *The Market Revolution: Jacksonian America, 1815-1846* (New York: Oxford University Press, 1991); Sean Wilentz, "Slavery, Antislavery, and Jacksonian Democracy," in *The Market Revolution in America: Social, Political, and Religious Expressions*, ed. Melvyn Stokes and Stephen Conway (Charlottesville: University of Virginia Press, 1996), 202–223; Arthur M. Schlesinger, Jr., *The Age of Jackson* (Boston: Little, Brown and Company, 1945), 451–452; Jonathan H. Earle, *Jacksonian Antislavery & the Politics of Free Soil, 1824-1854* (Chapel Hill: University of North Carolina Press, 2004), 1–3, 66–74, 132–139, 164–165. Michael Morrison, *Slavery and the American West: The Eclipse of Manifest Destiny and the Coming of the Civil War* (Chapel Hill: University of North Carolina Press, 1997), 39–77, sees Northern Democratic anti-extensionism as rooted in strict constructionism, in contrast to notions of national moral uplift that underpinned Northern Whigs' Proviso support. In making these distinctions, Morrison underplays similarities across the rhetoric employed by the Proviso's tri-partisan proponents.

6. David R. Roediger, *The Wages of Whiteness: Race and the Making of the American Working Class* (New York: Verso, 1991), esp. 140–144. Alexander Saxton, *Rise and Fall of the White Republic* (New York: Verso, 1990), esp. 153–154, acknowledges the divisiveness of the Proviso for Democrats but still sees it as consistent with their emphasis on white male supremacy. In an intricate argument about Northern racism, Thomas Hietala, *Manifest Design: American Exceptionalism and Empire*, rev. ed. (Ithaca: Cornell University Press, 2003), 122–130, presents the Northern Democrats who initiated the Wilmot Proviso as motivated primarily by racist free labor considerations. These congressmen felt betrayed, Hietala argues, since they acquiesced in Texas annexation only after Treasury Secretary Robert Walker had promised that the black population would be contained east of the Rio Grande if the country acquired additional territory.

7. Boston *Emancipator*, Sept. 16, 1846; Prairieville (WI) *American Freeman*, Sept. 1, 1846; JGW to Joseph Sturge, Aug. 28, 1846, in *Letters of JGW*, ed. Pickard, 2:30–31; AS to Samuel Webb, Dec. 11, 1846, Alvan Stewart Papers, NYHS; *Weekly Herald and Philanthropist*, Aug. 19, 1846.

8. JG to SPC, Sept. 18, 1846, Oct. 30, 1846, SPC Papers; *Ashtabula Sentinel*, Aug. 31, 1846;

BDW, Aug. 15, 1846; *Weekly Herald and Philanthropist*, Aug. 19, 1846; Michael F. Holt, *Rise and Fall of the American Whig Party: Jacksonian Politics and the Onset of the Civil War* (New York: Oxford University Press, 1999), 251, and Sean Wilentz, *The Rise of American Democracy: Jefferson to Lincoln* (New York: W. W. Norton & Company, 2005), 597. Though the Proviso seemed to have only minimal effect on most 1846 elections, there were exceptions. Hartford's Democratic mayor, for example, worried that "the late elections are of a character to stimulate the Whigs," owing to the "growing feeling that we have been used by the south about long enough." Calvin Day to Gideon Welles, Nov. 14, 1846, Gideon Welles Papers, microform, NYPL.

9. *CG*, 29th Congress, 2nd Session, 96, 105, 114, 303, 425–426, 555–556, 573. According to Wilmot's account two years later, Polk did not expect slavery to be extended into the conquered territory and had apparently persuaded Wilmot to let the appropriation pass without controversy, *CG Appendix*, 30th Congress, 2nd Session, 139; John George Nicolay and John Hay, *Abraham Lincoln: A History* (New York: The Century Co., 1890), 285; JG to Seth Gates, Jan. 25, 1847, GS Papers; *National Era*, Mar. 11, 1847, and "How it Was Done: Correspondence of the New York *Tribune*," in ibid., Mar. 25, 1847; JG to CFA, Jan. 25, 1847, Adams Family Papers, Microfilm Edition, Massachusetts Historical Society, Boston; Leonard Richards, *The Slave Power: The Free North and Southern Domination, 1780-1860* (Baton Rouge: Louisiana State University Press, 2000), 153, notes also that eighteen of the twenty-two Northerners who ultimately helped defeat the Proviso were serving as lame ducks.

10. Rachel A. Shelden, *Washington Brotherhood: Politics, Social Life, and the Coming of the Civil War* (Chapel Hill: University of North Carolina Press, 2013), 36–40, argues that heated speeches for and against the Proviso were intended primarily as appeals to constituents rather than to influence legislation and thus exaggerate the personal enmity among members. Shelden's point, however, underscores that divisions manifested in these debates, if not necessarily on the Washington social circuit once the gavel fell, reflected the accelerating polarization of the national electorate.

11. *Emancipator*, Mar. 31, 1847; *Annual Report of the American and Foreign Anti-Slavery Society* (New York: William Harned, 1847), 4–5; Waukesha (WI) *American Freeman*, Apr. 5, 1848.

12. *CG*, 29th Congress, 2nd Session, 355; *CG*, 30th Congress, 1st Session, 552. Examples of similar condemnations of slavery as a "moral and political evil" can be found in *CG*, 29th Congress, 2nd Session, 545, and 30th Congress, 1st Session, 545–547, 664. For additional examples of language condemning slavery as unchristian and uncivilized, see *CG*, 29th Congress, 2nd Session, 443–444, 477–78; *CG Appendix*, 29th Congress, 2nd Session, 334; and *CG*, 30th Congress, 1st Session, 883.

13. For Brinkerhoff's professing to be the Proviso's true author, see his letter to SPC, Nov. 22, 1847, SPC Papers. The old but lengthy historiography attempting to adjudicate this claim is summarized in Foner, "Wilmot Proviso Revisited," 262–265; *CG*, 29th Congress, 2nd Session, 377–380.

14. *CG Appendix*, 29th Congress, 2nd Session, 282; *CG*, 30th Congress, 1st Session, 994. For other examples of this common argumentative tack, see *CG* 29th Congress, 2nd Session, 115, 181, and 30th Congress, 1st Session, 1023; *Bradford Democrat*, quoted in *National Era*, May 27, 1847.

15. *CG*, 30th Congress, 198–200, 245–246. New to Congress in late 1847, Palfrey was an accomplished theologian, public servant, and amateur historian. With his deceased father a Louisiana slaveholder (as were his living brothers), Palfrey had inherited and then freed twenty of his father's slaves a few years before his election to Congress. On Palfrey, and his many careers, see Frank Otto Gatell, *John Gorham Palfrey and the New England Conscience*

(Cambridge, MA: Harvard University Press, 1963), and on his complicated relationship to his slaveholding family, see Edward E. Baptist, *The Half Has Never Been Told: Slavery and the Making of American Capitalism* (New York: Basic Books, 2014), 309-315. For a Proviso Democrat's version of these anti–Slave Power arguments, see *CG Appendix*, 29th Congress, 2nd Session, 177–180.

16. For a few examples of Northerners from across the political spectrum speaking on this theme, see *CG*, 29th Congress, 2nd Session, 365, 478, and *CG*, 30th Congress, 1st Session, 199, 601, 1023; *CG*, 29th Congress, 2nd Session, 454–455.

17. *CG Appendix*, 29th Congress, 2nd Session, 333; *CG*, 30th Congress, 1st Session, 1060; *Emancipator*, Oct. 6, 1847.

18. For a brief discussion of Liberty arguments that the Slave Power stifled the prosperity of Northern free labor, see ch. 3 above; *CG*, 29th Congress, 2nd Session, 354. Other examples of these sorts of free labor arguments can be found in a number of Democratic and Whig congressional speeches. See ibid., 114, 181, 402, 419, and *CG*, 30th Congress, 2nd Session 547–548, 1023; *CG*, 29th Congress, 2nd Session, 354–55; *CG*, 30th Congress, 1st Session, 1022, 199. For more on gendered dimensions of non-extension rhetoric, see Elizabeth R. Varon, *Disunion!: The Coming of the American Civil War, 1789-1859* (Chapel Hill: University of North Carolina Press, 2008), 186–189, which argues that Northern Democrats' concern with demonstrating the manliness of their anti-extensionism stemmed from a desire to disarm Southern attempts to depict them as feminized, sentimental abolitionists.

19. Foner, "Wilmot Proviso Revisited," esp. 276–278. For more on rising Whig antiwar sentiment, see also Amy S. Greenberg, *A Wicked War: Polk, Clay, Lincoln, and the 1846 U.S. Invasion of Mexico* (New York: Knopf, 2012), 194–199; for its spread beyond antislavery circles, see 233–238. Preston King to John Dix, Nov. 12, 1847, John A. Dix Papers, Rare Books and Manuscripts Library, Columbia University, New York. Also see King's speech in *CG*, 29th Congress, 2nd Session, 114–115; ibid., 136.

20. For a few excellent examples of the many Northern refusals to compromise on slavery extension, see *CG*, 29th Congress, 2nd Session, 72, 139, 196; *Weekly Herald and Philanthropist*, Dec. 1, 1846; *National Era*, Sept. 16, 1847.

21. This Missouri Compromise formula was first proposed as a substitute for the Proviso by Indiana doughface Rep. William Wick (D), *CG*, 29th Congress, 1st Session, 1218. Examples of Southern Democratic support can be found in in *CG*, 29th Congress, 2nd Session, 135–136, 360–362, 998, 1013. On Polk's eventual commitment to this solution, see Potter, *Impending Crisis*, 69–73.

22. On popular sovereignty, see ibid.

23. For assertions of slavery's unfeasibility in Oregon, see *CG*, 29th Congress, 2nd Session, 409, 477, and 30th Congress, 1st Session, 662, 804, 811, 871. For Northern concerns that Southerners might indeed transport slaves to Oregon if permitted, see ibid., 547, 805. Good examples of the antislavery and proslavery positions in House debates over Oregon can be found in *CG Appendix*, 30th Congress, 1st Session, 956–964. Attempts to write extension of the Missouri Compromise line into the bill organizing Oregon can be seen in *CG*, 29th Congress, 2nd Session, 169, 187, 409, and *CG*, 30th Congress, 1st Session, 875. On popular sovereignty, see *CG*, 30th Congress, 1st Session, 805, 808, 813; ibid., 805; *National Era*, Feb. 4, 1847. On racism in nineteenth-century Oregon, see Eugene H. Berwanger, *The Frontier against Slavery: Western Anti-Negro Prejudice and the Slavery Extension Controversy* (Champaign: University of Illinois Press, 1967), ch. 4.

24. On the Clayton Compromise, see Potter, *Impending Crisis*, 73–75, and Holt, *Rise and Fall of the American Whig Party*, 335–336; *CG*, 30th Congress, 1st Session, 950, 1002; ibid., 1007. Senate examples of criticisms similar to those made in the House can be seen in ibid., 992,

994. Oregon was ultimately admitted in the session's final hours without any alteration to its constitutional prohibition of slavery after the reluctant last-minute acquiescence of Thomas Hart Benton (D-MO) and Samuel Houston (D-TX), both vigorous expansionists. *CG*, 30th Congress, 1st Session, 1078.

25. *CG*, 29th Congress, 2nd Session, 322, 353–354; *Albany Evening Atlas*, July 1, 1847; *CG*, 30th Congress, 1st Session, 989.

26. JGW to the *Essex Transcript*, July 1, [1846] (originally printed as "Christianity in Politics," in *Essex Transcript*, July 2, 1846), in *Letters of JGW*, ed. Pickard, 2:27; Prairieville *American Freeman*, Sept. 1, 1846; Chicago *Western Citizen*, May 30, 1848; Henry I. Bowditch to JPH, Dec. 29, 1847, Hale-Chandler Papers, Rauner Special Collections Library, Dartmouth College Library, Hanover, NH; *Western Citizen*, May 23, 1848.

27. *CG*, 29th Congress, 333.

28. *CG*, 29th Congress, 2nd Session, 387–388; *CG*, 30th Congress, 1st Session, 661–662; *CG*, 29th Congress, 2nd Session, 188; *CG*, 30th Congress, 1st Session, 666.

29. Edward Wade to SPC, July 7, 1847, SPC Papers; JGW to GB, Dec. 1846, in *Letters of JGW*, ed. Pickard, 2:48–49; "What has the Liberty Party Done?" by "A Congregationalist Minister, *Of Undoubted Orthodoxy*," from *GMF*, quoted in *American Freeman*, Apr. 14, 1847; *Western Citizen*, Apr. 11, 1848; Don E. Fehrenbacher, *Chicago Giant: A Biography of "Long John" Wentworth* (Madison, WI: American History Research Center, 1957), 68–69, explains that Wentworth's shift stemmed from a multitude of concerns but "must always be viewed against the background of rising antislavery sentiment in his own district, which the recent election had so forcefully verified."

30. *Emancipator*, Mar. 29, 1848; *Weekly Herald and Philanthropist*, Dec. 1, 1846. Also see *Emancipator*, June 16, Oct. 13, 1847, and Edward Wade to SPC, July 7, 1847, SPC Papers.

31. *CG Appendix*, 29th Congress, 2nd Session, 281.

32. *CG*, 30th Congress, 1st Session, 601; *CG*, 29th Congress, 2nd Session, 189–190; ibid., 353–354. In 1840, in fact, Wilmot had spearheaded an effort to proscribe a planned abolitionist meeting from houses of worship and public buildings in Towanda, Pennsylvania. Philadelphia *Pennsylvania Freeman*, Feb. 6, 1840. Wilmot had reputedly even supported reinstatement of the gag rule in 1845. *Weekly Herald and Philanthropist*, Dec. 1, 1846.

33. *CG*, 29th Congress, 2nd Session, 443; *CG*, 30th Congress, 1st Sess., 72; *CG*, 29th Congress, 2nd Session, 86.

34. Ibid., 389–390; Preston King to Azariah Flagg, Feb. 22, 1847, Azariah Cutting Flagg Papers, NYPL; *CG*, 29th Congress, 2nd Session, 333. Numerous references to popular constituent support for the Proviso can be seen in Whig and Democratic speeches, in *CG*, 29th Congress, 2nd Session, 84, 124, 137, 146, 196–197, 421, 477–478, and *CG Appendix*, 29th Congress, 2nd Session, 333–335, 555.

35. *CG*, 29th Congress, 2nd Session, 138, 333. Also see ibid., 478; *CG Appendix*, 29th Congress, 2nd Session, 343.

36. Over the 1846–47 and 1847–48 sessions of Congress, resolutions opposing the extension of slavery were submitted to Congress at least once by the legislatures of New Hampshire, New York, Pennsylvania, New Jersey, Connecticut, Rhode Island, Ohio, Michigan, Maine, Vermont, Massachusetts, and the new state of Wisconsin. For many of these state legislative resolutions, see the speech of Rep. Sidney Lawrence (D-NY) in *CG Appendix*, 30th Congress, 1st Session, 680. For the Connecticut resolutions and the Wisconsin resolutions (not included in Lawrence's catalogue for the 30th Congress, 1st Session) see *CG*, 30th Congress, 1st Session, 51, 965; LT to AAP, Feb. 5, 1847, LT Papers; *National Era*, Mar. 11, 1847; *CG*, 29th Congress, 2nd Session, 542.

37. The extreme Southern position can be seen in *CG Appendix*, 29th Congress, 2nd Ses-

sion, 137–139, and *CG*, 30th Congress, 1st Session, 775, 876, 879, 906, 927, 1045; Alexander Sims (D-SC) perhaps best elaborated the biblical defense of slavery in *CG*, 29th Congress, 2nd Session, 291. The radical proslavery stance in these debates closely resembles Chief Justice Taney's infamous 1857 decision in *Dred Scott v. Sandford* (discussed further below). Even some Southerners who supported the Missouri Compromise solution out of expediency questioned its constitutionality, treating the proposal as a Southern concession. For example, see *CG*, 29th Congress, 2nd Session, 142, 178–179, and *CG*, 30th Congress, 1st Session, 903; *CG*, 30th Congress, 2nd Session, 66, 927. Also see examples of secession threats in *CG*, 29th Congress, 2nd Session, 543 and *CG*, 30th Congress, 1st Session, 903.

38. *CG*, 29th Congress, 2nd Session, 47, 554, 555–556; *CG*, 30th Congress, 1st Session, 149.

39. Holt, *Rise and Fall of the American Whig Party*, 253–255, 265–267; *National Era*, Sept. 16, Oct. 7, 1847; *Emancipator*, Dec. 22, 1847; SPC to JPH, Sept. 23, 1847, JPH Papers; SPC to JPH, May 12, 1847, in *The Salmon P. Chase Papers*, ed. John Niven (Kent, OH: Kent State University Press, 1993), 2:153; JG to CFA, Aug. 12, 1847, Adams Family Papers; Greenberg, *A Wicked War*, 190–199, 214–240, 256–264.

40. CS to JG, Mar. 6, 1848, in *Selected Letters of Charles Sumner*, ed. Beverly Wilson Palmer (Boston: Northeastern University Press, 1990), 1:223–225; Manisha Sinha, "The Caning of Charles Sumner: Slavery, Race, and Ideology in the Age of the Civil War," *Journal of the Early Republic* 23 (2003): 233–262, esp. 237–241; JG to SPC, Sept. 18, 1846, SPC Papers; GB to SPC, Sept. 14, 1847, in *SPC Papers*, ed. Niven, 2:157–158; Stanley Harrold, *Gamaliel Bailey and Antislavery Union* (Kent, OH: Kent State University Press, 1986), 127–129. Also see the brief discussion of Bailey's antislavery gatherings in the early 1850s in chapter 6 below.

41. *CG*, 30th Congress, 1st Session, 1022; ibid., 245, 818.

42. Rep. William Haskell (D-TN) asserted that these antislavery radicals "ought to swing as high as Haman." *CG*, 30th Congress, 1st Session, 653. Other Southern overreactions can be seen in ibid., 654, 657, 662. On the *Pearl* escape and the response in Washington, see Stanley Harrold, *Subversives: Antislavery Community in Washington, D.C., 1828–1865* (Baton Rouge: Louisiana State University Press, 2003), 116–145. Ultimately the crowd outside the *Era* office dispersed without committing violence or serious property damage.

43. Hale's bill would have made "any city, town, or incorporated place within the District liable for all injuries done to property by riotous or tumultuous assemblies." *CG Appendix*, 30th Congress, 1st Session, 500–510.

44. *CG*, 30th Congress, 2nd Session, 572, 591–592; *CG*, 30th Congress, 2nd Session, 592; ibid., 576–579, 599–602, 604.

45. *Utica Democrat*, quoted in *National Era*, May 27, 1847; *CG*, 30th Congress, 1st Session, 553; ibid., 394.

Interlude Three

1. CS to JG, Dec. 1, 1847, in *Selected Letters of Charles Sumner*, ed. Beverly Wilson Palmer (Boston: Northeastern University Press, 1990), 1:202. For more detail see James B. Stewart, *Joshua R. Giddings and the Tactics of Radical Politics* (Cleveland: Press of Case Western Reserve University, 1970), 141–146, and Frank Otto Gatell, "Palfrey's Vote, the Conscience Whigs, and the Election of Speaker Winthrop," *New England Quarterly* 31 (June 1958): 218–231.

2. *BDW*, Oct. 13, 16, 1847; *Ashtabula Sentinel*, Jan. 31, 1848.

3. JG to Seth Gates, Dec. 4, 1847, GS Papers; JGP to CFA, Dec. 6, 1847, Adams Family Papers, Microfilm Edition, Massachusetts Historical Society, Boston; JGP to Winthrop (draft), Dec. 5, 1847, Palfrey Family Papers, Houghton Library, Harvard University, Cambridge, MA.

As Amos Tuck summarized, Palfrey asked whether Winthrop would "so constitute the Committee on Foreign relations, and of ways and means, as to favor Peace; the committee on the Territories, so as to favor the prohibition of Slavery therein; the Committee on the Judiciary, so as to favor the repeal of the law of Feb. 12, 1793, denying a trial by jury to persons claimed as fugitive slaves; the Committee on the District of Columbia so as to favor the abolition of slavery and the slave trade therein." Tuck to George G. Fogg, Dec. 6, 1847, George G. Fogg Papers, NHHS; Winthrop to JGP, Dec. 5, 1847, Palfrey Family Papers.

4. *CG*, 30th Congress, 1st Session, 2; Washington (DC) *National Era*, Dec. 9, 1847; Tuck to Fogg, Dec. 6, 1847, George G. Fogg Papers; JGP to CFA, Dec. 6, 1847, Adams Family Papers; *Ashtabula Sentinel*, Jan. 31, 1848. For the story about Holmes walking out, see Gatell, "Palfrey's Vote," 223–224; Jeffery A. Jenkins and Charles Stewart III, *Fighting for the Speakership: The House and the Rise of Party Government* (Princeton: Princeton University Press, 2013), 139n71, correctly note, however, that, contrary to the portrayal in other secondary accounts, Holmes's abstention was not actually pivotal, as the same vote total (110) would have been required for a majority even if Holmes had participated (and brought the total number of votes up from 218 to 219). Philadelphia's Lewis Charles Levin, the lone American party man, had scattered his initial votes.

5. LT to JGP, Dec. 16, 1847, Palfrey Family Papers; JG to CS, Jan. 15, 1848, CS Papers. For examples of Conscience Whig sentiments, see Stephen C. Phillips to JGP, Dec. 9, 1847, Palfrey Family Papers; *Ashtabula Sentinel*, Dec. 27, 1847, Jan. 3, 1848; and *BDW*, Dec. 10, 11, 14, 16, 1847, Mar. 20, 22, 1848. For Liberty views, see *National Era*, Dec. 9, Dec. 16, 1847, and Boston *Emancipator*, Dec. 15, 1847.

6. Edward Wade to JPH, Dec. 13, 1847, JPH Papers; Henry B. Stanton to JG, Dec. 11, 1847, JG Papers; Henry I. Bowditch to JPH, Dec. 29, 1847, Hale-Chandler Papers, Rauner Special Collections Library, Dartmouth College Library, Hanover, NH; *Emancipator*, Dec. 22, 1847.

Chapter Five

1. The name "Barnburner," originally intended as a slur, analogized radical Democrats willing to destroy their party to a farmer who burnt down his barn to eliminate a rat infestation. Jonathan H. Earle, *Jacksonian Antislavery & the Politics of Free Soil, 1824-1854* (Chapel Hill: University of North Carolina Press, 2004), 62. David M. Potter, *The Impending Crisis: 1848-1861*, completed and edited by Don E. Fehrenbacher (New York: Harper & Row, 1976), 77–82, acknowledges Liberty elements of the Free Soil coalition only after discussing Barnburners and Conscience Whigs: "Along with these, there were also the Liberty men." Frederick J. Blue, *The Free Soilers: Third Party Politics 1848-54* (Urbana: University of Illinois Press, 1973), ch. 1–4, pays more attention to Liberty influences, especially the role of Salmon Chase, but concentrates closest on Barnburner Democrats. See also Chaplain Morrison, *Democratic Politics and Sectionalism: The Wilmot Proviso Controversy* (Chapel Hill: University of North Carolina Press, 1967), 145–157, and Joel Silbey, *Party over Section: The Rough and Ready Presidential Election of 1848* (Lawrence: University Press of Kansas, 2009). In contrast to Silbey, Joseph G. Rayback, *Free Soil: The Election of 1848* (Lexington: University Press of Kentucky, 1970), depicts the slavery extension issue as crucial in the 1848 campaign. Earle, *Jacksonian Antislavery*, 157–162, recognizes the influential role of Liberty coalitionists like Chase, but overemphasizes Jacksonian roots of popular political antislavery. Aileen S. Kraditor, *Means and Ends in American Abolitionism: Garrison and His Critics on Strategy and Tactics, 1834-1850* (Chicago: Ivan R. Dee, Inc., 1989 [1967]), 181–189, describes the Free Soil Party as betraying Liberty ideals. Reinhard O. Johnson, *The Liberty Party, 1840-1848: Antislavery Third-Party*

Politics in the United States (Baton Rouge: Louisiana State University Press, 2009), ch. 4, similarly sees the Liberty move into the Free Soil Party as politically unsuccessful and ideologically compromising, especially in forcing Liberty men to abandon the most radical antislavery interpretations of the Constitution, the importance and prevalence of which I believe Johnson overstates. The best discussion of coalitionist movements among Liberty men remains Richard H. Sewell, *Ballots for Freedom: Antislavery Politics in the United States 1837-1860* (New York: Oxford University Press, 1976), ch. 6-8. This chapter builds on Sewell's contributions by placing the emergence of the Free Soil Party in the context of the Liberty anti-Slave Power arguments described above.

2. JL to SPC, July 7, 1848, SPC Papers.

3. Johnson, *Liberty Party*, ch. 3, clearly identifies these mounting anxieties, but many Liberty leaders nonetheless remained optimistic about winning new converts, not least because of the example of the Hale movement in New Hampshire. In 1845, Connecticut's legislature modified its election laws so that a plurality on the first runoff would determine winners in state representative contests: ibid. 133. Maine also switched to requiring only a plurality for state representative elections in 1847: Hallowell, ME, *Liberty Standard*, May 18, 1848. In 1848, Vermont passed a law stipulating that congressional elections would initially require a majority, but that runoff elections would employ plurality rules: Charles L. Williams, *The Compiled Statutes of the State of Vermont* (Burlington: Chauncey Goodrich, 1851), 59; Michael J. Dubin, *United States Congressional Elections, 1788-1997: The Official Results of the Elections of the 1st Through 105th Congresses* (Jefferson, NC: McFarland & Company, 1998), 157.

4. Austin Willey to JPH, July 25, 1846, JPH Papers; *Liberty Standard*, Sept. 3, 1846. See also ibid. Sept. 17, 1846; John E. Godfrey to JPH, July 22, 1846, JPH Papers.

5. Letter from Samuel Fessenden to John Keep, from *Cleveland American*, quoted in *GMF*, Jan. 7, 1847; *Essex Transcript*, quoted in *GMF*, Jan. 7, 1847; Johnson, *Liberty Party*, 107-109; Austin Willey, *The History of the Antislavery Cause in State and Nation* (Portland, ME: Brown, Thurston, and Hoytt, Fogg & Donham, 1886), 304-307.

6. JGW to Joseph Sturge, Nov. 28, 1846, in *The Letters of John Greenleaf Whittier*, ed. John B. Pickard (Cambridge, MA: Belknap Press of Harvard University Press, 1975), 2:44; JGW to JPH, July 16, 1846, Hale-Chandler Papers, Rauner Special Collections Library, Dartmouth College Library, Hanover, NH; JGW to JGP, Sept. 21, 1846, in *Letters of JGW*, ed. Pickard, 2:36-37.

7. JG to SPC, Aug. 3, 1846, SPC Papers; JG to SPC, Aug. 31, 1846, in *The Salmon P. Chase Papers*, ed. John Niven (Kent, OH: Kent State University Press, 1993), 2:127-128. See also James B. Stewart, *Joshua R. Giddings and the Tactics of Radical Politics* (Cleveland: Press of Case Western Reserve University, 1970), 117-118; JG to SPC, Sept. 18, 1846, SPC Papers.

8. SPC to JG, Aug. 15, 1846, in *SPC Papers*, ed. Niven, 2:125-126; SPC to JG, Sept. 23, 1846, in ibid., 2:130-131; Ann Arbor *Signal of Liberty*, Aug. 8, 1846; Cincinnati *Weekly Herald and Philanthropist*, Aug. 26, 1846. Chase's Democratic affinities are manifested in letters to Hale, Jan. 30, 1846, and to JG, Aug. 15, 1846, in *SPC Papers*, ed. Niven, 2:122-123, 125-126. For more on Chase's interest in the idea of a "True Democratic" party and his attraction to Jacksonian economic stances, see John Niven, *Salmon P. Chase: A Biography* (New York: Oxford University Press, 1995), 95-96, and Earle, *Jacksonian Antislavery*, 155-159. Earle, however, overstates the degree to which these "True Democratic" coalitionist leanings indicated Chase's Democratic propensities. It should be noted that one of the most important antislavery Whig newspapers in Ohio was Hamlin's *True Democrat*; SPC to JG, Oct. 20, 1846, in *SPC Papers*, ed. Niven, 2:133-134. This "Anti-slavery League" idea Chase briefly floated was for a cross-party organization pledged to vote only for antislavery candidates. SPC to JPH, May 12, 1847, Papers

of Salmon P. Chase, LC. Chase had also discussed this concept in his letter to the 1846 Chicago North-Western Liberty Convention. See chapter 4 above, and Niven, *Salmon P. Chase*, 99–102.

9. GB to SPC, Sept. 14, 1847, in *SPC Papers*, ed. Niven, 2:156–158. On the founding of the *National Era* and its early success, see Stanley Harrold, *Gamaliel Bailey and Antislavery Union* (Kent, OH: Kent State University Press, 1986), ch. 7.

10. *GMF*, Mar. 4, 18, May 27, June 24, Sept. 16, Oct. 21, 1847; Johnson, *Liberty Party*, 185–86.

11. *GMF*, June 3, 1847; "Advice to Honest Men," quoted from Concord, NH, *Granite Freeman*, in *GMF*, Jan. 28, 1847.

12. Washington (DC) *National Era*, Apr. 29, May 13, Sept. 16, 1847; SPC to Edward Wade, June 23, 1847, Papers of SPC, LC; *Emancipator*, June 23, 30, 1847; Sewell, *Ballots for Freedom*, 136; *Emancipator*, Apr. 14, 21, May 12, June 6, 1847. For other examples of opposition to postponement, see also *Liberty Standard*, May 20, 1847; letter of Kiah Bailey in *GMF*, May 28, 1847; *GMF*, June 24, 1847; and Waukesha (WI) *American Freeman*, Oct. 13, 1847; *National Era*, Apr. 15, 29, May 13, 1847.

13. *Emancipator*, Mar. 31, Aug. 11, Sept. 1, 1847; For examples of Liberty leaders across New England requesting Hale appearances, see from JPH Papers: Henry B. Stanton to JPH, July 21, 1846; Daniel Hoit to JPH, Aug. 6, 1846; Stanton to JPH, Sept. 4, 1846; Joseph Poland to JPH, Sept. 10, 1846; Henry I. Bowditch to JPH, Sept. 15, 1846; Sherman M. Booth to JPH, Oct. 16, 1846; Chauncey L. Knapp to JPH, Dec. 10, 1846; and Austin Willey to JPH, Dec. 19, 1846. Stanton to JPH, Oct. 1, 1846, Hale-Chandler Papers. Leavitt announced his retirement as fulltime editor of the *Emancipator* in August of 1847, but remained an influential contributor until the spring of 1848, at which point the operation came fully under the control of publisher Curtis C. Nichols, with the aid of Joseph C. Lovejoy: *Emancipator*, Aug. 18, 1847; Hugh Davis, *Joshua Leavitt: Evangelical Abolitionist* (Baton Rouge: Louisiana State University Press, 1990), 236–237.

14. Fogg's Concord, NH, *Independent Democrat and Freeman* had been formed by merging the Liberty *Granite Freeman* and the *Independent Democrat*, which had been created as a Hale campaign paper; Stanton to SPC, July 17, 1847, SPC Papers; JGW to Samuel Fessenden, July 26, 1847, in *Letters of JGW*, ed. Pickard, 2:93; LT, JL, Stanton, Willey, JGW, and Charles D. Cleveland to JPH, July 26, 1847, Hale-Chandler Papers; JGW to JPH, July 30, 1847, in *Letters of JGW*, ed. Pickard, 2:93–94; LT to JPH, July 28, 1847, enclosed in LT et al. to JPH, July 26, 1847, Hale-Chandler Papers; Stanton to SPC, July 17, 1847, SPC Papers.

15. *Liberty Standard*, Sept. 23, 1847; *Emancipator*, Sept. 1, 15, 22, 1847. Stanton to JPH, Sept. 10, 1847, JPH Papers; JGW to JPH, [Nov. 2, 1847], in *Letters of JGW*, ed. Pickard, 2:95–96; JPH to JGW, Aug. 13, 1847, Hale-Chandler Papers; LT to SPC, Oct. 6, 1847, SPC Papers.

16. Blue, *Free Soilers*, 8–10; Sewell, *Ballots for Freedom*, 115–120; Johnson, *Liberty Party*, 64–65. For examples of support in Michigan for broadening the platform, see Theodore Foster to Birney, Mar. 30, 1846, in *Letters of James Gillespie Birney, 1831–1857*, ed. Dwight L. Dumond (1938; rep., Gloucester, MA: Peter Smith, 1966), 2:1007–1009, and *Signal of Liberty*, July 4, 1846; *Address of the Macedon Convention, By William Goodell, and Letters of Gerrit Smith* (Albany: S. W. Green, *Patriot* Office, 1847).

17. *American Freeman*, July 21, Aug. 25, 1847; *GMF*, June 24, 1847; Burlington, VT, *Liberty Gazette*, quoted in *Emancipator*, July 7, 1847; AS to Samuel Webb, Nov. 6, 1847, Alvan Stewart Papers, NYHS.

18. John St. John to JPH, Oct. 22, 1847, JPH Papers; Stanton to JPH, Oct. 22, 1847, Hale-Chandler Papers; *National Era*, Nov. 11, 1847; LT to JPH, Oct. 27, 1847, Hale-Chandler Papers.

19. JPH to Samuel Lewis, Jan. 1, 1848, Hale-Chandler Papers; Henry Bowditch to JPH, Feb. 27, 1848, ibid.

20. Stanton to JPH, Oct. 30, 1847, Hale-Chandler Papers; Zebina Eastman to JPH, Mar. 15, 1848, JPH Papers; JL to SPC, Feb. 21, 1848, SPC Papers; JL to JPH, Mar. 10, 1848, JPH Papers; *CG*, 30th Congress, 1st Session, 805; ibid., 81, 123, 341, 368; ibid., 63, 403, 520, 558, 567, 604, 617, 694; ibid., 723, 727; *CG Appendix*, 30th Congress, 1st Session, 500–510; "M," Chicago *Western Citizen*, May 23, 1848.

21. CS to SPC, Dec. 2, 1846, Papers of SPC, LC. See also Flamen Ball to SPC, Sept. 1, 1847, SPC Papers.

22. *BDW*, Sept. 28, 29, 30, Oct. 9, 13, 1846, Aug. 24, 1847; ibid., Dec. 31, 1846, Mar. 3, 1847; ibid., Nov. 17, Dec. 1, 1847, Jan. 27, 1848; CFA to GB, Aug. 15, 1847, Adams Family Papers, Microfilm Edition, Massachusetts Historical Society, Boston; Henry Clay, *Speech of Henry Clay at the Lexington Mass Meeting, 13th November 1847, Together with the Resolutions Adopted on that Occasion* (New York: George F. Nesbitt, 1847). On Clay's speech, see also Amy S. Greenberg, *A Wicked War: Polk, Clay, Lincoln, and the 1846 U.S. Invasion of Mexico* (New York: Knopf, 2012), 229–237; JG to CS, Jan. 4, 1847, CS Papers.

23. See Michael F. Holt, *Rise and Fall of the American Whig Party: Jacksonian Politics and the Onset of Civil War* (New York: Oxford University Press, 1999), 269–274; Amos Tuck to Moses Cartland, Jan. 6, 1847, Cartland Family Papers, Houghton Library, Harvard University, Cambridge, MA.

24. JG to CS, June 2, Aug. 5, 1847, CS Papers; *Ashtabula Sentinel* [Giddings's local political organ], Apr. 26, May 3, June 14, 28, July 12, 1847; Horace Greeley to Thurlow Weed, Jan. 13, 1847, Horace Greeley Miscellaneous Manuscripts, NYHS; Greeley to Schuyler Colfax, May 1, 1847, Horace Greeley Papers, microform, NYPL; CS to Thomas Corwin, Sept. 7, 1847, in *Selected Letters of Charles Sumner*, ed. Beverly Wilson Palmer (Boston: Northeastern University Press, 1990), 1:194–197; CS to JG, Nov. 1, 1847, ibid., 1:200–201; Holt, *Rise and Fall*, 267; Greeley to Colfax, Sept. 15, 1848, Greeley Papers, NYPL. See also Greeley to CS, June 25, 1848, CS Papers.

25. Jacob Brinkerhoff to SPC, Nov. 22, 1847, SPC Papers; New York *Evening Post*, Feb. 16, 1848.

26. *Albany Evening Atlas*, May 3, 1847; Leonard L. Richards, *The Slave Power: The Free North and Southern Domination, 1780–1860* (Baton Rouge: Louisiana State University Press, 2000), 137–148.

27. *Atlas*, Jan. 18, 20, 21, 25, Feb. 15, 18, 1847; *Evening Post*, quoted in *GMF*, Feb. 11, 1847; Preston King to Flagg, Sept. 24, 1847, Flagg Papers, NYPL; King to Flagg, Jan. 12, 18, Sept. 14, 1847, ibid.; King to SPC, Aug. 16, 1847, SPC Papers; *Atlas*, Feb. 3, Apr. 23, July 1, 1847; ibid. Mar. 14, Apr. 18, 1848; King to Gideon Welles, Sept. 11, 1847, Preston King-Simeon Smith Papers, St. Lawrence University, Canton, NY.

28. *Atlas*, Oct. 4, 5, 6, 1847; *Herkimer Convention; The Voice of New York!, Proceedings of the Herkimer Mass Convention of Oct. 26, 1847* (Albany *Atlas* Extra, Nov. 1847), quotes from 25–26.

29. SPC to CS, Dec. 2, 1847, in *SPC Papers*, ed. Niven, 2:160–162; Stanton to JPH, Oct. 30, 1847, Hale-Chandler Papers; Flagg to John A. Dix, Nov. 13, 1847, John A. Dix Papers, Rare Books and Manuscripts Library, Columbia University, New York; Stanton to JPH, Mar. 2, 1848, JPH Papers.

30. Stanton to JPH, Mar. 2, 1848, JPH Papers; SPC to CS, Feb. 19, 1848, CS Papers.

31. SPC to JG, Mar. 10, 1848, Papers of SPC, LC; Call for a "People's Convention," Mar. 23, 1848, Cincinnati, enclosed with letter of N. M. Sawyer to Thomas Morris, Apr. 1, 1848, SPC Papers.

32. JG to SPC, Mar. 16, 1848, SPC Papers; JG to SPC, Apr. 7, 1848, ibid.; JG to CS, Apr. 17, 1848, CS Papers; CFA to JG, Apr. 21, 1848, JG Papers; CS to JG, Apr. 21, 1848, in *Selected Letters of CS*, ed. Palmer, 1:232–233; *Ashtabula Sentinel*, Apr. 22, 29, 1848.

33. SPC to JPH, Apr. 29, 1848, JPH Papers; JL to SPC, Apr. 1, 1848, SPC Papers.

34. JG to CS, May 17, 1848, CS Papers; *BDW*, Mar. 10, 28, 30, May 19, June 6, 1848; Tuck to George Fogg, May, 10, 1848, George G. Fogg Papers, NHHS; JG to CS, May 1, 1848, CS Papers.

35. *Evening Post*, May 16, 1848; Jacob Brinkerhoff to SPC, Feb. 2, 1848, SPC Papers; Brinkerhoff to SPC, Mar. 28, 1848, in *SPC Papers*, ed. Niven, 2:168; David Wilmot to SPC, May 29, 1848, SPC Papers.

36. *The Utica Convention: Voice of New York* (*Albany Atlas* Extra, February 1848), quote from 17; *Evening Post*, Feb. 19, 1848; Earle, *Jacksonian Antislavery*, 74–76; *Atlas*, May 24, 25, 26, 1848; *National Era*, June 1, 1848; Potter, *Impending Crisis*, 70–71; *Evening Post*, May 22, 27, 1848; Donald Bruce Johnson, compiler, *National Party Platforms*, vol. 1, *1840–1956* (Urbana: University of Illinois Press, 1978), 11.

37. SPC to CS, June 5, 1848, CS Papers; GB to CS, May 31, 1848, ibid.

38. Henry Wilson, *History of the Rise and Fall of the Slave Power in America* (Boston: J. R. Osgood and Co., 1872–1877), 133–139; Tuck to Fogg, May 10, 1848, Fogg Papers; Johnson, *National Party Platforms*, 16; For a detailed discussion of the machinations involved in the 1848 Whig nominations, see Holt, *Rise and Fall*, ch. 10.

39. Holt, *Rise and Fall*, 334; Rayback, *Free Soil*, 205; Wilson, *History of the Rise and Fall of the Slave Power*, 142–144. Vaughan was an antislavery Whig who had worked for Kentucky abolitionist Whig Cassius Clay's Lexington *True American* and then founded his own Louisville *Examiner*. He later became editor and part owner of the Cleveland *True Democrat* and after that part owner of the Republican *Chicago Tribune*. Stanley Harrold, *Abolitionists and the South, 1831–1861* (Lexington: University of Kentucky Press, 1995), 29–30; Niven, *Salmon P. Chase*, 99–101.

40. SPC to CS, June 5, 1848, CS Papers; JG to SPC, Lynds Jones, E. S. Hamlin, and H. L. Chaffee, June 7, 1848, SPC Papers; JG to CS, June 17, 1848, CS Papers; *National Era*, July 6, 1848. Chase had carefully coordinated the timing of the Columbus Free Territory and Liberty Conventions. Niven, *Salmon P. Chase*, 107.

41. *Atlas*, May 27, 1848; MVB to Benjamin F. Butler, June 20, 1848, Butler Family Papers, Department of Rare Books and Special Collections, Manuscripts Division, Princeton University Library; *Atlas*, June 23, 1848; MVB to Samuel Westbury, David Dudley Field, and others, June 20, 1848, in O. C. Gardiner, *The Great Issue: Or the Three Presidential Candidates* (New York: Wm. C. Bryant & Co., 1848), 110–120; *Atlas*, June 24, 1848.

42. S. B. Parsons to CS, June 16, 1848, CS Papers; SPC to CS, June 20, 1848, ibid.

43. *BDW*, June 20, 1848; Wilson, *History of the Rise and Fall of the Slave Power*, 146–148; Rayback, *Free Soil*, 212; Bruce Laurie, *Beyond Garrison: Antislavery and Social Reform* (New York: Cambridge University Press, 2005), 153–159; letter of "G.W.L.," June 29, 1848, in *National Era*, July 13, 1848; letter from "C.," June 29, 1848, in ibid.; Blue, *Free Soilers*, 58–59.

44. Moses Cartland to JPH, July 20, 1848, JPH Papers; *Western Citizen*, July 4, 1848; *National Era*, July 13, 1848; Johnson, *Liberty Party*, 117–118; JL to SPC, July 7, 1848, SPC Papers.

45. Milwaukee (relocated from Waukesha) *American Freeman*, June 7, 14, 28, 1848; T. B. Hudson and J. H. Fairchild to JPH, July 24, 1848, Hale-Chandler Papers; *American Freeman*, Aug. 1, 1848; LT to JPH, Aug. 2, 1848, JPH Papers.

46. *GMF*, July 20, 1848; "The Crisis—What is Our Duty?" in ibid., July 27, 1848; JL to JPH, July 1, 1848, JPH Papers; J. W. Alden to JPH, July 21, 1848, ibid.; *National Era*, July 20, 1848; JGW to William Stevens Robinson, [June 1848], in *Letters of JGW*, ed. Pickard, 2:107; JGW, "Union," in *National Era*, Aug. 3, 1848.

47. JPH to SPC, June 8, 14, 1848, SPC Papers; *National Era*, July 13, 1848; Samuel J. Tilden to SPC, July 29, 1848, in *SPC Papers*, ed. Niven, 2:179–180; *National Era*, July 6, 1848; *Atlas*, June

30, 1848; David Dudley Field to CS, July 8, 1848, CS Papers; SPC to John Van Buren, June[sic, July] 19, 1848, in *SPC Papers*, ed. Niven, 2:176–178.

48. Oliver Dyer, *Phonographic Report of the Proceedings of the National Free Soil Convention at Buffalo, N.Y., August 9th and 10th, 1848* (Buffalo: G. H. Derby, & Co, 1848).

49. Stanton to JPH, Aug. 20, 1848, JPH Papers; Dyer, *Phonographic Report*, 12. The *Cincinnati Herald* reported that Butler credited SPC as "the author of the admirable set of resolutions which constitute the Free Soil platform [the *Herald*'s words]," quoted in *National Era*, Aug. 24, 1848. On these negotiations, see also Blue, *Free Soilers*, 70–74; Harrold, *Gamaliel Bailey*, 120–122; and Sewell, *Ballots for Freedom*, 156–157. SPC to James W. Taylor, Aug. 15, 1848, in *SPC Papers*, ed. Niven, 2:183–185; Dyer, *Phonographic Report*, 19.

50. Ibid., 19–20. In addition to the ten antislavery resolutions, a few others addressed "certain other questions of National policy," such as "River and Harbor improvements," a "tariff of duties as will raise revenue adequate to defray" the government's "necessary expenses" and debt payments, and a free land policy. SPC to James W. Taylor, Aug. 15, 1848, in *SPC Papers*, ed. Niven, 2:183–185. The tariff and free lands resolutions have been perceived as sops to ex-Democrats. The tariff resolution, however, should be understood as a compromise, endorsing a tariff as the primary source of federal revenue while emphasizing its revenue rather than protective objectives. In fact, it was a Whig who proposed the plank, to ensure that the platform didn't ignore tariff politics altogether.

51. Dyer, *Phonographic Report*, 24; *National Era*, Nov. 4, 1847. Douglass declined to speak beyond an explanation that he was recovering from a throat operation. *New York Herald*, quoted in *National Era*, Aug. 17, 1848; ibid., Aug. 31, 1848. On the racism of most Barnburners, see Eric Foner, "Politics and Prejudice: The Free Soil Party and the Negro, 1849–1852," *Journal of Negro History* 50 (Oct. 1965): 239–256.

52. On McLean's withdrawal (though with conflicting views on the details thereof) see Rayback, *Free Soil*, 226–27, and Blue, *Free Soilers*, 76. MVB to the New York Delegation in the Buffalo Convention, Aug. 2, 1848, Butler Family Papers, Department of Rare Books and Special Collections, Manuscripts Division, Princeton University Library; Oliver Dyer, *Great Senators of the United States Forty Years Ago, (1848 and 1849)* (New York: Robert Bonner's Sons, 1889), 100–102; Henry B. Stanton, *Random Recollections* (New York: Harper Brothers, 1887), 163–64. Dyer, *Phonographic Report*, 32, reports Van Buren's vote total as 244; Johnson, *Liberty Party*, 87, notes that Dyer's tabulation of each state's votes actually adds up to 254. However, 244 seems more likely to be correct, as the vote count listed for Ohio both by Dyer and Johnson exceeds the number of delegates to which the state was entitled by 9.

53. Dyer, *Phonographic Report*, 27; George W. Julian, *Political Recollections, 1840–1872* (Chicago: Jansen, McClurg & Company, 1884), 60–61; *Emancipator*, Aug. 16, 1848.

54. Fogg to JPH, Aug. 21, 1848, JPH Papers; JL to JPH, Aug. 22, 1848, ibid; *American Freeman*, Aug. 16, 23, 1848.

55. *National Era*, Aug. 24, 1848; letter of MVB in ibid., Aug. 31, 1848; JGW to Sturge, [October] 1848, in *Letters of JGW*, ed. Pickard, 2:118–119; JL to SPC, Aug. 21, 1848, in *SPC Papers*, ed. Niven, 2:188.

56. "Proceedings of the Colored Convention. Held at Cleveland, Ohio, Sept. 6, 1848," in Rochester *North Star*, Sept. 29, 1848; Blue, *Free Soilers*, 118–121; Samuel Ringgold Ward to John H. Thomas, Ebenezer F. Simons, and Hiram Gillet, Sept. 16, 1848, in *Black Abolitionist Papers*, vol. 4, *The United States, 1847–1858*, ed. C. Peter Ripley (Chapel Hill: University of North Carolina Press, 1991), 27–29; Blue, "Black Men Have No Rights Which White Men are Bound to Respect: Charles Langston and the Drive for Equality," *No Taint of Compromise: Crusaders in Antislavery Politics* (Baton Rouge: Louisiana State University Press, 2005), 68–69;

Stephen Kantrowitz, *More Than Freedom: Fighting for Black Citizenship in a White Republic* (New York: Penguin Press, 2012), 158–163.

57. JG to CS, Aug. 24, 1848, CS Papers; King to Simeon Smith, Sept. 2, 1848, Preston King-Simeon Smith Papers. In St. Lawrence County, Van Buren ended up winning 59 percent of the vote. Earle, *Jacksonian Antislavery*, table 2, 200. JL to SPC, Aug. 21, 1848, in *SPC Papers*, ed. Niven, 2:188; Boston *Emancipator and Free Soil Press*, Sept. 20, 1848.

58. Letter from JGW, from Newburyport *Beacon of Liberty*, Oct. 28, 1848, reprinted in *Letters of JGW*, ed. Pickard, 2:117–118. Knapp had relocated from Montpelier to Lowell in 1844: Laurie, *Beyond Garrison*, 136–137. For congressional election results (and consequently lists of candidates as well), see Dubin, *Congressional Elections*, 151–155; Johnson, *Liberty Party*, 110; *National Era*, July 13, 27, 1848.

59. Austin Willey to JPH, Sept. 22, 1848, JPH Papers; JGW to Sturge, [October] 1848, in *Letters of JGW*, ed. Pickard, 2:118–119; WJ to Jn Jay, Sept. 13, 1848, John Jay Collection, Rare Books and Manuscripts Library, Columbia University, New York; WJ to Ella Kingsfield Jay, Oct. 1, 1848, ibid.; Niles to Welles, Sept. 17, 1848, Welles Papers, NYPL; *National Era*, Sept. 7, Oct. 5, 1848.

60. Blue, *Free Soilers*, 141–151, and Earle, *Jacksonian Antislavery*, 169–180, provide thorough analyses of the results, with Earle contending that more ex-Democrats nationwide voted for Van Buren than ex-Whigs. My discussion of election results in this paragraph relies primarily on data from the tables in Blue, 142, and Earle's appendix, 200–210; Johnson, *Liberty Party*, 119; Jn Jay to CS, Dec. 8, 1848, CS Papers; *National Era*, Nov. 16, 1848.

61. Much of this maneuvering can be traced in Chase's correspondence. The following letters from the Papers of SPC, LC have been particularly helpful: Eli Nichols to SPC, Dec. 15, 1848; SPC to E. S. Hamlin, Jan. 20, 1849; Stanley Matthews to SPC, Jan. 24, Jan. 26, 27, 1849; B. F. Hoffman to SPC, Jan. 25, 1849. Also helpful are these from the SPC Papers: Hamlin to SPC, Jan. 18, 19, 20, 30, 1849; John F. Morse to SPC, Jan. 29, 1848; Flamen Ball to SPC, Feb. 8, 10, 17, 1849. Finally, these items from the Norton Strange Townshend Family Papers, William L. Clements Library, University of Michigan, Ann Arbor, also enabled the author to track these events: NST to Brewster Randall, Feb. 19, 1849; S. D. Griswold to NST, Jan. 23, 1849; Q. F. Atkins to NST, Jan. 26, 1849; Samuel Lewis to NST, Jan. 29, 1849; H. C. Taylor to NST, Jan. 30, 1849; [Joel] Tiffany and [Melancthon] Woolsey Welles to NST, Feb. 2, 3, 1849. The parts of the Black Laws that Chase worked to repeal were those barring black courtroom testimony against whites and an outrageous requirement that black immigrants into the state post a $500 bond. The best analysis of these two and a half months of complicated machinations can be found in Stephen E. Maizlish, *The Triumph of Sectionalism: The Transformation of Ohio Politics, 1844–1856* (Kent, OH: Kent State University Press, 1983), ch. 6. Chase's election to the Senate and the issues surrounding the question of coalition with Ohio Democrats are also described in Blue, *Free Soilers*, 162–171, Niven, *Salmon P. Chase*, 116–122, and Sewell, *Ballots for Freedom*, 168, 206–208.

62. SPC to Hamlin, Jan. 20, 1849, SPC Papers; H. C. Taylor to NST, Jan. 30, 1849, Norton Strange Townshend Family Papers; CS to SPC, Feb. 27, 1849, Papers of SPC, LC; S. Dana to JPH, Feb. 23, 1849, JPH Papers; Butler to SPC, Mar. 3, 1849, SPC Papers; John Van Buren to SPC, Mar. 6, 1849, ibid.; JL to SPC, Mar. 2, 1849, ibid.

63. *Wisconsin Freeman* (formerly the *American Freeman*), Nov. 15, 1848; Dubin, *Congressional Elections*, 155; Blue, *Free Soilers*, 137; Lewis D. Campbell to CS, Oct. 19, 1848, CS Papers; John Niles to Gideon Welles, Mar. 26, Apr. 5, 1849, Gideon Welles Papers, microform, NYPL; *National Era*, Nov. 16, 1848, May 3, July 5, Aug. 30, Oct. 11, 1849; *Wisconsin Free Democrat* (formerly the *Wisconsin Freeman*), Jan. 3, 1849.

Interlude Four

1. Jeffery A. Jenkins and Charles Stewart III, *Fighting for the Speakership: The House and the Rise of Party Government* (Princeton: Princeton University Press, 2013), 155–174, offer the best extant account of this contentious speakership contest, but still leave room for further analysis of Free Soilers' strategy of promoting sectional gridlock.

2. Washington (DC) *National Era*, Aug. 30, 1849; CS to JG, Aug. 20, 1849, in *Selected Letters of Charles Sumner*, ed. Beverly Wilson Palmer (Boston: Northeastern University Press, 1990), 1:268–269; JG to CS, Oct. 29, 1849, CS Papers.

3. JG to Laura Waters Giddings, Dec. 2, 1849, JG Papers. Estimates of expected Free Soil strength varied widely. Several incoming representatives had been supported by the Free Soil Party and ran on their anti-extension credentials but had not renounced their old party ties. One overestimate from the Boston *Republican*, quoted in *National Era*, Aug. 30, 1849, counted eighteen Free Soil votes including men elected with Free Soil support (and hoped for two more in New England runoffs). In a more measured assessment, the *National Era*, Oct. 11, 1849, counted ten or eleven (depending on Palfrey's fortunes in an upcoming runoff, which ultimately went unresolved) who would vote against the major-party candidates. Over the course of these proceedings, the number of free soil Whigs and free soil Democrats voting against their party's nominees fluctuated. On the first ballot, fourteen total representatives (with Indiana Free Soiler George Julian absent) cast anti-extension votes against the caucus candidates. *CG*, 31st Congress, 1st Session, 2; "From Our Regular Correspondent," New York *Evening Post*, Dec. 4, 1849.

4. *CG*, 31st Congress, 1st Session, 2; "31st Congress," *National Era*, Dec. 6, 1849. Six Southern Whigs and three South Carolina Democrats also scattered their votes to nominees more suitably proslavery than Winthrop or Cobb. Led by Georgia's Robert Toombs and Alexander Stephens, the disgruntled Southern Whigs became known derisively as the "impracticables." Michael F. Holt, *Rise and Fall of the American Whig Party: Jacksonian Politics and the Onset of Civil War* (New York: Oxford University Press, 1999), 467–470; Howell Cobb to his wife, Dec. 4, 1849, in *The Correspondence of Robert Toombs, Alexander H. Stephens, and Howell Cobb*, ed. Ulrich Bonnell Phillips (American Historical Association, 1913; rep., New York: Da Capo Press, 1970), 178.

5. *Evening Post*, Dec. 22, 1849; "Not Factious," *National Era*, Dec. 20, 1849.

6. *CG*, 31st Congress, 1st Session, 5–6, 13–14.

7. Ibid., 13; Durkee, "Letter from D.," Dec. 7, 1849, in Milwaukee *Wisconsin Free Democrat*, Dec. 19, 1849.

8. *CG*, 31st Congress, 1st Session, 16–18. Brown's personal position on the Wilmot Proviso was ambiguous. He had sided with the South many times, but had missed the opportunity to vote on the Proviso, since he did not sit in the 29th and 30th Congresses while serving as Assistant Postmaster General under President Polk. In that capacity, though, he proscribed Barnburners from patronage offices during their 1848 revolt. Jenkins and Stewart, *Fighting for the Speakership*, 161–163; Root, ex-Whig John Howe (PA), and Amos Tuck refused to support Brown. With decades of hindsight, George W. Julian, *Political Recollections, 1840–1872* (Chicago: Jansen, McClurg & Company, 1884), 74–76, argued that Brown's subsequent doughfaced record vindicated the Free Soilers who voted against him; *CG*, 31st Congress, 1st Session, 19, 21–22.

9. Orin Fowler to Artemas Hale, Dec. 12, 1849, Artemas Hale Papers, William L. Clements Library, University of Michigan, Ann Arbor; SPC to CS, December 14, 1849, in *The Salmon P. Chase Papers*, ed. John Niven (Kent, OH: Kent State University Press, 1993), 2:265.

10. For examples of support for Strong and Stevens, see the speech of Preston King in *CG*, 31st Congress, 1st Session, 36, and JG to Joseph Addison Giddings, Dec. 8, 1849, JG Papers.

11. "The Contest for Speakership," *National Era*, Dec. 13, 1849; *CG Appendix*, 31st Congress, 1st Session, 35.

12. *CG*, 31st Congress, 1st Session, 25–27. On lying and Southern honor culture, see Kenneth S. Greenberg, "The Nose, the Lie, and the Duel in the Antebellum South," *American Historical Review* 95 (Feb. 1990): 57–74.

13. JG to LMG, Dec. 16, 1849, JG Papers; JG to CS, Dec. 15, 1849, CS Papers; Charles Allen to JGP, Palfrey Family Papers, Houghton Library, Harvard University, Cambridge, MA; JG to Joseph A. Giddings, Dec. 25, 1849, JG Papers; letter from Charles Durkee, Dec. 14, 1849, in *Wisconsin Free Democrat*, Dec. 26, 1849.

14. *CG*, 31st Congress, 1st Session, 34, 47.

15. *CG*, 31st Congress, 1st Session, 49–50, 61–63, 66. Evincing the House's general uncertainty, Cobb privately reported that some Whig supporters of the plurality rule believed it likely to elect Cobb, but Cobb himself voted against the rule, assuming it would elect Winthrop. Howell Cobb to his wife, Dec. 20, 22, 1849, in *Correspondence of Toombs, Stephens, and Cobb*, 179–180; *CG*, 31st Congress, 1st Session, 67, 75–76.

Chapter Six

1. In addition to the primary sources cited below, my discussion of the Compromise of 1850 and debates preceding it draws on the syntheses of William W. Freehling, *The Road to Disunion*, vol. 1, *Secessionists at Bay, 1776-1854* (New York: Oxford University Press, 1990), 487–510; Elizabeth R. Varon, *Disunion!: The Coming of the American Civil War, 1789-1859* (Chapel Hill: University of North Carolina Press, 2008), 210–231; Sean Wilentz, *The Rise of American Democracy: Jefferson to Lincoln* (New York: W. W. Norton & Company, 2005), 633–645; and David M. Potter, *The Impending Crisis, 1848-1861*, ed. Don E. Fehrenbacher (New York: Harper & Row, 1976), 90–120. Potter demonstrates that this legislation was less a compromise than an "armistice," in which moderates staved off disaster without getting a majority of congressmen to agree on the settlement. Don E. Fehrenbacher, *The Slaveholding Republic: An Account of the United States Government's Relations to Slavery*, ed. Ward M. McAfee (New York: Oxford University Press, 2002), 66–68, 83–87, shows that even before the compromise, Washington City served more as a way station for transportation of slave "merchandise" than as an actual slave marketing center like Alexandria. On the often-overlooked Texas boundary issue, see Mark J. Stegmaier, *Texas, New Mexico, and the Compromise of 1850: Boundary Dispute and Sectional Crisis* (Kent, OH: Kent State University Press, 1996). On the border state tensions that shaped the new Fugitive Slave Act, see Stanley Harrold, *Border War: Fighting over Slavery before the Civil War* (Chapel Hill: University of North Carolina Press, 2010), 138–145. On the Fugitive Slave Act's controversial and legally innovative provision for federal commissioners to deputize citizen posses, see Gautham Rao, "The Federal *Posse Comitatus* Doctrine: Slavery, Compulsion, and Statecraft in Mid-Nineteenth-Century America," *Law and History Review* 26 (Spring 2008): 1–56.

2. Clay's initial resolutions can be found in *CG*, 31st Congress, 2nd Session, 246–247.

3. *CG*, 31st Congress, 1st Session, 451–455, 476–484. Calhoun also advocated an outlandish constitutional amendment to give Southerners a sectional veto over the Northern majority in Congress. Most Southern opponents of Clay's compromise, including future Confederate president Jefferson Davis (D-MS), made more conventional demands for extension of the Missouri Compromise line westward and division of California to leave the less settled south-

ern portion open to slavery, even though previous Congresses had clearly rejected this plan. Leonard L. Richards, *The California Gold Rush and the Coming of the Civil War* (New York: Alfred A. Knopf, 2007), 125–131.

4. *CG Appendix*, 31st Congress, 1st Session, 260–269; ibid., 1054–1065; ibid., 468–480; Flamen Ball to CS, May 22, 1850, CS Papers; SPC to Stanley Matthews, May 6, 1850, in *The Salmon P. Chase Papers*, ed. John Niven (Kent, OH: Kent State University Press, 1993), 2:291–294.

5. For one example of Free Soilers' use of this nickname for Foote, see *GMF*, Jan. 3, 1850. On the competing efforts of Foote and in-state rival Jefferson Davis to shape California's admission, see Richards, *California Gold Rush*, 102–109. Two key differences between Clay's omnibus and the separate bills that finally passed were that the omnibus had left Texas smaller than it ultimately became and had specifically barred the New Mexico and Utah territories from passing legislation concerning slavery, while the final bills tacitly endorsed popular sovereignty; *GMF*, May 2, Aug. 1, 1850.

6. On Douglas's financial interest in slavery, see Robert W. Johannsen, *Stephen A. Douglas* (New York: Oxford University Press, 1973), 208–211, 336–338; Stegmaier, *Texas, New Mexico, and the Compromise of 1850*, ch. 8, 11. See also Holman Hamilton, *Prologue to Conflict: The Crisis and Compromise of 1850* (Lexington: University of Kentucky Press, 1964), 136–138, 151–159; SPC to Edward S. Hamlin, Aug. 14, 1850, in *SPC Papers*, ed. Niven, 2:303; Rachel A. Shelden, *Washington Brotherhood: Politics, Social Life, and the Coming of the Civil War* (Chapel Hill: University of North Carolina Press, 2013), 66–68.

7. *CG*, 31st Congress, 1st Session, 1136–37, 1561–63; "Letter of Hon. Horace Mann to his Constituents on the Slavery Question," in Boston *Emancipator and Republican*, May 9, 1850; *GMF*, Aug. 1, 1850; Cleveland *Daily True Democrat*, Mar. 17, 1850.

8. *GMF*, Sept. 5, Oct. 10, 1850; Austin Willey to JPH, Oct. 14, 1850, JPH Papers; Jacob Brinkerhoff to SPC, Nov. 29, 1850, SPC Papers.

9. Fillmore's message, Dec. 2, 1850, in *CG*, 31st Congress, 2nd Session, 5; *CG Appendix*, 31st Congress, 2nd Session, 252–256; ibid., 237–249. Arguments like Mann's must also be appreciated against the backdrop of an extensive history of kidnapping raids in the free states. See Harrold, *Border War*, 29–33, 57–61.

10. *CG Appendix*, 31st Congress, 1st Session, 1299–1302; *Emancipator and Republican*, Sept. 19, 1850.

11. *GMF*, Mar. 28, 1847; JG to Joseph A. Giddings, Mar. 8, 1850, JG Papers; Jn Jay to CS, May 15, 1850, CS Papers.

12. For a useful recap of some of the most famous fugitive slave incidents, see Varon, *Disunion!*, 236–241, or Wilentz, *Rise of American Democracy*, 645–653. For a statistical summary of the alleged fugitives apprehended under this law, see Stanley W. Campbell, *The Slave Catchers: Enforcement of the Fugitive Slave Law, 1850–1860* (Chapel Hill: University of North Carolina Press, 1968), appendix, 199–207. Campbell, 154–157, shows that most cases prosecuted under the 1850 act resulted without incident in the remanding of the alleged fugitive to slavery. On the escalation of Underground Railroad activism, especially in New York City, in response to the Fugitive Slave Act, see Eric Foner, *Gateway to Freedom: The Hidden History of the Underground Railroad* (New York: W. W. Norton & Company, 2015), 126–171. For additional insights on the extraordinary, previously unheralded work of Louis Napoleon, see Sarah Levine-Gronningsater, "Delivering Freedom: Gradual Emancipation, Black Legal Culture, and the Origins of Sectional Crisis in New York, 1759-1870" (Ph.D. diss., University of Chicago, 2014), ch. 6.

13. Harrold, *Border War*, illuminates a preexisting pattern of repeated conflict over fugitive slave rendition on the North-South border; *Emancipator and Republican*, Oct. 10, 17, 1850;

Gary Collison, *Shadrach Minkins: From Fugitive Slave to Citizen* (Cambridge, MA: Harvard University Press, 1997), 79–85, 94–104; Stephen Kantrowitz, *More Than Freedom: Fighting for Black Citizenship in a White Republic* (New York: Penguin Press, 2012), 177–188.

14. Campbell, *Slave Catchers*, 117–120, 148–151. For more detail, see Collison, *Shadrach Minkins*, 110–150, 192–196.

15. Thomas P. Slaughter, *Bloody Dawn: The Christiana Riot and Racial Violence in the Antebellum North* (New York: Oxford University Press, 1991); Washington (DC) *National Era*, Oct. 23, 1851; Centreville *Indiana True Democrat*, Nov. 13, 1851.

16. *National Era*, Oct. 9, 1851; Milton C. Sernett, *North Star Country: Upstate New York and the Crusade for African American Freedom* (Syracuse: Syracuse University Press, 2002), 136–145. For more on May, see Donald Yacovone, *Samuel Joseph May and the Dilemmas of the Liberal Persuasion, 1797-1871* (Philadelphia: Temple University Press, 1991).

17. *CG*, 31st Congress, 2nd Session, 597–598, 660; CS to Horace Mann, Jan. 28, 1851, in *Selected Letters of Charles Sumner*, ed. Beverly Wilson Palmer (Boston: Northeastern University Press, 1990), 1:322–323; *CG Appendix*, 31st Congress, 2nd Session, 292–326; Chicago *Western Citizen*, Mar. 11, 1851; *GMF*, Feb. 27, 1851; *Indiana True Democrat*, Feb. 27, 1851.

18. *CG*, 31st Congress, 2nd Session, 247–249, 574–580; ibid., 401–402.

19. Stanley Harrold, *Gamaliel Bailey and Antislavery Union* (Kent, OH: Kent State University Press, 1986), 142–144.

20. *National Era*, July 3, 1851, Apr. 1, May 27, 1852; Joan D. Hedrick, *Harriet Beecher Stowe: A Life* (New York: Oxford University Press, 1995), 223, 233.

21. Letter of "S.E.M." of Arispe, IL, Dec. 29, 1851, in *National Era*, Jan. 29, 1852; Jn Jay to CS, July 5, Dec. 20, 1852, CS Papers; Chicago *Free West*, Feb. 1, May 4, 1853; JGW to WLG, May 1852, in *The Letters of John Greenleaf Whittier*, ed. John B. Pickard (Cambridge, MA: Belknap Press of Harvard University Press, 1975), 2:191.

22. John L. Brooke, "Party, Nation, and Cultural Rupture: The Crisis of the American Civil War," in *Practicing Democracy: Popular Politics in the United States from the Constitution to the Civil War*, ed. Daniel Peart and Adam I. P. Smith (Charlottesville: University of Virginia Press, 2015).

23. SPC to My dear friend [NST?], Aug. 2, 1851, SPC Papers. For a good example of Chase explaining his preference for the name Free Democrats, see SPC to CS, Feb. 26, 1851, CS Papers. On Chase's election to the Senate, see chapter 5 above. I. W. Gray to SPC, Apr. 17, 1849, SPC Papers; Hamlin to SPC, Apr. 8, 1849, ibid.; Edward Wade to SPC, Jan. 14, 1850, ibid.; JG to SPC, Aug. 12, 1851, ibid. On the complicated course of coalition in Ohio, see Richard H. Sewell, *Ballots for Freedom: Antislavery Politics in the United States, 1837-1860* (New York: Oxford University Press, 1976), 200–211; Stephen E. Maizlish, *The Triumph of Sectionalism: The Transformation of Ohio Politics, 1844-1856* (Kent, OH: Kent State University Press, 1983), 149–174; and Frederick J. Blue, *The Free Soilers: Third Party Politics 1848-54* (Urbana: University of Illinois Press, 1973), 168–172, 182–186.

24. Hamlin to SPC, Jan. 18, 1850, ibid.; SPC to Hamlin, Jan. 12, 1850, Papers of Salmon P. Chase, LC; *Daily True Democrat*, Aug. 24, 1850; Hamlin to SPC, Mar. 11, 1850, SPC Papers; Adams Jewett to SPC, Feb. 3, 1850, Papers of SPC, LC; John G. Breslin to SPC, Apr. 5, 1850, SPC Papers; Hamlin to SPC, Dec. 6, 1850, ibid.; SPC to NST, July 15, 1850, Aug. 10, 1850, May 24, 1851, Norton Strange Townshend Family Papers, William L. Clements Library, University of Michigan, Ann Arbor.

25. John F. Morse to SPC, Oct. 31, 1850, SPC Papers; Hamlin to SPC, Dec. 6, 1850, ibid.; JG to CS, Mar. 17, 1851, CS Papers; SPC to C. R. Miller, Aug. 25, 1851, in *National Era*, Sept. 11, 1851; Adams Jewett to SPC, Jan. 20, 1850, Papers of SPC, LC.

26. John Niles to Gideon Welles, Mar. 26, Apr. 5, 8, 1849, Gideon Welles Papers, micro-

form, NYPL; A. E. Burr to Gideon Welles, June 6, July 12, Aug. 8, 1849, ibid.; John Niles to JPH, Apr. 9, 1850, JPH Papers.

27. Sewell, *Ballots for Freedom*, 211-214; Ronald P. Formisano, *The Birth of Mass Political Parties: Michigan, 1827-1861* (Princeton: Princeton University Press, 1971), 210; Michael J. Dubin, *United States Congressional Elections, 1788-1997: The Official Results of the Elections of the 1st through 105th Congresses* (Jefferson, NC: McFarland, 1998), 158; Michael J. McManus, *Political Abolitionism in Wisconsin, 1840-1861* (Kent, OH: Kent State University Press, 1998), 55-78.

28. Benjamin F. Butler to SPC, July 30, 1849, SPC Papers; Preston King to JG, Sept. 19, 1849, JG Papers; Seth Gates to JG, Nov. 10, 1849, Nov. 16, 1850, ibid.; Blue, *Free Soilers*, 154-162, 179-182; Sewell, *Ballots for Freedom*, 223-229; Jonathan H. Earle, *Jacksonian Antislavery & the Politics of Free Soil, 1824-1854* (Chapel Hill: University of North Carolina Press, 2004), 187-190; Arthur Harry Rice, "Henry B. Stanton as a Political Abolitionist" (Ed.D. diss., Teachers College, Columbia University, 1968), 311-351.

29. Sewell, *Ballots for Freedom*, 216-218; John Roberts to Charles G. Eastman, May 1, 1849, Charles G. Eastman Papers, VHS; Levi Vilas to Eastman, Apr. 20, 1849, ibid.; John Cain to Eastman, May 4, 1849, ibid.; Barber to Eastman, May 13, 1849, ibid.; John Cain to Eastman, July 21, 1849, ibid.; D. W. Robinson to Eastman, Feb. 7, 1851, ibid.

30. This discussion of the Massachusetts coalition draws on Blue, *Free Soilers*, ch. 8; David H. Donald, *Charles Sumner and the Coming of the Civil War* (New York: Knopf, 1960), 177-204; Sewell, *Ballots for Freedom*, 218-223; and Earle, *Jacksonian Antislavery*, 184-187. The original conversation between Sumner and Whittier is recounted in JGW to Grace Greenwood, May 18, 1851, in *Letters of JGW*, ed. Pickard, 2:177; Dubin, *U.S. Congressional Elections*, 158, 161. Also, Whig congressman Orin Fowler's reelection represented an antislavery victory. Free Soilers had declined to challenge Fowler given his forceful denunciation of Webster and the Compromise.

31. SPC to CS, Nov. 18, 1850, CS Papers; JG to CS, Nov. 25, 1850, ibid.; GB to CS, Nov. 27, 1850, ibid.; JL to CS, Dec. 18, 1850, ibid.; JGW to CS, Jan. 16, 1851, in *Letters of JGW*, ed. Pickard, 2:171-172; Samuel Gridley Howe to Horace Mann, Jan. 23, Jan. 31, 1851, in *Letters and Journals of Samuel Gridley Howe*, ed. Laura E. Richards (Boston: Dana Estes & Company, 1909), 2:334-336. Among the other beneficiaries of the bargain, Democrat Nathaniel Banks became speaker of the state house, and Wilson became president of the state senate. Though unconfirmed, it seems likely that a few anti-Compromise Whigs switched their votes to elect Sumner.

32. *Indiana True Democrat*, May 8, 1851; Flamen Ball to CS, Apr. 25, 1851, CS Papers; E. A. Stansbury to CS, Apr. 25, 1851, ibid.; JGW to CS, "Second day Morning" [after Apr. 24, 1851], in *Letters of JGW*, ed. Pickard, 2:176; David Dudley Field to CS, Jan. 9, 1851, CS Papers; John Van Buren to CS, Feb. 20, Apr. 7, 1851, ibid.; SPC to CS, Apr. 28, 1851, ibid.

33. J. P. Blanchard to CS, Mar. 14, 1852, ibid.; Donald, *Charles Sumner*, 222-227; *CG*, 32nd Congress, 1st Session, 2371.

34. Sumner's speech and the extensive debate that followed can be seen in *CG Appendix*, 32nd Congress, 1st Session, 1102-1125. The speech was also published as *Slavery Sectional; Freedom National: Speech of Hon. Charles Sumner on his Motion to Repeal the Fugitive Slave Bill, in the Senate of the United States, Aug. 26, 1852* (Boston: Ticknor, Reed, and Fields, 1852); Harriet Beecher Stowe to CS, Nov. 7, 1852, CS Papers; Bradford Wood to CS, Nov. 10, 1852, ibid.; David L. Child to CS, Feb. 8, 1853, ibid.

35. Blue, *Free Soilers*, 234-235; SPC to My dear friend [NST?], Aug. 2, 1851, SPC Papers; Barber to Charles G. Eastman, Mar. 20, 1851, Charles G. Eastman Papers, VHS; Edward Hamlin to SPC, Dec. 3, 1851, SPC Papers.

36. "Call for a National Convention of the Friends of Freedom," in *Daily True Democrat*, July 15, 1851; ibid., Sept. 26, 27, 29, 1851; Sewell, *Ballots for Freedom*, 241–242; James B. Stewart, *Joshua R. Giddings and the Tactics of Radical Politics* (Cleveland: Press of Case Western Reserve University, 1970), 200–205; *National Era*, Dec. 11, 1851.

37. Milwaukee *Wisconsin Free Democrat*, Apr. 30, 1851; *Proceedings of the Democratic National Convention, Held at Baltimore, June 1–5, 1852* (Washington: Robert Armstrong, 1852); William E. Gienapp, *The Origins of the Republican Party, 1852-1856* (New York: Oxford University Press, 1987), 14–16.

38. Gienapp, *Origins*, 16–19; Donald Bruce Johnson, compiler, *National Party Platforms, Volume 1: 1840-1956* (Urbana: University of Illinois Press, 1978), 21.

39. *GMF*, June 24, 1852; *Indiana True Democrat*, Feb. 6, 1851; *Western Citizen*, Jan. 28, 1851. For more on the Union party movements see Michael F. Holt, *Rise and Fall of the American Whig Party: Jacksonian Politics and the Onset of Civil War* (New York: Oxford University Press, 1999), ch. 17–19, passim; Hartford *Republican*, June 17, 1852; *National Era*, July 15, 1852; Concord, NH, *Independent Democrat*, June 17, 1852; Austin Willey to JPH, June 21, 1852, JPH Papers; CS to CFA, [June 13, 1852], in *Selected Letters of CS*, ed. Palmer, 1:362; *GMF*, July 15, 1852; Resolutions of the "State Political Anti-Slavery Convention," *Indiana True Democrat*, May 27, 1852; SPC to Edward Keyes, July 5, 1852, in *GMF*, July 15, 1852.

40. Willey to JPH, June 21, 1852, JPH Papers; *GMF*, July 15, July 29, Sept. 9, 1852; *CG Appendix*, 31st Congress, 2nd Session, 886–892. Other good examples of Free Soilers attacking the major parties can be seen in speeches by NST and John W. Howe in ibid., 712–715, 882–886.

41. SPC to JPH, Aug. 5, 7, 1852, JPH Papers; George Fogg to JPH, Aug. 3, 1852, Hale-Chandler Papers, Rauner Special Collections Library, Dartmouth College Library, Hanover, NH; Amos Tuck to JPH, Aug. 5, 1852, JPH Papers; Richard H. Sewell, *John P. Hale and the Politics of Abolition* (Cambridge, MA: Harvard University Press, 1965), 144–147.

42. *National Era*, Aug. 26, 1852; Willey to JPH, Aug. 19, 1852, Hale-Chandler Papers; letter from Fogg, Aug. 9, 1852, in *Independent Democrat*, Aug. 26, 1852; Walt Whitman to JPH, Aug. 14, 1852, JPH Papers; JG to JPH, Aug. 16, 1852, Hale-Chandler Papers; letter from Fogg, Aug. 9, 1852, in *Independent Democrat*, Aug. 26, 1852; JPH to Henry Wilson, Sept. 6, 1852, in *National Era*, Sept. 23, 1852; Sewell, *John P. Hale*, 148–49.

43. Blue, *Free Soilers*, 248–49; Sewell, *Ballots for Freedom*, 246–247; Rochester *Frederick Douglass' Paper*, Oct. 29, 1852; James Oakes, *The Radical and the Republican: Frederick Douglass, Abraham Lincoln, and the Triumph of Antislavery Politics* (New York: W. W. Norton & Company, 2007), 23–24; Preston King to Francis P. Blair, Feb. 26, 1852, Blair and Lee Family Papers, Department of Rare Books and Special Collections, Manuscripts Division, Princeton University Library; Charles Allen to Moses Cartland, July 5, 1852, Cartland Family Papers, Houghton Library, Harvard University, Cambridge, MA; *GMF*, June 24, 1852.

44. Joseph Root to JG, Feb. 23, 1852, JG Papers; Willey to JPH, Aug. 19, 1852, Hale-Chandler Papers; letter from Fogg, Aug. 12, 1852, in *Independent Democrat*, Aug. 26, 1852.

45. Gienapp, *Origins*, 27–29.

46. Gienapp, *Origins*, 20–27, 30–35, 47–50; Potter, *Impending Crisis*, 234–246.

47. Blue, *Free Soilers*, 256; *Independent Democrat*, Dec. 2, 1852; *Ashtabula Sentinel*, Jan. 15, 1853. The declining salience of issues like banking and tariffs owed partly to the nation's economic prosperity in the early 1850s.

48. James Stewart, *Joshua Giddings*, 214–216; Henry Wilson to GS, Oct. 11, 1852, GS Papers. See also H. C. Taylor to GS, Nov. 8, 1852, and A. N. Cole to GS, Nov. 17, 1852, ibid.

49. Harrold, *Gamaliel Bailey*, 133–134; Kinsley S. Bingham to Mary Bingham, Jan. 26, 1851, Kinsley S. Bingham Papers, Michigan Historical Collections, Bentley Historical Library,

microform, University of Michigan, Ann Arbor; George W. Julian to his wife, Jan. 11, 1851, in Grace Julian Clarke, "Home Letters of George Julian, 1850–1851," *Indiana Magazine of History* 29 (1933): 156; Grace Greenwood, "An American Salon," in *Cosmopolitan*, Feb. 1890, 441–447, quote from George W. Julian on 447. See also Jonathan Earle, "Saturday Nights at the Baileys': Building an Antislavery Movement in Congress, 1838–1854," in *In the Shadow of Freedom: The Politics of Slavery in the National Capital*, ed. Paul Finkelman and Donald R. Kennon (Athens, OH: Ohio University Press, 2011), 83–96.

50. *Lockport Journal*, quoted in *Independent Democrat*, Jan. 6, 1853. See also "The Late Whig Party," quoting from *New-York Daily Tribune* and *Newburyport Herald*, in *Indiana True Democrat*, Nov. 25, 1852; *Ashtabula Sentinel*, Apr. 28, 1853; JG, in ibid., June 2, 1853; *GMF*, Apr. 7, July 14, 1853; JL to Roger Hooker Leavitt, Nov. 12, 1852, JL Papers.

51. Frustrations over Slave Power resistance to federal support for agricultural improvement would mature later in the decade in response to the defeat of Vermont Republican Justin Morrill's land grant agricultural college legislation. Ariel Ron, "Developing the Country: 'Scientific Agriculture' and the Roots of Republican Party" (Ph.D. diss., University of California Berkeley, 2012), ch. 5.

52. *Ashtabula Sentinel*, Apr. 14, 1853; *Independent Democrat*, Feb. 24, Mar. 10, 1853.

53. On the importance of the Maine Law and nativism in the disruption of party politics in the North and in the weakening of the Whig Party specifically, see Gienapp, *Origins*, 44–67; Hartford *Republican*, Feb. 5, 1852. For good examples of how Free Soilers took advantage of opportunities created by the expanded interest in temperance while still focusing on opposing the Slave Power, see *Ashtabula Sentinel*, Aug. 18, 1853, and *GMF*, Sept. 15, 1853.

54. *Independent Democrat*, Sept, 22, 1853; JGW to Edward A. Stansbury, Minthorne Tompkins, Monroe B. Brant, and George W. Rose, Sept. 23, 1853, in *Letters of JGW*, ed. Pickard, 2:233–235; *GMF*, Oct. 20, 1853.

55. Edward Wade to Salmon P. Chase, Oct. 17, 1853, SPC Papers; *National Era*, June 23, 1853; *Ashtabula Sentinel*, July 14, Sept. 15, Oct. 27, 1853; Sewell, *Ballots for Freedom*, 252–253; McManus, *Political Abolitionism in Wisconsin*, 80–84.

Chapter Seven

1. Concord, NH, *Independent Democrat*, Apr. 21, 1853, July 14, 1853; SPC to Charles D. Cleveland, May 27, 1853, SPC Papers; *Independent Democrat*, Dec. 23, 1852. President Polk had previously attempted to purchase Cuba. When the succeeding Whig administrations abandoned the project, Southern expansionists supported Narciso López's filibustering forays. Extant evidence suggests that Pierce initially welcomed new filibustering, but, by mid-1854, had come out against such an expedition and hoped to secure Cuba through diplomacy: Don E. Fehrenbacher, *The Slaveholding Republic: An Account of the United States Government's Relations to Slavery*, ed. Ward M. McAfee (New York: Oxford University Press, 2002), 128–129; Robert E. May, *Manifest Destiny's Underworld: Filibustering in Antebellum America* (Chapel Hill: University of North Carolina Press, 2002), 20–35, 119–123. On the Ostend Manifesto and its immediate background, see Michael Todd Landis, *Northern Men with Southern Loyalties: The Democratic Party and the Sectional Crisis* (Ithaca, NY: Cornell University Press, 2014), 91–95. On the broader proslavery vision that shaped American diplomacy regarding Cuba, see Matthew Jason Karp, "'This Vast Southern Empire': The South and the Foreign Policy of Slavery, 1833–1861" (Ph.D. diss., University of Pennsylvania, 2011), 362–390.

2. David M. Potter, *The Impending Crisis, 1848–1861*, ed. Don E. Fehrenbacher (New York: Harper & Row, 1976), 145–154, 178, 182–83; *GMF*, June 23, Sept. 8, 1853. On how the China

trade stimulated support for a Pacific railroad, see Dael Norwood, "Trading in Liberty: The Politics of the American China Trade, c. 1784–1862" (Ph.D. diss., Princeton University, 2012), esp. ch. 5.

3. Washington (DC) *National Era*, Apr. 17, 1853; *CG*, 32nd Congress, 2nd Session, 539–543, 556–565. The characterization of Richardson as Douglas's "Representative Shadow" appears in Chicago *Free West*, May 11, 1854. Letter from JG, Feb. 8, 1853, in *Ashtabula Sentinel*, Feb. 17, 1853; letter from JG, Feb. 15, 1853, in ibid., Feb. 24, 1853; *CG*, 32nd Congress, 2nd Session, 1116–1117.

4. *National Era*, Apr. 17, Nov. 17, 1853; *Independent Democrat*, Nov. 17, Dec. 15, 1853.

5. Letter from JG, Jan. 5, 1854, in *Ashtabula Sentinel*, Jan. 12, 1854; *GMF*, Jan. 12, 1854.

6. The F Street Mess included Senators Andrew Pickens Butler (SC), Robert M. T. Hunter (VA), and James Mason (VA), all proslavery zealots and all chairs of powerful Senate committees. For more, see Rachel A. Shelden, *Washington Brotherhood: Politics, Social Life, and the Coming of the Civil War* (Chapel Hill: University of North Carolina Press, 2013), 98–102, 117–119.

7. *CG*, 33rd Congress, 1st Session, 239–240; George W. Julian, *The Life of Joshua R. Giddings* (Chicago: A. C. McClurg and Company, 1892), 311–312; *National Era*, Jan. 24, 1854. Completed before Douglas's newest amendments, the initial version of the Appeal did not mention Kansas, but the Independent Democrats soon published a postscript. The *New-York Daily Times*, Jan. 24, 1854, initially misprinted the Appeal as coming from the "Senators and a majority of the Representatives from Ohio," a common misconception, replicated, for example, in the *New-York Daily Tribune*, Jan. 25, 1854. Chase hypothesized that this mix-up stemmed from the fact that the Independent Democrats had at first sought signatures from Ohio congressmen to issue an address to the people of that state, but when some representatives requested revisions, the Independent Democrats decided to avoid delay and issue the Appeal in its original form: *CG*, 33rd Congress, 1st Session, 280; Dick Johnson, "Along the Twisted Road to Civil War: Historians and the 'Appeal of the Independent Democrats,'" *Old Northwest* 4 (1978): 136–138.

8. Eric Foner, *Free Soil, Free Labor, Free Men: The Ideology of the Republican Party before the Civil War* (1970; rep., Oxford: Oxford University Press, 1995), 94–95. Roy F. Nichols, "The Kansas-Nebraska Act: A Century of Historiography," *Mississippi Valley Historical Review* 43 (Sept. 1956): 205–206, likewise viewed this "manifesto" as setting off "a chain reaction which gave Northern leaders their desired opportunity to mobilize the anti-Southern voting strength of the more populous north." For a counterargument that questions the importance and reach of the Appeal, see Mark E. Neely, Jr., "The Kansas-Nebraska Act in American Political Culture: The Road to Bladenburg and the *Appeal of the Independent Democrats*," in *The Nebraska-Kansas Act of 1854*, ed. John R. Wunder and Joann M. Ross (Lincoln: University of Nebraska Press, 2008), 13–46. Neely, however, overlooks the degree to which the Appeal enabled Chase and Sumner to structure the ensuing Senate debates around contesting the Slave Power's new demands.

9. For example, the Appeal appeared immediately, alongside editorial praise, in both the Democratic-leaning New York *Evening Post*, Jan. 25, 26, 1854, and the Whiggish *New-York Daily Times*, Jan. 24, 1854; Chicago *Free West*, Feb. 2, 1854; Concord, NH, *Independent Democrat*, Feb. 2, 1854.

10. *CG*, 33rd Congress, 1st Session, 275–282.

11. CS to Jn Jay, Jan. 12, 1854, in *Selected Letters of CS*, ed. Palmer, 1:399–400. See also CS to Jn Jay, Jan. 21, 22, 1854, in ibid., 1:401–403; JG to Grotius R. Giddings, Feb. 5, 1854, JG Papers; JG to Grotius R. Giddings, Feb. 12, 1854, G-J Papers; *New-York Daily Tribune*, Feb. 1, 1854;

Bruce Laurie, *Rebels in Paradise: Sketches of Northampton Abolitionists* (Amherst: University of Massachusetts Press, 2015), 136; *CG*, 33rd Congress, 1st Session, 580, 617–623; *Ashtabula Sentinel*, Mar. 16, 1854.

12. *New-York Daily Tribune*, Feb. 1, 1854; *CG Appendix*, 33rd Congress, 1st Session, 140, 269; WJ to CS, Apr.[?] 1854, William Jackson to CS, July 1, 1854, Francis Jackson to CS, July 4, 1854, CS Papers; Frederick Douglass to CS, Feb. 27, 1854, ibid.

13. *Ashtabula Sentinel*, Mar. 2, 1854; *GMF*, Apr. 13, 1854; *Free West*, Mar. 2, 1854; E. A. Stansbury to CS, Feb. 23, 1854, CS Papers; J. D. Baldwin to CS, Feb. 28, 1854, ibid.; Jn Jay to CS, Jan. 24, 1854, ibid.; *New-York Daily Times*, Jan. 20, 1854; *Springfield (MA) Daily Republican*, Feb. 8, 1854.

14. *CG*, 33rd Congress, 1st Session, 531–532; *National Era*, Mar. 16, 1854; *Independent Democrat*, Mar. 30, 1854; *GMF*, Mar. 30, 1854; *Ashtabula Sentinel*, Apr. 6, 1854.

15. *CG*, 33rd Congress, 1st Session, 1130–1249, passim; *CG Appendix*, 33rd Congress, 1st Session, 663, 986–989, 972–976.

16. William E. Gienapp, *The Origins of the Republican Party, 1852–1856* (New York: Oxford University Press, 1987), 78–79; Stanley Harrold, *Gamaliel Bailey and Antislavery Union* (Kent, OH: Kent State University Press, 1986), 160–161. In Committee of the Whole, Stephens moved to strike out the "enacting words" of the Senate bill. The committee then reported "this action" to the House, which rejected that report so as to make it possible for Richardson to now introduce his own Kansas-Nebraska bill as an amendment to substitute for all of the Senate bill after the enacting clause, even though Richardson's substitution differed from the original bill only in its excision of an anti-immigrant clause that John Clayton (W-DE) had added in the Senate. The Senate then abandoned the Clayton amendment and ratified the House bill, rather than risk another fight in Committee of the Whole. *CG*, 33rd Congress, 1st Session, 1240–1254; *National Era*, May 25, 1854.

17. Gienapp, *Origins*, 89–90; *Ashtabula Sentinel*, July 6, 1854; "Address to the People of the United States," in *National Era*, June 29, 1854; *GMF*, July 6, 1854.

18. Letter from JG, June 15, 1854, in *Ashtabula Sentinel*, June 22, 1854; *Springfield Daily Republican*, May 24, 1854; *Free West*, Apr. 20, 1854; Douglas, quoted in Robert W. Johannsen, *Stephen A. Douglas* (New York: Oxford University Press, 1973), 451; *Ashtabula Sentinel*, July 6, 1854.

19. *Free West*, Mar. 30, Sept. 21, 1854; James W. Stone to SPC, SPC Papers; letter from JG, June 15, 1854, in *Ashtabula Sentinel*, June 22, 1854; *Free West*, June 8, 1854.

20. *National Era*, June 1, 1854; *GMF*, June 1, 1854; Sean Wilentz, *The Rise of American Democracy: Jefferson to Lincoln* (New York: W. W. Norton & Company, 2005), 676–77; Bruce Laurie, *Beyond Garrison: Antislavery and Social Reform* (New York: Cambridge University Press, 2005), 239–242; *Springfield Daily Republican*, May 29, 1854.

21. Frederick J. Blue, "Freemen to the Rescue: Sherman M. Booth and the Fugitive Slave Act," *No Taint of Compromise: Crusaders in Antislavery Politics* (Baton Rouge: Louisiana State University Press, 2005), 127–135; *Reminiscences of the Busy Life of Chauncey C. Olin*, in Chauncey C. Olin, *A Complete Record of the John Olin Family* (Indianapolis: Baker-Randolph Co., 1893), liii–lxxiv; *GMF*, Apr. 26, 1855. Booth, however, ultimately faced incarceration after the U.S. Supreme Court decided against him on appeal in 1859. For more detail on the rescue and subsequent legal proceedings, see H. Robert Baker, *The Rescue of Joshua Glover: A Fugitive Slave, The Constitution, and the Coming of the Civil War* (Athens: Ohio University Press, 2006).

22. Michael J. McManus, *Political Abolitionism in Wisconsin, 1840–1861* (Kent, OH: Kent State University Press, 1998), 89–96, 138.

23. Richard H. Sewell, *Ballots for Freedom: Antislavery Politics in the United States, 1837-1860* (New York: Oxford University Press, 1976), 264; Gienapp, *Origins*, 104–106; *National Era*, July 20, 1854.

24. *GMF*, Aug. 17, Sept. 14, 1854; *Free West*, Sept. 21, 1854.

25. *Independent Democrat*, Aug. 24, 1854. On the role of antipartisanship in the Know Nothing movement, see Mark Voss-Hubbard, *Beyond Party: Cultures of Antipartisanship in Northern Politics before the Civil War* (Baltimore: Johns Hopkins University Press, 2002).

26. Tyler Anbinder, *Nativism and Slavery: The Northern Know-Nothings and the Politics of the 1850s* (New York: Oxford University Press, 1992), 57–68, 71–73; Gienapp, *Origins*, 109–110.

27. On the Know Nothing movement in Massachusetts, see Laurie, *Beyond Garrison*, 272–284; Samuel Gridley Howe to Horace Mann, Nov. 14, 1854, in *Letters and Journals of Samuel Gridley Howe*, ed. Laura E. Richards (Boston: Dana Estes & Company, 1909), 2:403; JGP to JG, Dec. 20, 1854, JG Papers.

28. My emphasis on this legislature's antislavery record should not be read as suggesting that Massachusetts Know Nothings were insincere in their nativism. In response to the explosion of the state's impoverished Catholic immigrant population in the wake of the Irish Potato Famine, nativist legislators in the 1850s also imposed stringent suffrage requirements designed to limit immigrants' political power, including a literacy test and a two-year waiting period after naturalization. Laurie, *Beyond Garrison*, 286.

29. *Free West*, Mar. 15, Apr. 12, 1855; Sewell, *Ballots for Freedom*, 271; *Independent Democrat*, Feb. 13, Mar. 8, 15, 22, 1855; Richard H. Sewell, *John P. Hale and the Politics of Abolition* (Cambridge, MA: Harvard University Press, 1965), 154–162.

30. Greeley to Colfax, Aug. 24, 1854, Sept. 7, 1854, Horace Greeley Papers, microform, NYPL; Gienapp, *Origins*, 176–178.

31. *National Era*, Feb. 15, May 17, 1855; *GMF*, Dec. 21, 1854; Bruce C. Levine, *Half Slave and Half Free: The Roots of Civil War* (New York: Hill and Wang, 1992), 199; Stephen E. Maizlish, *The Triumph of Sectionalism: The Transformation of Ohio Politics, 1844-1856* (Kent, OH: Kent State University Press, 1983), 198–206; John Bigelow to CS, Nov. 8, 1854, CS Papers; *Free West*, Oct. 26, 1854.

32. A classic argument for slavery trumping nativism can be found in Foner, *Free Soil, Free Labor, Free Men*. See also James L. Huston, *Calculating the Value of the Union: Slavery, Property Rights, and the Economic Origins of the Civil War* (Chapel Hill: University of North Carolina Press, 2003), 205–215. Two of the most important works arguing the other side of this question are Gienapp, *Origins*, and Michael F. Holt, *The Political Crisis of the 1850s* (New York: W. W. Norton & Co, 1978). For a synthesis that ultimately privileges antislavery, see Anbinder, *Nativism and Slavery*.

33. *Free West*, Dec. 14, 1854; *GMF*, Jan. 18, 1855. On Southern Know Nothings, see Freehling, *Road to Disunion*, vol. 2, *Secessionists Triumphant, 1854-1861* (Oxford: Oxford University Press, 2007), 85–94.

34. Maizlish, *Triumph of Sectionalism*, 209–210; Anbinder, *Nativism and Slavery*, 163–64; letter from "BY AUTHORITY," Mar. 20, 1855, in *New-York Daily Tribune*, Mar. 24, 1855; SPC to CS, June 19, 1855, CS Papers; "State Platform of the Know Somethings of New York," in Letter from "VIATOR," Aug. 2, 1855, in *New-York Daily Tribune*, Aug. 3, 1855.

35. Anbinder, *Nativism and Slavery*, 147–154; *GMF*, Feb. 1, 8, 1855; *National Era*, Feb. 15, 1855; SPC to Edward S. Hamlin, Feb. 9, 1855, in *The Salmon P. Chase Papers*, ed. John Niven (Kent, OH: Kent State University Press, 1993), 2:401–402.

36. *National Era*, Nov. 23, 1854; *Ashtabula Sentinel*, Nov. 2, 1854.

37. Ichabod Codding to Zebina Eastman, May 21, 1855, in *Free West*, May 24, 1855.

38. Anbinder, *Nativism and Slavery*, 165–174; Wilson, quoted in *GMF*, July 5, 1855; SPC to CS, June 19, 1855, CS Papers.

39. *New-York Daily Tribune*, July 9, 17, 1855; *Springfield Daily Republican*, July 16, 1855.

40. *Buffalo Commercial Advertiser*, June 18, 1855, quoted in *Evening Post*, June 20, 1855; ibid., June 15, 1855; *Springfield Daily Republican*, July 21, 28, 1855; *Free West*, June 21, 1855; Henry Wilson, speech delivered at New York City Republican Ratification Meeting, Oct. 9, 1855, quoted in *Evening Post*, Oct. 10, 1855.

41. SPC to Edward S. Hamlin, Nov. 11, 1854, and Jan. 22, 1855, in *SPC Papers*, ed. Niven, 2:388–390, 397–399; SPC to NST, June 21, 1855, SPC Papers; Maizlish, *Triumph of Sectionalism*, 207–224; SPC, quoted in *Springfield Daily Republican*, Aug. 30, 1855; SPC to CS, Oct, 15, 1855, CS Papers; Lewis Campbell to CS, Oct. 16, 1855, ibid.; SPC to James S. Pike, Oct. 18, 1855, in *SPC Papers*, ed. Niven, 2:425–426; *GMF*, Oct. 18, 1855; Jn Jay to CS, Oct. 13, 1855, CS Papers.

42. *Free West*, Apr. 5, 1855; *GMF*, Apr. 19, Aug. 2, 9, 1855; *Evening Post*, July 7, 1855; Nicole Etcheson, *Bleeding Kansas: Contested Liberty in the Civil War Era* (Lawrence: University Press of Kansas, 2004), 52–88; *Free West*, Apr. 5, 1855. On race and gender ideologies that shaped the contours of the Kansas conflict, see Kristen Tegtmeier Oertel, *Bleeding Border: Race, Gender, and Violence in Pre-Civil War Kansas* (Baton Rouge: Louisiana State University Press, 2009).

43. Wesley Bailey, Letter of Oct. 8, 1855, to New York City Republican Ratification Meeting, Oct. 9, 1855, quoted in *Evening Post*, Oct. 10, 1855.

44. "Prospectus of the Tenth Volume of the National Era," in *National Era*, Nov. 29, 1855; *Springfield Daily Republican*, Nov. 19, 1855.

Interlude Five

1. Thirteen of sixteen free states held elections for the 34th Congress during the summer or fall of 1854, and the remaining three had concluded their elections by April 1855. Kenneth C. Martis, *The Historical Atlas of the Political Parties in the United States: 1789–1989* (New York: MacMillan, 1989), 33–34. Martis notes that the Whig label was used in only six states, all of which held congressional elections between August and November 1854; Tyler Anbinder, *Nativism and Slavery: The Northern Know-Nothings and the Politics of the 1850s* (New York: Oxford University Press, 1992), 166–169; David M. Potter, *The Impending Crisis, 1848-1861*, ed. Don E. Fehrenbacher (New York: Harper and Row Publishers, 1976), 251; William E. Gienapp, *The Origins of the Republican Party, 1852-1856* (New York: Oxford University Press, 1987), 240–241, estimates the anti-Nebraska strength at 118. For additional information about this contest, and the institutional power it offered to antislavery Republican House members, see Jeffery A. Jenkins and Charles Stewart III, *Fighting for the Speakership: The House and the Rise of Party Government* (Princeton: Princeton University Press, 2013), 177–208.

2. New York *Evening Post*, Dec. 3, 11, 1855; Robert D. Ilisevich, *Galusha A. Grow: The People's Candidate* (Pittsburgh: University of Pittsburgh Press, 1988), 108; Charles Henry Jones, *The Life and Public Services of J. Glancy Jones* (Philadelphia: J. B. Lippincott Company, 1910), 1:266.

3. JG, *History of the Rebellion: Its Authors and Causes* (New York: Follett, Foster & Co., 1864), 383; George W. Julian, *The Life of Joshua R. Giddings* (Chicago: A. C. McClurg and Company, 1892), 322.

4. Gienapp, *Origins*, 241–242; Michael F. Holt, *Rise and Fall of the American Whig Party: Jacksonian Politics and the Onset of Civil War* (New York: Oxford University Press, 1999), 962–963.

5. *CG*, 34th Congress, 1st Session, 3–4, 7–8, 11–15; JG, *History of the Rebellion*, 384; Fred Harvey Harrington, "The First Northern Victory," *Journal of Southern History* 5 (May 1939):

192. Thirteen of the forty-one Fuller supporters were Northerners: Anbinder, *Nativism and Slavery*, 199. Fuller explained that if forced to vote on restoration of the Missouri Compromise, he would vote for it, but he "opposed" continued "agitation of the question." He further clarified his sentiments by averring his willingness to admit Kansas as a slave state if the territorial population so chose. *CG*, 34th Congress, 1st Session, 54–55; Washington (DC) *National Era*, Dec. 13, 20, 27, 1855. During the last week of January, Democrats switched to South Carolina's James Orr, in hopes he might fare better with Southern Know Nothings than Richardson had, but found no significant change, and then, as discussed below, William Aiken of the same state replaced Orr on the final ballots; Jeffery A. Jenkins and Timothy P. Nokken, "The Institutional Origins of the Republican Party: Spatial Voting and the House Speakership Election of 1855–56," *Legislative Studies Quarterly* 25 (Feb. 2000): 101–130, as well as Jenkins and Stewart, *Fighting for the Speakership*, 182–185, 201–205, show convincingly that ideological positions on slavery (computed from congressional voting data) were highly predictive of these speakership votes, and also that Banks organized most House committees to represent the antislavery sentiments of his winning coalition. For a countervailing and, I believe, less compelling argument, see Joel H. Silbey, "After 'The First Northern Victory: The Republican Party Comes to Congress, 1855–1856," *Journal of Interdisciplinary History* 20 (Summer 1989): 1–24.

6. Edwin B. Morgan to Henry and Richard Morgan, Dec. 12, 1855, in Temple R. Hollcroft, "A Congressman's Letters on the Speaker Election in the Thirty-Fourth Congress," *Mississippi Valley Historical Review* 43 (Dec. 1956): 450–451; *National Era*, Dec. 20, 1855; Gienapp, *Origins*, 245; JG, *History of the Rebellion*, 386; Solomon Haven to James M. Smith, Dec. 11, 1855, and Dec. 20, 1855, Solomon G. Haven Papers, William L. Clements Library, University of Michigan, Ann Arbor; Timothy Crane Day to John Bigelow, Dec. 30, 1855, John Bigelow Papers, NYPL. Prominent members of the steering committee included ex-Democrats Galusha Grow (PA) and Francis Spinner (NY), ex-Whigs Schuyler Colfax (IN, also a Know Nothing), William A. Howard (MI), Edwin B. Morgan (NY), Justin Morrill (VT), Benjamin Stanton (OH), Cadwallader Washburn (WI), Elihu Washburne (IL), and Israel Washburn, Jr. (ME), and ex-Free Soilers Anson Burlingame (MA) and Mason Tappan (NH), both also Know Nothings: Gienapp, *Origins*, 245, Harrington, "First Northern Victory," 195, Ilisevich, *Galusha A. Grow*, 112; JG to LMG, Jan. 27, 1856, G-J Papers.

7. Horace Greeley, editorial correspondence of Jan. 5, 1856, in *New-York Daily Tribune*, Jan. 7, 1856; New York *Evening Post*, Dec. 17, 1855; Edwin B. Morgan to Henry and Richard Morgan, Dec. 22, 1855, in Hollcroft, "A Congressman's Letters," 451. For examples of this derisive laughter at threats of disunion, see *CG*, 34th Congress, 1st Session, 61–62, and Greeley, editorial correspondence of Dec. 20, 1855, in *New-York Daily Tribune*, Dec. 24, 1855; Jenkins and Nokken, "Institutional Origins of the Republican Party," 124n22; *CG*, 34th Congress, 1st Session, 27, 58–59, 72, 149; *National Era*, Jan. 17, 1856; JG to LMG, G-J Papers, Jan. 11, 1856.

8. JG to LMG, G-J Papers, Jan. 11, 1856; *National Era*, Jan. 17, 1856; Edwin B. Morgan to Henry and Richard Morgan, Jan. 10, 1856, in Hollcroft, "A Congressman's Letters," 454. For more on drinking and drunkenness in Congress, see Rachel A. Shelden, *Washington Brotherhood: Politics, Social Life, and the Coming of the Civil War* (Chapel Hill: University of North Carolina Press, 2013), 26–30, 125–130; *CG*, 34th Congress, 1st Session, 170–199, Giddings quote on 199.

9. JG to Grotius Giddings, Dec. 12, 1855, JG Papers; Preston King to Francis P. Blair, Feb. 3, 1856, Blair and Lee Family Papers, Department of Rare Books and Special Collections, Manuscripts Division, Princeton University Library; LT to Sidney Dean, Jan. 5, 1856, LT Papers; Jn Jay to CS, Dec. 18, 1855, CS Papers; James W. Stone to SPC to Nathaniel P. Banks, Feb. 4, 1856, Papers of Nathaniel P. Banks, LC; JG to LMG, Feb. 1, 1856, G-J Papers.

10. Aiken was considered most likely to win support from Fuller voters because he had avoided the Democratic caucus that had condemned Know Nothingism. On the plurality vote, he did indeed win the votes of most Southern Know Nothings, but several Northern Know Nothings along with a Marylander and Delawarean scattered their votes to Fuller or Campbell, allowing for Banks's narrow triumph. *CG*, 34th Congress, 1st Session, 324, 335–337; Harrington, "First Northern Victory," 200–202; Gienapp, *Origins*, 246; Jenkins and Nokken, "Institutional Origins of the Republican Party," 114–115.

11. CS to CFA, Feb. 5, 1856, in *Selected Letters of Charles Sumner*, ed. Beverly Wilson Palmer (Boston: Northeastern University Press, 1990), 1:442–443; JG to LMG, Feb. 9, 1856, G-J Papers; Edwin B. Morgan to Henry and Richard Morgan, Feb. 3, 1856, in Hollcroft, "A Congressman's Letters," 457; Thurlow Weed to Nathaniel P. Banks, Feb. 3, 1856, Papers of Nathaniel P. Banks, LC; JG to LMG, Feb. 3, 1856, G-J Papers; JG, *History of the Rebellion*, 389; *New-York Daily Times*, Feb. 5, 6, 1856; *New-York Daily Tribune*, Feb. 5, 1856; *Chicago Tribune*, Feb. 5, 1856; "Chronological Resume of Lewis Tappan's life written by him," entry for Feb. 3, 1856, LT Papers.

12. *GMF*, Feb. 7, 1856; Concord, NH, *Independent Democrat*, Feb. 7, 1856; "The Triumph at Washington," *New-York Daily Tribune*, Feb. 4, 1856; Jenkins and Nokken, "Institutional Origins of the Republican Party," 118.

Conclusion

1. Ralph Plumb to JG, Dec. 1, 1862, JG Papers; Reinhard O. Johnson, *The Liberty Party, 1840–1848: Antislavery Third-Party Politics in the United States* (Baton Rouge: Louisiana State University Press, 2009), 365–366; Nat Brandt, *The Town That Started the Civil War* (Syracuse, NY: Syracuse University Press, 1990), 121–122, 125–126, 221–222, 232–236, 242, 248.

2. William Goodell, quoted in New York *Emancipator*, Aug. 15, 1839; ibid., Sept. 3, 1840.

3. Maurice Duverger, *Political Parties: Their Organization and Activity in the Modern State*, trans. Barbara North and Robert North (Cambridge, UK: Methuen & Co. Ltd., 1969), 217, and William H. Riker, "The Two-Party System and Duverger's Law: An Essay on the History of Political Science," *American Political Science Review* 76 (Dec. 1982): 753–766, show that in most cases single-member-district plurality rules produce a dominant two-party political system.

4. On late-nineteenth- and early-twentieth-century efforts to eliminate institutional supports for third-party challenges, see Peter H. Argersinger, *Structure, Process, and Party: Essays in American Political History* (Armonk, NY: M. E. Sharpe Inc., 1992), esp. 53–57, 150–164; Lisa Jane Disch, *The Tyranny of the Two-Party System* (New York: Columbia University Press, 2002); and Harold A. Scarrow, "Duverger's Law, Fusion, and the Decline of American 'Third Parties,'" *Western Political Quarterly* 39 (Dec. 1986): 634–647.

5. Stanley Harrold, *Gamaliel Bailey and Antislavery Union* (Kent, OH: Kent State University Press, 1986), 172–174; Washington (DC) *National Era*, Jan. 17, 1856.

6. *National Era*, Feb. 28, Mar. 6, 1856; Richard H. Sewell, *Ballots for Freedom: Antislavery Politics in the United States, 1837–1860* (New York: Oxford University Press, 1976), 277–279.

7. *CG Appendix*, 34th Congress, 1st Session, 530; David H. Donald, *Charles Sumner and the Coming of the Civil War* (New York: Knopf, 1960), 278–311; Elizabeth R. Varon, *Disunion!: The Coming of the American Civil War, 1789–1859* (Chapel Hill: University of North Carolina Press, 2008), 266–271; Sean Wilentz, *The Rise of American Democracy: Jefferson to Lincoln* (New York: W. W. Norton & Company, 2005), 688–693; SPC to Theodore Parker, June 23, 1856, SPC Papers.

8. On the 1856 Republican national convention and the events leading up to it, see

William E. Gienapp, *The Origins of the Republican Party, 1852-1856* (New York: Oxford University Press, 1987), ch. 10. For the platform, see Donald Bruce Johnson, compiler, *National Party Platforms*, vol. 1, *1840-1956* (Urbana: University of Illinois Press, 1978), 27-28. For a brief biography of Jessie Benton Frémont, with an emphasis on her antislavery views, see Frederick J. Blue, "Quite a Female Politician: Jessie Benton Frémont and the Antislavery Movement," *No Taint of Compromise: Crusaders in Antislavery Politics* (Baton Rouge: Louisiana State University Press, 2005), 238-264. For a more complex interpretation of her role in the 1856 campaign and the gender politics of the early Republican Party, see Michael D. Pierson, *Free Hearts and Free Homes: Gender and American Antislavery Politics* (Chapel Hill: University of North Carolina Press, 2003), ch. 5-6; JG to George W. Julian, June 24, 1856, G-J Papers.

9. David M. Potter, *The Impending Crisis, 1848-1861*, ed. Don E. Fehrenbacher (New York: Harper & Row, 1976), 264-65; Gienapp, *Origins*, 413-415.

10. Dismissing Taney's ruling on the territorial question, Republican analysts claimed (following the two dissenting justices) that that portion of the decision was nonbinding *obiter dicta* once the court denied Scott standing to file suit. Don E. Fehrenbacher, *The Slaveholding Republic: An Account of the United States Government's Relations to Slavery*, ed. Ward M. McAfee (New York: Oxford University Press, 2002), 280-283. For further analysis, see Fehrenbacher, *The Dred Scott Case: Its Significance in American Law and Politics* (Oxford: Oxford University Press, 1978).

11. For a detailed argument about the proslavery orientation of the Buchanan administration and its congressional allies, see Michael Todd Landis, *Northern Men with Southern Loyalties: The Democratic Party and the Sectional Crisis* (Ithaca, NY: Cornell University Press, 2014), 163-204. On controversy over the Lecompton Constitution, see also Varon, *Disunion!*, 305-314, and William W. Freehling, *Road to Disunion*, vol. 2, *Secessionists Triumphant, 1854-1861* (Oxford: Oxford University Press, 2007), 130-144. See ibid., 168-184, on the African slave trade issue, and 271-287, 297-303, on Southern Democrats' complicated political maneuvering around the issue of congressional slave codes for the territories. On Cuba, see Fehrenbacher, *Slaveholding Republic*, 130-31. On the New York case of *Lemmon v. The People*, see Paul Finkelman, *An Imperfect Union: Slavery, Federalism, and Comity* (Chapel Hill: University of North Carolina Press, 1981), 296-332; Sarah Levine-Gronningsater, "Delivering Freedom: Gradual Emancipation, Black Legal Culture, and the Origins of Sectional Crisis in New York, 1759-1870" (Ph.D. diss., University of Chicago, 2014), ch. 6; and Marie Tyler-McGraw and Dwight T. Pitcaithley, "The Lemmon Slave Case: Courtroom Drama, Constitutional Crisis and the Southern Quest to Nationalize Slavery" *Common-place* 14 (Fall 2013), accessed March 30, 2015, http://www.common-place.org/vol-14/no-01/mcgraw/#.VRoHHvnF9Og. On the physical resistance of slave escapes, see Stanley Harrold, *Border War: Fighting over Slavery before the Civil War* (Chapel Hill: University of North Carolina Press, 2010), 177-182. On the legal resistance of new personal liberty laws, see Thomas D. Morris, *Free Men All: The Personal Liberty Laws of the North, 1780-1861* (Baltimore: Johns Hopkins University Press, 1974), 166-201.

12. On Brown's raid and popular reactions to it, see Freehling, *Road to Disunion*, 2:205-221, and Varon, *Disunion!*, 326-334; John Sherman, *Recollections of Forty Years in the House, Senate, and Cabinet: An Autobiography* (Chicago: Werner Company, 1895), 138-146; David Brown, *Southern Outcast: Hinton Rowan Helper and "The Impending Crisis of the South"* (Baton Rouge: Louisiana State University Press, 2006), 152-170. The denouement of this lengthy contest can be followed in *CG*, 36th Congress, 1st Session, 634-647, 649-650. The speaker ultimately elected was New Jersey Republican William Pennington (cousin of former 1855-56 speaker candidate Alexander Pennington). See also Potter, *Impending Crisis*, 386-391, and

Richard Franklin Bensel, *Yankee Leviathan: The Origins of Central State Authority in America, 1859-1877* (Cambridge: Cambridge University Press, 1990), 47-57. Bensel also elucidates how tariff politics contributed to the standoff.

13. Brown, *Southern Outcast*, 170-173; Freehling, *Road to Disunion*, 2:265-268.

14. *Proceedings of the Republican National Convention, Held at Chicago, May 16, 17, and 18, 1860* (Albany: Weed, Parsons, and Company, 1860), 79-82; Sewell, *Ballots for Freedom*, 361-365; Potter, *Impending Crisis*, 418-430. The 1860 Republican platform's economic planks aimed to appeal to a broad cross-section of Northern farmers, workers, and manufacturers who together depended on a strong home market. For more on the development of a Northern economic nationalism favoring governmental action to stimulate the home market, see Ariel Ron, "Developing the Country: 'Scientific Agriculture' and the Roots of Republican Party" (Ph.D. diss., University of California, Berkeley, 2012); SPC to Jn Jay, Nov. 6, 1860, Jay Family Papers, Rare Books and Manuscript Library, Columbia University, New York; GS to JG, June 2, 1860, JG Papers.

15. GS to JG, June 2, 1860, JG Papers; James Oakes, *Freedom National: The Destruction of Slavery in the United States, 1861-1865* (New York: W. W. Norton & Company, 2013), 49-62.

16. SPC to Ruhamah Ludlow Hunt, Nov. 30, 1860, in *The Salmon P. Chase Papers*, ed. John Niven (Kent, OH: Kent State University Press, 1993), 3:37-40; Amos Tuck to John Tuck, Tuck Family Papers, Rauner Special Collections, Dartmouth University Library, Hanover, NH; Oakes, *Freedom National*, 70-73.

17. *CG Appendix*, 37th Congress, 1st Session, 42; Oakes, *Freedom National*, 118-143. War Department orders addressed the legal issue of dispossessing Unionist slaveholders by suggesting the prospect of compensation for masters whose loyalty could be proven at a later date.

18. *CG*, 37th Congress, 2nd Session, 1353, 1447-49. On the intriguing wartime developments in Washington, D.C., see Kate Masur, *An Example for All the Land: Emancipation and Equality in Washington, D.C.* (Chapel Hill: University of North Carolina Press, 2010).

19. *CG*, 37th Congress, 2nd Session, 194-195, 1340, 2041-42, 2068; *CG Appendix*, 37th Congress, 2nd Session, 364. On former Free Soiler Isaac Arnold, see James A. Rawley, "Isaac Newton Arnold, Lincoln's Friend and Biographer," *Journal of the Abraham Lincoln Association* 19 (Winter 1998): 39-56.

20. Oakes, *Freedom National*, 261-65; ibid., 434-35, shows that the fear that Unionist border state masters would ultimately claim as fugitives the thousands of slaves who had enlisted in the Union military was the primary motive for this uncontroversial repeal legislation.

21. *CG Appendix*, 37th Congress, 2nd Session, 184-86, 412-413; Oakes, *Freedom National*, 224-239. The role of slaves in their own emancipation has been uncovered especially by the work of the Freedman and Southern Society Project, a portion of which is nicely summarized in Ira Berlin, Barbara J. Fields, Stephen F. Miller, Joseph P. Reidy, and Leslie S. Rowland, *Slaves No More: Three Essays on Emancipation and the Civil War* (Cambridge: Cambridge University Press, 1993). See also Steven Hahn, "Did We Miss the Greatest Slave Rebellion in Modern History?," in *The Political Worlds of Slavery and Freedom* (Cambridge, MA: Harvard University Press, 2009), 55-114. Similar themes were presented earlier in Robert F. Engs's iconoclastic unpublished lecture "The Great American Slave Rebellion," first delivered to the Civil War Institute at Gettysburg College, June 27, 1991, which is cited, somewhat unfavorably, in James M. McPherson, "Who Freed the Slaves," in *Drawn with the Sword: Reflections on the American Civil War* (New York: Oxford University Press, 1996), 193, 195-196.

22. Oakes, *Freedom National*, 301-317, 340-345, 367-392.

23. Oakes, *Freedom National*, 421-429.

24. *CG*, 38th Congress, 1st Session, 1324, 1479-1483.

25. The standard account of Reconstruction's temporary successes and ultimate failures is Eric Foner's impressive *Reconstruction: America's Unfinished Revolution* (New York: Harper & Row, 1988).

26. A singular example of Southern postwar efforts to reshape historical memory of the antebellum conflict is ex–Confederate president Jefferson Davis's specious and insincere *The Rise and Fall of the Confederate Government* (New York: D. Appleton and Company, 1881). For an important discussion of Civil War memory, and amnesia, see David Blight, *Race and Reunion: The Civil War in American Memory* (Cambridge, MA: Harvard University Press, 2001).

Index

abolitionists: anti-extensionism and, 4, 10–12, 105–24, 137–49, 161–70, 188–93; black activism and, 3–6, 57–58, 81, 121, 149–50, 167–70, 238n16; British example and, 5, 28, 67, 237n14; civil rights movement and, 5, 225, 236n13, 256n11, 273n16; coalition politics and, 11–12, 15–17, 42, 44–49, 73–75, 96, 113, 258n22; constituent relations and, 116–24, 193–95, 253n54, 263n10; defense of Northern civil liberties and, 9, 213–14; definitions of, 233n5; development of, 5–11; direct actions of, 30, 84, 162, 195; dissension in, 32, 244n52; Free Soil Party and, 143–49; Garrison's faction and, 3, 13; moral animus of, 2–3, 5, 25, 27, 39, 50, 79, 84, 101–2, 110–11, 115–16, 119, 124, 139–40, 214–15; one idea strategy and, 32–42, 135–36, 173; petition strategy and, 8–9, 37; political strategies of, 4, 8–13, 22, 25–42, 47–72, 90–94, 107–16, 121, 133, 137, 163–70, 191; presidential campaigns and, 37–38, 41–42, 94–103; scholarship on, 3–5, 15–16, 26, 29, 40, 77–78, 91, 235n9, 236n13, 239n3, 252n44, 262n6; Slave Power rhetoric and, 3, 11–13, 16–32, 39–42, 86–90, 106; state-level politics of, 12, 16, 23–25, 48, 53, 110, 119, 131–37, 171–76, 215, 265n36; unpopularity of, 3–4, 6, 15–17, 21, 116–24, 192–93; women's roles as, 3, 22, 32, 34, 37, 48–49, 78–79, 182, 247n3. *See also specific parties and people*

Adams, Charles Francis, 58, 108, 137, 141, 145–46, 149

Adams, John Quincy: abolitionist partnerships with, 47–52, 57, 70–71, 74, 248n4, 248n10; *Amistad* case and, 56, 62, 70; death of, 121, 146; gag rule activism of, 49, 54–55, 64–68, 70, 175, 192, 248n6; Liberty Party's pursuit of, 95; petitioning strategy and, 19–20, 22; Whig Party participation of, 44, 61–62

African Americans: abolitionist activism by, 3–6, 57–58, 81, 121, 149–50, 167–70, 238n16; civil rights and, 5, 23, 57, 81, 136–37, 225, 242n27, 256n11, 273n16; District of Columbia and, 53; emancipations of, 221–23; fugitive slave laws and, 6–7, 26, 30, 53, 70–71, 122, 162–64, 166–70, 195–96, 198, 213–15; Northern racism and, 3–4, 9, 17, 21, 112–14, 118, 139–41, 147–48, 168–69; population of, 6; suffrage and, 30, 57–58

Aiken, William, 210–11, 286n10

Albany Atlas, 139, 144

Albany Convention (political abolitionists, 1840), 38–39

Albany Patriot, 53

Allen, Charles, 143, 152–53, 157–58, 174

Allen, Heman, 249n16

Alvord, James, 25, 57

American and Foreign Anti-Slavery Society, 64, 110

American Anti-Slavery Society, 17–20, 22, 24, 27–29, 33–34, 36, 52
American Colonization Society, 6
American Party, 126, 187, 197–205, 207–10, 219, 283n28, 286n10. *See also* Know Nothing Party
Amistad case, 34, 55–56, 62, 70, 86, 111, 122, 169
Andrews, Sherlock, 249n16
annexation: of Cuba, 187–88, 219, 280n1; of Texas, 23–25, 31, 96–103, 105–7, 111, 118, 120–21, 136–37, 251n32
anticlericalism, 32–33
antislavery advocates. *See* abolitionists; *and specific people*
"Appeal of the Independent Democrats," 190–91, 281n7
Arkansas, 223
Arnold, Isaac, 222
Articles of Confederation, 106
Ashmun, George, 118, 123
Ashtabula Sentinel (OH), 108, 141, 202
Atchison, David, 189, 205

Bailey, Gamaliel: editorial position of, 29, 72, 83–84, 121, 132–34, 137, 151, 156, 169–70, 201–2, 217; Republican Party's founding and, 216–17; strategizing of, 30, 32, 39, 55, 80, 83–84, 95, 132–34, 145, 174, 177, 182, 194
balance of power politics, 77–86, 90–94, 130, 155–60, 215
Baldwin, Roger, 56, 86, 88, 122
Bangor Gazette, 131
Banks, Nathaniel P., 1–2, 194, 207–11, 213, 216–17, 278n31
Baptist, Edward, 83
Barber, Edward, 58, 173, 177
Barnburners, 129–30, 137–48, 150, 173, 175, 180, 262n4, 267n1
Bell, John, 43–46, 246n4
Benson, Lee, 235n9, 238n22
Bibb, Henry, 57, 81, 102, 133, 148, 150, 167
Bingham, Kinsley, 182, 196
Birney, James, 18, 21, 26, 36, 38–39, 41, 81, 84, 88, 95–96, 98, 101, 151, 260n47
Black Laws, 30, 57–58, 132, 152, 171, 273n16
Blair, Francis P., 216–17

Blanchard, Jonathan, 57
Bleeding Kansas, 204–5, 217–18
Booth, Sherman, 149, 196
Booth, Walter, 153
Borden, Nathaniel, 53, 74, 249n16
Border Ruffians, 205
Boston Courier, 67
Boston Daily Whig, 108, 137, 141, 145
Boston Vigilance Committee, 167
Boutwell, Francis, 174
Bowditch, Henry I., 71, 127
Bradish, Luther, 30–31
Brainerd, Lawrence, 217
Brinkerhoff, Jacob, 110–11, 138, 141
Britain, 5, 28, 67, 237n14
Brooke, John, 170
Brooks, Preston, 217
Brown, John, 213, 219, 221–22
Brown, William, 157–59, 274n8
Bryant, William Cullen, 139
Buchanan, James, 218–19
Buel, Alexander, 173
Buffalo Convention (Free Soil, 1848), 136, 145–46, 148–53, 173, 177, 179
Burns, Anthony, 195, 198
Butler, Andrew, 217
Butler, Benjamin F., 144, 148, 272n49

Calhoun, John C., 45, 62, 112, 163, 218–19, 275n3
Calhoun, William, 249n16
California, 114–15, 121, 162, 164, 276n5
Camp, David, 58
Campbell, Lewis, 153, 194, 204, 208
Canada, 167–68, 196
Cass, Lewis, 138–39, 141, 145, 149, 151, 171–73
Catholicism, 126, 181, 197–99, 201, 203, 283n28
Central Corresponding Committee (abolitionist third party), 38, 41
Channing, William Ellery, 71
Channing, William F., 71
Chaplin, William, 23, 71, 122
Chase, Salmon: abolitionism of, 21; Bailey and, 83–84; coalition building of, 141, 143–49; Compromise of 1850 and, 163–64; 1856 House speakership battle and, 2;

Free Soil Party and, 143–48, 174, 272n49; governorship of, 204; Ohio state politics and, 16, 63, 66, 68, 132–33, 140–41, 171–72, 204, 273n16; political strategizing of, 39, 85, 95, 101–2, 106, 120–21, 134, 136–37, 140–41, 158, 177, 203, 239n4; Republican Party's founding and, 216–17, 221; senate career of, 152, 163–64, 169, 174–75, 179, 181–82, 190–93, 215, 220; Southern antislave politics and, 80; Supreme Court service of, 224

Chicago Tribune, 271n39

Child, David, 176

Cincinnati Philanthropist, 24, 29, 52, 83–84, 87, 89, 108

civil rights: African Americans and, 5, 23, 57–58, 81, 147–48, 225, 236n13, 242n27, 256n11, 273n16; normative masculinity and, 3, 37, 112–16, 119, 140–41, 165, 260n47, 262n6

Civil War, 11, 221–27

Clay, Cassius, 271n39

Clay, Henry: Compromise of 1850, 162–64, 275n3, 276n5; presidential aspirations of, 35–36, 69, 71, 86–90, 94–103; Whig partisanship and, 137–38, 141

Clayton, John, 114–15, 282n16

Clayton Compromise, 114–15

Clermont County Anti-Slavery Society, 26

coalitions. *See* abolitionists; *and specific parties*

Cobb, Howell, 156–57, 160, 275n15

Columbus Convention (Free Territory, 1848), 141, 143–45, 147

Committee of the Whole on the State of the Union, House of Representatives, 54, 193, 282n16

Compendium of the Impending Crisis of the South, 219–20

Compromise of 1850, 12, 161–77, 180–81, 184–85, 187, 190, 194

Confederate States of America, 223–27

Connecticut, 81, 85–86, 88, 183–84, 198, 268n3

Conscience Whigs, 125–27, 129–30, 134–45, 150, 156–57, 167

Constitution: abolitionist interpretations of, 7–8, 16, 19, 32, 101, 136, 176; amendments to, 225; *Dred Scott* decision and, 218–19, 265n37

Convention of the Friends of Freedom in the Eastern and Middle States (Boston, 1845), 101

conventions (political). *See specific cities and parties*

Corwin, Thomas, 89, 138

Craft, William and Ellen, 167–68

Creole, 67

"Crime Against Kansas" (Sumner), 217

Cuba, 187–88, 219, 280n1; slavery in, 34–35

Cushing, Caleb, 28, 175

Davis, David Brion, 236n13

Davis, Jefferson, 120, 275n3, 276n5, 289n26

Davis, John, 92, 261n2

Davis, Mary, 78

Declaration of Independence, 6, 148, 220

Declaration of Sentiments (American Anti-Slavery Society), 17

Delano, Columbus, 118

Delany, Martin, 81, 84–85

Delaware, 224

Delbanco, Andrew, 236n13

Democrats: antislavery faction in, 98–100, 105–8, 115–16, 118–19, 123, 130–43, 157; Barnburner faction of, 129–30, 137, 139–41, 146–48, 150, 173, 175, 180, 262n4, 267n1; cross-sectional appeal of, 3, 9, 16–17, 34, 120–21; economic policies of, 132, 171; 1848 presidential campaign and, 137–42; 1852 presidential campaign and, 176–85; emergence of, 7; Free Soil coalitions with, 100, 171–76; Hale's defection from, 99–100; Kansas-Nebraska Act and, 188–89; Northern defeats of, 197–98, 200, 207; partisanship and, 2, 16–17, 43–46, 56–57, 61, 77–78, 107–8, 125–27, 129–30, 138–39; racism of, 86, 112–16, 118, 147–48; Slave Power argument and, 12, 26–27, 29, 77, 133–34; speakership fights and, 43–46, 155–60; Texas issue and, 95, 97–103; third-party attacks on, 29, 31–32, 82, 90–94, 101–3, 110–12, 117, 137–43. *See also* Free Democrats; Hunkers; Independent Democrats; Second Party System; *and specific people* denationalization of slavery, 6, 84–85, 109–16, 143–49, 164–65, 190–96, 205, 214–27

De Witt, Alexander, 182, 190

dilatory tactics, 8–12, 22, 54, 90–94. *See also* abolitionists; House of Representatives; petitions; third-party politics

District of Columbia: abolition in, 213–14, 222; federal control of, 8, 18–19, 22; immediatists and, 8–9, 18, 22–23, 28, 34–35, 37, 49, 53–54, 58–61, 70, 121, 144–49, 155, 159, 173, 248n4, 251n32; slave trade in, 61, 162, 275n1; Van Buren's policy on, 34, 144–49

Dix, John, 119, 151

Dixon, James, 112

Dodge, Henry, 144

Donald, David, 236n13

Doty, James, 173

doughfaces, 20, 34, 82, 86, 115–16, 119, 138–40, 177, 218. *See also specific people*

Douglas, Stephen, 164, 179–80, 188–91, 193–95, 281n7

Douglass, Frederick, 100, 148, 150, 192

Dred Scott v. Sandford, 218–20, 265n37

Duer, William, 159

Durkee, Charles, 151–53, 157, 159, 173, 178–79, 196

Earle, Thomas, 38, 268n8

economic policy: abolitionists and, 7, 15–16, 41, 82–83; Democratic Party and, 107–8, 171; Republican Party and, 220; Whig Party politics and, 40–41, 44–45, 63

Electoral College, 7

Emancipation Proclamation, 213, 223

Emancipator (New York, Boston): abolitionist disseminations and, 29, 36, 43–44, 50–51, 54, 62–63, 67, 92, 109–10, 127, 134, 149; editorship of, 31, 59, 91, 269n13

Emancipator and Republican (Boston), 166

ethnoculturalists, 4, 235n9

evangelical Protestantism, 17–18, 21, 110. *See also* abolitionists; Catholicism; nativism; slavery

Examiner (Louisville), 271n39

expansionism: 1844 presidential campaign and, 95–103; No Territory strategy, 120, 123–24. *See also* Cuba; slavery; territories; Texas; *and specific people*

Fairbanks, Erastus, 89

federal government: anti-extensionism and, 4, 6, 8, 10–12, 105–24, 137–49, 161–70, 183, 188–93; civil rights and, 136–37; constitutional authority and, 7–8, 16, 19, 32–42; denationalization strategies and, 84–85, 109–16, 143–49, 164–65, 190–96, 205–6, 214–15, 218–19, 221–27; fugitive slave enforcement and, 162–70; jurisdiction over District of Columbia and, 18–19, 121; Slave Power argument and, 15–19, 25–32, 34, 48–49, 80, 82–84, 119–20; territories and, 10, 18, 106–8, 113–14, 119–20, 138–39, 162, 188. *See also specific houses of congress and political figures*

Federalists, 7, 25

Fessenden, Samuel, 131, 151

Fifteenth Amendment (to the Constitution), 225

Fillmore, Millard, 73, 143, 164, 166, 168–69, 200, 218

"Financial Power of Slavery" (Leavitt), 82, 246n72

First Confiscation Act, 221

First Congress, 6

First Party System, 7

Fitzhugh, George, 45

Fogg, George, 134, 180

fomenting insurrection (charge), 17, 50, 122

Foner, Eric, 83, 107, 190, 239n4

Foote, Henry, 122, 163–64, 276n5

Fort Sumter, 221

Foster, Theodore, 85

Fourteenth Amendment (to the Constitution), 225

Free American (Boston), 91

Free Democrats, 177–78, 180–85, 188, 197. *See also* Free Soil Party; Independent Democrats

Freehling, William, 19, 238n22

free labor movement, 4, 37, 112–22, 135–41, 149–53, 163–67, 195–96, 239n4, 262n6

Free Soil Party: coalition politics and, 2, 171–76, 274n3; Compromise of 1850 and, 163–70; founding of, 10, 12, 129–30, 141;

Kansas-Nebraska Bill and, 187, 190–95; national aims of, 13; platform of, 143–53, 173, 216; presidential politics and, 176–85; Slave Power argument and, 10–11, 183–85; speakership fights and, 155–62; state-level politicking of, 149–53, 171–76, 195–97. *See also* abolitionists; third-party politics; *and specific people*
Free West (Chicago), 200
Frelinghuysen, Theodore, 94–95
Frémont, John C., 218, 221
French Revolution, 1848, 123
Friend of Man (Utica), 31
Friends of Freedom meeting (Cleveland, 1851), 177, 194
Friends of the Integrity of the Union convention (Harrisburg, 1837), 57
Fries, George, 111
F Street Mess, 189
Fugitive Slave Act of 1793, 6–8, 16–17, 70, 155–58, 162–63, 196, 198, 205, 219
Fugitive Slave Act of 1850, 164–67, 171–79, 185, 195–96, 222
Fuller, Henry, 208–11, 284n5, 286n10
fusionists, anti-Nebraska, 195–206

Gadsden, James, 188
gag rules: House of Representatives versions, 9, 18–22, 27, 31, 37, 58–59, 64–68, 70–71, 111, 117, 119, 222; Senate versions of, 240n15
Garland forgery, 97
Garnet, Henry Highland, 58, 81–82, 133
Garrison, William Lloyd, 3–6, 13, 17, 32–38, 50, 57–58, 85, 99–100, 150, 167, 233n5
Gates, Seth, 35–36, 44, 52–62, 65, 67–70, 72–75, 113, 151, 246n5, 251n32
Gay, Sydney Howard, 167
gender (attacks on), 3, 37, 112–16, 119, 140–41, 165, 260n47, 262n6
Genesee County (New York) Anti-Slavery Society, 35, 44, 60
Gentry, Meredith, 120
Giddings, Joshua: congressional service of, 152, 155–60, 166–67, 181–83, 189–90, 192–93, 195, 213; Free Soil Party's creation and, 143–50, 174; Hale and, 100; histories by, 4–5; Leavitt and, 63, 65–66, 89; speakership battles and, 1–2, 73–75, 155–60, 208–9; speeches of, 54–55; Whig Party membership of, 44, 46, 53, 62–63, 67–69, 71, 86–87, 108, 113, 120–21, 123, 125–26, 131–32, 137–38, 141, 172
Gillette, Francis, 85
Glover, Joshua, 196
Godfrey, John, 131
Goodell, William, 31, 87, 135, 180
Gordon, Samuel, 118–19
Gouverneur, Samuel, 18
Granite Freeman (Concord, NH), 269n14
Greeley, Horace, 138, 199, 211
Greenberg, Amy, 121
Green Mountain Freeman (Montpelier), 182–83, 189, 205
Grimké, Sarah, 22, 49, 65
Grimké(-Weld), Angelina, 22–23, 65
Grover, Martin, 113, 119
Grow, Galusha, 193–94

Haiti, 222
Hale, John P.: antislavery coalition leadership of, 134–36, 140–41, 201, 224, 268n3; Democratic Party membership of, 99–100; Foote's threats against, 122, 163–64; presidential campaign of, 179–81, 184; senate election of, 100, 103, 117, 122–23, 131, 152, 163, 169, 174, 178–79, 199, 215; Van Buren and, 146–48
Hamlin, Edward, 132, 137, 171–72, 268n8
Hamlin, Hannibal, 115–16, 182
Hammond, James Henry, 19
Hanway, Castner, 168
Hard Shell Democrats, 173, 199
Harper's Ferry, 213, 219
Harrison, William Henry, 36, 39–40, 61, 63, 73–75, 88
Haven, Solomon, 209
Hawthorne, Nathaniel, 236n13
Helper, Hinton R., 219–21
Henry, William "Jerry," 168
Herkimer Convention (Barnburners, 1847), 140
Hietala, Thomas, 262n6
Holley, Myron, 31–32, 36
Holmes, Isaac, 126
Holt, Michael F., 235n9, 239n3

House Divided speech (Lincoln), 193
House of Representatives: abolitionist debate strategies and, 8–12, 22, 42, 48–53, 62, 67, 72, 121, 133, 137, 191; committee powers and, 127, 155–57, 209–10, 266n3; constituent pressure and, 116–24; election strategies and, 28–29, 149; gag rules of, 9, 16–20, 22–23, 27, 37, 49–59, 61, 64–66, 68, 70–71, 111, 117, 160; majority-rule elections, 90–94, 158–60, 198, 259n32; speakership contests in, 1–2, 12, 43–46, 73–75, 125–27, 155–62, 173, 207–11, 215–17, 219–20; Wilmot Proviso debate in, 109–16. *See also specific congressmen and parties*
Howe, Samuel Gridley, 175
Hunkers, 139–41, 173–74, 183
Hunter, Robert M. T., 44–45, 73, 175

Illinois, 38, 102
immediatists, 5, 8–9, 18–19, 27, 37–39, 49, 53–60, 70, 121, 155, 173, 248n4, 251n32
Independent Democrat (Concord, NH), 100, 269n14
Independent Democrats, 100, 131, 133–45, 187–95, 199. *See also* Free Democrats
Independent Order of the Friends of Equal Rights, 201. *See also* Know Somethings
Indiana, 21, 178, 197
interrogatory strategy, 28–30, 34, 38–39
Iowa, 112, 197

Jackson, Andrew, 7–8, 15–16, 18, 26, 51, 77–78, 107
Jackson, William, 249n16
James, Francis, 249n16
Jay, John, 167, 191–92
Jay, William, 25–27, 30, 39, 50–52, 67, 95, 151
Jefferson, Thomas, 7, 106
Johnson, Andrew, 157
Johnson, Reverdy, 120
Johnson, William Cost, 37, 61, 64
Joliffe, John, 151
Jones, John, 43–46, 246n4
Julian, George, 148–49, 179, 182, 223–24

Kansas-Nebraska Act, 12, 187–94, 204–5, 208–9, 282n16
Kansas Territory, 189–90, 204, 219

Kendall, Amos, 18
Kentucky, 30, 35–36, 224
kidnapping, 26, 167–70, 276n9
King, Daniel P., 259n38
King, Leicester, 63, 68, 136
King, Preston, 109, 113, 119, 139, 141, 147, 150, 153, 158, 173, 180, 194, 216–17
Knapp, Chauncey, 39, 58, 150
Knapp, Isaac, 50
Know Nothing Party, 126, 181, 187, 197–211, 217, 219, 286n10. *See also* American Party
Know Somethings, 201, 204

Lahm, Frederick, 123
Langston, Charles Henry, 150
Latimer, George, 70–71
Laurie, Bruce, 29, 91, 256n11
Leader (Cleveland), 201
League of Freedom (Boston), 167
Leavitt, Joshua: editorship of, 31–32, 43–44, 52–53, 88–89, 91, 137, 269n13; Free Soil Party activism of, 143–53, 174, 182–83; lobbying by, 59–72, 85; political strategizing of, 35, 42, 48, 61–62, 74, 79, 82, 92, 95, 130, 134, 136, 141, 147–48, 174, 182, 252n42, 252n44
LeMoyne, Francis, 85
Le Roy Gazette (New York), 60, 73
Lewis, Samuel, 39, 133, 140–41, 172, 184
Liberator (Boston), 17, 50
Liberia, 222
Liberty League, 135, 150
Liberty Party: abolitionist support for, 39, 121, 256n11; black activism in, 57; coalition politics and, 12, 42, 59–75, 86–94, 96, 113, 120–27, 129–30, 259n38, 260n47; conventions of, 70–71, 95, 101–2, 132, 134, 136, 147; 1840 election and, 47–49, 81, 215; founding of, 3, 9–10, 16–17, 46, 49, 59–60, 225; free labor politics and, 112–16; Free Soil Party's creation and, 131–37, 140–53, 158; platforms of, 59, 82; state-level activism and, 57–59, 68, 81–84, 90–94, 101, 119, 131–37, 255n5; strategies of, 9–10, 48–59, 77–86, 129–37; Wilmot Proviso and, 117–24. *See also* abolitionists; third-party politics; *and specific people*
Liberty Standard (Hallowell, ME), 131

Lincoln, Abraham, 2, 109, 193, 213, 220–24
lobbying, 42, 47–53, 59–72, 194, 209, 247n1
Loguen, Jermain, 81, 84–85, 168
Louisiana (state), 223
Louisiana Purchase, 113–14, 188
Lovejoy, Elijah P., 21
Lovejoy, Joseph C., 134, 147, 269n13
Lovejoy, Owen, 85, 117, 217, 222
Lundy, Benjamin, 24, 51–52, 242n27

Macedon Lock (New York) Convention, 135
Madison, Dolley, 122
Magdol, Edward, 236n13
Maine, 24, 93–94, 111, 131, 268n3
Maine Law (1851), 181, 183–84
majority-rule elections, 12, 90–94, 158–60, 198, 259n32
Mann, Horace, 121, 165–66, 174, 276n9
Marcy, William, 18, 30–31
Maryland, 223
masculinity, 3, 37, 112, 114–16, 119, 140–41, 165, 260n47, 262n6
Mason, James, 162–64
Massachusetts: abolitionist strategy in, 32–33, 38, 130–31; black activism in, 58; Free Soil Party in, 145, 147, 150–53; Know Nothing Party in, 197–98, 201–2, 283n28; Liberty Party of, 82, 91–93, 102
Massachusetts Abolitionist (Boston), 33, 44, 52
Massachusetts Abolition Society, 33
Massachusetts Anti-Slavery Society, 25, 33, 51
Massachusetts Female Emancipation Society, 33
Massachusetts House of Representatives, 23, 93–94
Massachusetts legislature, 24
Massachusetts Whig Party, 50
Matthews, Stanley, 140–41, 143
Mattocks, John, 74, 86, 88–89, 249n16
May, Samuel, 168
Mayhew, David R., 247n2
McDuffie, George, 18
McKay, F. C. D., 60
McLean, John, 141, 148
Meade, Richard, 159

Medill, Joseph, 201
Melville, Herman, 236n13
Mexican-American War, 10, 12, 25, 71–72, 100–116, 120–21, 125, 131
Mexico, 23, 51, 114
Miami County (OH) Liberty Convention, 95
Michigan, 38, 57, 81, 102, 138, 153, 172, 196–97
Minkins, Shadrach, 168
Mississippi, 24
Missouri (state), 204–5, 223
Missouri Compromise, 7, 16–17, 113–16, 189–90, 194, 265n37, 275n3, 284n5
mob violence, 21, 84, 119, 122, 137, 241n18
moral suasion strategy, 17, 39–40, 50, 79, 84, 101–2, 110–11, 119–20
Morris, Thomas, 25–26, 30, 52–53
Morrison, Chaplain, 107–8
Morse, John F., 152, 172
Morton, Marcus, 92–93

Napoleon, Louis, 167
National Convention of Colored Freemen, 150
National Era (Washington, DC), 114, 121–22, 132–34, 145, 151, 156–58, 169–70, 190, 201–2, 206, 217
National Hotel, 156
National Intelligencer (Washington, DC), 47, 66
Native Americans, 114. *See also* Second Seminole War
nativism, 126, 181, 183–85, 196–204, 207–8, 283n28, 286n10
Nebraska Territory, 188–89
Needham, Horatio, 184
New England. *See specific states*
New Hampshire, 82, 99–100, 131, 183, 197–99
New Jersey, 38
New Mexico, 105, 114–15, 162, 164–65
New York: abolitionist party politics in, 38, 81, 143–49, 238n16; Democratic Party of, 98–99, 129–30, 138–40, 180–81, 262n4; Know Somethings in, 201; state-level politicking in, 30–31, 38. *See also* Barnburners; Hunkers; *and specific parties and people*
New York Assembly, 23–24, 119

New York Association for the Political Elevation and Improvement of the People of Color, 58
New-York Daily Times, 190, 281n7
New York Evening Post, 98, 139
New York Manumission Society, 238n16
New York State Anti-Slavery Society, 4, 30–31, 41, 71, 78, 83
New York State Vigilance Committee, 167
New-York Tribune, 97, 138, 192, 199
New York Whig Party, 69
Nichols, Curtis C., 269n13
Niles, John, 112, 151
nonvoting strategy, 33, 38, 150, 233n5
North, the: abolitionism's relative appeal in, 3–6, 15–17, 21, 116–24, 192–93; economy of, 26, 82–83; free labor movement and, 4, 17, 37, 112–16, 121–22, 135, 139–41, 149–53, 163–70, 195–96, 239n4, 262n6; nativism in, 181, 183–85; racism in, 3–4, 9, 17, 21, 37, 112–16, 118, 121–22, 135, 139–41, 147–53, 163–67, 195–96, 187, 213–14, 239n4, 256n11, 262n6; speakership representation from, 155–60. *See also specific people and states*
North-Western Liberty Convention (Chicago, 1846), 102, 132
Northwest Ordinance, 106
No Territory strategy, 120, 123–24, 138

Oberlin-Wellington slave rescue, 213
Ohio: abolitionism in, 4, 29–30, 38, 130–33, 200, 204; Black Laws of, 30, 132, 152, 171, 273n16; Free Soil Party and, 143–49, 151–52, 171–72; Liberty Party of, 16, 84–85, 89, 119, 140–41; Whig Party of, 67–68, 184–85. *See also* Chase, Salmon
Ohio Free Press (Xenia), 62–63
one-idea strategy, 32–42, 80–82, 102, 135–36, 173, 213–14
Opposition Party, 219
Order of the Star Spangled Banner, 197, 201. *See also* Know Nothing Party
Oregon territory, 109, 114–15, 262n4, 264n24
Orleans Territory, 7
Ostend Manifesto, 188
Owsley, Frank, 235n12

Palfrey, John G., 111, 121–22, 126–27, 152–53, 263n15, 266n3
panic of 1837, 52
partisanship: abolitionist politics and, 56–57, 79, 86–90, 107–8; Second Party System and, 2, 31–32, 44, 99, 125–27, 138–39, 274n3. *See also* Democrats; Second Party System; Whig Party
paternalism, 256n11
patronage: House politicking and, 12–13, 156–57, 201, 209–10, 214, 219–20, 266n3; presidential prerogatives and, 34, 109, 214–15, 262n4
Pearl affair, 122, 137
Pennington, Alexander, 208
Pennington, James W. C., 81, 84–85
Pennington, William, 287n12
Pennsylvania, 6–7, 20, 57, 119, 197, 202
Pennsylvania Freeman (Philadelphia), 37
People's Party (of Ohio), 200
People's Party (of Wisconsin), 184
petitions, 8–9, 16–25, 35, 37, 49–59, 61–72. *See also* gag rules
Phelps, Amos A., 33, 52
Philadelphia Convention (American Party, 1855), 202–5
Philadelphia Convention (Republican Party, 1856), 217–18
Phillips, Stephen C., 141, 145, 249n16
Pierce, Franklin, 99, 177–80, 183–85, 187–88, 195, 198, 205, 210
Pinckney, Henry Laurens, 19–20
Pittsburgh Convention (Free Soil Party, 1852), 177, 179
Pittsburgh Convention (Republican Party, 1856), 217
Plumb, Ralph, 213
plurality rules, 1, 90, 93, 97, 130, 155–60, 173–74, 199, 207–10
political abolitionists. *See* abolitionists; *and specific people*
Polk, James K., 95, 103, 105–7, 109, 114, 121, 125, 131, 136, 139, 262n4, 280n1
popular sovereignty, 113–15, 138–39, 162, 164, 189, 204–5, 219
postal campaigns, 17–25, 31
Preliminary Emancipation Proclamation, 213, 223

presidency: 1840 campaign for, 61–63; 1844 campaign for, 94–103, 133; 1848 campaign for, 124, 129–30, 138–43; 1852 campaign for, 176–85; 1856 campaign for, 211, 216–19; patronage and, 34, 37–38, 109; Slave Power argument and, 37–38, 86–90. *See also specific parties and presidents*

Prigg v. Pennsylvania, 70

property rights, 18–19, 23, 84, 176, 213–14, 218–19

Quakers, 48, 247n1
Quincy Patriot (MA), 50
Quist, John W., 236n13

racial equality, 11, 54, 139, 224, 237n14, 256n11
racism (Northern), 4, 37, 112–22, 139–41, 149–53, 163–67, 195–96, 239n4, 262n6
Randolph, John, 20
Rankin, John, 26
Rantoul, Robert, 56, 174
Rathbun, George, 141
Ray, Charles B., 40, 81, 84–85, 167
religious arguments, 3, 5, 17, 21, 25, 48, 101, 110. *See also* Catholicism; evangelical Protestantism; moral suasion strategy
Republican Party: 1855–56 speaker battle and, 1–2, 205–11; 1859 speaker battle and, 219–21; founding of, 2, 12, 187, 194, 197–98, 202–3, 205–6, 211, 216–17; Kansas-Nebraska Act and, 195–206; platform of, 4, 10, 64, 220, 288n14. *See also specific people*
Republicans (Jeffersonian), 7
revisionist historiography, 4–5, 235n12, 289n26
Revolutionary War, 6
Rhode Island, 24, 90, 183, 198
Richards, Leonard, 258n22
Richardson, William, 189, 193–94, 208–9, 282n16
Riddle, Albert G., 85–86
Rise and Fall of the Confederate Government (Davis), 289n26
Roediger, David R., 262n6
Root, Joseph, 116, 119, 145, 152, 157, 160, 180

runoffs, 12, 90–94, 98, 100, 174, 268n3, 274n3

Sabbatarian campaign, 48, 247n2
scattering strategy, 27–29, 31, 44, 173, 211, 246n4
Schenck, Robert, 157
Scott, Winfield, 177–80
Second Bank of the United States, 26
Second Confiscation Act, 223
Second Great Awakening, 17
Second Party System: creation of, 7–8, 35; definitions of, 2; defusion of sectionalism and, 3, 64, 99; Slave Power argument and, 3, 9, 15–17, 26, 80, 90–94; third-party openings in, 9–10, 32–46, 77–90, 102–3, 107–8, 118, 143, 160, 171–85, 215, 225. *See also* Democrats; Whig Party
Second Reconstruction, 225
Second Seminole War, 34, 55
sectionalism: gender roles and, 205; Kansas-Nebraska Act politics and, 187–206; Know Nothing Party and, 200–204, 207; Second Party System and, 3, 34, 47; third-party politics and, 103, 117–27, 137–43, 171–76; Wilmot Proviso and, 105–7, 109–16, 120–24. *See also* North, the; South, the
Sedgwick, Theodore III, 98
Senate (US): Chase's career in, 152, 163–64, 169, 174–75, 179–82, 190–93, 215, 220; gag rules in, 240n15; Hale's career in, 100, 103, 117, 122–23, 131, 152, 163, 169, 174, 178–79, 199, 215; Wilmot debate in, 115–16
Seventh of March Speech (Webster), 163, 174
Sewall, Samuel, 93, 98, 102, 174
Seward, William, 30–31, 95, 182, 193, 199, 201
Shelden, Rachel, 8, 263n10
Sherman, John, 219–20
Slade, William, 19, 35–37, 45, 52–54, 57, 61, 63–65, 68, 73–75, 87–89, 96, 113
Slave Power argument: abolitionists' unpopularity and, 3, 47–49, 117–24; annexation and, 69, 71–72, 96–103, 105–7, 111, 125, 136–37, 161–62; anti-extensionism and, 10, 18–19, 23–24, 109–16, 129–30; Compromise of 1850 and, 161–77, 180–87, 190, 194; federal control and, 10–12, 18–22, 59,

Slave Power argument (*continued*)
77, 80, 82–84, 143–49; formulation of, 9, 15–17, 20, 25–32, 34, 215; free labor movement and, 112, 114–16; Free Soil articulations of, 173–85; gag rules and, 16–25, 49–50, 62–72; the House speakerships and, 12, 43–46, 73–75, 155–60, 207–11; Know Nothing Party and, 199–201; Liberty Party strategies and, 59–72, 81–83, 86–94, 97–98, 121, 129–37; presidential elections and, 61–63, 94–103, 129–30, 133, 138–53, 176–85; proslavery outbursts and, 10–11, 18, 47–49, 51, 54–55, 61, 64, 71, 122, 193–94, 214; Second Party System and, 3, 13, 86–90; third-party politics' necessity and, 39–40, 86–90, 190–95, 263n10; Wilmot Proviso and, 109–24

slavery: anti-extensionism and, 4, 10, 12, 105–7, 109–24, 137–49, 161–70, 188–93; British abolition of, 5, 28, 67, 237n14; the Constitution and, 7–8, 16, 19, 32, 101, 136, 176, 214; debates over, 8–12, 22, 42, 48–53, 62, 67, 72, 107–8, 121, 133, 137, 191, 195–96; denationalization movement and, 6, 8, 15–17, 84–85, 143–49, 163–65, 178, 191–96, 205–6, 214–15, 218–19, 221–27; economic inefficiency of, 82–83, 214; free labor movement and, 4, 17, 37, 112–16, 121–22, 135, 139–41, 149–53, 163–67, 195–96, 239n4, 262n6; moral opposition to, 2–3, 5, 50, 79, 84, 101–2, 110–11, 115–16, 119–20, 124, 139–40, 214–15; property rights and, 18–19, 23, 84, 176, 213–14, 218–19; slave trade and, 7–8, 18, 57, 61, 162, 214, 219, 222, 275n1. *See also* federal government; Slave Power argument; South, the; territories

Slavery Sectional, Freedom National (Sumner), 175–76

Smith, Gerrit: congressional victory of, 182, 190, 192–93; immediatism and, 27, 53; Liberty League and, 135–36, 150, 168, 179–80, 220–21; Liberty Party's creation and, 42; lobbying by, 59–60, 63; New York politicking by, 30–31; political strategizing of, 69, 80, 135

Soft Shell Democrats, 173, 199

Sorin, Gerald, 236n13

Soulé, Pierre, 188

South, the: antislavery politics in, 78–80; disproportionate influence of, 7–9, 11, 25–32, 48, 64–65, 83, 131; disunion threats and, 120, 155–60, 163, 193–94, 219–21; federal powers and, 32–33, 113–14, 119–20, 183, 265n37; proslavery faction's aggressiveness and, 10–11, 47–49, 51, 54–55, 61, 71, 102–3, 122, 190–95, 214; Reconstruction in, 224–25; revisionist histories of, 4–5, 235n12, 289n26; slavery's extension and, 12, 23–25, 105–7, 109–16, 125, 187–94, 204–5, 208–9, 215–16, 219

South Carolina, 221

Southern and Western Liberty Convention (Cincinnati, 1845), 101

Spain, 187–88

special legislation, 48

Sprague, William, 153

Sprigg, Ann, 65–67

Springfield Republican (MA), 193

Stanton, Elizabeth Cady, 33

Stanton, Henry B., 20, 23, 29–39, 52, 127, 135, 140–41, 145, 148, 180

States' Rights faction, 43–45

Stephens, Alexander, 193–94, 274n4, 282n16

Stevens, Thaddeus, 57, 158, 182, 250n26

Stewart, Alvan, 18, 20, 23, 31–32, 95, 136, 244n51

Stewart, James, 4

Stowe, Harriet Beecher, 169–70, 176, 182, 185

Strong, William, 158

Sumner, Charles, 121–27, 131, 138–45, 159, 169, 174–76, 181–82, 190–92, 215–24

Supreme Court (US), 56, 62, 70

Swisshelm, Jane Grey, 78

Taney, Roger, 218, 265n37, 287n10

Tappan, Arthur, 74

Tappan, Lewis: *National Era* establishment and, 72; political strategizing of, 38, 46, 48, 51–52, 56, 69, 71, 85, 95–97, 134–45, 147, 167, 177, 182

Tappan, Mason, 199

Taylor, Zachary, 138, 141, 143, 145, 149, 152, 162, 164

temperance movement, 95, 181, 183–85, 197

territories: federal powers over, 113–15, 119–20, 138–39, 188, 287n10; popular sovereignty idea and, 113–15, 138–39, 162, 164, 189, 204–5, 219; Wilmot Proviso and, 18, 105–8, 117, 222. *See also specific territories*
Texan War of Independence, 23, 51
Texas: annexation of, 57, 68–69, 96–99, 105–7, 111, 118, 120–21, 139, 164, 251n32; proslavery expansion and, 16–17, 23–25, 31, 51–52, 57
third-party politics: American history of, 2; balance of power politics and, 9–10, 77–86, 155–60, 214–15; Compromise of 1850 and, 161–77, 180–87, 190, 194; lobbying and, 47–53, 59–72; majority-rule rules and, 12, 90–94, 158–60, 198, 259n32; scholarship on, 235n9; sectionalism and, 137–49; universal reform idea and, 134–37. *See also* abolitionists; Free Soil Party; Know Nothing Party; Liberty Party
three-fifths clause, 7, 25, 27
Thurman, Allen, 118
Tilden, Samuel, 141
Tocsin of Liberty (Albany), 53
Torrey, Charles, 32–33, 53, 71, 84
Townshend, Norton Strange, 152, 172
Tracy, John, 30
transcontinental railroad, 188–89
Treaty of Guadelupe-Hidalgo, 120–21
True American (Lexington, KY), 271n39
True Democrat (Cleveland), 271n39
Tuck, Amos, 99, 113, 126–27, 134, 138, 165, 221, 266n3
Tyler, John, 36, 52, 63, 68, 73–75, 97

Uncle Tom's Cabin (Stowe), 169–70, 176, 185
Underground Railroad, 53, 71, 84–85, 167, 195, 222
Union party movement, 177–78
U.S.S. Grampus, 35
Utah territory, 162, 165
Utica Convention (Barnburner, 1848), 144–45, 148
Utica Democrat, 123

Van Buren, John, 180
Van Buren, Martin, 7, 19, 34–35, 39–40, 44–45, 56, 88, 95–96, 140–41, 143–51

Vance, Joseph, 30
Vaughan, John C., 143, 201, 271n39
Vermont: abolitionist party politics in, 38, 91, 133, 135–36, 197, 199–200, 268n3; Free Soil Party in, 145, 151, 173–74, 178; Know Nothings in, 199–200, 203; Liberty Party's growth in, 81–82, 93–94; temperance movement in, 183–84; Whig-Republican Coalition in, 197
Vermont Anti-Slavery Society, 58
Vermont legislature, 23–24, 268n3
View of the Action of the Federal Government in Behalf of Slavery (Jay), 25–27, 52
Voice of Freedom (Montpelier, NH), 150
vote scattering, 27–29, 31, 44, 173, 211, 246n4

Wade, Benjamin, 172, 182, 193
Wade, Edward, 39, 55, 67, 127, 171, 190, 193, 210
Waldo, Loren, 153
Walker, Robert, 122
Walters, Ronald G., 236n13
Ward, Samuel R., 81, 150
War of 1812, 7
Webster, Daniel, 97, 120–21, 163–64, 166–67, 174
Weed, Thurlow, 31, 199, 201, 211
Weld, Theodore Dwight, 22, 51–52, 65–67, 69
Wentworth, John, 116–17
Western Reserve, 54–55, 85–87, 133, 152, 171. *See also* Ohio
Whig Party: abolitionist coalitions and, 11, 19, 35, 41–42, 47–49, 53–54, 58, 60–75, 108, 137–43, 249n16; collapse of, 143, 161, 176–85, 187, 199, 207; Conscience Whigs and, 125–27, 129–43, 145, 167; conventions of, 36, 126, 143; cross-sectional appeal of, 3, 9, 16–17, 34, 120–21; economic policies of, 40–41, 44–45, 63, 73, 125; 1839 speakership battle and, 43–46; 1840 presidential race and, 36–37, 40–41; 1841 speakership election and, 73–75; 1844 presidential race and, 94–103; 1847 speakership election and, 125–27; 1849 speakership fight and, 155–60; 1852 presidential campaign and, 176–85; formation of, 7; No Territory strategy and, 120–21;

Whig Party (*continued*)
  partisanship and, 2, 16–17, 43–46, 56–57, 77–78, 107–8, 125–27, 129–30, 138–39, 143; Slave Power argument and, 12, 26–27, 47, 59, 77, 133–34; third-party attacks on, 29–32, 40–41, 61–62, 64–72, 85–94, 96–103, 117, 125–27, 129–30, 137–43, 196, 258n22, 260n47. *See also specific people*
White, John, 74
whiteness, 9, 37, 112–22, 135–41, 149–53, 163–67, 195–96, 225–27, 239n4, 262n6
Whittier, John Greenleaf: abolitionist strategizing and, 22, 28–29, 135, 174; candidacy of, 92; lobbying efforts of, 52; political strategizing of, 39, 50, 56, 61, 103, 117, 131–32, 134–47, 149, 151, 170, 175, 182; Slave Power argument and, 27–29; Whig affiliations of, 27–28, 56
Wilentz, Sean, 235n9
Willey, Austin, 131, 134–45, 151, 165, 178, 180
Wilmot, David, 105–8, 113, 118, 141, 153, 155–60
Wilmot Proviso: abolitionism's connection to, 116–24, 131, 138–39, 218–19, 274n8; antislavery coalition's formation and, 131–49, 161–62; Congressional debate on, 109–16; description of, 105–8, 261n2; 1849 speakership battle and, 155–60; No Territory strategy and, 120, 123–24, 138; Republican policy and, 222
Wilson, Henry, 4–5, 143, 174, 179, 182, 201, 203, 222, 224
Winthrop, Robert, 126, 155–58, 160, 266n3
Wisconsin, 110, 112, 115–16, 135, 141, 151–53, 173, 184–85, 196
Wise, Henry, 65
women, 3, 22, 32–34, 37, 48, 78–79, 182, 205, 247n3
Wood, Bradford, 119, 176
Woodbury, John, 99
Worcester Convention (Free Territory, 1848), 144–45
Wright, Elizur, Jr., 24, 32–33, 97, 168
Wright, Theodore S., 81

Young Whigs. *See* Conscience Whigs

www.ingramcontent.com/pod-product-compliance
Lightning Source LLC
Chambersburg PA
CBHW021936290426
44108CB00012B/860